The Canterbury and York Society

GENERAL EDITOR: A. K. McHARDY

M.A., D.Phil.

DIOCESE OF CANTERBURY

The Register of
John Morton

ARCHBISHOP OF CANTERBURY

1486—1500

VOLUME I

EDITED BY

CHRISTOPHER HARPER-BILL

Privately Printed for
the Canterbury and York Society
by Duffield Printers, Leeds
1987

PART CXLVIII   VOL. LXXV

FIRST PUBLISHED 1987
© CANTERBURY AND YORK SOCIETY
ISSN. 0262 - 995X

This volume is published with
the help of a grant from
the Isobel Thornley Bequest

Details of previous volumes available from the
Hon. Treasurer of the Society, St. Anthony's Hall, York YO1 2PW

CONTENTS

		page
Introduction		vii
Collation of the Manuscript		xxii
Abbreviations		xxiv
References		xxvi
REGISTER OF ARCHBISHOP MORTON		1
APPENDIX: The Archbishop's Secular Commissions		171
INDEX OF PERSONS AND PLACES		173
INDEX OF SUBJECTS		221

INTRODUCTION

John Morton's Career

John Morton[1] was born about the year 1420 at either Bere Regis or
Milborne St Andrew, Dorset. His family can probably be traced back to
the early fourteenth century, when it was established in Nottingham-
shire, of which county his great-great-grandfather, Sir Robert Morton,
was sheriff in 1364.[2] Sir Robert had an only son, Charles, who
himself had two sons. The elder remained in the Midlands while the
younger, William, the archbishop's grandfather, moved south to Dorset.
William had two sons, the younger, William, serving as member of
Parliament for Shaftesbury in 1437. John came, therefore, of a family
of middling gentry, who were prominent in the affairs of the county,
but took little part in national politics. His own younger brother,
Richard, was sheriff of Dorset and Somerset in 1483.

Morton's early life and education are obscure. Anthony Wood's
assertions that he was educated at Cerne abbey, and subsequently at
Balliol, cannot be substantiated.[3] His first appearance in official
records is in a papal faculty to the bishop of Salisbury, dated 7
October 1447, permitting him to confer on John Morton, clerk, the
office of notary public, provided that he was found fit and had
completed his twenty-fifth year.[4] The following year he proceeded
Bachelor of Civil Law at Oxford, by November 1451 he was described as
Bachelor of Both Laws, and he was incorporated as Doctor of Civil Law
in March 1452. Meanwhile, between 1448 and 1451 he had practised as a
proctor in the university Chancellor's court, and in 1451 was serving
as Commissary and Official of the Chancellor, Mr George Neville. His
selection by this man, subsequently a noted patron of scholars, perhaps
indicates some academic distinction. In 1452 Morton was principal of
the Oxford civil law school, and in September 1453 he was admitted as
principal of Peckwater Inn.

In January 1453 he obtained his first benefice, Shellingford in
Berkshire.[5] From this year he ceases to appear regularly in the
records of the university, and it is probable that he had begun to
practise in the Court of Arches.[6] The archbishop of Canterbury, Thomas
Bourgchier, was at this time Chancellor of England, and this may well
have eased Morton's transition from practise as an ecclesiastical
lawyer to royal service. In September 1456 he was appointed chancellor
to Edward, Prince of Wales,[7] and this important position immediately
made him the recipient of ecclesiastical patronage. In 1459 he was
already considered a suitable candidate for a bishopric, being
suggested as his successor by John Bere, the aged and infirm bishop of
St David's, but nothing came of this.[8]

Morton was, perhaps inevitably, drawn into the developing political
crisis in England. In the Parliament of 1459 he was one of the triers
of Gascon petitions,[9] and as a distinguished lawyer closely connected
with the government, he was concerned with the drafting of the act of
attainder against Richard of York and his supporters.[10] In 1461 his
association with Margaret of Anjou led him to reject the opportunity

open to civil servants to safeguard their own position by anonymous neutrality, and was one of the twenty-two men specifically excluded by Edward IV from the pardon offered after his seizure of the throne.[11] After the Lancastrian defeat at Towton he was captured at Cockermouth while attempting to escape to Scotland,[12] imprisoned in the Tower and included in the bill of attainder of 4 November 1461.[13] Soon, however, he managed to escape to join Margaret of Anjou in exile in France.[14] Appointed keeper of the privy seal in the government in exile, he was one of the embassy which, in June 1462, negotiated the Treaty of Tours with Louis XI of France.[15] He accompanied the queen on both her unsuccessful Northumbrian expeditions, and was present at the defence of Dunstanborough Castle against Warwick.[16] After the Readeption, when Lancastrian hopes had finally been dashed at Tewkesbury, Morton, who had hitherto not wavered in his loyalty, at last came to terms with the de facto king of England. On 3 July 1471 he received a royal pardon,[17] and by Michaelmas he was at work in the Chancery.[18] His attainder was reversed the following year, when he became Master of the Rolls.[19] He was a member of the Council by December 1473.[20] Morton's change of heart represented no opportunism, but political realism. According to Thomas More, he admitted twelve years later that he would have preferred Edward, Prince of Wales, to have the crown, but saw no point in backing a dead man against the live occupant.[21] More also states that Edward IV actively sought Morton's support,[22] and certainly the subsequent rapid elevation of one of the most consistent opponents of the house of York is a further indication of his outstanding ability.

Morton's new eminence resulted in the accumulation of benefices on a grand scale. At the time of his elevation to the episcopate he held four cathedral prebends and five archdeaconries, and by August 1474 he had been appointed Dean of Arches. His governmental functions must, however, have absorbed most of his time. As Master of the Rolls, he provided an important strand of continuity, serving under three Chancellors during a crucial period in the history of Chancery, when the volume of litigation increased fourfold, overtook that in the Exchequer and approached that of King's Bench, while the Chancery masters ceased to be mere clerks, and were increasingly recruited from the most able of the academic lawyers.[23] At the same time Morton was constantly engaged on diplomatic missions.[24] Thus, in the last years of Edward IV's reign Morton stood at the centre of governmental activities, and he was elevated to the bishopric of Ely by papal provision on 30 October 1478.[25] Dominic Mancini noted how the king relied on his counsel,[26] and since their reconciliation Morton had done nothing to betray Edward's confidence in him.

With the assumption of power by Richard, duke of Gloucester, Morton's fortunes changed, although it is not clear whether he was guilty of the alleged treason for which he was arrested in the council chamber on 13 June 1483.[27] In the following January he suffered a second attainder.[28] He was transferred from the Tower to the custody of the duke of Buckingham at Brecon. It is not clear whether he prompted the duke to rebellion, or whether Buckingham drew Morton into a pre-existing conspiracy.[29] The rebellion failed, and Morton, with a price on his head, escaped to Flanders. In January 1485 he was in Rome with his nephew Robert and Mr Oliver King, perhaps preparing the _curia_ for the coming coup.[30] After Bosworth he returned to England where the new king, completely innocent of governmental experience, desperately needed the service of reliable administrators. The attainder against Morton was reversed, and he became a member of the king's council. On 6 March 1486 he was appointed Chancellor, a position which he was to retain for the remainder of his life.[31] Following the death of Cardinal Bourgchier, Morton was in October 1486 translated to the archbishopric of Canterbury, and on 20 September 1493 he was created cardinal priest of St Anastasia.[32]

Throughout his pontificate Morton remained at the centre of secular government. A study of his role in the formation of early Tudor government is a serious need, but so far Mr Pronay has only given some indications of what may one day emerge.[33] The original secretarial functions of Chancery changed little, but the equitable jurisdiction of the Chancellor's court continued the expansion inaugurated during the Yorkist period. Statutes of the early years of Henry's reign laid additional judicial responsibilities on the Chancellor, so that the drive against disorder and criminality came under his general supervision. Morton's most important function was, however, surely political; he was the closest of the king's advisers, was present at nearly all the council meetings of which record has survived, and was responsible for explaining royal policy to Parliament. Foreign ambassadors and reports consistently recognised the archbishop's key role in the formulation of policy.[34]

Within the realm Morton was blamed for the heavy taxation which characterised the first twelve years of Henry VII's reign. Although that famous device 'Morton's Fork' was the invention of Francis Bacon rather than of the archbishop, there can be no doubt that the Cornish rebels of 1497 were particularly hostile to Morton.[35] Nevertheless, by the time of his death those with political perception had come to appreciate his role in government. It is not necessary to rely upon the eulogy of Sir Thomas More; even the London chronicler, representing a group which had suffered more than most from the fiscal policies of the government, considered him 'a man worthy of memory for his many great acts and specially for his great wisdom, which continued to his decease, passing four score years and odd; in our time was no man like to be compared with him in all things, albeit he lived not without the great disdain and hatred of the commons of this land'.[36] Vergil believed that after the deaths of Morton and Bray, it was quite obvious to all that they were responsible not for aggravating royal harshness, but for restraining it.[37] The archbishop's determination to establish security within the realm had been tempered by a concern for justice, whereas those closest to the king after 1500 participated in a campaign of financial terrorism.

An attempt has been made elsewhere to examine the general characteristics and significance of Morton's archiepiscopate,[38] and the introduction to a later volume will consider the records of _sede vacante_ administration, which constitute such a large proportion of this register.[39] The archbishop's relations with the abbey of St Albans, the priory of Folkstone and the bishop of London have been the subject

of separate treatment.[40] The structure of his household and administration, and the exercise of his patronage, have also been examined in
some detail.[41] Here it must suffice to say that while the register
inevitably contains a great number of routine documents and much common
form, in comparison with many such records of the fifteenth century it
contains much of individual interest from which a picture of the archbishop's policies may emerge. The overall view must be of an episcopate
characterised by the aggressive assertion and extension of the trad-
itional rights of the church of Canterbury – the amplification of the
power of the _legatus natus_ to embrace exempt religious houses,[42] the
defence of the prerogative testamentary jurisdiction,[43] the extension
of financial and administrative rights in vacant sees.[44] Yet there
are indications that, in an age when the jurisdictional and financial
structure of the church was increasingly criticised by the literate
laity, Morton intended to centralise ecclesiastical authority in his
own hands in order to achieve a measure of reform, and that he was
frustrated in this by the particularism and the accumulated privileges
of individual churches.[45]

One aspect of Morton's activities which is hardly reflected in the
register is his building programme. At Ely he rebuilt the episcopal
palace at Hatfield and the castle at Wisbech, and cut a great dyke
through the fens from Peterborough to Wisbech;[46] he was 'the first
person not only to project but also to carry into effect a large design
of draining'.[47] At Canterbury cathedral the Angel Steeple was
completed, certainly with his encouragement and assistance, and fines
were levied in vacant dioceses for the repair of his cathedral church.[48]
He apparently intended to duplicate his drainage achievements in Kent,
and to make a new haven at Thanet.[49] In July 1493 licence was granted
for the impressing of stonecutters and bricklayers for a programme of
building and repairs on the manors of the church of Canterbury in Kent,
Surrey and Sussex.[50] The obvious results were the rebuilding of the
archbishop's palace at Croydon,[51] and the great brick tower which still
dominates the entrance to Lambeth. Leland also attributed to him work
at Maidstone, Allington Park, Charing and Ford.[52]

The personal preoccupations and affections of Morton's last years
are reflected in his will and last testament.[53] The estates which he
had accumulated over forty-five years of interrupted political influence
were distributed to his surviving nephews and to the church of
Canterbury. He made bequests to the king, and to Henry VII's mother,
wife and daughter, and provided for his own clerical and secular
servants. He requested that his body should be buried at Canterbury,
under a marble slab without elaborate adornment before the statue known
as Our Lady of the Undercroft, and left money to provide for masses for
twenty years to be celebrated by two monks at Canterbury, one monk at
Ely, and a hired chaplain at Bere Regis. He bequeathed a sum of money
to every individual monk at Canterbury and Ely, and left a thousand
marks for the needy sick. The most interesting provision, however, was
for the payment for twenty years of £128 6s 8d _per annum_ to maintain at
least thirty poor students, of whom two thirds, including two monks of
Christ Church, were to be at Oxford, and one third at Cambridge, of
both of which universities the archbishop was Chancellor. Shortly after
these provisions were made, the archbishop died at Knole on 15 September

1500, during the outbreak of pestilence which also carried off Archbishop Rotherham and Bishops Langton, Alcock and Jane.

Contents of the Register

The present volume contains those entries in the register relating to the diocese of Canterbury and the province in general. The various sede vacante registers will be printed in subsequent volumes. Attention may be drawn to the following documents of particular interest.

Papal documents: apart from the routine bulls of provision and translation, the register contains bulls issued at the instance of the English government to facilitate the transfer of power to the new regime (8, 11-12, 43), and to give ecclesiastical support to Henry VII's campaign to restrain disorder and criminality, particularly by restriction of the rights of sanctuary (10).[54] The Papacy also responded to the king's request for the transfer of a number of Franciscan houses to the Observants (188),[55] and issued commissions for enquiry into the sanctity of King Henry VI and Anselm of Canterbury (185, 211).[56] There are documents relating to the extension of the archbishop's powers to permit the visitation of exempt religious houses (9, 48), and an authorisation for the separation of the parish church of Folkestone from the priory (212). Two papal indulgences were offered, to contributors to the crusade and to the expenses of the Roman church (47, 187).[59] Two indults were granted to the archbishop (208-9), and the testamentary prerogative and sede vacante jurisdiction of the church of Canterbury was confirmed (nos. 204-6, 213, 215, 219). Most interesting, perhaps, are the long sequences of documents relating to litigation between the archbishop and Bishop Hill of London, concerning probate (189-203), and between the archbishop and the prior and convent of the cathedral church of Winchester, concerning revenues and jurisdiction in churches appropriated to the episcopal mensa during the vacancy of the see (221-66).

Records of Convocation: although Archbishop Morton presided over five meetings of the Convocation of the Province of Canterbury, only the records of the 1487 and 1489 assemblies are recorded in the register (85-128), together with a detailed analysis of contributions from the diocese of Canterbury to the subsidy of 1489 (129-79).[58]

Archiepiscopal Documents: among the mass of routine documents, there are those relating to the reform of religious houses (13-15, 50, 71, 76-83) and the discipline of the secular clergy (31, 62). The archbishop extended his protection to the charterhouse of Witham in its difficulties (38), and granted indulgences or commendations for various institutions (23-5, 55, 59-60, 67). Indulgences were also granted in association with mandates for prayers and processions for the safety of the king and the realm (33, 56, 74-75). Apart from the dispute with the bishop of London, there is other evidence for the determination to safeguard the testamentary prerogative (57-58, 70). Archiepiscopal commissions for the administration of the estates of

intestates are noted in the register only for the years 1487-89
(267-345).

Miscellaneous documents: these include a long account of the criteria
for canonisation and the expenses involved, no doubt related to the
attempts to obtain the canonisation of Henry VI and Anselm (181-83),
and also an interesting account of the translation of the relics of
St Swithun in 1476 (184). Also transcribed in this register are
charters of Archbishops Edmund Rich and Thomas Arundel (53-54), the
foundation statutes of Ellis Davy's almshouse at Croydon (180), and
various documents concerning the college at Bredgar, including the
emendation of its statutes (346).

Institutions to Benefices: (347-430, 449-753): the institution list
appears to be complete, apart from a gap in the middle months of 1489.
A total of 385 institutions are recorded for the fourteen years of
Morton's tenure of the see of Canterbury, an average of 28 per annum,
compared with 31 per annum during Bourgchier's archiepiscopate. It is
unlikely, therefore, that there are many omissions. The information
which can be drawn from the institutions is best presented in tabular
form:

Number of Institutions

Diocese of Canterbury and immediate jurisdiction within England   331
Jurisdiction of Calais (all benefices in royal gift)   28
Other dioceses sede vacante   26

Total   385

Presentations within the diocese and immediate jurisdiction in England

	Total	Graduates presented	Religious presented
Archbishop	149	87	4
Archdeacon of Canterbury	10	7	–
Religious corporations	106	19	10
Other clergy	14	3	–
The king	5	1	–
Other lay patrons	47	6	1
	331	123 (=37%)	15

These figures emphasise the domination of the archbishop in the field
of ecclesiastical patronage, and also the favour which he showed to
graduate clergy. A comparison with other periods is instructive.

Archbishop Chichele, 1414-43   1334 institutions recorded, 128
    graduates, 9.5%[59]
Archbishop Warham, 1503-32   898 institutions recorded, 347
    graduates, 39%[60]

Or, taking totals of those already beneficed and newly instituted:

xii

Archbishop Bourgchier, 1454–86   1122 clergy named, 238 graduates, 22%[61]
Archbishop Morton, 1486–1500   426 clergy named, 145 graduates, 34%

This indicates very clearly the steadily increasing prospects of graduate employment in the course of the fifteenth century, and the abatement of the crisis which had caused Chichele such concern.[62]

Ordination Lists: as transcribed in the register, these are far from complete, and are of little value for any statistical analysis. There were six days during the year when ordinations might be celebrated – the four Ember Saturdays, the fifth Saturday of Lent and Holy Saturday. In Bourgchier's time ordinations were held on average four times a year. Morton's register contains details of five ordinations celebrated by Richard Martyn, Bishop in the Universal Church and superior of the Canterbury Franciscans, between 14 April 1487 and 20 September 1488, and subsequently on 18 September 1490 and 24 September 1491. Apart from these, the only ordinations recorded are those celebrated by the archbishop himself in his cathedral church every Holy Saturday from 1491 to 1499. Although Holy Saturday was normally the occasion of the largest ordination of the year, and the monks of Christ Church in particular would wish to be ordained by their titular abbot rather than by a suffragan, it is extremely unlikely that this was the only ceremony, and it is probable that Martyn continued to ordain on other occasions until his death in 1498.

The register records the ordination of 73 secular priests and 186 religious, and these figures are in approximately the same ratio as those for Bourgchier's pontificate. Institutions to benefices within the diocese can be traced for only fifteen of the seculars ordained.

The numbers of religious ordinands by houses is as follows: Christ Church, Canterbury, 50; St Augustine's, Canterbury, 17; Franciscans of Canterbury, 15; Leeds, 12; Faversham, 11; Boxley, 8; Dominicans of Canterbury, 6; Carmelites of Sandwich, 6; St Radegund's, Bradsole, 5; St Martin's, Dover, 5; St Gregory's, Canterbury, 4; West Langdon, 4; Austin friars of Canterbury, 3; Combwell, 3; Moatenden, 3; Carmelites of Lossenham, 2; Bilsington, 1; Domus Dei, Dover, 1; Austin friars of London, 3; Bayham, in Chichester diocese, 1; Franciscans, house unspecified, 1; friar, Order uncertain, 1.

The great majority of secular ordinands were ordained to the title of a religious house; the exceptions were normally members of the archbishop's own household or administration or the fellows of Oxford colleges. The number of titles granted by religious houses was as follows:

Within Canterbury diocese:

St Gregory's, Canterbury, 12; St Sepulchre's, Canterbury, 5; Domus Dei Dover, and Leeds, 2 each; St Radegund's Bradsole, Christ Church Canterbury, Ospringe and Wye college, 1 each.

Outside Canterbury diocese:

Barnwell, St John the Evangelist Cambridge, Haliwell, Tonbridge, 2 each; Barking, Bermondsey, St Guthlac's Hereford, St Mary without Bishopsgate,

St Thomas Acon (both London), Hagnaby, Oseney, Revesby, Syon, 1 each.

The ordination lists therefore provide further illustration, but not clarification, of this process. The predominance of St Gregory's and St Sepulchre's, both houses of modest income, is an indication that the convent gained some profit from the guarantees which it provided. This impression is strengthened by reference to the ordination lists for the diocese of Bath and Wells in 1491 (vol. ii, 53, 65, 75). There three titles were granted by Worspring priory and two by Bridgenorth hospital in the very year when they were exempted from payment of the tenth because of their poverty. The presence in the Canterbury ordination lists of titles supplied by distant houses such as Barnwell and St John the Evangelist, Cambridge, suggests that they too specialised in this service. One of the most surprising features is the lack of correspondence between the provenance of the ordinand and the house which granted the title. St Gregory's provided titles for men from London and Lincoln dioceses, St Sepulchre's for a man from Neath, and Wye for a Scots ordinand.

The Register

Archbishop Morton's register is bound in two volumes, the first containing exclusively records of his pontificate, the second a composite volume which also contains parts of the registers of his predecessors William Courtenay and Thomas Bourgchier, and of his immediate successor Henry Deane. The present, and almost certainly original, binding was executed, as was that of the companion volumes in the Lambeth series, in all probability by a Londoner whose work on printed books spans the period 1515 to 1523.[63]

The register is far less systematic than those of Chichele or Kempe earlier in the fifteenth century, and in this it is akin to that of Bourgchier. There is, for example, no section reserved for papal bulls of provision or royal writs. There are indications, however, of some attempt to organise the material. Folios 1-8 and 17-24 are largely devoted to papal documents, or to the acta of the archbishop as commissary of the apostolic see. Folios 9-12 and 25-32 contain, for the most part, the archbishop's commissions and acta as diocesan and metropolitan. The division of material was not, however, rigidly maintained.

Neither is the register as complete as that of Chichele, although more material has been preserved for the fifteen year archiepiscopate of John Morton than for Bourgchier's thirty-two years. It is obvious that some quires were mislaid before binding. The first quire ends with an incomplete document (42) by which it is noted: vacat quia registratur in alio quaterno. This should occur in a sede vacante register for the diocese of Rochester for the years 1492-93, which is not bound into either volume. On 14 December 1495 Mr John Barett, the registrar, produced for scrutiny a quire which he had recently found in the registry; it contained a mandate for the release of the spiritualities of the diocese of Winchester which is not included in the bound register (243).

There are various indications that the register was not a working record, but was compiled some time later than the documents which it contains. There is no chronological sequence within the various quires of litterae diversae. The first section contains documents dated 1486–93, the second, documents dated 1493–98, but within the two sections chronological order is not maintained. It also appears that the sede vacante registers were, in some cases at least, fair copies, compiled at Lambeth after the end of the vacancies which they describe. It is possible that in 1496 the quire used in Lichfield was taken by Mr Potkyn to Rochester, where he utilised the blank folios, but it is unlikely that the second quire of the Exeter register was taken to Wells two years later, while quire B includes the final part of one sede vacante register, the whole of another, and at the end of the quire a group of litterae diversae which predate the sede vacante registers. The ordination lists provide a further indication of delay in registration. The dating of these is frequently erroneous and confused, and the record ends abruptly in the middle of a list, because the scribe had not allowed himself sufficient space. There is every indication that at some date the scribe set out to transcribe those ordination lists which he had to hand, and these were surely far from a complete record for Morton's pontificate. A final corroboration may be provided by the unwillingness of the registry at Lambeth to hand over to the prior and convent of Christ Church, after the archbishop's death, the records of spiritual administration.[64] Is it possible that Morton's demise prompted an effort to gather together, in the form of a register, those quires and original documents from the previous fourteen years which could still be found?

The Handwriting

The greater part of the register is written in a single hand. The exceptions are: Vol. 1, fos. 94–98, appointment of Official sede vacante, Lincoln diocese, in 1495, and mandates issued by him. This is most likely the hand of Mr William Miller, notary public and subsequently chapter clerk at Lincoln, who was on the archbishop's instructions appointed as scribe of the acts of Mr John Walles, the Official.[65] Vol. 1, fos. 227–250, account of proceedings before papal commissaries in the case between the archbishop and the prior and convent of Winchester. This is a most distinctive humanist book hand, compared to the business hand in which most of the register is written. The record is of two distinct processes, before Mr Hutton at Lambeth and before the abbots of Hyde and Titchfield at Southampton. The only notary public who was present on both occasions was Mr William Imbroke, and it is likely that he, who had previously been employed as a scribe to one of the archbishop's commissaries, produced this account for the register. Vol. 2, fos. 50v–60, 87–121. These folios record wills proved by, and visitations conducted by, Mr John Vaughan, one of the two commissaries appointed by Mr Roger Framingham, monk of Norwich and visitor of the diocese sede vacante. The scribe accompanying Mr Vaughan was Mr William Curtes, whose hand this almost certainly is. Vol. 2, fos. 162–168. The institutions to vacant benefices from 1497 are recorded in a new hand, which has not appeared before in the register. It is impossible to identify, beyond the obvious observation that it belonged to one of the clerks of the Lambeth registry.

There remains the hand which wrote the remainder of the register.
At first glance identification is easy. The same scribe compiled the
Registrum Album, a precedent book compiled from extracts in the archiepiscopal registers. An index to this work was compiled in the later
sixteenth century by Mr Thomas Yale, Ll.D., Chancellor to Archbishop
Parker, who on fo. 11, the first folio of the original compilation
which he had indexed on the previous ten folios, wrote: manus magistri
Barret quondam registrarii etc. Barret became registrar after the
death of John Beele, Archbishop Bourgchier's registrar, in 1489, so
this identification was obvious. But there is reason to suppose that
the register was written not by him, but by his deputy and future
brother-in-law, Mr William Potkyn. The clue to this identification is
provided by the Norwich sede vacante register. Potkyn had accompanied
Mr Roger Church, the archbishop's Official, to the vacant diocese, as
he usually did in the later years of the pontificate. Those sections
of the Norwich register which record the acta of Mr John Vaughan were
written by his scribe, Mr Curtes. The transition from one hand to
another within this sede vacante register does not correspond to the
division of the quires, which suggests that each scribe wrote up the
account of those visitations at which he had been present at Norwich
after completion of the visitations, rather than at Lambeth, for there
is no indication that Mr Curtes was normally in the archbishop's
employment. If this is the case, the main hand in the Norwich register
is that of Mr Potkyn, rather than of some minor Lambeth clerk. This
identification is strengthened by the fact that the Norwich register
includes judgements in the consistory court, as registrar of which
Potkyn had been appointed by the archbishop. Once it is established
that Potkyn himself recorded Church's acta in the diocese of Norwich,
it is obvious that he wrote the bulk of the whole register, which is
written in the same hand. Perhaps Mr Barett, the principal registrar,
who was responsible also for the registration of proceedings in the
Court of Audience and before the Commissaries of the archbishop's
Prerogative, delegated the registration of the archbishop's acta to
Potkyn. This would explain, incidentally, two features of the
register as it is bound up. The paucity of material, other than sede
vacante registers, after 1494, may be a result of Potkyn's frequent
employment from 1495 onwards as scribe to the Official in vacant sees;
he was often away from Lambeth, and possibly copies of the archbishop's
acta which he would have entered in the register were mislaid during
his absence. Also, a man who had spent so much of his time engaged
in sede vacante administration may have developed an enhanced view of
the importance of this activity, and this would explain the preponderance
of such material in the register, which is in marked contrast to the
inclusion of only one such record in Bourgchier's register.

Editorial Method

This calendar attempts to include the essential information contained
in each entry in the register. Where a document has been published in
full, the calendar entry is somewhat abbreviated and a reference given
to the published edition; where a document has recently been calendared
elsewhere, the entry is here reduced to the briefest note.

The modern equivalent of all place names is given, except in those few cases where there is some doubt as to identification. For ease of reference, the county has been added to those places not in Kent, and this is an exception to the general rule that any editorial addition to the information contained in the ms. is placed in square brackets. Personal names have been retained in the form in which they appear in the ms., even when that form varies within the same entry. Marginalia have not been noted unless they contain information not in the text. The historical year beginning on January 1 has been used throughout. The folio numbers of the ms. are given in the calendar at the head of the first entry which begins on that folio. Thus, in the case of long entries which extend over several folios, the intervening foliation is not given; and indeed, in the case of verbose and repetitious entries relating, for example, to legal proceedings, which are here radically abbreviated, it would be impossible to indicate the precise point of turn.

Acknowledgements

This volume is the first of three which will present a calendar of Morton's Canterbury register, and includes material relating to diocesan and provincial business. Vol. ii will contain sede vacante registers from various dioceses, and vol. iii the register for the vacancy of the diocese of Norwich in 1499.

The calendar is based upon that submitted in 1977 for the degree of Doctor of Philosophy in the University of London. I am extremely grateful to Professor Robin Du Boulay, who supervised my thesis, and to my examiners, Professor Rosalind Hill and Dr David Smith, for many helpful suggestions. My thanks are due to the authorities of King's College London for the award of the Inglis scholarship and a post-graduate tutorial studentship, during the tenure of which the initial work on this project was accomplished; to the Central Research Fund of the University of London for grants which facilitated research; and to the former head of the history department of St Mary's, Martyn Dyer, for his constant interest.

The Society acknowledges with thanks the permission granted by His Grace the Archbishop of Canterbury for the publication of this calendar, and I wish to record my gratitude to Dr E.G.W. Bill, Lambeth Librarian, for extending to me the facilities of the library. Miss Melanie Barber, archivist at Lambeth, has been an unfailing source of encouragement from the first day that I began work on the register. My wife Ruth has helped in very many ways.

NOTES

1. See W.F. Hook, Lives of the Archbishops of Canterbury (1861–84), v, 387–499; R.L.K. Woodhouse, Archbishop John Morton (1895); Dictionary of National Biography; and most recent and reliable, A.B. Emden, Biographical Register of the University of Oxford to A.D. 1500 (Oxford, 1957–59), ii, 1318–20.

2. A genealogical table is provided by J. Hutchins, History and

Antiquities of the County of Dorset, (3rd ed., 1861-70), ii, 594-95.
Such pedigrees are very hard to substantiate and are based to a large
extent on local tradition. There is no information about his father,
Richard, save that he occurs in 8-9 Henry VI (ibid., ii, 593).
According to Anthony Wood, he may have been a member of the corporation
of shoemakers (Athenae Oxonienses, ed. P. Bliss, (Oxford, 1813-20), i,
643).

3. Wood, op.cit., ii, 683-88. N. Orme, Medieval Education in the West
of England (Exeter, 1976), makes no mention of any educational
establishment at Cerne.

4. CPL 1447-55, p. 373.

5. Reg. Beauchamp, Sarum, i, pt. i, fo. 21.

6. In July 1455 he was appointed a commissioner to hear an appeal from
the Court of Admiralty, a task traditionally assigned to practitioners
in the Court of Canterbury (CPR 1452-61, p. 246).

7. CPR 1452-61, p. 323.

8. CPL 1455-64, p. 556.

9. Rot. Parl., v, 345.

10. Paston Letters and Papers of the Fifteenth Century, ed. N. Davis
(Oxford, 1971-76), ii, no. 617.

11. CCR 1461-68, p. 55.

12. Paston Letters, ii, no. 625.

13. Rot. Parl., v, 477, 480; CPR 1461-67, p. 30.

14. Historical Collections of a London Citizen, ed. J. Gairdner (Camden
Soc., n.s. xvii, 1876), p. 218.

15. C.L. Schofield, The Life and Reign of Edward IV (1923), ii, 220,
231, 252.

16. Ibid., ii, 264, 301; Three Fifteenth-Century Chronicles, ed.
J. Gairdner (Camden Soc., n.s. xxvii, 1880), p. 158.

17. CPR 1467-77, p. 261.

18. R.J. Knecht, 'The Episcopate and the Wars of the Roses', University
of Birmingham Historical Journal, vi (1957), 119.

19. CPR 1467-1477, p.334.

20. J.R. Lander, Crown and Nobility 1450-1509 (1976), p. 312.

21. T. More, The History of King Richard III, ed. R.S. Sylvester
(Complete Works, Yale edition, ii, 1963), p. 92.

22. Ibid., p. 91.

23. N. Pronay, 'The Chancellor, the Chancery and the Council at the end
of the Fifteenth Century', in British Government and Administration,
ed. H. Hearder and H.R. Loyn (Cardiff, 1974), pp. 87-103.

24. For details, see BRUO, ii, 1319.

25. Handbook of British Chronology (2nd ed., 1961), p. 224.

26. D. Mancini, The Usurpation of Richard III, ed. C.A.J. Armstrong (Oxford, 1936), p. 32.

27. More, Richard III, pp. 49, 127.

28. Rot. Parl., vi, 250.

29. Polydore Vergil believed that Buckingham informed Morton of his intention of declaring for Henry Tudor (Polydore Vergil's English History, ed. H. Ellis (Camden Soc., xxix, 1844), p. 194). More thought that Morton attached Henry's claim to a plot originally intended to be in favour of Buckingham himself (Richard III, pp. 91-3).

30. S.B. Chrimes, Henry VII (1972), p. 106, n. 2.

31. Rot. Parl., vi, 273; The Anglica Historia of Polydore Vergil, A.D. 1485-1537, ed. D. Hay (Camden Soc., 3rd series, lxxiv, 1950), p. 7; CCR 1485-1500, no. 67.

32. Handbook of British Chronology, p. 211. The grant of the temporalities of Canterbury on 13 July 1486 preceded papal translation by three months (CPR 1485-94, p. 119). Henry VII had hoped for his elevation to the cardinalate in 1488 (CSP Venetian, i, nos. 537, 553).

33. Cf. Pronay, art. cit.

34. CSP Venetian, i, nos. 562, 597; CSP Milan, i, no. 525; CSP Spanish, i, nos. 221, 292.

35. C.L. Kingsford, Chronicles of London (Oxford, 1905), p. 216; Vergil, ed. Hay, p. 92.

36. Chronicles of London, p. 232.

37. Vergil, ed. Hay, pp. 92, 132-34.

38. C. Harper-Bill, 'Archbishop John Morton and the Province of Canterbury, 1486-1500', JEH, xxix (1978), 1-21. The study by C. Jenkins 'Cardinal Morton's Register', Tudor Studies presented to A.F. Pollard, ed. R.W. Seton-Watson (1924), pp. 26-74, concentrates on evidence relating to the registry at Lambeth, and on the state of the church as revealed by the visitation documents.

39. For the present, see C. Harper-Bill, 'A Late Medieval Visitation – the Diocese of Norwich in 1499', Proceedings of Suffolk Institute of Archaeology and History, xxxiv, pt. i (1977), 35-47.

40. M.D. Knowles, 'The Case of St Albans Abbey in 1490', JEH, iii (1951), 144-58; C. Harper-Bill, 'The Priory and Parish of Folkestone in the Fifteenth Century', Archaeologia Cantiana, xciii (1977), 195-200; C. Harper-Hill, 'Bishop Richard Hill and the Court of Canterbury, 1494-96', Guildhall Studies in London History, iii (1977), 1-12.

41. C. Harper-Bill, 'The Familia, Administrators and Patronage of Archbishop John Morton', Journal of Religious History, x (1979), 236-52.

42. Below, nos. 9, 13-15, 48, 50, 71; see also Letters from the English Abbots to the Chapter at Citeaux, 1442-1521, ed. C.H. Talbot (Camden Soc., 4th series, iv, 1967), nos. 50, 56, 61, 64, 66, 73, 77, 96, 100-101, 103, 105.

43. Below, nos. 189-203.

44. Below, nos. 221-66.

45. For amplification, see JEH, xxix, 19-21.

46. J. Bentham, History and Antiquities of the Conventual and Cathedral Church of Ely (2nd ed., Norwich, 1812), p. 181.

47. H.C. Darby, The Medieval Fenland (Cambridge, 1940), p. 167.

48. C.E. Woodruff and W. Danks, Memorials of Canterbury Cathedral (1912), pp. 207-10; below, ii, 380, 481; iii, 263, 266-8, 271, 274-5.

49. The Itinerary of John Leland in or about the Years 1535-1543, ed. L.T. Smith (1909), iv, 60.

50. CPR 1485-94, p. 443.

51. VCH Surrey, iv, 267-8

52. Leland, op.cit., iv, 62.

53. Sede Vacante Wills, ed. C.E. Woodruff (Kent Archaeological Soc., Records Branch, iii), pp. 85-93.

54. See I. Thornley, 'The Destruction of Sanctuary', in Tudor Studies presented to A.F. Pollard, pp. 183-207.

55. See A.G. Little, 'The Introduction of the Observant Friars into England - a Bull of Alexander VI', PBA, xxvii (1941), 155-66.

56. The testimony of witnesses and other relevant documents relating to the attempted canonisation of Henry VI were edited by P. Grosjean, Henrici VI Angliae Regis Miracula Postuma ex Musei Britannici Regis 13 C VIII (Brussels, 1935). Selections in translation are in R. Knox and S. Leslie, The Miracles of Henry VI (Cambridge, 1923). For the best discussion of the cult, see J.W. McKenna, 'Piety and Propaganda, the Cult of King Henry VI', in Chaucer and Middle English Studies, ed. B. Rowland (1974), pp. 72-88. For Anselm, see R.W. Southern, St Anselm and his Biographer (Cambridge, 1963), pp. 341-3.

57. See W.E. Lunt, The Financial Relations of the Papacy with England, 1327-1534 (Medieval Academy of America Publications, lxxiv, Cambridge, Mass., 1962), 595-60.

58. The grants to the crown by the 1491 and 1495 meetings of Convocation are detailed in CFR 1485-1509, nos. 140, 555. For 1491, see also below, ii, nos. 60, 62. For 1497, see M. Bowker, The Secular Clergy in the Diocese of Lincoln 1495-1520 (Cambridge, 1968), p. 138. For the charitable subsidies granted to the archbishop, see F.R.H. Du Boulay, 'Charitable Subsidies granted to the Archbishops of Canterbury, 1300-1489', BIHR, xxiii (1950), 147-64.

59. Reg. Chichele, i, 129-348.

60. These figures were calculated by M. Kelly, <u>Canterbury Jurisdiction and Influence during the Episcopate of William Warham, 1503–32</u> (Cambridge Ph.D. thesis, 1963).

61. <u>Reg. Bourgchier</u>, p. xxxix.

62. See E.F. Jacob, <u>BJRL</u>, xxix (1945–6), 304–25; <u>JEH</u>, i (1950), 172–86.

63. Cf. <u>Reg. Chichele</u>, i, xvi.

64. PRO, Early Chancery Proceedings, C1/238/2.

65. Vol. ii, no. 136. See also K. Major, 'The Office of Chapter Clerk at Lincoln in the Middle Ages', in <u>Medieval Studies presented to Rose Graham</u>, ed. V. Ruffer and A.J. Taylor (Oxford, 1950), p. 187.

I am grateful to Dr. C.S.L. Davies for a copy of his article 'Bishop John Morton, the Holy See and the accession of Henry VII', which was received after this introduction was written but is shortly to appear in <u>The English Historical Review</u>, and also for drawing my attention to the problem indicated in the note to 89.

COLLATION OF THE MANUSCRIPT

Folio numbers	Quire mark	Volume and number of entry in calendar	Nature of Entries
Vol. 1			
1–16v		i, 1–42	Papal bulls, commissions, letters, 1487–93.
17–24v	b	i, 43–54	Papal bulls, letters, 1487–92.
25–32v	c	i, 55–84	Commissions, letters, etc., 1488–93.
33–36v	d	i, 85–96	Minutes of Convocation, 1487.
37–46v		i, 97–123	Minutes of Convocation, 1489.
47–54v	f	i, 124–179	Documents relating to taxation of clergy, 1489.
55–62v	g	ii, 1–43	Sede vacante register, Lichfield diocese, 1490–1.
63–77v (77 blank)	h	ii, 44–76	Sede vacante register, Wells diocese, 1491.
78–85v	k	ii, 77–105	Sede vacante register, Winchester diocese, 1492–3.
86–93v (93 blank)	l	ii, 106–134	Sede vacante register, Winchester diocese, 1492–3.
94–117v (98v–101v blank)	m	ii, 135–263	Sede vacante register, Lincoln diocese, 1495.
118–132v	q	ii, 264–332g	Sede vacante register, Exeter diocese, 1492–3.
133–141v (140–1 blank)	s	ii, 332h–365	Sede vacante registers, Exeter diocese 1492–3 and Wells diocese, 1495.
142–166v (157v–8, 163–6 blank)	t	ii, 366–451	Sede vacante registers, Lichfield and Rochester dioceses, 1496.
167–174v	v	ii, 452–475	Sede vacante register, Worcester diocese, 1498.
175–182v (181–2 blank)	A	ii, 476–488	Sede vacante register, Worcester diocese, 1498.

183–206v (183, 190, 197v–8 blank, 188–9 excised)	B	ii, 489–558, i, 180–188	<u>Sede vacante</u> registers, Worcester diocese, 1498 and Salisbury diocese, 1499; statutes of Croydon almshouse, papal bulls, letters.
207–214v	C	i, 189–198	Letters, litigation at court of Rome.
215–226v	D	i, 199–222	Papal bulls, letters etc., 1494–96.
227–234v	E	i, 223–234	Litigation before papal commissaries.
235–250v	F	i, 234–266	Litigation before papal commissaries.
251–256v	H	i, 267–345	Commissions to administer estates of intestates.

Vol. 2

2–17v (1 wanting)	iii, 1–79	<u>Sede vacante</u> register, Norwich diocese, 1499; institutions, ordinations, synods, wills.
18–25v	iii, 80–101	Norwich wills.
26–33v	iii, 102–122	Norwich wills.
34–41v	iii, 123–143	Norwich wills.
42–49v	iii, 144–158	Norwich wills.
50–57v	iii, 159–179	Norwich wills.
58–61v	iii, 180–189	Norwich wills.
62–73v	iii, 190–195	Norwich accounts.
74–81v	iii, 196–262	Norwich accounts, consistory court cases, visitations.
82–99v	iii, 263–379	Norwich visitations.
100–111v	iii, 380–604	Norwich visitations.
112–121v	iii, 605–800	Norwich visitations.
122–127	i, 346	Ordinances for Bredgar college.
128–136v	i, 347–430	Canterbury institutions.
137–152v	i, 431–539	Canterbury institutions and ordinations.
153–168v	i, 540–753	Canterbury institutions.

ABBREVIATIONS

English and Welsh Counties

Bd.	Bedfordshire		Lei.	Leicestershire
Bk.	Buckinghamshire		Li.	Lincolnshire
Brk.	Berkshire		Mx.	Middlesex
Ca.	Cambridgeshire		Nf.	Norfolk
Carn.	Carnarvonshire		Np.	Northamptonshire
Chs.	Cheshire		Ox.	Oxfordshire
Co.	Cornwall		Ru.	Rutland
Db.	Derbyshire		Sa.	Shropshire
De.	Devonshire		Sf.	Suffolk
Do.	Dorset		So.	Somerset
Ess.	Essex		St.	Staffordshire
Gl.	Gloucestershire		Sx.	Sussex
Ha.	Hampshire		Sy.	Surrey
He.	Herefordshire		Wa.	Warwickshire
Hrt.	Hertfordshire		Wlt.	Wiltshire
Hu.	Huntingdonshire		Wo.	Worcestershire
La.	Lancashire		Yk.	Yorkshire

Other abbreviations

abp.	archbishop		d.	death
app.	appendix		D.C.L.	Doctor of Civil Law
archd.	archdeacon		Decr.B.	Bachelor of Canon Law
B.C.L.	Bachelor of Civil Law		Decr.D.	Doctor of Canon Law
bp.	bishop		dioc.	diocese
br.	brother		dy.	deanery
B.V.M.	Blessed Virgin Mary		esq.	armiger, esquire
can.	canon		fo.	folio
cath.	cathedral		I.	inductor
ch.	church		inst.	institution
chap.	chaplain		inv.	inventory
coll.	college, collegiate		J.U.B.	Bachelor of Both Laws

J.U.D.	Doctor of Both Laws
kt.	knight
l.d.	letters dimissory
m.	monk
Mr	Master
n.s.	new series
O. Carm.	Carmelite Order
O. Carth.	Carthusian Order
O. Cist.	Cistercian Order
O.E.S.A.	Order of Augustinian Friars
O.F.M.	Order of Friars Minor
O.P.	Order of Preachers
O.S.A.	Order of Augustinian Canons
O.S.B.	Order of St Benedict
O.S.J.J.	Order of the Hospital of St John at Jerusalem
O. Trin.	Order of Trinitarians
P.	patron
pr.	priest
pres.	presentation
r.	rector
res.	resignation
S.T.B.	Bachelor of Theology
S.T.P.	Doctor of Theology
t.	title
temp.	temporalities
vac.	vacant
v.	vicar
vic.	vicarage

REFERENCES

BIHR   Bulletin of the Institute of Historical Research

BJRL   Bulletin of the John Rylands Library

BRUC   A.B. Emden, Biographical Register of the University of Cambridge to A.D. 1500 (Cambridge, 1963)

BRUO   A.B. Emden, Biographical Register of the University of Oxford to A.D. 1500 (Oxford, 1957-59)

CCR   Calendar of the Close Rolls preserved in the Public Record Office (London, H.M.S.O., 1892-1963)

CFR   Calendar of the Fine Rolls preserved in the Public Record Office (London, H.M.S.O., 1911-63)

CPL   Calendar of Entries in the Papal Registers relating to Great Britain and Ireland: Papal Letters (vols i - xiv London, H.M.S.O., 1894-1961; vol. xv Dublin, Irish Historical MSS Commission, 1978)

CPR   Calendar of the Patent Rolls preserved in the Public Record Office (London, H.M.S.O., 1891-)

CSP Milan   Calendar of State Papers and Manuscripts existing in the archives and collections of Milan, 1385-1618 (London, H.M.S.O., 1913)

CSP Spanish   Calendar of Letters, Despatches and State Papers relating to the negotiations between England and Spain, preserved in the archives of Simancas and elsewhere (London, H.M.S.O., 1862-1964)

CSP Venetian   Calendar of State Papers and Manuscripts relating to English affairs existing in the archives and collections of Venice and in other libraries of Northern Italy (London, H.M.S.O., 1864-1947)

C & Y   Canterbury and York Society

Churchill   I.J. Churchill, Canterbury Administration (2 vols, 1933)

Decretum   in Corpus Iuris Canonici, ed. E. Friedberg, vol. i (Leipzig, 1879)

EHR   English Historical Review

Foedera   Foedera, Conventiones etc., ed. T. Rymer, 20 vols (1704-35)

JEH   Journal of Ecclesiastical History

Literae Cantuarienses   Literae Cantuarienses, ed. J.B. Sheppard (3 vols, Rolls Series lxxxv, 1887-9)

Mansi	*Sacrorum Conciliorum Nova et Amplissima Collectio*, ed. J.D. Mansi (31 vols, Florence, 1759-98)
Monasticon	*Monasticon Anglicanum* of William Dugdale, ed. J. Caley et al. (6 vols in 8, 1817-30)
PBA	*Proceedings of the British Academy*
PCC	Prerogative Court of Canterbury Will Registers, now in PRO, PROB 11
Pollard	A.F. Pollard, *The Reign of Henry VII from Contemporary Sources* (3 vols, London 1913-14)
PRO	Public Record Office
Reg. Bourgchier	*Registrum Thome Bourgchier, Cantuariensis Archiepiscopi 1454-86*, ed. F.R.H. Du Boulay (C & Y, liv)
Reg. Chichele	*Register of Henry Chichele, Archbishop of Canterbury 1414-43*, ed. E.F. Jacob (C & Y, xlv-xlvii)
Reg. Ep. Peckham	*Registrum Epistolarum Fratris Iohannis Peckham, Archiepiscopi Cantuariensis*, ed. C.T. Martin (3 vols, Rolls Series lxxvii, 1882-6)
Reg. Langham	*Registrum Simonis Langham, Cantuariensis Archiepiscopi 1366-68*, ed. A.C. Wood (C & Y, liii)
Reg. Pecham	*Registrum Johannis Pecham, Cantuariensis Archiepiscopi 1279-92*, ed. F.N. Davis and D.L. Douie (C & Y lxiv-lxv)
Reg. Pontissara	*Registrum Johannis de Pontissara, Episcopi Wyntoniensis 1282-1304*, ed. C. Deedes (C & Y, xix, xxx)
Reg. Stillington	*The Registers of Robert Stillington, Bishop of Bath and Wells 1466-91, and Richard Fox, Bishop of Bath and Wells 1492-94*, ed. H.C. Maxwell Lyte (Somerset Record Society, lii)
Reg. Winchelsey	*Registrum Roberti Winchelsey, Cantuariensis Archiepiscopi 1294-1313*, ed. R. Graham (C & Y, li-lii)
Rot. Parl.	*Rotuli Parliamentorum; ut et Petitiones, et Placita in Parliamento* (6 vols, 1832)
Taxatio	*Taxatio Ecclesiastica Angliae et Walliae auctoritate Papae Nicholai IV* (1802)
TRHS	*Transactions of the Royal Historical Society*
VCH	*The Victoria County Histories of England*
Wilkins	*Concilia Magnae Britanniae et Hiberniae...446-1718*, ed. D. Wilkins (4 vols, 1737)
X	'Decretales', in *Corpus Iuris Canonici*, ii, ed. E. Friedberg

VI   'Liber Sextus Decretalium D. Bonifacii Papae VIII',
          in <u>Corpus Iuris Canonici</u>, ii, ed. E. Friedberg

1   [fo.1] REGISTER OF THE MOST REVEREND FATHER IN CHRIST AND LORD JOHN MORTON, D.C.L., FIRST BISHOP OF ELY AND THEN POSTULATED TO THE ARCHBISHOPRIC OF CANTERBURY AND TRANSLATED BY POPE INNOCENT VIII FROM THE CHURCH OF ELY TO THAT OF CANTERBURY ON 6 OCTOBER 1486, IN THE THIRD YEAR OF THE PONTIFICATE OF THAT POPE.

Bull of Pope Innocent VIII directed to John bp. of Ely, translating him from the church of Ely to that of Canterbury, vacant by the d. of Thomas Bourgchier, cardinal priest of St Ciriac in Thermis. Before taking possession of the church of Canterbury he is to swear the accustomed oath of fealty, according to the form enclosed, in the presence of the bps. of London and Rochester. St Peter's Rome, 6 Oct. 1486.

    [Calendared: CPL 1484-92 (xv), no.198.]

2   [fo.1v] Bull directed to John bp. of Ely. Concurrent absolution from the bonds by which he is bound to the church of Ely. St Peter's Rome, 6 Oct. 1486.

3   [fo.2] Bull directed to the suffragans of the church of Canterbury, enjoining due obedience and reverence to the abp. St Peter's Rome, 6 Oct. 1486.

4   Bull directed to the vassals of the church of Canterbury, enjoining them to swear fealty to the abp. and to perform their accustomed services. St Peter's Rome, 6 Oct. 1486.

5   [fo.2v] Bull directed to the clergy of the dioc. of Canterbury, enjoining them to show due honour and obedience to their diocesan. St Peter's Rome, 6 Oct. 1486.

6   Bull directed to the people of the dioc. of Canterbury, enjoining them to show due honour and obedience to their diocesan. St Peter's Rome, 6 Oct. 1486.

7   Memorandum that on 9 Dec. 1486, in accordance with custom, William Sellyng, S.T.P., prior of Christ Church, Canterbury, delivered to John Morton, as he sat before the high altar of the chapel of Le Ely Inne in the suburbs of London, the cross of the church of Canterbury. After the prior had delivered a solemn sermon, the abp. received the cross, kissed it and handed it to his crossbearer. This was done in the presence of Mr Robert Morton, Master of the Rolls, Mr David William, Decr. D., Mr Thomas Cooke, D.C.L., Sir Edmund Mountford, Mr John Hervy, canon of Hereford, and many others.

    [fo.3v blank]

8   [fo.4] Confirmation by Pope Innocent VIII of the dispensation for the marriage of King Henry VII and Elizabeth of York. St Peter's Rome, 27 March 1486.

   [Printed: Foedera, xii, 297-9; calendared: CPL 1484-92 (xiv),p.2.]

9   [fo.5] Bull[1] of Pope Innocent VIII, authorising the abp. to visit and reform houses of the Cluniac, Cistercian, Premonstratensian and other orders, notwithstanding their exemption. St Peter's Rome, 6 Aug. 1487.

   [1. For the reissue of this bull, and printed text, see 48.]

10   [fo.6] Bull of Pope Innocent VIII permitting the apprehension of those malefactors who sally forth from sanctuary to commit further crimes, and then return to their refuge. St Peter's Rome, 6 Aug. 1487.

   [Printed: Foedera, xii, 541-2, from the exemplification by Pope Alexander VI, calendared: CPL 1484-92 (xiv), p.35.]

11   [fo.7] Commission of Pope Innocent VIII to the abp., at the petition of King Henry VII, to absolve in person or by deputy those who have incurred excommunication by their opposition to the marriage and succession of the king, and who humbly seek absolution, administering to them an oath that they will not in future commit such acts nor aid and counsel those acting thus, and imposing on them a suitable penance. St Peter's Rome, 6 Aug. 1487.

   [Printed: Foedera, xii, 324-5.]

12   [fo.7v] Confirmation by Pope Innocent VIII of the dispensation granted by James bp. of Imola for the marriage of King Henry VII and Elizabeth of York. St Peter's Rome, 23 July 1486.

   [Printed: Foedera, xii, 313-4; calendared: CPL 1484-92 (xiv), p.27.]

13   [fo.8] Citation of the abbot of Waltham Holy Cross. Addressed to all rs. etc. within the province of Canterbury. Wishing to obey the papal mandate [9] and to fulfil the obligations of his office, the abp. has directed his attention to the abbey of Waltham Holy Cross (Sancte Crucis de Waltham), O.S.A., London dioc. This house was piously founded long ago by the illustrious kings of England, and once religion flourished and the Rule of St Augustine was notably observed, but it has now suffered a disastrous decline in spiritualities and temporalities, and the abp. is informed that this is due for the most part to the guilt and deficiencies of the abbot, so that with the neglect of God's service true religion has been perverted into error, holy obedience into obstinate rebellion, and votive charity into licencious self-gratification. Most of the manors, granges and other buildings are on the verge of ruin, the movable goods and valuables of the monastery, which were provided in profusion by the founders and other faithful benefactors, together with the ancient treasures and the stock of the manors, are alienated and consumed, and the house is greatly burdened with debt. These evils, and the want of reform in the head and some of the members, are mostly attributable to the negligence of the current abbot, and this brings almost irreparable harm to the monastery, grave peril to his soul, shame upon holy religion, and sets a bad example to the multitude. The abp., therefore, orders the recipients of this mandate to cite peremptorily, or cause to be cited, Br Thomas, abbot of Waltham, to appear before the abp. or his commissaries in the chapel at Lambeth on the tenth day after the delivery of the citation or the next judicial day thereafter, to answer in person certain articles to be put to him by apostolic authority, and to receive judgement according to the tenor of the papal letters. The executor of this mandate is to certify the abp. or his commissaries of the action taken. Lambeth, 9 Feb. 1488.

14   [fo.8v] Citation of the priors [sic] of St Andrew's, Northampton. Addressed to all rs. etc. within the province of Canterbury. The abp. has recently received papal letters [9] . Since the monastery of St Andrew at Northampton, of the Cluniac order, Lincoln dioc., in which the observance of religion once flourished, has cast aside the yoke of sweet contemplation and for some long time past has declined in fervour, it urgently requires the office of correction and reformation. Because of the incessant struggle, still undecided, between Thomas Sudbury and William Breknok, Cluniac monks, for the office of prior, the pure norm of life has been abandoned, the service of God is largely neglected, the devout ordinance of the founders is turned into a mockery, and the religious, who should live according to the monastic rule, on occasion even take up bloody arms, and lead a warlike and dissolute life, to the peril of their souls etc. The abp. therefore orders the recipients of this mandate to cite peremptorily, or cause to be cited, the foresaid Thomas and William, pretended priors, to appear before the abp. or his commissaries on the fifteenth day after delivery of the citation or the next judicial day thereafter, etc. [as 13]. Lambeth, 6 Feb. 1488.

15   Mandate to all rs. etc. within the province of Canterbury. Since the abp. directed letters of citation to Thomas and William, pretended priors of St Andrew's, Northampton, Thomas Sudbury has shown himself prepared to appear, but William Breknok has gone into hiding, so that he cannot be cited in person. So that his disgraceful self-concealment does not appear to avail him, the abp. has decreed, as justice demands, that he should be cited in the following manner. He orders the recipients of this mandate, jointly or singly, that they should peremptorily cite, or cause to be cited, the foresaid William Breknok, in person if he can be apprehended and there is safe access to him, otherwise by public citation posted on the doors of the monastery and of the parish church of Northampton nearest to the house, or through his known friends and neighbours, or by other legal ways and means, so that in all probability the citation will come to his notice, to appear before the abp. or his commissaries on the fifteenth day after delivery etc. [as 13]. Lambeth, 27 Feb. 1488.

[For discussion, see R. Graham, 'The English Province of the Order of Cluny in the Fifteenth Century', TRHS, 4th series, vii (1924), 98–130.]

16   [fo.9] Commission with power of canonical coercion to Mr Thomas Cooke, D.C.L., as Auditor of Causes in the Court of Audience. Lambeth, 15 Jan. 1487.

[See Churchill, ii, 212-3, for form.]

17   Commission with power of canonical coercion to Mr Thomas Cooke, D.C.L., and Mr Humphrey Hawardyn, D.C.L., as Commissaries of the Prerogative. Mortlake (Mortelak'), 3 March 1487.

[See Churchill, ii, 179-80, for form.]

18   [fo.9v] Commission with power of canonical coercion to Mr Thomas Cooke, D.C.L., and Mr Humphrey Hawardyn, D.C.L., jointly or singly, as Auditors of Causes in the Court of Audience. Lambeth, 3 March 1487.

[See Churchill, ii, 212-3, for form.]

19   Commission with power of canonical coercion to Mr Adam Redesheff, Decr.D., and Mr William Shaldoo, M.A., as commissaries of the abp. in the town of Calais (Calesie) and the surrounding district in the dioc. of Therouanne subject to the king of England. Lambeth, 20 Feb. 1487.

[Printed: Churchill, ii, 219-20.]

20   [fo.10] Commission to Nicholas Wynnysbury, literate, as Apparitor General in the province of Canterbury. Lambeth, 29 Jan. 1487.

[See Churchill, ii, 182-3, for form.]

21   Commission to John Medewall, literate, as apparitor in the deanery of Arches in London, with powers relating to testamentary business within the city of London and the borough of Southwark. Lambeth, 29 Jan. 1487.

22   [fo.10v] Commission with power of canonical coercion to Mr William Shaldoo, S.T.B., as dean of Croydon, in the abp.'s immediate jurisdiction. Lambeth, 8 Jan. 1487.

[See Churchill, ii, 26, for form.]

23   [fo.11] Injunction for the reception of the questors of the hospital of St Thomas Acon (de Accon), London, addressed to all rs. etc. within the province of Canterbury, exhorting all clergy and people to observe as inviolable the privileges and indulgences granted by various popes to the hospital over a period of many years. Because the master and brethren have complained that some persons in the province, both ecclesiastical and lay, have frequently and to the great prejudice of the hospital prevented their messengers and proctors from announcing these privileges and indulgences, the abp. orders all recipients of these letters, on pain of the penalties for contempt, to receive with the greatest favour the questors of the hospital, which is one of the four places permitted by a provincial constitution to collect aids[1], is situated at the birthplace of the glorious martyr, and where his memory is venerated second only after the church of Canterbury, not less even than in the hospital of St Thomas in Rome. Once a year at least they should allow them to declare to the people in church, on a Sunday or feast day, the privileges and indulgences of the hospital, as listed in the attached schedule; they should encourage the people by word and example, should permit collection without any disturbance, and should deliver what is collected without any subtraction, on pain of excommunication. To exhort the faithful to contribute more readily, the abp., confident of the immense mercy of God and the merits of the BVM, SS Peter and Paul, and SS Alphege and Thomas his patrons, grants to all truly penitent, contrite and confessed who contribute to the hospital forty days indulgence as often as they make a grant. Rebels and objectors shall be cited peremptorily to appear before the abp. or his Auditor of Causes on the fifteenth day after citation or the next judicial day thereafter. Lambeth, 12 Dec. 1487.

[1. Reg. Chichele, iv, 261-2.]

24 [fo.11v] Schedule of indulgences and pardons granted to those who with their alms visit or relieve the hospital of St Thomas Acon, where the glorious martyr was born and which long ago was admitted by Convocation as one of the four places permitted to gather the alms of Christian people for the health of their souls. Pope Alexander IV[1] remitted a seventh part of penance enjoined to all those who help or relieve the hospital with their goods or alms, or who join the fraternity and make a yearly payment.

Pope Benedict XII commanded all places to allow the proctors of the hospital to expound freely their indulgences to clergy and people. If the proctors come to any city, castle or town under interdict, once yearly they have the power to open the church doors so that divine service may be said, accursed persons put out by name and the dead buried in the churchyard, and they that do public penance that day shall be released and spared. Also, all who give to the hospital a certain quantity of their goods, make a yearly payment and on their deathbeds bequeath any goods to the hospital, may choose each year able and discreet confessors who may absolve them of all sins for which they are contrite and have confessed, excepting such as are reserved to the court of Rome, and may dispense them from all vows which they may not conveniently or profitably keep, excepting only the vow of Jesus and the Holy Cross. Every brother shall have written letters of fraternity, and burial shall not be denied him in whatever manner or from whatever disease he may die, except if he is accursed by name by ecclesiastical censure.

5

Pope Boniface IX remitted, for each feast day, [blank] days of penance enjoined to all those penitent and shriven, who devoutly visit or relieve the hospital each year at the feasts of the Nativity and Circumcision of Our Lord, Epiphany, Easter, Ascension, Corpus Christi, Whitsun, the Nativity, Purification and Assumption of BVM, the Nativity of St John the Baptist, SS Peter and Paul, the dedication of the church of St Thomas, his Translation and Martyrdom, and All Hallows, and furthermore in the octaves of the feasts of the Nativity of Our Lord, Epiphany, Ascension, Corpus Christi, the Nativity and Assumption of BVM, St John the Baptist, SS Peter and Paul, and within six days of Whit-Sunday.

Pope Pius II[2] mercifully remitted for evermore seven years and seven Lentens of penance enjoined to all penitent and shriven persons who devoutly visit yearly, in person or by deputy, every Tuesday from Quinquagesima to the octave of Easter, and the four days after Easter, and also every day within the octaves of the feasts of the Translation and Martyrdom of St Thomas, and give on any day charitable subsidy.

Pope Paul II[3] mercifully remitted five years and five Lentens of penance to all who devoutly visit the chapel of Our Lady within the church of St Thomas, and there give alms for the conservation of that place.

Popes Boniface IX, Eugenius IV, Calixtus III, Pius II and especially Sixtus IV, by his leaden bulls issued by apostolic authority, confirmed, ratified and established all the liberties, franchises, privileges and pardons granted by their predecessors to the master and brethren, and have charged that no man should be so foolhardy as to break or contradict their grant and confirmation, on pain of incurring the indignation of Almighty God and the apostles Peter and Paul. Given at St Peter's, Rome, 16 Jan. 1472.

Henry Chichele, abp. of Canterbury, granted to all benefactors of the said place forty days pardon, and in Convocation ordained the hospital to be one of the four places which the province admitted before other places in the realm, as had been the usage in olden times.

John Stafford, John Kempe and Thomas Bourgchier, abps., confirmed and ratified the same, and granted to all their subjects within the province who are shriven, contrite and repentant and who relieve the hospital with their alms one hundred days of pardon. John, now abp. of Canterbury, has confirmed these and granted forty days pardon to all the foresaid benefactors.

[1. CPL 1198-1304, p.339
 2. CPL 1455-64, pp.515-6
 3. CPL 1458-71, pp.454-5]

25   [fo.12] Indulgence granted to the benefactors of the hospital of
     St Thomas Acon. The abp., confident of the mercy of Almighty God,
     etc., mercifully grants indulgence of forty days of enjoined penance
     to all those truly penitent, contrite and confessed who visit the
     church on each of the feasts of the Nativity and Circumcision of Our

Lord, Epiphany, Easter, Pentecost, Holy Trinity, Corpus Christi, the
Nativity, Annunciation, Purification, Assumption and Visitation of the
BVM, All Saints, Holy Cross, the apostles and evangelists, St Thomas
the Martyr and the dedication of the church, and throughout the octaves
of those feasts that have octaves, and each day during the whole of
Lent, in order to pray devoutly and perform a pilgrimage, and who lend
helping hands to the repair of the fabric and to the other necessities
of the church, or who in their testaments leave, or donate or procure
charitable subsidies, publicly or secretly, and who say a Lord's Prayer
with an Ave Maria for the health of the universal church, the realm of
England, the benefactors of the said church who are alive and the souls
of those who are dead, and for the souls of all the faithful departed,
and to those who at any other time of the year preach or hear the word
of God in that church, especially in Lent, whenever and however often
they do any of the above things. The abp. also constitutes them
participants and coheirs in all the prayers and benefits of the church
of Canterbury and the adjoining churches. Lambeth, 23 Feb. 1488.

26 [fo.12v] In the parish church of St Mary, Lambeth, in the presence of
Mr Thomas Cooke, Auditor of Causes, John Choo, r. of Dowdeswell
(Dowdyswell'), Gl., acknowledged his obligation to pay, by reason of
his church, an annual pension of 40s to Mr John Burton, S.T.P., r. of
Withington (Wythyndon'), Gl. Notarial exemplification by Mr John Beele,
notary public, in the presence of Mr Richard Nikkys, D.C.L., Mr James
Hutton, D.C.L., and Mr Robert Myddylton, D.C.L. 29 Jan. 1487.

27 Licence granted, because of his learning and moral virtues, to Mr John
Veysy, M.A., to preach in Latin or the vernacular to clergy and people
in churches and other suitable places throughout the province of
Canterbury, provincial constitutions to the contrary notwithstanding,
with a grant of forty days indulgence to those in a state of grace who
hear his sermons. Lambeth, 8 Feb. 1487.

28 [fo.13] Licence granted to Mr William Holcombe, precentor of the
collegiate church of St Mary Ottery (Beate Marie de Oterey), Exeter
dioc., to celebrate divine office in chapels, oratories and other
suitable places throughout the province, or to have divine office
celebrated in his presence by a suitable chaplain, so long as no
prejudice is suffered thereby by the parish church to which the chapel
or oratory is annexed, provincial constitutions to the contrary
notwithstanding. Lambeth, 26 March 1487.

29 Licence granted to Mr William Holcombe to preach in Latin or the
vernacular [as no.27, but without grant of indulgence]. Lambeth,
26 March 1487.

30 Licence granted to Sir John Dynham, Lord Dynham, Treasurer of England,
and to Elizabeth Wylleby, daughter of Robert, Lord Wylleby of Broke,

that their marriage may be celebrated in any church, chapel or oratory within the province of Canterbury, so long as no prejudice results thereby to Elizabeth's parish church and there is no canonical impediment to the marriage. [Undated.]

31   Monition to the r. of All Saints, Canterbury to reside. Addressed to all rs. etc. within the province of Canterbury. In the recent provincial council at St Paul's, London, it was decreed that, on pain of the law, all rs., vs., and other curates should reside in their benefices, laying aside canonical impediment and other legitimate causes of absence, so that they might instruct their parishioners by word and example. The abp. has received reliable information that Mr Alan Hyndmerrsh, r. of All Saints, Canterbury, does not reside in accordance with this ordinance, yet receives all the fruits and revenues of the church, in contempt of the canonical rulings on this matter, hence the church is defrauded of the proper divine services and the cure of souls is neglected. Wishing that, as the r. is maintained by the stipend of the church, so he should undertake the cure and the burdens incumbent upon him, the abp. orders the recipients of these letters that they should warn Mr Alan, in person if he may be apprehended, otherwise in the person of his proctor if he has left such in his church, or if not by public monition in his church before his acquaintances and parishioners, that within six months of this monition he should come to his church and reside in person, as the cure requires, on pain of deprivation. If he does not obey within six months, the abp. will proceed to his deprivation and will provide for the church as seems best in accordance with the will of God and with justice. Those executing this mandate are to certify the abp. of the action they have taken. Lambeth, 5 July 1488.

32   [fo.13v] Licence granted to Mr John Ryse, r. of Sampford Courtney (Sampford Courteney), De., to celebrate divine office in person or by a suitable chaplain in the chapels of St Nectan and St Leonard in the same parish, so long as no prejudice results thereby to the parish church, provincial constitutions to the contrary notwithstanding. Lambeth, 3 July 1488.

33   Mandate for the organisation of processions, directed to Mr Richard Lichfield, D.C.L., the abp.'s Official in London dioc. sede vacante. The king has asked the abp. to enjoin prayers for himself and his armies engaged in the defence of the church in England, the realm and his royal rights. The abp. therefore orders his Official in London dioc. to instruct the suffragans of the province that they should order the clergy and laity to arrange processions for the welfare of the universal church and of the king and realm, and for the tranquillity and peace of all Christian people, in all cathedral, conventual, collegiate and parish churches, to be held three times a week in cities and larger towns and twice a week in lesser centres, with chanting of the litany and with masses, if possible, and in any case with three collects, for the state of the universal church, for the

8

successful expedition of the king and his armies, and for peace and tranquillity, with supplications that almighty and merciful God will hearken to their prayers and will grant success to the king and his kingdom, the nobles and all the faithful of the realm in their enterprises, will protect and defend them from the assaults and wiles of their enemies, and will grant to the faithful a long-awaited peace. The Official shall himself organise such processions in the city and dioc. of London. In order to encourage the faithful in their supplications, the abp., confident of the mercy of Almight God etc., grants forty days indulgence to all the faithful who are contrite and confessed when they participate in such processions. Lambeth, 13 May 1489.

34 [fo.14] Certificate of the dean and chapter of St Paul's, sealed in the chapter house, containing the names of those nominated by them to the abp., from whom he is to choose his Official in the vacancy of the see following the death of Bishop Thomas Kempe, according to the composition between the dean and chapter and Abps. Boniface of Savoy and Robert Kilwardby. Those nominated are Mr Thomas Jayn, Decr.D., archd. of Essex, Mr Richard Lichfield, D.C.L., archd. of Middlesex, and Mr Walter Oudeby, Decr.D. London, 30 March 1489.

35 Commission to Sir John Don and Edward his son as bailiffs of the archiepiscopal manor of Tring (Treng), Hrt., the office to be exercised in person or by deputies acceptable to the abp. and his successors, for the duration of the lives of John and Edward, for a wage of 40s p.a. to be paid at Michaelmas by the abp.'s receiver from the profits of the manor. All ministers, officials and tenants of the manor are to render them obedience in the execution of their office. Lambeth 15 July 1489.

36 Johannes permissione divina etc., dilectis filiabus mulieribus in domo mulierum . . . [incomplete document].

37 [fo.14v] Bull of Pope John XXII directed to the abp. of Canterbury and the bps. of Lincoln and Bath and Wells. Since the priors and convents of Carthusian houses have complained to the pope of the detention of their possessions by ecclesiastical and lay persons, and since it is difficult to bring every complaint to the apostolic see, the pope appoints the abp. and bps. conservators of the possessions and privileges of the Carthusian order, with powers of canonical coercion extending to the invocation of the secular arm, and power to act outside their own diocs. Avignon, 4 July 1318.

38 [fo.15] Letter of conservation for the Carthusian brethren. The abp., as conservator of the privileges of the Carthusian order, to all archdeacons and their Officials, rural deans, rs. etc. within the province of Canterbury. The prior and conv. of the Charterhouse at

Witham (Wytham), So., have complained that certain sons of iniquity, whose names they do not know, have occupied and detained spiritual and temporal possessions of the priory, and that some of them have repeatedly threatened and molested the prior and conv., and this they do daily, to the peril of their souls etc. Therefore, as it is difficult to have recourse to the apostolic see for every complaint, they have humbly begged the abp. to provide a remedy. He, wishing to aid the prior and conv. against their molestors and to discourage others from such acts, commands all recipients of this mandate, by the apostolic authority by which he acts in this matter, that they shall order all occupiers or detainers of the possessions of Witham, and those who have made any threat or assault against the prior and conv., to restore any such possessions within fifteen days – five days for the first, five for the second and five for the third and peremptory warning – and also to make satisfaction for any injuries relating to these possessions, on pain of major excommunication which the abp. by these letters promulgates against any guilty person who does not obey this monition. After fifteen days the recipients of this mandate, when so requested by the prior and conv., shall publish the excommunication of such persons in church on Sundays and festivals, not ceasing from their denunciation until the molestors return to the bosom of Holy Mother Church and merit absolution, having made condign satisfaction according to the law, or until other instructions are received from the abp. Those requested to act shall certify the abp. of the action taken. Lambeth, 22 March 1491.

39   [fo.15v] Bull of Pope Alexander VI notifying the abp. of the provision of William Smith to the see of Coventry and Lichfield, vacant by the d. of John Halse. St Peter's Rome, 1 Oct. 1492.

40   [fo.16] Bull of Pope Innocent VIII notifying the abp. of the translation of Edmund Audley from the see of Rochester to that of Hereford, vacant by the d. of Thomas Myllyng. St Peter's Rome, 22 June 1492.

41   Bull of Pope Alexander VI notifying the abp. of the provision of Thomas Savage to the see of Rochester, vacant by the translation of Edmund Audley to the see of Hereford. St Peter's Rome, 3 December 1492.

42   [fo.16v] Undated. To Mr Ralph Hannyes, clerk. Since the pope has provided Mr Thomas Savage, D.C.L., dean of the chapel royal, to the see of Rochester, vacant by the translation of Bp. Edmund to the see of Hereford...[incomplete document; marginal note: vacat quia registratur in alio quaterno].

43   [fo.17] Mr Thomas Cooke, Auditor of Causes, appeared before the abp. and on behalf of the king and queen presented apostolic letters, which were required to be exhibited in distant parts, requesting him to examine these letters and cause them to be transcribed and exemplified. There follows a bull of Pope Innocent VIII, clarifying that the prohibition of resistance to the king extends to Ireland and other places outside the realm subject to the king, and extending this prohibition to ecclesiastical persons in England, Ireland and the king's other dominions. St Peter's Rome, 17 May

1488[1]. Having pronounced the letters to be authentic, the abp. ordered that they should be transcribed, exemplified, signed and sealed by a notary public, so that the transcripts might have the authority of the originals. Notarial exemplification by Mr John Beele, clerk of Bath and Wells dioc. and notary public by apostolic authority, in the presence of Mr Rumpayne of Bath and Wells dioc. and John Ryche, chaplain of Canterbury dioc.

> [1. Printed: Foedera, xii, 341-2; calendared: CPL 1484-92 (xiv) pp.33-4. Printed: Wilkins, iii, 630-2; Pollard, iii, no.40.]

44 [fo.18] Consent of William the subprior and the conv. of Christ Church Canterbury, required by the decrees of Abps. Thomas Becket and Edmund Rich,[1] to the consecration of Mr Richard Fox, D.C.L., elect and confirmed of Exeter, elsewhere than in the cathedral church of Canterbury. Canterbury, 3 Apr. 1487.

> [1. For this privilege of Christ Church, see C.R. Cheney, 'Magna Carta Beati Thome; Another Canterbury Forgery', BIHR, xxxvi (1963), 1-26.]

45 [fo.18v] Profession of Richard Fox, elect of Exeter.

In the name of God, Amen. I Richard, bp. elect of the church of Exeter, to be consecrated by you, most reverend father and lord John, abp. of Canterbury, primate of all England and legate of the apostolic see, declare and promise due and canonical obedience, reverence and subjection in all matters to you and your canonical successors in the church of Canterbury, according to the decree of the Roman pontiffs, and I will be an aid in the defence, retention and conservation of your rights and those of the church of Canterbury, saving my order. So help me God and the Holy Gospels. I confirm the above by subscription with my own hand.

46 Bull of Pope Innocent VIII notifying the abp. of the translation of Peter Courtenay from the see of Exeter to that of Winchester, vacant by the d. of William Waynflete. St Peter's Rome, 29 Jan. 1487.

47 Mr John de Giglis, J.U.D., papal collector in England, and Perseus de Malintiis, dean of the church of St Michael de le Profeto at Bologna, papal chamberlain, specially deputed commissaries in this matter, presented to the abp. in a low parlour at Lambeth a papal bull containing certain indulgences, and requested him to examine these letters and cause them to be transcribed and exemplified, so that the exemplification might have the same authority as the original.

Pope Innocent VIII announces that the Turks and Tartars, who have previously occupied many Christian lands, now intend to attack the territory of Casimir, king of Poland, and will afterwards descend on Italy, Sicily and Malta. To assist the war against them, the pope decrees that until the revocation of this indulgence, all those in the

dominions of the king of England who contribute between one and four
gold florins, or such amount as may be ordained by the pope's
commissaries, may choose a suitable confessor who once in their
lifetime may grant absolution from all ecclesiastical censures and
penalties in any matter whatsoever, and may grant absolution whenever
it is sought in matters not reserved to the apostolic see; once in
their lifetime and in articulo mortis (even if they are in this
condition more than once) the confessor may grant full absolution and
remission from all their sins, with the full indulgence which
accompanies a visit to the threshold of the apostles, etc., and he
shall impose salutary penance. He may also commute to the benefit of
the holy expedition any vows, save those of chastity and religion. All
other indulgences, save those for the war against the Turk, are
suspended. The papal commissaries shall appoint preachers to publicise
the indulgence. The commissaries may accept money acquired by usury,
rapine or spoliation where it is not known to whom restitution should
be made, and they may, with certain safeguards, absolve those making a
contribution from the penalties for simony, marriage within the
prohibited degrees and ordination below the canonical age, and may
restore those for any reason deprived of their ecclesiastical dignity.
The commissaries may interpret any uncertainties in this bull, and may
use canonical coercion, extending to the invocation of the secular arm.
Those who promise a contribution and then withdraw are subject to
excommunication and eternal malediction. The collectors shall take
only a reasonable and moderate salary. The commissaries are to have
the help of the diocesan authorities when it is requested. St Peter's
Rome, 18 Sept. 1488.[1]

After the abp. had examined these letters and pronounced them to be
authentic, he ordered them to be transcribed and exemplified by a
notary public. He declared John de Giglis and Perseus de Malintiis to
be the legitimate commissaries of the pope, according to papal letters
dated at St Peter's, 18 September 1488,[2] and entrusted them with the
administration of the indulgences and faculties contained in the bull.
The transcript and exemplification of the bull should have the full
authority of the original. Notarial exemplification by Mr Nicholas
Turnour, B.C.L., of London dioc., notary public by apostolic authority
and proctor general of the Court of Canterbury, in the presence of John
Rocche and James Dutton, literates dwelling in London. Lambeth,
9 March 1489.

    [1. Printed: Wilkins, iii, 626–9
     2. CPL 1484–92 (xiv), pp.52–3.]

48   [fo.21] Reissue by Pope Innocent VIII of the bull Quanta in Dei
Ecclesia [9], permitting the visitation and reform of exempt religious
houses, with the addition of a clause permitting visitation by suitable
deputies. St Peter's Rome, 6 March 1490.

    [Printed: Wilkins, iii, 630–2; Pollard, iii, no.66; calendared:
    CPL 1484–92 (xiv), p.51.]

49   [fo.22] Bull of Pope Innocent VIII addressed to John abp. of Canterbury, permitting the investigation and reform of those churches claiming privileges of sanctuary. St Peter's Rome, 18 March 1490.

    [Calendared: CPL 1484–92 (xiv), p.35.]

50   [fo.22v] Monition directed to William Wallingford, abbot of St Albans, issued by authority of the bull Quanta in Dei Ecclesia [9]. The abp. rehearses the defects in the monastery that have been brought to his attention: the abbot is notorious for his simony, usury and the dilapidation of the possessions of his house, and for his laxity and negligence in administration. The abbot and not a few of his monks have abandoned the Rule and set the pious intentions of the founders at naught. Among other grave crimes, the abbot admitted to the nunnery of St Mary de Prae (Pray), and subsequently made prioress, Helen Germyn, a married and licentious woman. Thomas Sudbury, a monk of St Albans, fornicated with her, and other monks went to her and her sisters as to a brothel. At St Mary de Prae and Sopwell (Sapwell) the abbot has changed prioresses at will, substituting for good women the evil and corrupt, and deputing brethren to rule these nunneries and the other monastic cells as wardens, who dissipate and consume the goods of the priories. At St Albans the abbot has wasted the valuables of the house and has felled and sold wood to the value of eight thousand marks. Immorality, simony and theft flourish in the abbey, and the abbot defends rather than punishes the culprits, while oppressing the virtuous. Therefore, the abbey urgently needs the office of visitation and correction. The abp. has already charitably admonished the abbot, but he has neglected to effect reform. The abp. now   peremptorily orders the abbot to reform himself, his abbey and the nunneries within thirty days, and the more distant cells within sixty days, otherwise the abp. will proceed in accordance with the terms of the apostolic mandate. So that he may know of the abbot's obedience or contempt, he is to certify the abp. of the action he has taken. A transcript of the papal bull is attached. Notarial exemplification by Henry Medwall, notary public by papal authority, in a high chamber at Lambeth, in the presence of Mr Thomas Maddes, S.T.B., of Norwich dioc., and Mr Rompayne of Bath and Wells dioc. Lambeth, 5 July 1490.

    [Printed: Wilkins, iii, 532–4; Pollard, iii, no.67. For discussion see Knowles, JEH iii (1951), and also further papal bulls calendared in CPL 1484–92 (xv), nos. 464 and 478.]

51   [fo.23v] Bull of Pope Innocent VIII notifying the abp. of the translation of Richard Fox from the see of Exeter to that of Bath and Wells, vacant by the d. of Robert Stillington. St Peter's Rome, 7 Feb. 1492.

52   [fo.24] Bull of Pope Alexander VI notifying the abp. of the provision of Oliver King to the see of Exeter, vacant by the translation of

13

Richard Fox to the see of Bath and Wells. St Peter's Rome, 30 Sept. 1492.

53 Grant of lands in Chevening and Chipstead by Abp. Edmund Rich. Notification that, by virtue of the concession made by King John to Abp. Hubert Walter and his successors in perpetuity that the lands which the men of the fee of the church of Canterbury hold in gavelkind may be converted into fees, and that the services other than money from those lands, that is provisions (exennia), carrying service and the like, may be converted to the equivalent money rent, together with the maintenance of the customary money rent,[1] Abp. Edmund grants to John de Chepstede a quarter of a sulung of land in Chipstead (Chepstede) and ten acres of land in Chevening (Chevenyng), with all their appurtenances, which he holds in the tenement of Otford (Otteford), to be held of the abp. and his successors freely and quietly, pacifically and honourably, by hereditary right, by the services of a tenth part of one knight's fee and by the service of 29s 2d in annual rent, to be paid at the four terms of the year, that is 7s 4d at each of Christmas, Easter and the Nativity of St John the Baptist and 7s 2d at Michaelmas, which 29s 2d is in substitution for all the services and customs which he or his predecessors ever owed to the abp. or his predecessors. The abp. grants that John and his heirs shall hold the foresaid land with all its appurtenances fully and wholly, freely and quietly by the foresaid service, and in all things they shall have in perpetuity the same liberty in the land as the other military tenants of the church of Canterbury and their heirs in the lands which they hold in fee of the church of Canterbury. The abp. and his successors shall have in perpetuity the same power and liberty over John and his heirs as over the other military tenants and their heirs. Sealed in the presence of Mr Richard de Wich, the abp.'s chancellor, Mr Nicholas de Bureford, Mr Reginald London, Mr Richard de Witlyngton and Mr Roger de Leycestre, abp.'s clerks, Henry Wintersel, Adam de Chivening, Hamo de Vielston' and Richard de Puntfrait', knights, Henry Luvel, John de Chevening, Simon de Chivening, Alan de Sunderhesse, Nicholas de Twitham, Thomas de Sibburn, Peter de Kersyng [sic in MS, rectius Kemsyng], clerk, and others. [Undated, Spring 1235 – Autumn 1240.[2]]

> [1. See Lambeth MS 1212, p.48, and F.R.H. DuBoulay, The Lordship of Canterbury, p.69f.
> 2. Mr Richard de Wich did not become chancellor until Spring 1235 at the earliest; before the archbishop's departure from England.]

54 [fo.24v] Letters testimonial of Abp. Thomas Arundel concerning the tenure of lands in Chipstead (Chipstede) and Chevening (Chevenyng). John Chipstede, son and heir of John Chipstede, holds, as his ancestors have held of the abps. of Canterbury from time immemorial, the lands and tenements, rents, services and mills with their appurtenances which the said John Chipstede has by hereditary right after the death of his father in Chipstead and Chevening in the abp.'s manor of Otford (Otteford) by the service of a tenth part of a knight's fee and the service of 29s 2d p.a., payable to the abp. and his successors at the four customary terms. All these lands and tenements in Chipstead and Chevening are held of the abp. by the foresaid services, except for thirty-three and a half acres of land in gavelkind which William Chipstede, John's uncle, recently acquired from the ancestors of John Kyngesdowne. William Courtenay, the abp.'s predecessor, had custody of John Chipstede when he was a minor, and of all the issues and profits of the said lands and tenements, and John rendered homage to Abp. William and also to the present abp., who earnestly requests that the recipients of these letters should when so required testify according to justice in this matter, to the salvation of the rights of the church of Canterbury and of the hereditary right of John Chipstede, the abp.'s tenant. Lambeth, 13 Nov. 1405.

[Note: nos. 51 and 52 were collated with the originals by Mr John Barett, whose notarial sign is here written in the register.]

55 [fo.25] Grant by the abp. of forty days indulgence to all those in the province of Canterbury who are penitent, contrite and confessed and who grant, leave or assign anything from their goods to John Danyell or any collector deputed by him for the repair and reconstruction of Rochester bridge (Rowchester brigge), which at the moment is almost ruined, and unless it is soon repaired will crumble from its foundations, to the grave peril and intolerable inconvenience of those wishing to cross it. Indeed, some who recently wished to cross the dangerous passage over which it is built had their boat wrecked and were drowned; by the repair of the bridge these and similar dangers may quickly and effectively be avoided. 2 Nov. 1489.

56 Mandate to Mr Richard Lychefeld, D.C.L., the abp.'s Official in London dioc. sede vacante. Since the abp. sent letters ordering processions [33] there have been torrential downpours of rain, and unless God remedies this situation, which He may do more quickly if Christian people resort to His mercy by the intercession of prayer, most of the harvest will be ruined. The abp. has learned that the processions, especially in London have already stopped, although for the most urgent of reasons they should continue. He orders the Official that he should, as far as he is able, ensure the continuance of the general processions and those in each church, organising general processions on six days a week and on the seventh at his discretion, with masses or other accustomed prayers for the church, the king, the kingdom and their peace and tranquillity, with litanies and collects, the first of All Saints, the second for the church, the third for the king, the fourth for the kingdom, and the fifth for fair weather, not ceasing these processions until receipt of the abp.'s mandate. Croydon, 4 Aug. 1489.

57 Mandate for the citation of Joan Chadworth. Addressed to all rs. etc. within the province of Canterbury. The abp. has learned that the lady Anne Crosby, widow and executrix of John Roger, generosus, who at the

15

time of her death held goods in various diocs. of the province, made
her last testament.[1] in which she appointed as executrix, among others,
Joan Chadworth. In her testament, among other bequests, she left
certain goods and valuables to her son John Crosby, a minor, which were
left in the hands of Joan Chadworth to his use until he came of age.
These goods and valuables she used for her own purposes until they were
almost entirely wasted, so that they may not be rendered to John when
he comes of age. Therefore, so that these goods may be disposed
according to the will of the testator and may be preserved safely, the
said Joan Chadworth is to be cited, in person if possible, otherwise by
public citation, to appear before the abp. or his commissary in the
parish church of Lambeth on the fourth day after citation to exhibit
the goods and valuables in question and to demonstrate how she will
ensure that they may be delivered to John Crosby when he comes of age,
and to submit to justice in this matter. Those who deliver this
citation are to certify the abp. of the action taken. Lambeth, 20 Oct.
1489.

[1. PCC 3 Milles. She was a parishioner of St Helen's within
Bishopsgate, London.]

58 [fo.25v] Inhibition directed to the abbot of Burton upon Trent. The
abp. has learned from Cecily the widow and Thomas the son of Henry Punt
and from Richard Salforde, the executors of the said Henry Punt of
Littleover (Parva Ovre), Db., that although Henry held goods in various
diocs. of the province and made a legitimate last testament,[1] appointing
Cecily, Thomas and John as his executors, and although the abp. by
virtue of his Prerogative legitimately sequestered the goods of the
deceased and cited the executors to exhibit the testament for probate,
nevertheless the abbot of Burton upon Trent (Burton super Trent),[2] who
knew all this, unjustly procured the exhibition of the testament before
him and attempted to grant probate, commit administration and
excommunicate the executors if they did not produce an inventory on a
certain day, thus impeding administration of the testament, to the
grave peril of his soul, the prejudice of the executors and in manifest
contempt of the Prerogative of the church of Canterbury. The abp.
orders that the abbot and his officials be inhibited by archiepiscopal
authority from any action prejudicial to the Prerogative of the church
of Canterbury or to the executors. The abbot should be cited to appear
before the abp. or his commissary on the fifteenth day after delivery
of the citation or the next judicial day thereafter to reply to
articles concerning this contempt of the Prerogative and impediment
of the testament, in a cause ex officio at the promotion of the
executors. [Undated.]

[1. PCC 20 Milles, dated 1489.
2. For the peculiar jurisdiction of the abbot of Burton upon Trent,
see VCH Staffordshire, iii, 209-10]

59 [fo.26] Littera questuaria in favour of the hospital of St Mary of
Bethlehem, Bishopsgate (extra Bysshopisgate, London'). The abp.
commends those seeking alms from the faithful for the poor, demented

16

and sick of the hospital, who have no other means of support. He
exhorts all within the province that when Thomas Large, literate,
proctor of the hospital, or any deputy, comes to their locality, they
should receive him favourably, out of reverence for SS Alphege and
Thomas, the abp.'s patrons. These letters are to be valid during the
abp.'s pleasure. Knole (Knoll'), 2 Jan. [? 1490].

60   Grant for the duration of one year of forty days indulgence to all
Christians within the province of Canterbury who are truly penitent,
contrite and confessed, who contribute to the relief of the parish
church of St Michael Queenhithe (apud Le Quenehithe) in the city of
London, the most part of whose vestments and ornaments were lately
destroyed by fire. Lambeth, 20 Nov. 1489.

61   In a high chamber at Lambeth the abp., who had certain business at the
Roman curia, appointed as his proctors John Kendall, prior provincial
of the Hospitallers in England, John de Gerona, John de Venetiis, John
Cloose, dean of the cath. church of Chichester, Hugh Spaldyng,
John de Verona, Nicholas de Parma, Bartholomew de Perusia, James de
Pistio and John de Nepolis, all resident in the Roman curia, and
William Wareham, D.C.L., jointly and singly with full powers to
represent the abp. Notarial exemplification by Richard Spencer, clerk
of Lincoln dioc., notary public by apostolic and imperial authority,
in the presence of Mr Thomas Cooke, D.C.L., of Norwich dioc., Auditor
of Causes, Mr John Camberton, S.T.P., of York dioc., and Mr John Barett
of London dioc., notary public. Lambeth, 18 Jan. 1490.

62   [fo.27] Mandate to Mr Edward Payne, the abp.'s Commissary General, and
to all rs., etc. within the province of Canterbury. The abp. has been
informed that Walter Briston, v. of Patrixbourne (Patriksborne), does
not maintain continual residence, but has been continually absent for
more than six months, although receiving the fruits and revenues of his
vic. in full. Willing therefore that as the v. is maintained by the
stipend of that church so he should exercise the cure and bear the
incumbent burdens, the abp. orders the Commissary General to cite him
peremptorily, or cause him to be cited, according to that decretal of
Pope Innocent III which begins Ex tue dilectionis[sic],[1] leaving ten
days between each citation. He is to be cited, in person if he may be
apprehended, otherwise by public citation at his vic. and before his
friends, acquaintances and parishioners, to appear and take up
continual residence within six months of delivery of the citation, on
pain of the law. If he fails so to do, the abp. intends to proceed
against him, to punish his contumacy and to provide for the vic. in
accordance with God's will and the sanctions of the canons. After six
months the abp. is to be certified of action taken. 15 July 1489.

   [1. c.11, Ex tue devotionis, X iii 4.]

63   Licence granted to John Baker, of Bath and Wells dioc., that he may

procure the celebration of mass by a suitable chaplain in the chapel
newly constructed by him in honour of the archangel Gabriel in the
parish of North Petherton (<u>Northpederton</u>), So., so long as no prejudice
is thereby suffered by the parish church, provincial constitutions to
the contrary notwithstanding. Lambeth, 16 Feb. 1490.

64 [<u>fo.27v</u>] Mandate to Mr John Stokys the Warden and the Fellows of All
Souls College, Oxford, that since the right of presentation has
devolved upon the abp. through their neglect, according to the statutes,
they should admit John Fairehede, born in the city of London and a
scholar and artist of the university of Oxford, to the vacant
scholarship in arts, to which the abp. by these presents provides him.
Lambeth, 3 May 1490.

65 Citation of the prior and conv. of Christ Church Canterbury to submit
to visitation on 22 April. Certificate of Prior William and the conv.
dated 17 April. Lambeth, 3 March 1490.

66 Commission to Mr Thomas Cooke, D.C.L., Auditor of Causes, to conduct
the visitation of Christ Church Canterbury, which the abp. is bound
to undertake before visitation of his province, but cannot conduct in
person because of the pressure of business upon him. Mr Cooke is to
receive the certificate of the prior and conv. and to adjourn the
visitation to 22 April 1491.[1] The archiepiscopal palace at Canterbury,
19 Apr. 1490.

    [1. A purely formal account of Mr Cooke's visitation is in
    Canterbury Dean and Chapter muniments, Priory Register S, fos
    359v-60.]

67 [<u>fo.28</u>] Archiepiscopal confirmation for Whittington College. The
college was founded in the city of London and the abp.'s immediate
jurisdiction by Richard Whittington, to the honour of the Holy Spirit,
the BVM, St Michael the Archangel and All Saints, with provision for a
warden who is to be a professor of sacred theology, four chaplains who
are to be masters of arts, two clerks and two choristers. The abp. has
received the supplication of Mr Edward Underwoode, S.T.P., the warden,
and the chaplains, clerks and choristers, that as they have founded a
fraternity of Holy Wisdom, in honour of Jesus Christ, His mother the
BVM, SS Paul the Apostle, John the Evangelist, Jerome the Priest,
Augustine bp. of Hippo and Mary Magdalen, called the guild of Holy
Wisdom, to the end that a solemn public reading or lecture may be given
freely and publicly in the college, so that sound doctrine and fruitful
preaching may be presented to Christ's people, the abp. should by his
ordinary and metropolitan authority confirm it in perpetuity. The abp.
therefore commends, ratifies, approves and validates the fraternity as
far as in him lies, and declares that, so that it may stand forever,
apostolic confirmation should be sought and obtained. He exhorts the
faithful to the maintenance of this fraternity, that they should be

copartners with the brothers and sisters and grant them alms, and he grants to those Christians present and future who lend helping hands forty days indulgence, whenever they so do. Lambeth, 4 Apr. 1490.

68 [fo.28v] Grant to John Children, whom, because of his outstanding merits, the abp. wishes to aid in his old age, of a corrody in the hospital of Maidstone (Maidiston), wherein he shall have a dwelling for the rest of his life. The prior is ordered to maintain him in victuals, clothing and other necessities, in accordance with the ordinances of the hospital. Lambeth, 27 Sept. 1490.

69 Mandate to Mr Henry Cooper, Decr.B., the abp.'s Commissary General. A dispute has recently arisen between Christ Church Canterbury and St Martin's Dover, patrons respectively of the parish churches of Fairfield (Feyrfeld') and Appledore (Appuldurr'), as to the boundaries of certain marshlands known as Le Ketermerrsh and Bekard. Mr Cooper is to examine witnesses produced by the prior and conv. of Dover as to the extent, limits and rights of tithe of the disputed marshes, and to transmit a notarialized copy of proceedings before him to the abp. or his commissary in this matter. Lambeth [undated].

70 Mandate to the preacher at Paul's Cross in London and to all rs. etc. within the province of Canterbury. The abp. has ordered Roger Shelley, esq., and William Maryner, his apparitor, to sequestrate all the goods and debts of Roger Appulton, late of Dartford (Dertford') in the dioc. of Rochester, who died intestate with goods in various diocs., so that the abp. may discharge his debts and dispose of his goods in pious uses for the health of his soul. The recipients of this mandate are to announce publicly that all his creditors and others with a claim on his estate should appear before the abp. or his commissary to state their claim in the parish church of Lambeth on 10 October. Lambeth, 10 Aug. 1491.

71 [fo.29] In the great chapel at Lambeth, in the presence of Mr John Barett, notary public, and of witnesses, there appeared before the abp. as he sat judicially Thomas Sutbury, professed monk and pretended prior of St Andrew's Northampton, who read from a paper schedule his resignation and release of the priory, as follows: In the name of God, Amen. Before you, most reverend father John abp. of Canterbury etc., I William Breknok[sic][1], professed monk and prior of the priory of St Andrew in the dioc. of Lincoln, desiring for certain genuine and legitimate reasons to be released from the cure and administration of the house, not compelled by any coercion, fear or guile, but purely, freely, simply and absolutely resign into your hands, as delegate of the apostolic see, such rights, status, dignity, title and possession as I have or have had in the said office of prior and in the government and administration of the house, and in this document I totally renounce these rights etc., in due legal form, and I swear on the holy Gospels that I will never in the future revoke this resignation or contravene

19

it, but will in all wise observe it.

This resignation was read publicly by the said Thomas, and was accepted by the abp., who declared the office of prior, as far as the said Thomas was concerned, to be vacant. Notarial exemplification by Mr John Barett, clerk of London dioc. and notary public by apostolic authority. Lambeth, 16 Feb. 1491.

[1. See 14-15, and CPR 1485-94, p.372.]

72 Certificate of Mr John Combe, B.C.L., that in obedience to the abp.'s mandate he examined the election of Richard Banham, monk of Tavistock (Tavistok'), De., O.S.B., as abbot of that house, citing objectors to appear on 28 May, and finding the election to be canonical, in the abp.'s name he confirmed it and installed the abbot. Sealed with the seal of Mr John Millett, Decr.D., Official of the archd. of Middlesex, as his own seal was not to hand. 10 June 1492.

73 [fo.29v] Letters dimissory for ordination to minor and major orders granted to Richard Lute and John Wroteley, brethren of the hospital of St Thomas at Southwark (Suthwerk), Sy, the see of Winchester being vacant. Lambeth, 12 Dec. 1492.

74 Mandate to the bp. of London for the organisation of processions. The king has requested the abp. to commend to God the king and his armies, since for the protection of the church in England and of the realm, and for the recovery of his rights which are unjustly and forcibly witheld by Charles, who calls himself king of France, and the restoration of which he has been unable to obtain, despite peaceful and lawful requests, he has declared war on Charles. The abp. orders the bp. of London to instruct all the suffragans of the province to admonish and exhort their subjects to pray for the welfare of the universal church and of the king and the magnates, and for the successful expedition of the king's armies. The clergy are to hold special processions each day in their cathedral, collegiate and conventual churches, and the laity are to participate in processions in their parish churches on Mondays, Wednesdays and Fridays, while in towns and other well-populated places both clergy and laity should humbly and devoutly go in general processions on Wednesdays and Fridays, or at least on Fridays, with chanting and mass if possible, praying that almighty and merciful God will guide the church, the king and his faithful magnates in all their enterprises, will protect them from the wiles and assaults of the enemy, and will grant the peace so long awaited by Christians. The bp. is to organise processions in the city and dioc. of London. So that the faithful may be encouraged in such prayers, the abp., confident of the immense mercy of almighty God, etc., grants to those faithful who are contrite, penitent and confessed forty days indulgence as often as they take part in such processions. [Undated, probably Oct. 1492.][1]

[1. Henry VII crossed to the continent and beseiged Boulogne in October 1492; by 27 October he was consulting his councillors on the peace proposals which led to the Treaty of Etaples.]

75   [fo.30] Similar mandate directed to Mr Henry Cooper, the abp.'s Commissary General, for the organisation of processions in the city and dioc. of Canterbury. [Undated, probably Oct. 1492.]

76   Commission to Mr William Warham, D.C.L., advocate of the Court of Canterbury, to investigate the crimes and excesses of the prior of Folkestone (Folkeston').[1] The abp. has heard that the observance of the Rule has lapsed and the prior has long absented himself, consuming the revenues of the house and allowing it to fall into decay and ruin and to become burdened with debt. He is to enquire especially into the extent and causes of the dilapidation and to determine the names of the creditors. Definitive sentence is reserved to the abp. Lambeth, 25 Oct. 1491.

> [1. For discussion of 76–82, see Harper-Bill, Archaeologia Cantiana, cxiii (1977).]

77   [fo.30v] Commission to Mr Henry Cooper, the abp.'s Commissary General. Although he answered the citation [79] , Thomas Banys, prior of Folkestone, has refused to reply to the articles against him, wherefore Mr Cooper is instructed to cite the prior to appear before him in the parish church of Folkestone at 10 a.m. on the tenth day after citation, to hear the testimony of witnesses against him and contest it if he so wishes. These witnesses are to be examined even if he does not appear. Mr Cooper is to send the abp. an account of proceedings attested by a notary public, including a transcript of the testimony. Lambeth, 8 March 1493.

78   Public instrument reciting a commission, dated 25 Oct. 1491, to Mr Thomas Cooke, Auditor of Causes, to investigate the conduct of the prior of Folkestone and the state of the priory [in the same terms as 76], which commission Mr Cooke, out of reverence for the abp., undertook. Lambeth, 12 Feb. 1493.

79   [fo.31] Mandate for the citation of the prior of Folkestone, addressed to all rs. etc. within the province of Canterbury. Since Thomas Banys, prior of Folkestone, has abandoned his house to live at Westminster, and has caused the priory to fall into debt and dilapidation, and if he takes no action the abp. will incur blame for this, he orders the recipients to cite the prior, in person if possible, otherwise by public citation, to appear before the abp. or his commissary on the fourth day after citation or the next judicial day thereafter in the chapel at Lambeth to show any reason why he should not be deprived of office. The executor of this mandate is to certify the abp. or his commissary. Lambeth, 7 Feb. 1493.

80 Articles proposed ex officio by the abp. against Thomas Banys, prior of the priory of SS Mary and Eanswith, Folkestone, O.S.B., or his proctor, to which he seeks a reply, under threat of legal penalties. First, that he has been prior for the past twenty or thirty years, and has received, administered and disposed of the fruits of the house; that the administration of spiritualities and temporalities, together with the cure of souls of the parishioners of the parish church canonically annexed and appropriated to the priory, were committed to him by one with sufficient power so to do; that while he was prior, he received the fruits of the priory himself or through his agents and administered them himself, but he oppressed the priory with a great burden of debt, entering into obligations for huge sums of money under the common seal of the priory in the name of the prior and conv., but without consulting the conv., which is today by his actions and guilt indebted to various creditors for around £700; that these large sums borrowed were not and are not used for the benefit of the priory, but that he has squandered them, while openly allowing the priory and its buildings to fall into ruin; that he was admonished by the abp., both verbally and in writing, to go to the priory, take up residence and serve his cure, but nevertheless for twenty years or more he has been continually absent and has lived elsewhere, and in the meantime has defrauded the house of the office of prior and has neglected the cure of souls, the administration of temporalities and spiritualities, the divine cult and regular observance; that all the above articles are true and are public knowledge, and the subject of common discussion in the parish of Folkestone and many other places in the dioc.

81 [fo.32] Sequestration of the revenues of Folkestone priory. Although the prior's proctor, John Fownten, appeared to answer the articles against him, he continually refused to make any answer to the charges. Wishing, therefore, to punish such contumacy with moderation and to reform the priory, the abp. ordered the sequestration of the revenues of the priory, forbidding Thomas Banys any part of their administration. The decree was read on 19 March in an inner chamber at Lambeth, in the presence of Mr Thomas Cooke, D.C.L., the abp.'s chancellor, the prior of Dover and Mr John Barett, scribe of the acts. The prior's proctor appeared and sought letters of appeal (apostillos). The abp. instructed him to prosecute his business on Friday 28 March between 1 p.m. and 2 p.m., and delegated Mr Cooke to refuse him letters of appeal against his definitive sentence, but he did not appear at the time assigned to him. Lambeth, 19 March 1493.

82 Notification of the deprivation of the prior of Folkestone, addressed to all the faithful etc. The abp. rehearses the neglect and administration of the priory for the past twenty years, while the prior has dwelt in the monastery of Westminster, a privileged place. He has cited Prior Thomas Banys, and has put to his proctor various articles, and has examined witnesses, and it has become obvious that there is in the priory little service of God and no norm of religion or morals, that the temporalities are devastated, and that the priory is burdened with debts of more than seven hundred marks. This is due not only to

22

the prior's negligence, but to his manifest culpability. The abp.,
therefore, wishing to avert the total ruin of the house, forbids
Thomas Banys any part in the government and administration of
spiritualities and temporalities, and judicially removes him from the
office of prior. Lambeth, 2 June 1493.

83 [fo.30v] Commission to Mr Ralph Haynyes, canon of the Augustinian
priory of Reigate, issued in the vacancy of the see of Winchester
following the death of Bp. Peter Courtenay. Because the prior is
prevented by old age and sickness from efficient government and
administration of the house, in order that the religious life and
financial stability of the priory may be preserved, Mr Ralph Haynyes
is commissioned to provide for the maintenance of holy religion
according to the Rule and the institutes laudably observed there of
old, and to manage the revenues, with power to cite all who meddle in
the priory's finances or unjustly occupy its possessions to appear
before the abp. or his commissary on the fifteenth day after citation
or the next judicial day thereafter. A full account is to be rendered
to the abp. whenever he may require it. Lambeth, 27 Feb. 1493.

84 Commission with power of canonical coercion to Mr Thomas Rowthale,
Decr.D., as Commissary of the Prerogative. Lambeth, 6 Oct. 1493.

   [See Churchill, ii, 179-80, for form.]

[fo.33] CONVOCATION OF THE PRELATES AND CLERGY OF THE PROVINCE OF CANTERBURY HELD BY AUTHORITY OF THE ARCHBISHOP IN THE CATHEDRAL CHURCH OF ST PAUL IN LONDON FROM 13 FEBRUARY 1487, IN THE FIFTH INDICATION OF THE PONTIFICATE OF POPE INNOCENT VIII AND THE FIRST YEAR OF THE ARCHBISHOP'S TRANSLATION.

[Note: the records of this Convocation are printed in part by Wilkins, iii, 618 ff. Wilkins omits the two schedules preserved in the archiepiscopal register, nos.93 and 94, but includes the fourth which is mentioned, concerning clerical discipline, from the Ely register of Bp.John Alcock; Pollard, iii, no.84.]

85 On 13 Feb. 1487 the abp. came to the cathedral church of St Paul where he celebrated a mass of the Holy Spirit. He then went to the chapel of St Mary with the bps. of Exeter, Worcester, Norwich, Hereford, Lincoln, Rochester and Salisbury and the other prelates and clergy, and a sermon was preached by Mr William Grasonn on the text Quid statis hic otiosi tota die.[1] The certificate of the bp. of London was then exhibited.

[1. Matthew, 20, 6.]

86 Certificate of Thomas bp. of London of the abp.'s mandate for the summoning of Convocation, dated at Lambeth, 28 Dec. 1486, which rehearses the royal writ to the abp., dated at Westminster, 16 Nov. 1486. Fulham, 12 Feb. 1487.

87 [fo.34] On 13 Feb. the abp. deputed Mr Thomas Cooke, D.C.L., Mr Humphrey Hawarden, D.C.L., and Mr Richard Lichefeld, D.C.L., to receive the certificates and letters of proxy of the bps. and clergy, and then adjourned Convocation to the following Friday in the chapter house.

88 On 16 Feb. the abp., sitting judicially with the forementioned bps., except the bp. of Hereford, pronounced contumacious all those who had been summoned and failed to attend, reserving punishment to himself. He then fluently explained the cause of the summons, and instructed the clergy to withdraw to the lower house and elect a prolocutor. They elected Mr Thomas Cooke, D.C.L., whom the dean of St Paul's presented to the abp. and prelates, and whom the abp. accepted. Then, because it was late, the abp. adjourned Convocation to the next day.

24

89 On Saturday 17 Feb. the abp., with the bps. of Exeter, Ely, Norwich, Lincoln, Rochester and Salisbury, communed at length with Convocation concerning reforms which should be implemented in the church. There was then produced a certain priest, William Symonds, aged twenty-eight, who before the prelates and clergy, and before the aldermen and sheriffs of the City of London, publicly confessed that he had abducted the son of an organmaker of Oxford University and had taken him to Ireland, and the boy was taken for the earl of Warwick, and that subsequently he had been with Lord Lovell in <u>Fernesfelles</u>. After his confession the abp. asked the mayor and sheriffs to conduct him to the Tower, since he was holding one of Symond's associates and had only one prison at Lambeth. After their departure, the abp. discussed with the prelates and clergy the necessary reforms. There was raised the issue of the abuse of the privileges of the Prior of the Hospital of St John in England. It was also complained that the preachers at Paul's Cross railed against the church and against ecclesiastical persons in their absence, and this before lay persons, who were always hostile to the clergy. It was determined that the Prior of the Hospitallers and two of the senior brethren from each mendicant house in the City, and other learned theologians beneficed there, should be summoned to discuss these matters on the following Tuesday. The prolocutor requested that the prelates and clergy summoned to this council should enjoy the ancient privileges and liberties, to which the abp. replied that insofar as it lay with him he wished this to be so. He then adjourned Convocation to the following Monday.

[The production in Convocation in February 1487 of William Symonds does not conform to the received version of the course of Lambert Simnel's rising. Polydore Vergil (<u>The Anglica Historia of Polydore Vergil, AD. 1485-1537</u>, ed. D. Hay, Camden Soc. 3rd series, lxxiv, 1950), 24, states that Simnel was captured with his mentor Richard Symonds at the battle of Stoke on 16 June 1487, but he was of course writing long after the event. Francis Lord Lovel landed at Furness on 4 June 1487, but in the previous year, following the collapse of the Stafford rebellion, he had taken refuge in Sir Thomas Broughton's house in north Lancashire, and it must be to this period that the register refers when it states that the priest was with Lovel in <u>Fernesfelles</u>. This entry suggests that Symonds was captured some time after he had taken Simnel to Ireland. The whole episode obviously needs further investigation.]

90 On 19 (or 20) Feb.[1] there appeared, before the forementioned bps. and Robert bp. of Worcester, the Prior of the Hospitallers, who protested that by his personal appearance he did not intend to diminish his privileges. If any gross abuses had been committed in places appropriated to his order by any chaplains or servants of himself and his brethren, he was most willing that they should be corrected, and he was willing to exhibit the apostolic letters granted to him and to have them reformed. He then left the assembly. The abp. was then told that certain lords of the king's council were in the church and wished to enter his presence. These lords were met by his episcopal colleagues, and he received them with honour. Their presence was

explained by Lord John Deneham, Treasurer of England, who said that
the king was grateful to the clergy for their benevolence and their
prayers, and asked them to maintain these. He then demonstrated the
extent of the king's expenditure for the defence of the realm and of
the church in England, and for measures against rebels, and asked the
abp., prelates and clergy to extend their help to him. The abp.
replied that he would confer with Convocation and convey its reply to
the king. Then, in the presence of the lords and of the mayor,
aldermen and sheriffs of London and of many others, the earl of
Warwick, son of the duke of Clarence, was led in by the earl of Derby,
and the abp. had him stand before him, so that he might be seen by
everybody. Then the lords sought his permission to withdraw, leaving
the earl of Warwick, whom the abp. took to Lambeth after he had
adjourned Convocation. Then the abp. ordered the preachers at Paul's
Cross and other places in the province of Canterbury to appear before
him on the following Wednesday, and adjourned Convocation to the
following day.

> [1. The chronology of the register becomes confused at this point.
> The Prior of the Hospitallers had been cited to appear on Tuesday
> 20 Feb., but from the register, unless the proceedings of some
> days have been entirely omitted, he seems to have appeared on
> Monday 19 Feb. The next firm date which is given by the scribe
> is 24 Feb. - a Saturday. The obvious explanation for this
> confusion is that the proceedings of some days were totally
> omitted by the scribe, and this is understandable in view of the
> extreme brevity of some of the daily entries in 1489; but it
> appears impossible to determine whether the omissions are for the
> first or second half of the week. See Reg. Chichele, iii,
> prefatory note.]

91   [fo.34v] On 24 Feb. there appeared before the abp. and his fellow
bps. many learned men, both secular and religious, who preached at
St Paul's Cross, and after a long discussion, the abp. admonished
them that they should not in future preach against the church and
ecclesiastical persons in sermons delivered to the laity, and if they
knew of any spiritual person who lived dishonourably, they should
denounce such a person to their ordinary, and if the ordinary did not
correct the malefactor, they should denounce him to the abp., and if
the abp. did not punish him, then he wished that they should preach
against the abp., and against no other. As it was late, he then
adjourned Convocation to the next day.

92   The next day there appeared before the abp. and the other bps. some
priests of the city of London, to whom the abp. emphasised the ill
repute that they had earned there because every day they frequented
inns, taverns and alehouses, and loitered there all day. The abp.
admonished them to avoid such places in future, and urged that twelve
or thirteen of them should eat communally; they should also cut their
long hair and not wear open gowns. They then withdrew from Convocation.
The abp., with the consent of the prelates, promulgated the following
constitution.

93 Provincial constitution regulating the obsequies of bps. The abp. with the approval of Convocation, decrees that henceforth, whenever one of the bps. of the province dies, his death shall be notified as soon as possible to the other bps., and within a month of receiving such notice, they shall in person or by deputy celebrate his funeral obsequies and six masses for his soul, as they wish to avoid the punishment of the canons imposed on those who wilfully transgress.

94 [fo.35] The prolocutor, in the name of the clergy, then presented to the abp. four schedules, the first concerning one whole tenth to be granted to the king, the second a subsidy to be granted to the abp., the third the Feast of the Transfiguration,[1] which the abp. with the consent of prelates and clergy ordained should be observed each year by nine readings on 7 Aug.,[2] and the fourth the correction of the clothing and life of priests.[3]

> [1. See R.W. Pfaff, New Liturgical Feasts in Later Medieval
> England (Oxford, 1970), chapter 2.
> 2. Recte 6 Aug. The Feast of the Name of Jesus, ratified by
> Convocation in 1489, fell on 7 Aug. (Pfaff, op.cit., p.xix);
> calendared in Reg. Stillington, no.861.
> 3. Printed in Pollard, iii, no.65 and calendared in Reg.
> Stillington, no.862.]

95 Charitable subsidy granted to the abp.,[1] for the praise of God and the defence of the church in England, payable on the feast of the Translation of St Thomas the Martyr [7 July] by all chaplains, both secular and religious, including those of the exempt orders, even the mendicants, receiving stipends of 8 marks, or 4 marks with food and drink, or the equivalent, each of whom is to pay 6s 8d, and no more than this up to a stipend of 10 marks; and if they receive 10 marks p.a. they shall pay 20s, and so on pro rata, with the following exemptions:

   i) all vicars choral and chaplains of cathedral and collegiate churches bound to personal residence and continually serving in divine office by day or by night.

   ii) all chaplains who from 11 March 1485 until the dissolution of the present Convocation are indicted, accused or imprisoned by the lay power on a charge of felony or of any other transgression or crime, or who are so burdened from the date of dissolution to the date of payment, if the certificate of their ordinary is produced.

   iii) poor chaplains in the universities of Oxford and Cambridge, and all religious living under their rule in cloister or studium and receiving no pension from outside sources.

   iv) sick or aged chaplains who cannot personally serve at the divine office, where this is certified by their ordinaries.

   v) all priests who maintain a parent at their own charge.

The subsidy is payable by all chaplains receiving corrodies in religious houses, or receiving pensions from ecclesiastical benefices,

or for rights in or titles to benefices resigned by them, whether or
not these have been established by their ordinary and whether conceded
to them or to others for their use. It is payable by all chaplains
holding chantries, hospitals, free chapels, or parish churches without
parishioners; if such benefices yield 8 marks, they shall pay 6s 8d,
if 10 marks then 13s 4d, if £10 then 20s, and so on, with the
provision that those holding hospitals shall pay only according to the
net revenue of the master after the exhibition of the poor and all
ordinary expenses have been deducted, and with the exception of
hospitals afflicted by grave poverty, as certified by the ordinary.
If any chaplain or clerk moves from one dioc. or one archdeaconry to
another, so that it is difficult for the collectors to levy the
subsidy from him, and the collectors or the ordinary signify his name
to the abp., then the collectors shall be exonerated for the sum in
question after taking an oath that they have not collected it. All
persons paying to the king with the laity a tenth, a fifteenth, an
aid or a subsidy shall be excused from the payment of this subsidy to
the abp., whatever sum they thus pay with the laity. No alienation
of the subsidy shall be authorised by reason of which the collectors
should have to account at the king's treasury or in any other secular
court. Diocesan bps. shall certify the abp. or his commissaries by
7 July of the names of those liable to payment, the sums due and the
names of the collectors in their diocs.; they shall appoint suitable
clerks as collectors, who are to receive for their expenses 12d in
the pound, and shall make payment and render account to the abp. or
his commissaries in St Paul's cathedral in London, and shall then be
acquitted. Each collector shall have, by the authority of Convocation,
power to sequestrate the fruits of those who fail or refuse to pay,
after due canonical monition, with the requisite means of canonical
coercion.

[1. See F.R.H. DuBoulay, 'Charitable Subsidies granted to the
Archbishop of Canterbury, 1300-1489', BIHR, xxiii (1950), 147-64.]
[Partially calendared: Reg. Stillington, no.863.]

96 [fo.35v] Grant to the king, for the defence of the church in England
and of the realm, of one whole tenth from ecclesiastical benefices and
possessions in the province of Canterbury, taxed and untaxed, which
by custom pay such a tenth, including the possessions of alien priories,
in whosoever's hands they now are, ecclesiastical or lay. One half is
to be paid at the feast of the Nativity of St John the Baptist
[24 June] and the other half at the feast of St Andrew [30 Nov.].
With the following exemptions:

i) the benefices and ecclesiastical possessions of poor religious,
    poor nuns and other poor and pious places in the province.
ii) the benefices and ecclesiastical possessions of religious and
    other ecclesiastical persons whose houses, possessions or
    benefices are destroyed, impoverished or diminished by flood,
    fire, ruin or other causes, or suffer thus between the date of
    this concession and the date of payment, as is certified by the
    ordinary to the king or the Treasurer and Barons of the
    Exchequer before the final date for payment. With the provision

28

that the diocesans shall include in their certificates of
exemption the following houses, possessions and benefices
specified by name [the transcript ends here].[1]

[1. For the royal writ, containing a complete list of
exemptions, see CFR 1485-1509, no.140.]

[The remainder of fo.36 is blank; fos.37-9 wanting; fo.40 blank.]

[fo.41] CONVOCATION OF THE PRELATES AND CLERGY OF THE PROVINCE OF
CANTERBURY HELD BY AUTHORITY OF THE ARCHBISHOP IN THE CATHEDRAL CHURCH
OF ST PAUL IN LONDON FROM 14 JANUARY 1489, IN THE SEVENTH INDICTION OF
THE PONTIFICATE OF POPE INNOCENT VIII AND THE THIRD YEAR OF THE
ARCHBISHOP'S TRANSLATION, UNTIL 23 OCTOBER 1489.

[Note: the records of this Convocation are printed in part by
Wilkins, iii, 625 ff. and Pollard, iii, no.85.]

97   Mandate to Thomas bp. of London, ordering him to summon Convocation to
meet at the cathedral church of St Paul on 14 Jan. 1489, rehearsing
the royal writ to the abp. dated at Westminster, 19 Nov. 1488.
Lambeth, 21 Nov. 1488.

98   [fo.41v] Mandate to Mr Edward Payne, Decr.B., the abp.'s Commissary
General, to summon to Convocation the clergy of Canterbury dioc. The
prior of Christ Church Canterbury, the archd. of Canterbury and the
abbots and priors of exempt and non-exempt religious houses are to
attend in person, and the chapter of Christ Church Canterbury are to
appoint one proctor and the clergy of the dioc. and the immediate
jurisdiction two proctors. Lambeth 16 Nov. 1488.

99   On 14 Jan. 1489 the abp. went by river from Lambeth to le Powlys
Warffe, and thence to the cathedral, where a mass of the Holy Spirit
was celebrated at the high altar by Robert bp. of Worcester. The abp.
then went to the chapel of St Mary with the bps. of Norwich, Rochester,
St Asaph's, Hereford, Lincoln, Chichester, Exeter, St David's,
Salisbury and Worcester, and other prelates. A sermon was preached
by Mr Thomas Maddes, S.T.B., on the text Translato sacerdotio necesse
est ut legis translatio fiat,[1] and the certificate of Thomas bp. of
London was exhibited and read aloud by Mr John Barett, notary public.

[1. Sic, rectius:translato enim sacerdotio necesse est ut et legis
translatio fiat, Hebrews, 7, 12.]

100   [fo.42] Certificate of Thomas bp. of London of the abp.'s mandate
for the summoning of Convocation. Fulham, 10 Jan. 1489.

101 [fo.42v] The abp., with the prelates and clergy, then went to the chapter house, and with the consent of his suffragans he deputed Mr Thomas Cooke, D.C.L., Mr Humphrey Hawarden, D.C.L., Mr Richard Lichefeld, D.C.L., and Mr Thomas Jane, Decr.D., to receive the certificates and letters of proxy of the bps. and clergy. He then adjourned Convocation until 17 Jan.

102 On 17 Jan. the abp., sitting judicially with the forementioned bps. and many abbots and priors of his province, ordered the deans, archds. and proctors of the clergy to withdraw to the lower house, that is the Long Chapel, to elect one of their number as prolocutor. After about an hour they returned to the chapter house and Mr Thomas Worsley, dean of St Paul's, presented to the abp. Mr Humphrey Hawarden, D.C.L., whom he accepted as prolocutor. Accepting this office, Mr Hawarden humbly requested that Holy Mother Church and the clergy attending this Convocation might enjoy their accustomed privileges and liberty, and the abp. conceded this, insofar as it lay with him. The abp. appointed the bps. of Norwich, St Asaph's, Hereford and Chichester jointly and singly as his commissaries to preside over and adjourn Convocation in his absence. He pronounced contumacious those summoned to Convocation who had failed to appear, reserving punishment to himself, and adjourned Convocation until Monday 19 Jan.

103 On 19 Jan. there entered the chapter house John Dynham, Treasurer of England, John earl of Oxford, Thomas earl of Derby and others of the king's council, sent by the king. The Treasurer elegantly explained that the king was enormously grateful for the charity and the concern they had shown for his majesty and the honour of his realm, and asked for their perseverence in this, promising to be a willing defender of the rights and liberties of the church in England. He then announced that the king, partly because of the request of the community of the realm expressed in the present Parliament, partly and more especially to counter the threat posed to the realm by the king of France, was anxious to defend the realm, and in this enterprise he needed the succour of the prelates and clergy of the province, not only their prayers, but also their financial aid. The abp. said that he would confer with Convocation, and as it was late adjourned proceedings to the following day.

104 [fo.43] On 20 Jan. there appeared in Convocation the bps. of Norwich, Hereford, Salisbury and St Asaph's, and after certain discussions, the bp. of Norwich adjourned Convocation until the following day.

105 On 21 Jan. the abp., after long and diverse discussions, adjourned Convocation until 23 Jan.

106 On 23 Jan. the abp., after diverse discussions, adjourned Convocation until the following Friday, 30 Jan.

107 On 30 Jan., among other business, a complaint was made by Mr Michael
Clyve, Chancellor or commissary of the bp. of Winchester, and by
various others, concerning the abuse of privileges in houses of the
Order of St John of Jerusalem, namely that chaplains presiding over
these houses asserted that their privileges permitted them to absolve
persons excommunicated by their ordinary in ex officio and instance
cases without the ordinary's authority, and even to solemnise
marriages in contravention of divine and canon law, and often one of
the parties to such a marriage was involved in litigation, or the
banns had not been called. Therefore the Prior Provincial of the
Hospitallers was summoned, and he denied that he was party to such
abuses. Examination of this matter was delegated to the chancellors
or Officials of the bps. in whose diocs. there were Hospitaller
houses.

108 Meanwhile John Dynham the Treasurer and the earls of Oxford and Derby
had entered the chapter house, with many other members of the king's
council. The Treasurer announced that the king had heard that the
king of France was preparing an army for an invasion and final conquest
of England, and hence he desired that the prelates and clergy should
without delay grant him a subsidy, lest the king of France achieve his
end. The abp. discussed this matter with Convocation, and as it was
late, he adjourned proceedings to the next day, 4 Feb. [sic].

109 On 4 Feb. the bps. of Norwich, Chichester and Hereford appeared in
Convocation, and the bp. of Norwich adjourned proceedings to the next
day.

110 On 5 Feb. the bp. of Norwich, in the presence of the bp. of Hereford,
adjourned Convocation to the next day, Friday 6 Feb.

111 On 6 Feb. the abp., after some discussion, adjourned Convocation to
Tuesday 10 Feb.

112 [fo.43v] On 10 Feb. it was determined that stipendiary chaplains
should pay a subsidy. The abp. then adjourned Convocation until the
following Saturday.

113 On 14 Feb., after further discussion, the abp. adjourned Convocation
to 20 Feb.

114 On 20 Feb., there appeared in Convocation the bps. of Norwich,
Winchester, Worcester, Ely, Lincoln, Chichester, Hereford, Rochester
and St Asaph's, and after certain discussions the bp. of Norwich
adjourned Convocation to the next day.

115   On 21 Feb. the bp. of Norwich, in the presence of the bp. of Hereford, adjourned Convocation to the next day.

116   On 22 Feb. the abp., after certain discussions, adjourned Convocation to 26 Feb.

117   On 26 Feb., after discussion of the great subsidy of £25,000 to the king and of two lesser subsidies to the abp., he adjourned Convocation to 27 Feb.

118   On 27 Feb., in the abp.'s presence, the prolocutor granted to the king, in the name of all the clergy, a great subsidy of £25,000 to be paid in two instalments, and as two tenths of the province would scarcely amount to the total of this subsidy, he conceded two whole tenths from ecclesiastical benefices and possessions, taxed and untaxed, which by custom paid tenths, with this provision, that when the subsidy of £25,000 had been paid, the prelates and clergy should be acquitted and exonerated from any further payment. He also granted two charitable subsidies to the abp., for the praise of God and the defence of the church in England. The suffragans and other prelates assented to these grants. The abp. gave his consent to the great subsidy of £25,000 and graciously accepted the two lesser subsidies. The prolocutor, on behalf of the clergy of the province, presented to the abp. a quire of paper containing the feast of the Name of Jesus,[1] which the abp. decreed should be observed in future according to the form detailed in this quire. The prolocutor also presented three other schedules containing details of the subsidies.

[1. See Pfaff, New Liturgical Feasts, chapter 4.]

119   [fo.44] Grant to the king, for the defence of the church in England and of the realm, of a subsidy of £25,000, the first moiety of £12,500 being due at the feast of the Annunciation of the BVM [25 March] and payable to the king by 1 May, the second moiety being due at Michaelmas and payable to the king by 1 November, in the following form: from the dioc. of Canterbury and the immediate jurisdiction of Christ Church, £1303 7s 10½d[1]; from the dioc. of Ely, £557 19s 7d; Norwich, £1740; Winchester, £1050; Salisbury, £1203 15s 3d; Chichester, £420; Rochester, £133 17s 9d; Bath and Wells, £600; the jurisdiction of St Albans, £66 13s 4d; the dioc. of Exeter, £456; Coventry and Lichfield, £510; Hereford, £280; Worcester, £550; London, £845 7s 4d; Lincoln, £2650; St David's, £58[2]; St Asaph, £40; Llandaff, £13 6s 8d; Bangor, £15 12s 2½d; which together constitute £12,500. Diocesans shall appoint collectors of the two moieties in their dioc. by 15 March and 15 September, and shall certify the Treasurer and Barons of the Exchequer of their names, and if there is a division between collectors, of the sum to be collected by each individually. If any collector is not able to collect the sum due from any person, and he signifies to the Exchequer the name of the defaulter and the sum due, the collector and the prelates and clergy of the province

32

shall be exonerated for this sum, and the Treasurer and Barons of the Exchequer shall proceed only against him who has not paid; in this matter the certificate of any collector or his attorney shall be sufficient without further inquisition or delay. Furthermore, if it happens that the war lasts for the next year or two years, so that there is need of the same expenditure by the clergy for defence, the Convocation grants the king a similar subsidy for each of the two years, on the same terms. If as time passes it becomes obvious that such enormous expense is not necessary for defence for either of these years, then Convocation wills that the subsidy should be reduced as circumstances allow, but the prelates and clergy of the province grant the king such a lesser subsidy for each of the next two years, in the same proportion to the sum granted by the community of the realm as is the present £25,000. This grant is not to be taken as a precedent, as it is unprecedented, because in former times the province of Canterbury has acknowledged and borne such burdens only in times of urgent necessity.

[1. Recte £1304 7s 10½d; cf. no. 128.
2. In CFR 1485-1509, no.267, the St David's figure is £63.]

120   [fo.44v] Terms of the grant. Convocation grants two whole tenths of ecclesiastical benefices and possessions, taxed and untaxed, including the possessions of alien priories in whosoever's hands they are, ecclesiastical or lay, payable in two moieties, on condition that when the sum of £25,000 is paid the clergy shall be acquitted and exonerated from all other payment. The following are to be exempt from payment: benefices and ecclesiastical possessions of all the colleges and collegiate halls of the universities of Oxford and Cambridge, of the college near Winchester founded by William Wikham, once bp. of Winchester, and the college of St Mary at Eton near Windsor; of the house of SS Saviour, Mary and Brigette at Syon, and of all Carthusian houses in the province; and of monasteries, colleges, churches and other pious places which the diocesan considers ought to be exempt and whose name he signifies to the Treasurer and Barons of the Exchequer, which certificate shall be accepted without further inquisition or delay. Each collector shall, by the authority of Convocation, have power to punish and coerce any person refusing to pay, by means of suspension, excommunication, interdict and sequestration, until full payment is made, with reimbursement of expenses incurred: once such payment is made, the collector may grant absolution and relax any process arising from this matter. Each collector shall have for his remuneration 2 groats for each pound collected.

121   [fo.45] Certificate of the royal writ,[1] dated at Westminster, 28 Feb. 1489, ordering the abp. to appoint trustworthy clerics of his diocese to collect that portion assigned to Canterbury dioc. of the moiety of the subsidy of £25,000, which amounts to £1304 8s 10½d.[2] The abp. is to certify the Treasurer and the Barons of the Exchequer of the names of the collectors of the first moiety by 15 March, and of the second moiety by 15 Sept. By the authority of this writ and of Convocation,

the abp. has appointed as collectors of the first moiety the abbot and convent of Boxley, with the provisions for the safe-guarding of the collectors detailed in the grant. Lambeth, 7 March 1489.

[1. Calendared: CFR 1485-1509, no.267.
2. Recte £1304 7s 10½d, cf. no. 128.]

122 [fo.45v] Notification to the king of the grant by Convocation of a subsidy of £25,000 [as detailed in nos. 119-20]. Lambeth, 28 Feb. 1490.

123 [fo.46] Mandate to the abbot and convent of Boxley to collect that portion of the first moiety of the subsidy which is due from Canterbury dioc. by 1 May, which amounts to £950, according to the attached schedule [nos 129-79 infra], with the modifications detailed in the grant, with power of canonical coercion against defaulters. [Undated.]

124 [fo.47] Mandate to Thomas bp. of London directing him to communicate to the abp's suffragans, and to the vicars-general of absent diocesans, instructions for the collection of the two minor subsidies granted to the abp. by Convocation, the first of which is due on 1 May, the second at Michaelmas, and which is to be taken at the following rates from all chaplains, secular and religious, including those of the exempt orders, even the mendicants: those receiving an annual stipend of 40s and their food and drink are to pay 3s 4d; those receiving 7 marks or 4 marks with their food and drink, 6s 4d;[1] those receiving 10 marks, 10s; those receiving 12 marks, 13s 8d;[2] and those receiving £10, 16s 8d, and so on, pro rata. Exemptions are as in 1487 [no.95], with the omission of chaplains indicted by the lay power and those maintaining a parent at their own charge. The subsidies are payable by all chaplains receiving annuities, pensions etc. from religious houses, or pensions from benefices or from the resignation of the office of abbot or prior, whether or not these have been established by their ordinary and whether conceded to them or to others for their use, at the following rates: those receiving 40s to pay 3s 4d; those receiving 7 marks, 6s 8d; those receiving 10 marks, 13s 4d; those receiving £10, 20s, and so on pro rata. The subsidies are payable by chaplains holding chantries, hospitals, free chapels and parish churches without parishioners, at the following rates: those receiving 4 marks to pay 3s 4d; those receiving 7 marks, 6s 8d; those receiving 10 marks, 10s; those receiving 12 marks, 20s, and thenceforth a tenth part of the benefice, with the exemptions as in 1487. The subsidies are payable by chaplains holding benefices with cure worth 12 marks or less which are not bound by their ordinaries to payment of the great subsidy granted to the king by this Convocation, when the true value of these benefices is today 10 marks or more. They are to be certified to the collectors by the ordinary, and shall pay 6s 8d, with provisions as in 1487. Collectors are to receive 12d for every pound collected. The diocesans, through the

34

collectors, are to conduct an inquisition into the names of all those
liable to payment of the first subsidy by 1 Nov. [sic], and are to
certify the names of the collectors of the first subsidy by 15 March
and of the second subsidy by 15 Sept. They shall admonish the
collectors, on pain of the law, to render account for all money
collected by them to the abp. or his commissaries at the forementioned
times. The bp. of London is also to do these things in his own dioc.
Lambeth, 1 March 1489.

[1. and 2. Sic in MS. The figures 6s 8d and 13s 4d seem more
likely; cf. DuBoulay, 'Charitable Subsidies', p.162.]

125 [fo.48] Mandate to the archd. of Canterbury or his Official[1] to
collect the two minor subsidies granted to the abp. by Convocation
within Canterbury dioc., and to account for the sums collected to the
abp. or his commissaries by 1 May and 1 Nov. respectively. Lambeth,
7 March 1489.[2]

[1. Margin, in later hand: Mandatum directum commissario Cant'.
2. MS: 1485.]

126 [fo.48v] Commission, with power of canonical coercion, to Mr Thomas
Jane, Decr.D., archd. of Essex, Mr Richard Lichefeld, D.C.L., archd.
of Middlesex, and Mr Robert Shirborne, M.A., to collect and take
custody of the minor subsidies granted to the abp. in the cathedral
church of St Paul's, London, keeping the money in a chest with three
keys, one to be retained by each of them, and to issue letters of
acquittance to the collectors and account to the abp. or his
commissaries. Lambeth, 29 March 1489.

127 Tenths of the possessions of the bps of the province of Canterbury:
the abp. of Canterbury, £223 16s 8d; the bp. of Ely, £200; Norwich,
£69; Winchester, £297 15s 7d; Salisbury, £103 16s 9½d; Chichester,
£47 4s 10d; Rochester, £30 0s 6d; Bath and Wells, £57 7s 10d; Exeter,
£46 3s 10d; Coventry and Lichfield, £37 18s; Hereford, £51 7s;
Worcester, £55 12s 7d; London, £100; Lincoln, £110 17s 4d; St David's,
£13 16s 5d; St Asaph, £18 17s 2½d; Llandaff, £11 10s 2½d; Bangor,
£15 12s 2½d.

128 [fo.49] Division of the subsidy granted to King Henry VII in the
fourth year of his reign: from Canterbury dioc. and the immediate
jurisdiction of Christ Church, £950, and the minor subsidy granted to
the abp., £354 7s 10½d, which total £1304 7s 10½d; from Ely dioc.,
£557 19s 7d; Winchester, £1050; Salisbury, £1203 15s 3d; Chichester,
£420; Rochester, £133 17s 9d; Bath and Wells, £600; the jurisdiction
of St Albans, £66 13s 4d; Exeter dioc., £456; Norwich, £1740; Coventry
and Lichfield, £510; Hereford, £280; Worcester, £550; London, £845 7s
4d; Lincoln, £2650; St David's, £58; St Asaph, £40; Llandaff,
£13 6s 8d; Bangor, £15 12s 2½d; which together total £12,500.

TAXABLE VALUE OF BENEFICES AND ECCLESIASTICAL POSSESSIONS IN THE
DIOCESE OF CANTERBURY.

129 [fo.49v] A moiety of a tenth of the spiritualities and temporalities
of the abp. of Canterbury.

Spiritualities: in Westbere dy., Reculver (Reculvere), £5 13s 4d; in
Charing dy., Cranbrook (Cranebrook), £1 6s 8d; in South Malling dy.
in Chichester dioc., Mayfield (Maghfeld), £3; in Rochester dioc., two
parts of Northfleet (Northflete) church, taxed at 100 marks apart from
newly endowed vicarage, £2. TOTAL: £12.

Temp.: in Canterbury dioc., £67 15s 5d; in Croydon dy. in Winchester
dioc., £3 15s 9d; in South Malling and Pagham dys. in Chichester dioc.,
£17 4s 0½d; in London and Middlesex archdeaconries in London dioc.,
£6 10s 9d; in Tring in Huntingdon archdeaconry in Lincoln dioc., £4 2s 5d.
TOTAL: £99 18s 4½d.[1]

TOTAL OF A MOIETY OF A TENTH: £111 18s 4½d.

TOTAL OF A WHOLE TENTH: £223 16s 9d.

  [1. Recte £99 8s 4½d.]

130 Tenth of the prior and conv. of Christ Church Canterbury.

In Pagham dy., Pagham (Paggeham), £110; in Bridge dy., Godmersham with
chapel, £43 6s 8d; in Charing dy., Westwell, £30; in Shoreham dy.,
Meopham (Mepeham), £16 13s 4d; in Dover dy., West Cliffe (Westcleve),
£18; in Westbere dy., Monkton (Monketon), £23 6s 8d; in Sandwich dy.,
Eastry, £43 6s 8d; temps. in Canterbury dioc., £771 7s 8d; in
Rochester dioc., £215 0s 5d; in Chichester, London, Winchester, Lincoln
and Norwich dioc., £313 4s 4d. TOTAL: £1664 5s 8d, of which a tenth
is £166 8s 7d.

  [1. Recte £1584 5s 9d.]

131 Tenth of the archd. of Canterbury.

St Mary's Sandwich (de Sandwico), £8; St Clement's Sandwich, £5 6s 8d;
in Canterbury dy., Hackington (Hakenton), £13 6s 8d; in Ospringe dy.,
Teynhan (Tenham), £133 6s 8d; in Lympne dy., Lympne (Lymmene), £20;
miscellaneous revenues, £20; TOTAL: £200, of which a tenth is £20.

132 Tenth of the abbot of St Augustine's Canterbury.

In Canterbury dy., Sturry (Turrey), £13 6s 8d; St Paul's Canterbury,
£8; in Westbere dy., Chislet (Chistelett), £23 6s 8d; Minster in
Thanet (Mynstre), £133 6s 8d; in Bridge dy., Preston near Wingham
(Preston), £20; Littlebourne (Litelborn), £20; in Sandwich dy.,
portions of the chamberlain of Deal (Dale) in Sandwich church, £1 10s;
in East Langdon (Est Langdon) church, £4; in Ripple (Riple) church,
£3 10s; in Pissing (Pising) church, £1; in Charing dy., Tenterden, £20;

Kennington (Keniton), £40; in Sutton dy., Lenham, £33 6s 8d; in
Sittingbourne dy., Milton (Middleton), £26 13s 4d; in Ospringe dy.,
Faversham (Feversham), £36 13s 4d; abbot's portion in vic. of, £10;
Selling, £20; in Lympne dy., Willesborough (Wyvelesberh), £16 13s 4d;
Stone in Oxney (Stone) £20; Brookland (Brokeland), £13 6s 8d; temp.,
including those of Plumstead (Plumstede), £808 1s 0¼d. TOTAL: £1234
1s 0¼d,[1] tenth £123 8s 1½d.

[1. Recte £1272 14s 4¼d.]

133   [fo.50] Tenth of the prior of Dover (Dovorr').

In Sandwich dy., Coldred (Colrede) and Popeshale, £13 6s 8d; in Dover
dy., Hougham (Hucham), £16 13s 4d; Guston, £10; St Margaret's, £16;
Buckland (Buklonde), £9 6s 8d; in Lympne dy., Appledore (Appuldore),
£20; temp., in Canterbury dioc., £188 10s. TOTAL: £273 16s 8d, tenth
£27 7s 8d.

134   Tenth of the abbot of Battle (de Bello).

In Bridge dy., Wye (Wy), £43 6s 8d; in Lympne dy., pension in Kingsnorth
(Kingesnorth) church, £2; in Charing dy., pension in Hawkhurst
(Hawkehurst), 5s; temp., in Canterbury dioc., £195 5s; TOTAL: £240 16s
8d, tenth £24 1s 8d.

135   Tenth of the abbot of Faversham.

In Ospringe dy., Boughton under Blean (Bocton), £60; Preston next
Faversham (Preston), £19 11s 2d; pension in Newnham (Newenham) church,
£3 6s 8d; pension in Luddenham (Lodyngham) church, £1 13s 4d; temp.,
in Canterbury dioc., £155 6s 2d; TOTAL: £239 17s 5d, tenth £23 19s 9d.

136   Tenth of the abbot of Boxley (Boxle).

In Sittingbourne dy., Eastchurch (Estchurch), £33 6s 8d; temp., in
Canterbury dioc., £62 14s 7d; temp., of abbey of Les Dunes (Dunes'),[1]
£2 18s 4d; TOTAL: £98 19s 7d, tenth £9 17s 11½d.

[1. See VCH Kent, ii, 153. In 1314 licence was granted to Boxley
to acquire from Les Dunes land in, and the advowson of, Eastchurch
in Sheppey.]

137   Tenth of the abbot of West Langdon (Langdon).

In Sandwich dy., Oxney (Oxene), £2; Walmer (Walmere), £10; West
Langdon (Westlangdon), £6 13s 4d; Waldershare (Waldershar), £12;
portion in Coldred (Colrede) church, £1 10s; in Dover dy., Lydden
(Ledane), £6 13s 4d; in Sittingbourne dy., Tong (Tonge), £30; temp.,
in Canterbury dioc., £25 17s 10d; TOTAL: £90 14s 6d,[1] tenth £9 1s 5½d.

[1. Recte £94 14s 6d.]

37

138 [fo.50v] Tenth of the abbot of St Radegund's (<u>Sancte Radegundis</u>), Bradsole.

In Sandwich dy., Sibertswold (<u>Sibertiswoode</u>), £9 13s 4d; in Dover dy., River (<u>Riparia</u>), £5 6s 8d; Alkham (<u>Alkeham</u>), £14; in Elham dy., Postling, £8; in Sittingbourne dy., Leysdown (<u>Leisdon</u>), £8; temp. in Canterbury dioc., £27 19s 8d; TOTAL: £72 19s 8d, tenth £7 5s 11½d.

139 Tenth of the prior of Rochester (<u>Roffen</u>') in Canterbury dioc.

In Sittingbourne dy., Hartlip (<u>Hartlepe</u>), £13 6s 8d; in Shoreham dy., Darenth (<u>Darent</u>), £6 13s 4d; in Sandwich dy., portion in Woodnesborough (<u>Wodnesbergh</u>) church, £1 5s; in Ospring dy., pension in Norton and Oare (<u>Ores</u>) churches, £1 10s; in Sutton dy., Boxley (<u>Boxle</u>), £32; temp. in Darenth, £16 8s 4d; in Shoreham dy., revenues in Cliffe (<u>Cleve</u>) and the Isle of Grain (<u>Grene</u>),£9; temp. in Canterbury and Elham, £1 18s 10d; TOTAL: £82 2s 2d, tenth £8 4s 2½d.

140 Tenth of the prior of Leeds (<u>Ledys</u>).

In Westbere dy., Sarre (<u>Serrey</u>), £3 6s 8d; in Sandwich dy., Woodnesborough (<u>Wodenesbergh</u>), £30; tithes of St Albans in Woodnesborough, £9 6s 8d; pension in Ham (<u>Hamme</u>) church, £2; tithes in Hartanger (<u>Hertangre</u>), 6s 8d; in Elham dy., pension in Acrise (<u>Acrese</u>) church, £2; in Sutton dy., Bersted (<u>Berghstede</u>), £8; Chart Sutton (<u>Charte</u>), £16 13s 4d; Goudhurst (<u>Gouthirst</u>), £13 6s 8d; Leeds, £13 6s 8d; Boughton Monchelsea (<u>Bocton Chensy</u>), £10; Stockbury (<u>Stokbury</u>), £27 6s 8d; Borden, £20; Rainham (<u>Renham</u>), £26 13s 4d; in Charing dy., Ashford (<u>Estchetesford</u>), £10 13s 4d; in Ospringe dy., pension in Oare (<u>Ores</u>) church, 8s; temp. in Canterbury dioc., £37 18s; TOTAL: £231 6s, tenth £23 2s 7¼d.

141 [fo.51] Tenth of the prior of St Gregory's, Canterbury

In Canterbury dy., Thanington (<u>Tanynton</u>), £11 6s 8d; Northgate, £3 6s 8d; Westgate, £5; St Dunstan's, £2 13s 4d; Nackington (<u>Nacyndon</u>), £4; in Westbere dy., tithes in Rushbourne (<u>Risheborne</u>), £1; in Bridge dy., Bekesbourne (<u>Lyvingesburn</u>), £10; tithes in Ash (<u>Esh</u>), £10; portion in Bishopsbourne (<u>Bisshopisborn</u>), £2; Waltham, £11 6s 8d; Elmstead (<u>Elmstide</u>), £16; in Charing dy., Bethersden (<u>Batrychisden</u>), £12; pension in Pluckley (<u>Plukle</u>) church, £1 6s 8d; in Shoreham dy., portion in Northfleet (<u>Northflete</u>) church, £2; in Ospringe dy., Stalisfield (<u>Stallesfeld</u>), £12; Oare (<u>Ores</u>), £4; temp. in Canterbury dioc., £25 15s; TOTAL: £133 15s, tenth £13 7s 6d.

142 Tenth of the prior of Monks Horton (<u>Horton</u>).

In Elham dy., Brabourne (<u>Braborn</u>), £30; in Lympne dy., tithes in Hope, £3 6s 8d; temp. in Canterbury dioc., £65 10s; TOTAL: £98 16s 8d;, tenth £9 17s 8d.

143 Tenth of the prior of Combwell.

In Charing dy., Benenden (Benynden), £20; in Sutton dy., Thornham (Thorneham) with chapel of Aldington, £13 6s 8d; in Dover dy., Beauxfield (Bewsfelde), £12; temp. in Canterbury dioc., £20 15s 10d; TOTAL: £66 2s 6d, tenth £6 12s 3d.

144 [fo.51v] Tenth of the prior of Bilsington.

In Lympne dy., Bilsington, £16 13s 4d; temp. in Canterbury dioc., £33 16s 5d; TOTAL: £50 9s 9d, tenth £5 0s 11d.

145 Tenth of the prior of Merton.

In Bridge dy., Patrixbourne (Patryksborn), £33 6s 8d; temp. in Harrietsham (Heriettysham), £1 6s 8d; TOTAL: £34 13s 8d, tenth £3 9s 4d.

146 Tenth of the abbot of Lessnes (Lesenes).

In Sutton dy., Marden (Merden), £26 13s 4d; in Sittingbourne dy., Newington (Newenton), £26 13s 4d; temp. in Canterbury dioc., £7 6s 8d; TOTAL: £60 13s 4d, tenth £6 1s 4d.

147 Tenth of the abbot of St Osyth (Sancti Osithe).

In Bridge dy., Petham, with temp., £20 17s, of which a tenth is £2 1s 8d.

148 Tenth of the abbess of Malling.

In Shoreham dy., East Malling (Estmalling), £16 13s 4d; temp. in same dy., £45; in Charing dy., temp. in Westwell, £3 0s 10d; TOTAL: £64 14s 2d, tenth £6 9s 5d.

149 Tenth of the abbot of Westminster (Westmon') in Canterbury dioc. Temp. in Luddenham (Lodenham), £1, of which a tenth is 2s.

150 Tenth of the abbot of Robertsbridge (Ponte Roberti). Temp. in Canterbury dioc., £12 10s 10d, of which a tenth is £1 5s 1d.

151 Tenth of the abbot of Bayham (Begham). Temp. in Canterbury dioc., £3, of which a tenth is 6s.

152 [fo.52] Tenth of the dean of St Paul's, London.

39

Temp. in Barnes (Bernes), Sy, in Croydon dy., £12, of which a tenth
is £1 4s.

153 Tenth of Throwley (Trughle), pertaining to Syon (Sion).[1]

In Bridge dy., Chilham (Chillham), £40; in Ospringe dy., Throwley,
£40; temp. in Canterbury dioc., £1 5s 6d; TOTAL: £81 0s 6d, tenth
£8 2s 0½d.

> [1. A cell of St Bertin at Omer, granted to Syon in 1424 by
> Thomas duke of Exeter and others, and confirmed by Henry VI in
> 1443 (CPR 1441–46, p.234).]

154 Tenth of the prior of Folkestone (Folkeston).

In Dover dy., Folkestone, £26 13s 4d, of which a tenth is £2 13s 4d.

155 Tenth of Ogbourne St George (Okerborn).[1]

In South Malling dy., Glynde, Sx., with pension £14 13s 4d, of which
a tenth is £1 9s 4d.

> [1. Dependency of Bec, dissolved in 1415. Glynde was subsequently
> granted to the royal free chapel of Windsor.]

156 Tenth of the abbess of Guines (Guynce).[1]

In Dover dy., Newington near Hythe (Newenton), £20; in Lympne dy.,
Brenzett (Brensete), £13 6s 8d; Broomshill (Bromeshell), £10 13s 4d;
temp. in Newington and Dover (Dovorr'), £1 1s 10d; TOTAL: £45 1s 10d,
tenth £4 10s 2¼d.

> [1. The possessions of Guines in Artois were granted in 1439 to
> Archbishop John Kempe, with licence to grant them to his new
> foundation of Wye college (CPR 1436–41, p.312.]

157 Tenth of St Mary's, Ile-Dieu (Insula Dei), Normandy.

In Sittingbourne dy., Upchurch,[1] £23 6s 8d; temp. of same church,
£2 9s 2¾d.

> [1. Granted to All Souls College, Oxford (CPR 1436–41, p.386).]

158 Tenth of the prior of Lewes.

Revenues in Dover (Dovorr'), £1 1s 8d, of which a tenth is 2s 2d.

159 Swingfield (Syntyngfelde)[1] in Dover.

Revenues, 15s, of which a tenth is 1s 6d.

> [1. A small Hospitaller house, attached to Buckland; see Knowles

and Hadcock, <u>Medieval Religious Houses, England and Wales</u>, 2nd ed.
(1971) p.307.]

160 Tenth of the abbot of Pontigny (<u>Pontenace</u>).[1]

In Lympne dy., New Romney (<u>Romene</u>) with chapel, £20, of which a tenth
is £2.

> [1. New Romney had been a cell of Pontigny from 1264; in 1439 the
> church was granted to All Souls College, Oxford (<u>VCH Kent</u>, ii,
> 239; <u>CPR 1436-41</u>, p.261).]

> [The list of churches which follows (nos. 161-79) corresponds
> closely to, but is not identical with, the <u>Taxatio</u> of 1291, and
> reflects minor shifts in ecclesiastical geography and valuation
> since that date. For the majority of churches, both value and
> tenth is listed. Within some deaneries, however, the value only
> of some benefices is given, and in such entries, the order of the
> ms. list has in this calendar been disturbed, for the sake of
> brevity and clarity, and the two categories of valuation have
> been listed separately. Those benefices here listed as untaxed
> are described in the ms. as <u>non taxata</u>.]

161 Dy. of Canterbury.

[<u>Both value and tenth listed</u>]

Fordwich (<u>de Fordewico</u>), £6 13s 4d, 13s 4d; St Mary Magdalene's
Canterbury, £5 6s 8d, 10s 8d; St George's Canterbury, £6 13s 4d, 13s
4d; Lower Hardres (<u>Parva Hardes</u>), £12, £1 4s; St Michael's Harbledown
(<u>Harbaldon</u>), £13 6s 8d, £1 6s 8d; St Martin's Canterbury, £10, £1;
vic. of Hackington (<u>Hakington</u>), £4 13s 4d, 9s 4d; St Nicholas
Harbledown, £6, 12s; St Andrew's Canterbury, £8, 16s; St Mildred's
Canterbury, £5 6s 8d, 10s 8d.

[<u>Value only listed</u>]

St Paul's Canterbury, £3 6s 8d; St Peter's Canterbury, £4; All Saints
Canterbury, £4; St Margaret's Canterbury, £4; St Alphege's Canterbury,
£4; St Mary <u>de castro</u>, Canterbury, £3 6s 8d; vic. of Thanington
(<u>Tanyngton</u>), £4; vic. of Westgate, £4; vic. of Northgate, £3 6s 8d;
vic. of Nackington (<u>Nacyndon</u>), £4; vic. of St Dunstan's Canterbury,
£4; St Michael Burgate, Canterbury, £4; Milton near Canterbury, £3 6s
8d; St Edmund's Canterbury, £2 13s 4d; St John's Canterbury, £3 6s 8d;
St Mary Bredin (<u>de Bredon</u>), £3 6s 8d; St Mary Bredman (<u>de Brednam</u>),
£2 13s 4d.

162 [fo.52v]] Dy. of Sandwich (<u>Sandewici</u>).

[<u>Both value and tenth listed</u>]

Barfreston (<u>Beverston</u>), £5 6s 8d, 10s 8d; Eythorne (<u>Eyethorn</u>), £12,
£1 4s; vic. of Woodnesborough (<u>Wodnesberth</u>), £10, £1; Deal (<u>Dale</u>),

£20, £2; vic. of Eastry, £10, £1; Great Mongeham (<u>Magna Muncham</u>), £30,
£3; Ham by Sandwich (<u>Hamme</u>), £11 6s 8d, £1 2s 8d; Knowlton (<u>Knolton</u>),
£13 6s 8d,[1] £1 6s 8d; vic. of Northbourne (<u>Northborn</u>), £6 13s 4d,
13s 4d; East Langdon (<u>Estlangdon</u>), £10, £1; Ringwould (<u>Ridingweld</u>),
£17 6s 8d, £1 14s 8d; vic. of Waldershare, £4, 8s; vic. of Tilmanstone
(<u>Tylmanston</u>), £10, £1; vic. of St Clement's Sandwich, £5, 10s;
St Peter's Sandwich, £6 13s 4d, 13s 4d; Stonar in the Isle of Thanet
(<u>Stonor</u>), £5, 10s; Little Mongeham (<u>Parva Mongeham</u>), £5 6s 8d, 10s 8d;
Betteshanger (<u>Betteshangre</u>), £11 6s 8d, £1 2s 8d; Ripple (<u>Ripley</u>),
£10, £1.

[Value only listed]

Vic. of St Mary's Sandwich, £3 6s 8d.

Not taxed:

Vic. of Eythorne; Tilmanstone (<u>Tilmaston</u>); Stokton.

    [1. MS: £12 6s 8d, cf. <u>Taxatio</u>, p.2.]

163   Dy. of Westbere.

[Both value and tenth listed]

Westbere, £6 13s 4d; 13s 4d; Swalecliffe (<u>Swalclyve</u>), £6 13s 4d, 13s 4d;
Whitstable (<u>Whitestaple</u>), £26 13s 4d, £2 13s 4d; vic. of Reculver
(<u>Reculvere</u>), £16 13s 4d, £1 13s 4d; vic. of Minster in Thanet (<u>Mynstre
in Thaneto</u>), £20, £2; vic. of St Lawrence in the Isle of Thanet, £5,
10s; vic. of St Peter's in the Isle of Thanet, £5, 10s; vic. of St
John's Margate, £5 6s 8d, 10s 8d; vic. of Chislet (<u>Chestelett</u>),
£5, 10s.

[Value only listed]

Vic. of Sarre (<u>Serre</u>), £3 6s 8d; portion of almoner of Christ Church
Canterbury in Monkton (<u>Monketon</u>), £33 6s 8d; vic. of Seasalter
(<u>Sesaltre</u>), £3 6s 8d.

Not taxed:

St Nicholas at Wade (<u>de Woode</u>), Isle of Thanet.

164   [<u>fo.53</u>] Dy. of Dover (<u>Dovorr'</u>).

[Both value and tenth listed]

Vic. of Alkham, £6 13s 4d, 13s 4d; vic of Hougham (<u>Hugham</u>), £5, 10s; vic. of
St Margaret's Dover, £4 13s 4d, 9s 4d; Charlton (<u>Charleton</u>), £10, £1;
St Nicholas Dover, £5, 10s; St James Dover, £5 6s 8d, 10s 8d;
Cheriton, £12, £1 4s ; vic of   Newington by Hythe (<u>Newenton</u>), £5 6s
8d, 10s 8d; St Peter's Dover, £6, 12s; Hawkinge (<u>Hawkyng</u>), £4 6s 8d,
8s 8d; Beauxfield (<u>Beuxfeld</u>), £12, £1 4s.

[Value only listed]

Vic. of Ewell, £3 6s 8d; vic. of River (<u>Riparia</u>), £3 6s 8d; vic. of
Guston, £3 6s 8d; vic. of Beauxfield (<u>Beaugfeld</u>), £4; St Mary's

Dover, £5 6s 8d; St John's Dover, £3 6s 8d.

Not taxed:

Vic. of Folkestone (Folkeston); Swingfield (Swynesfeld); Ewell.

[1.   MS: £3 13s 4d; cf. Taxatio, p.2.]

165   Dy. of Elham.

Vic. of Elham, £10, £1; Elham, £63 6s 8d, £6 6s 8d; Acrise, without pension, £8, 16s; Stowting (Stutyng), £13 6s 8d, £1 6s 8d; Monks Horton (Horton), £6 13s 4d, 13s 4d; vic. of Brabourne (Braborn), £6, 12s; Hastingleigh, £10, £1; Lyminge (Lymmyng), with chapel, £60, £6; vic. of Lyminge, £8, 16s; Saltwood (Saltwode), £43 6s 8d, £4 6s 8d; Wootton (Wotton), with pension, £10, £1; Denton, with portion, £10 6s 8d, £1 0s 8d; Bircholt (Byrcholt), £3 6s 8d, 6s 8d.

Not taxed:

Vic. of Postling.

166   Dy. of Lympne (Lymmene).[1]

Burmarsh (Borwermerssh), £9 6s 8d, 16s 8d; Bonnington (Bonynton), £6 13s 4d, 13s 4d; Ostenhanger (Hostinghanger), £4 13s 4d, 9s 8d; Dymchurch (Demechurch), £11 6s 8d, £1 2s 8d; Kingsnorth (Kyngesnoth), £10 13s 4d, £1 1s 4d; Ruckinge (Rokynge), £16 13s 4d, £1 13s 4d; Snargate (Snaregate), £17 13s 4d, £1 14s 8d; Woodchurch (Wodechurch), £20, £2; vic.[2] of Brenzett (Brensette), £4 13s 4d, 9s 4d; Kenardington (Kenardynton), £13 6s 8d, £1 6s 8d; vic. of Stone in Oxney (Stone), £6 13s 4d, 13s 4d;[3] vic. of Appledore (Appuldore), £6 13s 4d, 13s 4d; Aldington, with chapel, £30, £3; vic. of Aldington, £5, 10s; vic. of Brookland (Brokelond), £5 6s 8d, 10s 8d; Snave (Snaves), £13 6s 8d, £1 6s 8d; Wittersham (Wytrechysham), £20, £2; Warehome (Warehom), £16 13s 4d, £1 13s 4d;[4] Newchurch, £26 13s 4d, £2 13s 4d; Ivychurch (Ivechurch), £35 6s 8d, £3 10s 8d; Old Romney (Veteri Romenale), £18 13s 4d, £1 17s 4d.

[1.   See also no.168.
2.   MS. ecclesia; cf. Taxatio, p.2.
3.   Marginal note in 16th century hand: non taxatur ad decimam.
4.   MS. £1 6s 8d.]

167   [fo.53v] Dy. of Bridge (Bregge).

Wingham (Wyngham), provost's portion, £40, £4; Wingham, canons' portion, £160, £16; Stourmouth, with pension, £12 13s 4d, £1 5s 4d; vic. of Preston near Wingham (Preston), £4 13s 4d, 9s 4d; Adisham (Adesham), with chapel, £53 6s 8d, £5 6s 8d; Chillenden (Chillynden), £5 6s 8d, 10s 8d;. Wickham (Wykham), with vic., £38 13s 4d, £3 17s 4d; Kingston (Kyngeston), £12, £1 4s; Bishopsbourne (Bisshopisborn), with chapel, £33 6s 8d, £3 6s 8d; vic. of Petham, £4 6s 8d, 8s 8d; vic. of Waltham, £4 13s 4d, 9s 4d; Chartham, £26 13s 4d, £2 13s 4d; vic. of

Chilham, £6 13s 4d, 13s 4d; Upper Hardres (<u>Magna Herdys</u>), with chapel £26 13s 4d, £2 13s 4d; Crundale (<u>Crumdale</u>), £11 6s 8d, £1 2s 8d; Brook (<u>Broke</u>), £6 13s 4d, 13s 4d; vic. of Wye (<u>Wy</u>), £10 13s 4d, £1 1s 8d; Boughton Aluph (<u>Bocton Alulphi</u>), £40, £4; vic. of Godmersham, £10, £1; Ickham (<u>Ikham</u>), £30, £3; Elmstone (<u>Elmerstone</u>), £10, £1; Lyvingesburn (<u>Levyngesborne</u>), £10, £1.

Not taxed:

Vic. of Lyvingesburn; vic. of Patrixbourne (<u>Patrykisborn</u>).

168   Dy. of Lympne (<u>Lymmene</u>).[1]

[<u>Both value and tenth listed</u>]

Mersham, £25 13s 4d, £2 11s 8d; Lydd (<u>Lydde</u>), £36 13s 4d, £3 13s 4d; vic. of Lydd, £16 13s 4d, £1 13s 4d; Sevington (<u>Seventon</u>), £10, £1; Orlestone (<u>Orlaston</u>), £5 6s 8d, 10s 8d; St Mary in the Marsh (<u>in Marisco</u>), £20, £2; Hinxhill (<u>Henxhill</u>), £10, £1; Hope in the marsh of Romney (<u>Hope</u>), £13 6s 8d, £1 6s 8d; Midley (<u>Mydley</u>), £4 6s 8d, 8s 8d.

[<u>Neither value nor tenth listed</u>]

Shadoxhurst (<u>Saddokysherst</u>); Blackmanstone (<u>Blakmanston</u>); Eastbridge (<u>Estbrige</u>); Orgarswick (<u>Orgarswik</u>); vic. of Willesborough (<u>Willysborgh</u>); vic. of Lympne; vic. of Stone; vic. of Sellinge (<u>Sellyng</u>).

   [1. See also no. 166. The whole of this second Lympne section is written over an erasure.]

169   Dy. of Sutton

[<u>Both value and tenth listed</u>]

Harrietsham (<u>Heriottisham</u>), £16, £1 12s; Maidstone (<u>Maydeston</u>), with chapel, £106 13s 4d, £10 13s 4d; vic. of Lenham (<u>Leanham</u>), £6 13s 4d, 13s 4d; vic. of Marden (<u>Merden</u>), £6 13s 4d, 13s 4d; vic. of Goudhurst (<u>Goutherst</u>), £6 13s 4d, 13s 4d; Ulcombe (<u>Olcombe</u>), £20, £2; Hollingbourne (<u>Holyngborn</u>), £40, £4; vic. of Boxley (<u>Boxle</u>), £8, 16s; Otham, £6 13s 4d, 13s 4d; Staplehurst (<u>Stapulhurst</u>), £20, £2; Wormshill (<u>Wormeshill</u>), £14 13s 4d, £1 9s 4d; Sutton Valence (<u>Sutton</u>), with chapel, £33 6s 8d,[1] £3 6s 8d; vic. of Sutton Valence, £5 6s 8d, 10s 8d; Langley, £6 13s 4d, 13s 4d.

[<u>Value only listed</u>]

Vic. of Bersted (<u>Bergstede</u>), £3 6s 8d.

Not taxed:

Vic. of Boughton Monchelsea (<u>Bocton Chenesey</u>); vic. of Staplehurst (<u>Staplehirst</u>); Lullingstone (<u>Lullyngton</u>).

   [1. MS. £39 6s 8d; cf. <u>Taxatio</u>, p.3.]

170   Dy. of Sittingbourne (<u>Sydingbourne</u>).

[Both value and tenth listed]

Vic. of Upchurch, £5 6s 8d, 10s 8d; vic. of Hartlip (Hartlepe), £5,[1]
10s; vic. of Newington near Sittingbourne (Newenton), £6 13s 4d,
13s 4d; vic. of Borden, £5 6s 8d, 10s 8d; vic. of Eastchurch, £13 6s
8d, £1 6s 8d; vic. of Leysdown (Leysden), £5, 10s; vic. of
Sittingbourne (Sethingborn), £6 13s 4d, 13s 4d; Tunstal (Dunstalle),
£23 6s 8d, £2 6s 8d; vic. of Rainham (Reynham), £10, £1; Elmley
(Elmele), £6 13s 4d, 13s 4d; vic. of Milton near Sittingbourne
(Middilton), £8, 16s; Merston, £17 6s 8d, £1 13s 8d; Bapchild
(Bakchilde), £22, £2 4s; vic. of Tong (Tonge), £5 6s 8d, 10s 8d;
Bicknor (Bignor), £5 6s 8d, 10s 8d; vic. of Bapchild, £6 13s 4d, 13s
4d; Warden in the Isle of Sheppey (Wardon), £6 13s 4d, 13s 4d; Lower
Halstow (Halstowe), £6 13s 4d, 13s 4d; vic. of Lower Halstow, £4 13s
4d, 9s 4d; Sittingbourne (Sedyngborne), appropriated to the nuns of
Clerkenwell, £23 6s 8d, £2 6s 8d; Milstead (Milstede), £13 6s 8d,
£1 6s 8d; Wichling (Wycheling), £12, £1 4s.

[Value only listed]

Kingsdown (Kyngesdon), £4.

Not taxed:

Bredgar (Bradgare).

   [1. MS. £5 13s 4d; cf. Taxatio, p.3.]

171 [fo.54] Dy. of Ospringe (Ospring).

[Both value and tenth listed]

Vic. of Ospringe, £10, £1; vic. of Faversham, £10, £1; vic. of
Throwley (Trulegh), £8, 16s; vic. of Preston next Faversham (Preston),
£9 15s 6d, 19s 6¾d; Badlesmere (Baldesmere), £8 13s 4d, 17s 4d; Norton,
£18 13s 4d, £1 17s 4d; Graveney (Greane), £5 6s 8d, 10s 8d; vic. of
Selling, £6 13s 4d, 13s 4d; vic. of Boughton under Blean (Bocton),
£5 6s 8d, 10s 8d; vic. of Hernhill (Harnehill), £5, 10s; vic. of
Teynham (Tenham), £8 13s 4d, 17s 4d; vic. of Lynsted (Lynstede), £5,
10s; Goodnestone near Faversham (Gudneston), £5 6s 8d, 10s 8d;
Luddenham (Ludenham), £13 6s 8d, £1 6s 8d; vic. of Sheldwich
(Sheldwhich), £5, 10s; Eastling, £40, £4; Otterden (Otryndon), £6 13s
4d, 13s 4d; Leaveland (Levelond), £6 13s 4d, 13s 4d.

[Value only listed]

Vic. of Stalisfield (Stalfeld), £4; Buckland (Buklond), £2.

172 Dy. of Pagham (Pageham), Sx.

Vic. of Pagham (Paggeham), £16 13s 4d, £1 13s 4d; East Lavant
(Estlavent), £20, £2; Tangmere, £13 6s 8d, £1 6s 8d; Slindon (Slyndon),
£10, £1; vic. of Slindon, £4 13s 4d, 9s 4d; West Tarring (Terring),
£66 13s 4d, £6 13s 4d; vic. of West Tarring, £8, 16s; Patching, £20,
£2; vic. of Patching, £5, 10s; vic. of South Bersted (Southberghstede),
£6 13s 4d, 13s 4d.

173 Dy. of Shoreham, in the immediate jurisdiction of Christ Church Canterbury.

[Both value and tenth listed]

Shoreham, with chapel, £53 6s 8d, £5 6s 8d; Eynsford (Eynesforde), £20, £2; Darenth, £6 13s 4d, 13s 4d; Bexley (Bixle), £20, £2; vic. of Bexley, £6 13s 4d, 13s 4d; Crayford [alias Earde], £26 13s 4d, £2 13s 4d; vic. of Crayford, £26 13s 4d, £2 13s 4d; vic. of Meopham (Mepeham), £10, £1; Cliffe (Cleve), £73 6s 8d, £7 6s 8d; vic. of Isle of Grain (Greane), £10, £1; East Farleigh (Farleigh), £6 13s 4d, 13s 4d; vic. of East Farleigh, £6 13s 4d, 13s 4d; Hunton (Huntyngdon), £10, £1; East Peckham (Pecham), £23 6s 8d, £2 6s 8d; vic. of East Peckham, £8, 16s; Wrotham (Wroteham), £53 6s 8d, £5 6s 8d; vic. of Wrotham, £13 6s 8d, £1 6s 8d; Ickham (Icham), £13 6s 8d, £1 6s 8d; Sevenoaks (Sevenoke), £33 6s 8d, £3 6s 8d; vic. of Sevenoaks, £6 13s 4d, 13s 4d; vic. of Gillingham, £13 6s 8d, £1 6s 8d; Penshurst (Penseherst), £20, £2; Chiddingstone (Chedingston), £20, £2; Hever, £10, £1; Brasted (Bradestede), £26 13s 4d, £2 13s 4d; Sundridge (Sundrisshe), £20, £2; Chevening (Chevenyng), £16 13s 4d, £1 13s 4d; Orpington (Orpenton), £40, £4; vic. of Orpington, £5 6s 8d, 10s 8d; Keston (Kestane), £5, 10s; Hayes (Heese), £6 13s 4d; 13s 4d; vic. of East Malling (Estmalling) £8, 16s; vic. of East Farleigh, £6 13s 4d, 13s 4d; Halstead (Halstede), £5, 10s; Woodland (Wodlond) [alias Week], £4 13s 4d, 9s 4d.

[Value only listed]

Vic. of Darenth (Derunth), £3 6s 8d; Ifield (Ifeld), £3 6s 8d.

Not taxed:

Farningham (Ferningham); vic. of Farningham.

174 Dy. of South Malling (Southmalling), Sx.

Vic. of Mayfield (Magfelde), £7 6s 8d, 14s 8d; Buxsted (Bukstede), £32, £3 4s; Isfield (Ifelde), £10, £1; Edburton, £14 13s 4d, £1 9s 4d; Stanmer, £10 13s 4d, £1 1s 8d; Framfield (Freyngfeld), £10, £1; vic. of Wadhurst (Wadehirst), £6 13s 4d, 13s 4d; prebend of the dean of the collegiate church of South Malling, £40, £4; treasurer's prebend, £20, £2; chancellor's prebend, £20, £2; precentor's prebend, £20, £2.

175 [fo.54v] Dy. of Croydon, Sy.

Croydon, £40, £4; vic. of Croydon, £10, £1; Hayes (Heese), Mx., £23 6s 8d, £2 6s 8d; portion of the prior of Ogbourne (Okerborne) in Hayes, £2 6s 8d, 4s 8d; portion of the prior of Rochester in Hayes, £1, 2s; Harrow (Harowe), Mx., £40, £4; vic. of Harrow, £6 13s 4d, 13s 4d; Cheam (Cheyham), £23 6s 8d, £2 6s 8d; Merstham (Merstan), £23 6s 8d, £2 6s 8d; Charlwood (Cherlwode), £13 6s 8d, £1 6s 8d; East Horsley (Horstleigh), £12, £1 4s; Burstow (Borstowe), £8, 16s; Newington (Newenton), £14 13s 4d, £1 9s 4d; Wimbledon (Wymbaldon), £40, £4; Barnes, £14 6s 8d, £1 8s 8d.

176 Dy. of Bocking (Bokkyng), Ess.

Bocking (Bokking), £40, £4; Stisted (Stystede), £20, £2; Hadleigh (Hadlee), £40, £4;[1] portion of Hadleigh in Boxford (Boxforde), Sf., £1 6s 8d, 2s 8d; Monks Eleigh (Ilegh Monachorum), Sf., £20, £2; Latchingdon (Lachedon), £13 6s 8d, £1 6s 8d; Southchurch, £26 13s 4d, £2 13s 4d; Moulton (Moleton), Sf., £26 13s 4d, £2 13s 4d;[2] Ashbocking (Assh), Sf., £4 6s 8d, 8s 8d.

   [1. MS. £40 6s 8d, £4 2s 8d, shillings and pence figures struck
   through.
   2. MS. 13s 4d.]

177 Dy. of Risborough (Rysebergh), Bk.

Monks Risborough (Risebergh), £16 13s 4d, £1 13s 4d; Newington (Newenton), Ox., £26 13s 4d, £2 13s 4d; Halton, £10, £1; portion of prior of Wallingford (Walingford), £1, 2s.

178 Dy. of Arches, London.

St Vedast, £6 8s 4d, 13s 4d; St Dunstan [in the East], £8 6s 8d, 16s 8d; St Leonard [Eastcheap], £5, 10s; St Michael[Crooked Lane], £6, 12s; St Mary Aldermarychurch (de Aldermary Chirch), £4 13s 4d, 9s 4d; St Mary Arches (de Arcubus), £13 6s 8d, £1 6s 8d; All Hallows Lombard St (Omnium Sanctorum in Graschurch), £4 6s 8d, 8s 8d; St Pancras, £5, 10s.

179 Dy. of Charing (Cherring).

[Both value and tenth listed]

Frittenden (Frithenden), £10, £1; Sandhurst (Sandhirst), £16 13s 4d, £1 13s 4d; vic. of Benenden (Benyndon), £8, 16s; Rolvenden (Rolveden), £33 6s 8d, £3 6s 8d; vic. of Rolvenden, £6 13s 4d, 13s 4d; Hawkhurst (Haukeherst), £20, £2; vic. of Tenterden, £10, £1; vic. of Headcorn (Hedcrone), £8, 16s; High Halden (Halden), £10, £1; Biddenden (Bedyngden), £20, £2; Pluckley (Pluklee), £10, £1; Eastwell (Estwell), £10, £1; Boughton Malherbe (Bocton Maleherbe), £20, £2; vic. of Westwell, £10, £1; Hothfield (Hotfelde), £10, £1; Great Chart [alias Chart](Magna Chart alias Estchart), £20, £2; vic. of Ashford (Esshetesford), £5 6s 8d, 10s 8d; vic. of Kennington (Kenynton), £6 13s 4d, 13s 4d; Charing (Charryng), with chapel, £53 6s 8d, £5 6s 8d; vic. of Charing, £8 13s 4d, 17s 4d; Smarden (Smerden), £20, £2; Little Chart (Parva Chart), £16 13s 4d, £1 13s 4d; Newenden (Newendon), £9 6s 8d, 18s 8d.

[Value only listed]

Frinstead (Frenstede), £1 6s 8d; Pett, £3 6s 8d; Pevington (Pevynton), £4.

Not taxed:

Vic. of Bethersden (Beatrichden).

47

180   [<u>fo.199</u>] Foundation statutes of Ellis Davy's Almshouse, Croydon
(<u>Croydoun</u>), Sy. Ellis Davy, citizen and mercer of London, by
authority of royal letters patent dated 25 Dec. 1445,[1] has established
on land purchased from the abbot and conv. of Bermondsey (<u>Barmondsey</u>)
a perpetual almshouse for seven poor people from the town of Croydon
and four miles thereabout, who may be men only, or men and women, and
one of whom is to be tutor. The regulations for the almshouse are set
out in great detail, the most important points being that they shall
constitute a corporation and shall have a common seal. The governors
are to be the v. of Croydon, the two churchwardens and four of the
most worthy householders, and the overseers are to be the wardens of
the Mercers Company of London. On a vacancy in the office of tutor,
the governors shall appoint a successor within twenty days, and then
appointment shall devolve upon the overseers. When a vacancy occurs
among the other inmates, the churchwardens shall nominate two
candidates, from whom the tutor and brethren shall make an election,
and if they fail to do so within fifteen days, the churchwardens shall
provide to the place. Each inmate is to have his own place within the
almshouse, and is not to disturb his fellows. Of the total annual
revenue of £24 p.a., £15 12s shall be for the sustenance of the
inmates, that is, the tutor is to have 12d per week and the others 10d
each, and they shall not beg, on pain of expulsion. They shall attend
the parish church of Croydon each day, and say specified prayers, and
especially after the death of the founder they shall pray for his soul
around his burial place. They shall reside continually, and shall
dress soberly. Those sound in body, particularly any female inmates,
shall minister to those who are sick. They shall have a common chest
for their valuables and seal, and it shall have three keys, no man to
hold all three, and no document shall be sealed without the consent of
the founder, or after his death of the governors and overseers. They
should strive to increase the resources of the almshouse, and in no
way dissipate them. No leper, madman or person intolerably diseased
shall be admitted, and if any inmate becomes so diseased they shall
be put out, but shall have their 10d each week so that they may be
maintained elsewhere. If any inmate acquires or inherits 4 marks or
more they shall be put out, and if any acquires a sum less than 4 marks,
half of it shall be put in the common chest. Their behaviour is to be
sober, chaste and honest. Fines are to be imposed by the tutor for
breaches of discipline, and at the third offence the culprit shall be
expelled. The governors and overseers shall exercise a similar
discipline over the tutor, and after the founder's death they are to
have the power to make such statutes and ordinances as seem best to
them. The tutor and poor people are to keep the founder's anniversary,
and shall pay the v. of Croydon, the churchwardens and other priests
for its observance. They shall also pay the expenses of annual
visitation by two of the four wardens of the Mercers Company. Four
cottages granted to the almshouse shall be rented annually for the
best rent obtainable, for the increase of the common fund. The
foundation and ordinances shall be read to the tutor and poor people
every quarter. 26 April 1447.

[1. <u>CPR 1441-46</u>, p.318.]

[Printed: G. Steinman, <u>History of Croydon</u> (1834), Appx. VIII, p.267 ff.]

181 [fo.202] Order for the Canonisation of Saints.

Canonisation of saints is reserved to the Apostolic See, as
demonstrated by the texts cited by Johannes Andreae in Glossa
Ordinaria ad Librum Sextum[1] in the gloss on c. unicum VI iii 22 De
reliquiis et veneratione sanctorum. The twelve stages in the process
of canonisation are described, following Hostiensis, In Quinque
Decretalium Libros Commentaria,[2] in the gloss on c. 1 Audivimus X iii
45: supplication should be made to the pope several times, so that
there is time to see if miracles continue; the pope will commission a
preliminary enquiry in the locality, to test opinion and report
whether an inquisition into the candidate's sanctity should be
conducted. The pope will consult the cardinals, and if they consider
it right, he will appoint a commission to enquire into the truth of
the candidate's reputation, life and miracles. When this inquisition
has been returned, examination will be delegated to some chaplains of
the curia, who will draw up rubrics, which will then be examined by
the pope and cardinals, and if the pope considers that canonisation
should proceed, he will announce this first to the cardinals, then in
public consistory to those bishops present at the curia, seeking their
opinion. A day will be appointed, on which the pope will preach a
sermon recounting the process and the proof; while the pope prays, a
suitable hymn or antiphon will be sung, then the pope will rise and
declare that the candidate should be added to the catalogue of saints,
and that his feast should be observed on a specified day. Sometimes
matters may be expedited more easily, especially in the case of
martyrs, as is explained by Hostiensis and Innocent IV,[3] in their
glosses on c. 52 Venerabili fratre X ii 20 De testibus.

It is to be noted that both outstanding life and miracles are
necessary for canonisation, as demonstrated by the texts cited by
Panormitanus[4] in his gloss on c. 52 Venerabili fratre X ii 20 De
testibus.

The matters which require investigation are outlined: the quality
of the candidate's life, for which see Decretum, D. lxi c. 5 Miramur,
C. xii q. ii c. 27 Quatuor, C. vii q. i c. 36 Omnis qui, C. vii q. i
c. 49 Ibi adunati, and C. i q. i c. 65 Vide quantum. With regard to
miracles, four things are necessary: that the miracle should proceed
from God, that it should be contrary to nature, that it should be
effected not by the power of words, but by the merits of the candidate,
and that it should be for the corroboration of the faith, as is
demonstrated by the texts cited by the commentators on c. 52
Venerabili fratre X ii 20 De testibus, by Johannes Andreae in his
gloss on c. unicum VI iii 22, and by Hostiensis[5] in his commentary on
X iii 45 De reliquiis et veneratione sanctorum, where he states that
a less exhaustive examination is necessary of the miracles of martyrs.

If the church were to err in canonisation, prayers in honour of such
a person would still be acceptable, and one may offer private prayers,
but not solemn public prayers, to an uncanonised person believed to be
a saint, according to the commentaries of Innocent IV, Hostiensis and

Panormitanus on c. 1 <u>Audivimus</u> X iii 45 <u>De reliquiis et veneratione</u> <u>sanctorum</u>.

For the nature of a miracle, see the Archdeacon's commentary[6] on <u>Decretum</u>, C.xxvi q. v c. 14 <u>Nec mirum</u> and C. i q. i c. 56 <u>Teneamus</u>. For the manner in which miracles should be proved and witnesses examined, see Johannes Andreae, Dominic de San Geminiano[7] and Johannes Monachus[8] on c. 1 <u>Statuimus</u> VI ii 9 <u>De confessis</u>, and the Decretalists on c. 52 <u>Venerabili fratre</u> X ii 20 <u>De testibus</u>, Baldus de Ubaldis[9] in his gloss on c. 4 <u>Solam</u> iv 20 <u>De testibus</u>, and the Archdeacon's commentary on <u>Decretum</u>, C. xxvi q. v c. 14 <u>Nec mirum</u>.

[1. Johannes Andreae, <u>Glossa Ordinaria ad Librum Sextum</u> (Venice, 1507).

2. Hostiensis, <u>In Quinque Libros Decretalium Commentaria</u> (Venice, 1581).

3. Innocent IV, <u>In Quinque Libros Decretalium Commentaria</u> (Venice, 1578).

4. Panormitanus, <u>Lectura super Quinque Libris Decretalium</u> (Lyons, 1586).

5. Hostiensis, <u>Summa Aurea super Titulis Decretalium</u> (Cologne, 1612).

6. Guido de Baysio, <u>Rosarium, seu in Decretorum Volumen Commentaria</u> (Venice, 1577).

7. Dominic de San Geminiano, <u>Lectura super Sexto Libro Decretalium</u> (Trent, 1522).

8. Johannes Monachus, <u>Glossa Aurea super Sexto Decretalium Libro</u> (Paris, 1535).

9. Baldus de Ubaldis, <u>Commentaria in Codicem</u> (Lyons, 1545).]

[Printed: Wilkins, iii, 636-8, and with corrections, but omitting canonical references, in P. Grosjean, <u>Henrici VI Angliae Regis</u> <u>Miracula Postuma ex Musei Britannici Regis 13 C VIII</u> (Brussels, 1935), pp. 171-5.]

182 [<u>fo.203v</u>] Customary Order of Canonisation.

First a king, or some lords or other authoritative persons should several times make supplication for canonisation to the pope, who may commit investigation to two or three prelates, who shall send their findings to the pope in the form of a public instrument. The pope should then confer in consistory with the cardinals and decree according to the merits of the candidate. If there is to be a canonisation, the following procedure should be followed in the basilica of St Peter. A large wooden enclosure should be erected in the middle of the basilica; it should have one door, with an enclosed ladder leading up to it. Within the enclosure there should be set a wooden altar, and benches for the cardinals and other prelates and officials. There should be a scarlet carpet on which the pope may kneel, a frontal of brocade with a white fringe, and two chairs for the pope, for whom also there should be a white baldachin embroidered with gold brocade, with crimson pendants on which are to be depicted the arms of the church, the arms of the pope, the image of the person to be canonised, the arms of whomsoever has paid the expenses, and of the city where the saint was born or where his remains lie. From the door of the church to the entry to the enclosure should be set up to eighty candles, each about four pounds in weight, and there should be twelve similar candles for the veneration of the elevation of the Host. There should be two white candles of twelve pounds for the pope in procession, and each participant in the procession should have a candle of varying weight, according to his status. If the lord who has procured the canonisation has a banner, it should be borne and displayed before the offertory.

The Offertory.

The first commissary, a cardinal, should offer two loaves covered with saffron coloured brass foil, and two loaves covered with brass foil, and over each of the loaves there should be a cloth of the finest material, eight hands in length. The second commissary, a cardinal, should offer four casks of wine, similarly covered with brass foil. The third commissary, a cardinal, should offer four great candles of ordinary wax, each ten pounds in weight. The first orator, proctor or solicitor of the canonisation should offer a painted casket, on which are depicted white doves, one of which at least should be shown flying. The second of them should offer a similar casket, full of live little birds. Any other orators, proctors or solicitors should each offer a candle of ordinary wax weighing six pounds. Besides the forementioned candles there should be seven others of white wax, each of two pounds, which are to be carried in seven candlesticks in the papal procession from the robing chamber to the church of St Peter. There should be two similar candles for the credence for the sacred vessels, and seven similar candles for the altar at which the pope will celebrate. This is the accustomed procedure and ceremonial, in addition to the order for the celebration of mass.

[Printed: Wilkins, iii, 638-9.]

183 [fo.204] The Expenses of Canonisation.

There follow the expenses entailed in the commission of the cause and the conduct of the process, discounting the expenses of the commission, the cause and the process, since no accurate estimate of those may be given.

To the lord pope, in gold and silver, 100 ducats; for four yards of red cloth to be set at his feet, 20 ducats; for six lengths of white cloth to be set before him, 8 ducats; for the wine, 8 ducats; for the three commissaries of the canonisation, in jewels or money, 190 ducats; for wine to be given to them, 10 ducats; for a banquet of venison, chicken, sweetmeats, etc., for the pope and the three cardinals, 70 ducats; for the building of the enclosure in the middle of the church, 100 ducats; for the painting of shields, arms and spears, 15 ducats; for the clergy of St Peter's for the decoration of the church, 12 ducats; for the papal farriers, for the decoration of the enclosure,

7 ducats; for the consistorial advocate for his sermon, 80 ducats; for the cantors of the chapel and the papal sacrist, in all 24 ducats; for the bellringers and clerks of the chapel of St Peter's, in all, 3 ducats; for the clerks of the ceremonies, 12 ducats; for the notaries recording the process, 20 ducats; for the papal grooms and sweepers, 4 ducats; for the cardinals' grooms, 3 ducats; for the deacon and subdeacon, in all, one ducat; for the papal chamberlain, 20 ducats; for the masters of the doors, 8 ducats; for the sergeants, 8 ducats; for the keepers of the iron door, 4 ducats; for the keepers of the first door, 2 ducats; for the papal guards, 5 ducats; for the procurator fiscal, 4 ducats; for the bulls, 60 ducats; for the solicitor who has conducted the whole business, more or less according to the merits of him who has been canonised and the labours of the petitioners, estimated at 50 ducats, although today, as in other business, greater salaries are sought, and because of the importunity of the petitioners are often enough impetuously and unduly paid.

[Printed: Wilkins, iii, 639.]

184   [fo.204v] Translation of the relics of St Swithun on 14–15 July 1476.

On the vigil of the feast of the translation of the relics of St Swithun, bp. and confessor, some of the monks of the cathedral church of Winchester (Winton') took from the sacristy, where it had rested for almost twenty years, an ebony coffin covered with a fine cloth, in which rested the relics of St Swithun. They carried it with great reverence to the high altar, where they set it down. Shortly afterwards the bp. of Winchester celebrated Vespers, and, as some of the brethren have stated, when Matins also had been sung before the dead of night, according to ecclesiastical custom, the brethren rested, apart from two or three guarding the relics. The next day, at the appointed hour, they gathered in the choir and formed a solemn procession, which included the bps. of Winchester and Chichester (Cicestren'), the suffragan of the bp. of Winchester, the prior of Mottisfont (Mottesham), the abbot of Hyde (Hida) and the prior of Winchester, clad in pontificals, and the monks and ministers of the church, vested in albs and copes according to the solemnity of the occasion. The abbot of Hyde and the prior of Winchester approached the high altar and took the coffin on a wicket on their shoulders, and leaving the church, they processed around the greater part of the city, praising God. The coffin was in the middle of the procession, with the abbot in front and the prior behind it, and on either side William Downley, earl of Arundel, and Lord Storton, carrying it on their shoulders, and a huge crowd of people followed the procession. The bp. of Winchester celebrated mass, and after the gospel and offertory the bp. of Chichester preached in the vernacular. After mass the prelates, vested in pontificals, reverently lifted the relics from the high altar and bore them to their present resting place, to the accompaniment of singing and the music of the organ and other instruments, processing to the marble tomb constructed for the glorious saint, on which a silver reliquary, decorated with gold, had been placed. Those prelates who were able climbed a ladder on

the east side of the tomb up to the reliquary, and the bp. and prior
of Winchester placed the coffin with its glorious relics in the
reliquary, through an opening made for that purpose. The bp. of
Winchester then entered the reliquary, reverently kissed the relics
and stepped out, and in turn the other prelates and certain magnates
did the same. The opening was then sealed and the ladder removed, and
when they had prayed to God and His glorious saint Swithun, those who
had entered withdrew.

185   Mandate of Pope Alexander VI to the abp. of Canterbury and the bp. of
       Durham (Dunelmen'). The pope has learned from letters of King Henry
       VII of the merits and miracles of King Henry VI, the concourse of
       pilgrims to his tomb, and the general belief that his name should be
       added to the catalogue of saints. In accordance with the king's
       wishes, and following the example of his predecessor Innocent VIII who
       issued a similar commission, the pope orders them to proceed to the
       collegiate church within Windsor (Windesore) Castle, where Henry VI is
       buried, and to enquire into the life of the king and the miracles
       wrought during his lifetime and after his death, examining witnesses
       and documentary evidence. They should communicate their findings to
       the curia by sealed letters close. St Peter's Rome, 4 Oct. 1494.

           [Printed: Wilkins, iii, 640.]

186   [fo.205] Petition of King Henry VII that the remains of King Henry VI
       may be translated to Westminster (Westm') Abbey. Having persecuted
       Henry VI during his lifetime, Edward IV after his death ordered the
       burial of his body at Chertsey (Chertesey) Abbey, a remote place
       entirely unsuitable for a royal grave. When miracles occurred at the
       tomb, Richard III ordered the body to be exhumed and reburied in the
       collegiate church within Windsor Castle, where it now rests. The
       remains are now claimed by Westminster Abbey, where Henry VI's parents
       are buried and where the kings of England are crowned, and which lies
       close to the king's principal palace, and the king now petitions the
       pope to authorise the translation, whether or not the dean and chapter
       of Windsor give their consent.[1]

            [1. The competing claims of Windsor and Westminster for the remains
            were heard by the king's council sitting in the Star Chamber in
            Feb. 1498. The council decided in favour of Westminster, but the
            translation never took place. The case is printed by Grosjean,
            op.cit., pp.180-94, and discussed by J.W. McKenna, 'Piety and
            Propaganda: the Cult of King Henry VI', Chaucer and Middle English
            Studies, ed. B. Rowland (1974), pp.80-4.]

           [Printed: Wilkins, iii, 635-6.]

187   Mr. Robert Castellesi, clerk of Volterra (Vulteran') and papal
       protonotary, appeared in a high chamber at Lambeth with a papal
       commission addressed to himself, which he requested the abp. to
       inspect, and if he found it to be valid to cause it to be transcribed

by a notary public in the form of a public instrument having the validity of the original.

Mandate of Pope Alexander VI addressed to Mr. Robert Castellesi. The pope has in the last two years incurred great expense in the maintenance of troops for the defence of the Patrimony, and every day he needs to hire more mercenaries. Therefore the help of the faithful is greatly to be desired, and the pope wishes to provide for the salvation of souls, and also for his own necessary expenditure. He therefore commissions Robert, in person or by deputy, to grant to all rs., vs. and curates of parish churches within the dominions of King Henry VII who within eight months contribute a noble or more, as they compound with Robert, to the expenses of the Roman church, the faculty of granting absolution, full indulgence and remission of all sins, even those where the apostolic See should be consulted, once during the person's lifetime and in articulo mortis, to all their parishioners who are penitent, confessed and in the obedience of the Roman church, except those who have incurred excommunication or other ecclesiastical censures for rebellion [nos. 8, 43]. He is also commissioned to grant to all ecclesiastical persons, both native and alien, except the forementioned rebels, who similarly compound with Robert or his deputies, the faculty of choosing a suitable confessor, who having heard their confession may similarly absolve them and grant full indulgence and remission, once in their lifetime and in articulo mortis. He is to interpret any doubtful point in these letters, and he and his deputies are to have full authority to suspend all indulgences and faculties to absolve in reserved cases for a period of eight months. Notwithstanding apostolic, provincial or conciliar decrees to the contrary. St Peter's Rome, 30 May 1497.

After the abp. had examined these letters and pronounced them to be authentic, he ordered them to be transcribed and exemplified by a notary public, and declared that the transcript and exemplification should have the full authority of the original. Notarial exemplification by Mr John Barett, notary public, in the presence of Mr Hugh Payntewyn, D.C.L., and Mr Thomas Rowthale, Decr.D. Lambeth, 17 Feb. 1498.

188 [fo.206] In a high chamber of the palace of Westminster certain bulls were presented on behalf of the king to the abp., and it was requested that, as the king needed to exhibit these letters in various distant places, he should inspect them and, if he found them to be valid, should order them to be transcribed in the form of a public instrument.

Mandate of Pope Alexander VI addressed to the abp. of Canterbury and the bps. of Durham (Dunelmen') and Ely (Elien'). The pope has received a petition from King Henry VII, informing him that although there are fifty-seven Franciscan houses in England, only in the convent at Greenwich does the regular observance flourish. Elsewhere, in the Conventual houses, there are some who live a reprobate life, and there had once been more friars in twenty-five houses than there now are in fifty-seven. The house of friars of the Observance at Greenwich is full to capacity of brethren living an exemplary life, and as for various reasons it is not expedient to found new houses, the king petitions that five of the Conventual friaries noted for their laxity may be given to the friars of the Observance, and the brethren therein transferred to more reputable Conventual houses, unless they will live in obedience to the ultramontane general of the Observants and his vicars. The pope therefore orders the recipients of this mandate, or one or two of them, to take with them two or three professed in the Rule of the Observance and to visit five Conventual houses where the warden and friars live reprobate lives, to conduct an investigation, and unless they will conform to the Rule of the Observance, to transfer the brethren to other Conventual houses and to introduce friars of the Observance, and to grant the houses with their appurtenances to the use of the wardens and brethren of the Observance under the ultramontane general and the vicars of the province, with no appeal and enforcing these measures by ecclesiastical censures extending even to the invocation of the secular arm. Notwithstanding the agreements made between the Conventual and Observant friars, by which the Observants are prohibited from receiving Conventual houses for their habitation, and the letters of Popes Pius II, Paul II and Sixtus IV[1] confirming this agreement, etc. St Peter's Rome, 22 Apr. 1498.

After the abp. had examined these letters and pronounced them to be authentic, he ordered them to be transcribed and exemplified by a notary public, and declared that the transcript and exemplification should have the full authority of the original. Notarial exemplification by Mr Peter Carmelianus, notary public, in the presence of Giles Lord Dawbeney, the king's chamberlain, and Sir Richard Culford, the king's comptroller. Collation of the enregistered transcript with the original by Mr John Barett. Westminster, 15 Nov. 1498.

[1. The bulls Inter Assiduas Curas of 12 Jan. 1464, Cum Sacer Ordo of 18 February 1467, and Dum Singulos of 27 Apr. 1474.]

[Printed: A.G. Little, 'The Introduction of the Observant Friars into England: a Bull of Alexander VI', PBA, xxvii (1941), 162-6.]

189   [fo.207] Appointment by the abp. as his proctors at the court of Rome of Adrian Castellensis, protonotary of the apostolic see, John Gerona, clerk of the Apostolic Camera, and Hugh Spaldyng, warden of the English hospice in Rome, to represent him jointly or singly in all matters pertaining to the office of cardinal priest of St Anastasia. Notarial exemplification by [blank], in the presence of Mr John Canerton, S.T.P., and Mr Thomas Madeys, S.T.P. Lambeth, 17 March 1494.

190   [fo.207v] Appointment by the abp. as his proctors at the court of Rome of Adrian Castellensis, protonotary of the apostolic see, Thomas Routhale, Decr.D., William Robynson, Decr.D., John Gerona, clerk of the Apostolic Camera, Hugh Spaldyng, warden of the hospital of St Thomas the Martyr, and John Laurencii, Decr.D., of Tortosa (Dertusen') dioc., to represent him jointly or singly, with full powers,

including appointment of deputies. Notarial exemplification by
[blank], in the presence of Mr John Camberton, S.T.P., and Mr Thomas
Madeys, S.T.P. Lambeth, 10 Dec. 1494.

191 [fo.208v] Appeal to the court of Rome on behalf of the bp. of
London made by Mr Richard Draper, the bp.'s Official, in the house of
Richard Tripland in the parish of St Nicholas Shambles (ad Macellas).
He rehearses the testamentary rights of the bp. according to legatine
and provincial constitutions and ancient custom. When an appeal had
already been lodged by the bp., who feared that some attempt would be
made by the abp. and his officials against these rights, Mr Richard
Blodwell, Commissary General of the bp. in the deaneries of Middlesex
and Barking, cited to appear before him John Swarder and Robert
Dobson, executors of Richard Symson of the parish of All Hallows the
Less, and assigned a day for them to appear again to exhibit his
testament. When they failed to appear, and made no excuse, he
pronounced them contumacious and excommunicated them. Then, when
Mr Blodwell cited Robert Eryk and Thomas Robyns, executors of John
Eryk, who had died in the town and dy. of Barking (Berkyng), with
goods in that dy. and in London dioc., the abp., at the promotion of
the two forementioned pairs of executors, proceeded ex officio,
asserting that the deceased, at the time of their deaths, held goods
in various dioceses of the province, and that probate pertained to
him by virtue of the Prerogative of the church of Canterbury. The
abp., combining in himself the functions of judge and litigant,
inhibited Mr Blodwell from proceeding any further with probate and
from any action against the executors and, moreover, he cited
Mr Blodwell to appear before him, at short notice and in an unsafe
place, to answer certain articles relating to his contempt of the
Prerogative of the church of Canterbury and the impediment of the
last will of the foresaid deceased. In these and other ways the abp.
harassed the bp. of London and his officials in their probate
jurisdiction, and threatened, as he still does, to pronounce the
commissary a contumacious perjurer and to punish him as such, to
summon testaments and executors within the jurisdiction of the bp. of
London before himself or his commissary by virtue of his pretended
Prerogative, to grant probate of these testaments, and to defend his
actions by ecclesiastical censure and other legal penalties. These
actions are null, iniquitous and unjust, to the grave prejudice of
the rights and jurisdiction of the bp. and the cathedral church of
London. Since it is dangerous to conduct litigation before a suspect
judge, especially when he strives to give judgement in his own cause,
the bp.'s proctor appeals on all these counts to the apostolic see,
swearing that not ten days have elapsed since the bp. learned of
these injuries, and that he dares not approach the abp. to notify
him of the appeal within the time prescribed by law. The abp. will
be notified after the departure of Mr Draper for Rome. The present
appeal will be corrected, as is customary, in its style and legal
form. Notarial exemplification by John Barkeley, clerk of Norwich
dioc., in the presence of Mr Thomas Saynte, Decr. D., Mr John Mowbrey,
M.A., and Robert Fox, literate. London, 20 Oct. 1494.

192 [fo.209v] Notification by Peter de Accoltis de Arctio, J.U.D., papal chaplain and Auditor of the Sacred Palace, that he has lately been presented by papal messengers with two paper schedules containing supplications:

i) Petition of the bp. of London, outlining the testamentary rights of the bp. and the assaults that have been made upon them. He is appealing to the pope because the matter concerns the episcopate as a whole, and because he does not believe that he can obtain justice outside the court of Rome, because of the power and influence of the abp. He begs that the pope will commit to one of the Auditors of the Sacred Palace the major issue of the right of testamentary jurisdiction together with that of the specific wrongs committed by the abp. in this matter, notwithstanding that these causes have not legitimately devolved to the apostolic see, and should not by legal necessity be conducted and concluded there. At the bottom of the supplication was written: By order of the pope, let Mr Peter hear this case etc. At the very bottom of the lower margin: the pope approves. John cardinal of Alessandria (Alexandrin').

ii) A further matter of dispute has arisen, wherefore Richard bp. of London appeals again to the pope. After the first appeal, the abp. induced Mr Blodwell, either by incentives or, more likely, by terrorisation, to consent to the withdrawal and cancellation of the acts and processes, and absolved the executors excommunicated by Blodwell, by virtue of their pretended appeal to the metropolitan. This was unjust and to the detriment of the rights of the petitioner, and the bp. therefore appeals once more to the pope, begging that he will commit investigation into the injustice of such an agreement and the actions of Mr Blodwell to one of the Auditors of the Sacred Palace, and if it pleases him to Mr Peter de Accoltis, who is hearing the first appeal, so that the case may not be divided. Subscribed as i) above.

After the examination of reliable witnesses produced on behalf of the bp. of London to testify to the lack of safe access to the abp., and the request by the bp.'s proctor, Mr Peter de Luca, that he should issue a citation to the abp. and others involved, with an inhibition, both in the court of Rome and in partibus, the auditor cited the abp. and others involved by public edict, to be read in the Court of Contradicted Letters and to be affixed to the doors of St Peter's basilica and of the Court of Apostolic Audience, and also to the doors of the cathedral church of London and the parish church of St Magnus. They are to appear before the auditor, either in person or by their proctor, on the hundredth day after citation or the next judicial day thereafter, at Rome or wherever the papal court may be. He inhibited all action in contempt of the jurisdiction of the apostolic see and to the prejudice of the bp. of London while the case was pending. The letters of citation and inhibition posted on the doors of public places should have the same validity as if personally delivered. All this was done in the auditor's residence in the presence of Mr Anthony Corrunti of Autun (Eduen') dioc. and Mr Gerard Gerhard of Cambrai (Cameracen') dioc., notaries public and clerks to the auditor. Rome, 21 Feb. 1495.

193 [fo.211] Memorandum that the foresaid letters of citation were affixed to the doors of St Paul's cathedral on 11 and 13 July, and on the doors of the parish church of St Magnus in London on 23 July, with the following subscription: Be it knowen to all Cristen peopill that whoosumever he be that attemptith, contempnyth or takith away this copies of the inhibicioun and citacioun had oute of the courte of Rome is accursed in the deede doyng, and he canne not be assoyled onthisside the saide courte of Rome.

194 [fo.211v] In the Audience of Contradicted Letters in the church of St Celsus, Lelius de Cheramo, scriptor of the apostolic letters and lector of the Audience, read aloud the letters of citation. Mr Peter de Luca, proctor of the bp. of London, requested Pampulus de Miscua, notary public and scribe of the Audience, to draw up one or more public instruments in the presence of Mr John Mercelli and Anthony Farragene, proctors of the Audience. On the same day, the said notary affixed citations to the doors of St Peter's, in the presence of Venetus Jareterii and Peter Quelnek, clerks of Besancon (Bismitten') dioc., and to the doors of the Audience, in the presence of Natrelus Dudan, clerk of Cambrai (Cameracen') dioc., and Peter Urilband, clerk of Minercen'[1] dioc.

[1. Sic in MS, probably Mindensis, Minden diocese.]

195 Mr. John Barett, registrar of the abp.'s Prerogative, appeared in the Long Chapel by the north door of St Paul's cathedral, bearing the letters of inhibition and citation, and copies of the same, and in the presence of Mr Richard Draper, Official of the London consistory court and advocate of the Court of Canterbury, who was seeking the delivery of these letters to himself, he protested that the publication of these letters would cause uproar in London and elsewhere, especially since the abp. was engaged in the defence of the kingdom, as the king's enemies had come with a great force to within eight miles of Canterbury.[1] Moreover, he was retaining the letters for inspection to ascertain whether the English subscription [no.193] could be construed from the originals, with which he wished to collate the copies. Once this was done, he would release the originals to Mr Draper. At Mr Barett's request John Copland alias Johnson, clerk of Lincoln dioc. and notary public, drew up a public instrument to this effect, in the presence of Mr William Bottern of Winchester dioc., notary public, and William Curteys, literate of London dioc. London, 11 July 1495.

[1. A contingent of Perkin Warbeck's forces landed at Deal on 3 July.]

196 [fo.212] Appeal to the court of Rome on behalf of the abp. of Canterbury made by Mr John Reed, proctor of the Court of Canterbury, in his residence in Ivy Lane. Although the abp. maintains several proctors at the court of Rome, and will in person or by these proctors

58

answer any complaint brought against him and obey any papal mandate, and although both before and after his elevation to the cardinalate he has frequently been apprehended and cited in cases brought by persons far inferior in rank to the bp. of London, and has done them no injury in retribution, and although this was well known to Bp. Richard, and also to Mr Edward Vaghan, Mr Richard Draper and Mr Richard Blodwell, advocates of the Court of Canterbury, and Richard Spencer, registrar of the same court, who have taken an oath not to diminish, but rather to maintain the rights of the church of Canterbury, and to Mr John Hill and Mr Thomas Browne, canons of St Paul's, and Richard Foster, literate of London, nevertheless the bp., who at the time of his consecration had professed obedience, obtained from Peter de Accoltis de Arctio, Auditor of the Sacred Palace, through the wicked machinations of Mr Peter de Luca and Mr Draper, letters of inhibition and citation, to be posted on the doors of St Paul's, to the shame of the abp. These letters were obtained through the false assertion that there was no safe access to the abp., yet before the receipt of the letters both the bp. and his officials had discussed with the abp. in his residence, the reasons for the conflict between them, without the abp. exerting any undue pressure on them. The bp., moreover, told the abp. that he had these letters, which he had hitherto out of malice concealed, and that he would publish them so that he might combat his metropolitan by enlisting public opinion against him. He had these letters affixed to the doors of St Paul's by Draper, Blodwell, Hyll, Browne and Forster on 11 July, and they remained there for six hours, fixed so high that nobody could get to them without their permission, and although Mr Humphrey Hawardyn, D.C.L., Official Principal of the Court of Canterbury, and Mr John Barett, registrar of the Prerogative, with certain others of the abp.'s household approached them and offered a surety of 3000 ducats that the abp. would answer the citation in person or by his proctor, and that one of the bp.'s officials might approach the abp. in person to deliver the citation, and thus would be avoided the scandal which would arise from publication in London, especially serious since the abp. was engaged in the defence of the realm, or alternatively that the Official and registrar would themselves deliver the letters to the abp., the bp.'s servants refused to accept this proposal, and some of them announced to the large crowd of bystanders that the abp. had been cited to Rome, or even that he had been excommunicated by apostolic authority, and when Hawardyn and Barett asked to see the originals, or at least a collated copy, they mocked them, saying, 'If you can't see from the ground, then you must get some ladders to look at them.' Then, when Hawardyn and Barett had with great difficulty obtained copies, they put up other copies on the doors of St Paul's on 11 and 12 July; these were signed by Mr Richard Spencer, and subscribed in English [no.193], to the shame and disparagement of the abp. Therefore the abp.'s proctor appeals to the court of Rome against these injuries, swearing that not ten days have elapsed since the abp. and he learned of these injuries. The present appeal will be corrected and reformed according to the counsel of men learned in the law. Notarial exemplification by Mr William Falk, clerk of Norwich dioc., in the presence of Mr William Wytton, Decr. D., and Mr Roger Church, Decr. D., advocates of the Court of Canterbury. London, 21 July 1495.

197 [fo.213] Notification by George, cardinal bp. of Alba (Albanen'),
abp. of Lisbon (Ulixbonen'), that he has lately been presented by
papal messengers with a paper schedule containing a papal commission,
as follows: the pope has lately learned, through his procurator
fiscal, of the action of the bp. of London and his officials [no.196],
from which there arose grave scandal to the honour of the cardinalate
and to the archiepiscopal dignity, and unless a remedy is provided,
it is to be feared that worse will happen. Knowing, therefore, that
the canons decree the most severe penalties against those attacking
cardinals of the Roman church, realising that injury may be done as
much to one's reputation as to one's body, and wishing that injuries
to the cardinalate should not go unpunished and that similar
scandalous acts should not be perpetrated in the future, the pope at
the instance of his procurator fiscal orders George cardinal bp. of
Alba to inform himself of these matters extra-judicially, and if he
finds the allegations to be true, to cite Bp. Richard and his
officials and servants who are guilty in this matter, the bp. on pain
of suspension from the celebration of divine office and the
administration of his church, the officials on pain of excommunication,
to appear before him, the bp. in person or by his proctor, the others
in person. Whether or not they appear he is, without giving judgement,
to receive the necessary information and proof and to refer it to the
pope and the other cardinals in secret consistory, so that the pope
may impose condign punishment on Bp. Richard and his guilty servants,
stem these scandals, purge the stain from the cardinal and remove all
suspicion from the minds of men. Notwithstanding apostolic and other
constitutions to the contrary. At the foot of the commission were two
subscriptions: By order of the pope, let the cardinal summarily and
extra-judicially inform himself concerning these assertions and the
lack of safe access, and cite the bp. in person or by proctor and the
others in person, and having summarily informed himself, let him
refer the matter as requested. The second subscription: The pope
approves. John cardinal of Alessandria (Alexandrinus).

The cardinal then received another paper containing a supplication
and commission: Since the bp. incited his officials to these actions,
he should be cited and punished more, or at least as much, as those
whom he ordered to act thus. Therefore Nicholas, the procurator
fiscal, who is willing to prove his allegations, begs the pope to
order the cardinal bp. of Alba to cite the bp. to appear in person
under the penalties described in the commission. At the foot of this
supplication were two subscriptions: Let the cardinal summarily and
extra-judicially inform himself, and let him issue the citation as
requested. The second subscription: The pope approves. John
cardinal of Alessandria (Alexandrinus).

After witnesses had been produced by Nicholas de Parma, papal
procurator fiscal, and the cardinal was satisfied that the foregoing
was true and that there was no safe access to the bp. and his servants,
he ordered a public edict to be read in the Audience of Contradicted
Letters and to be posted on the doors of St Paul's cathedral and of
the church of St Magnus and at Paul's Cross in London, and elsewhere
where this might be done with safety. Nevertheless, any Christian so
requested by Nicholas de Parma should cite Bp. Richard and his

servants, on pain of excommunication etc., to appear on the eightieth
day after publication or the next judicial day thereafter before the
cardinal bp. of Alba or any other judge to whom the case might be
delegated, who will proceed notwithstanding their absence. He also
inhibited any action to the contempt or prejudice of Nicholas de Parma
while the case was pending. Notarial exemplification by Jaspard
Duceti, clerk of Lyons (Lugdunen') dioc., in the presence of Paul
Jupsi, priest of Venice (Venetiarum), and Peter Burges, papal scribe.
Rome, 18 Dec. 1495.

198   [fo.214] Appointment by Nicholas de Parma as his proctors in London
for the publication of the forementioned letters of Mr John Anthonius,
S.T.P., and Mr John Baptista, S.T.P., clerks resident in London, with
the power to commission deputies. Notarial exemplification by Aymo
Chichonis, clerk of Lyons (Lugdunen') dioc., in the presence of Paul
de Alexiis, clerk of the court of Rome, and Igrobus Waillant, clerk of
Bardunen'[1] dioc. Rome, 24 Dec. 1495.

    [1. Sic in MS; possibly Barchinonen', Barcelona diocese.]

[fo.215v blank]

199   [fo.216] Mandate of Pope Alexander VI to the abbots of St Augustine's
Canterbury, and of Bermondsey (Bermundesey) and to the prior of Ely
(Elien'). Having heard the complaints of the abp. of Canterbury
against the bp. of London and his named servants, and the supplication
that he should commit to some honest men in partibus all the causes to
be moved by the abp. against the bp. of London, the pope orders them,
or one or two of them, to summon Bp. Richard and the others who should
be summoned, to hear the propositions and to decide these matters in
accordance with justice, appellatione remota, enforcing their decree
by papal authority as regards the bp. and by ecclesiastical censure as
regards the others. Notwithstanding the constitution of Pope Boniface
VIII relating to judges outside their own dioc., but with the proviso
that not more than two days journey shall be involved, or other
apostolic constitutions and ordinances, and notwithstanding any indult
to Bp. Richard, his officials or others that they may not be
interdicted, suspended or excommunicated or summoned to judgement
other than in a specified place by apostolic letters not making express
and verbatim reference to that indult. St Peter's Rome, 1495.

200   Mr Peter de Luca, proctor of the bp. of London, appeared before Mr Peter
de Accoltis in his residence, in order to demonstrate that there was
no safe access to the abp. of Canterbury, and that therefore neither
he nor his principal might fulfil the auditor's mandate. He produced
as witnesses Richard Crofte, clerk, and John Edwardes, layman, of
London, who swore on oath that they were well acquainted with the
cardinal, who was primate of England [sic] and chancellor of the king,
that the cardinal did not permit the execution of any papal letters

against him, and that they would not dare execute this mandate by citing him in person at his accustomed residence, because if anyone attempted this they would undoubtedly not escape unharmed. This was done in the presence of Mr Anthony Corrunti of Autun (Eduen') dioc., and Mr Gerard Gerard of Cambrai (Cameracen') dioc., notaries public and scribes to the auditor. Notarial exemplification by Nicholas Voes, clerk of Cologne (Colonien') dioc., on behalf of John Dubreuquet, the exemplification being based on the notes of Alfonso Fernandus de Inena, clerk of Seville (Ispalen') dioc., who had been present, but was now absent from the curia and in Spain. Rome, 21 Feb. 1495.

201   [fo.216v] Mandate of Pope Alexander VI to the bps. of Ely (Elien'), Hereford (Hereforden') and Rochester (Roffen'), instructing them to investigate the complaints of the cardinal abp. of Canterbury against the bp. of London concerning the malicious publication of letters of citation and inhibition, and to reach a decision appellatione remota, etc. [as 199]. St Peter's Rome, 19 Aug. 1495.

202   Mandate of Pope Alexander VI to the abbots of St Augustine's, Canterbury, and of Bermondsey (Bermondesey), and to the prior of Ely (Elien'). The pope has recently received a supplication made on behalf of John, cardinal priest of St Anastasia, that although all the advocates, proctors and other officials of the Court of Arches at the time of their admission take an oath to show due reverence and obedience to the abp. and to conserve and defend the privileges, etc., of the church of Canterbury, nevertheless Edward Vaghan, Richard Draper and Richard Blodwell, advocates, Richard Spencer, proctor, and some other officials of the court have perpetrated various illicit acts in violation and contempt of the jurisdiction of the church of Canterbury, thus incurring the charges of conspiracy, rebellion and perjury: wherefore it is petitioned that the pope shall commit all causes to be moved by the cardinal abp. against the forementioned and other clergy and laity to some honest men in partibus. The pope therefore orders them, or one or two of them, to summon the foresaid officials, clerks and laymen, to hear the propositions, and to decide these matters in accordance with justice, appellatione remota. Notwithstanding etc. [as in no.199]. St Peter's Rome, 25 Oct. 1495.

203   [fo.217] Mandate of Mr Peter de Accoltis to all ecclesiastical persons in the city and diocese of London to whom these letters may come. Having received from the pope the first petition of the bp. of London [192], and having proceeded to the hearing of the case between the proctors of the abp. of Canterbury and those of the bp. of London, at the request of Mr John Laurencii, the abp.'s proctor, and notwithstanding the absence of Mr Peter de Luca, the bp.'s proctor, who was adjudged contumacious, the auditor issued general letters compulsory, to be executed on pain of excommunication of individuals and interdict upon churches. Any ecclesiastical person to whom these letters are presented by the abp. or his representative shall within

six days go to the ecclesiastical persons or institutions which are
named to him, and shall order them, on pain of excommunication or
interdict, that within twelve days they shall produce all acta, letters,
processes, instruments, etc., relating to the dispute between the abp.
and the bp. of London, in their original form or as authentic
transcripts, shall deliver the same to the abp. or his proctor, and
shall allow them to be transcribed, exemplified and authenticated by
their seals and by a notarial sign manual and to be conveyed to Rome
to the auditor or to any other judge acting in his stead. Any to whom
satisfaction is due shall be content with reasonable payment. If
such muniments are concealed or not delivered, production may be
compelled by ecclesiastical censure, appellatione remota. The
executors of this mandate are to inform the auditor of the action they
have taken. Absolution from any sentence incurred in this matter is
reserved to the auditor or to a superior authority. Notarial
exemplification by Nicholas Voes, clerk of Cologne (Colonien') dioc.,
in the presence of Leonard de Castilione, clerk of Milan (Mediolanen')
dioc., and Gerard Gerard, clerk of Cambrai (Cameracen') dioc.,
notaries public. Rome, 23 Dec. 1495.

204   [fo.218v] Bull of Pope Alexander VI confirming the testamentary
jurisdiction of the abp. of Canterbury. The pope has learned that the
laws of England forbid any executor or administrator of the goods of
deceased persons to bring a case for the recovery of the debts of the
deceased unless he can demonstrate that he has been commissioned as
executor or administrator under the seal of the diocesan who has
proved and enregistered the testament and granted administration of
the goods. Because it often happens that various ordinaries grant
probate of one testament, as the goods of the deceased are distributed
over several dioceses, and the administration of the goods is granted
to various persons, and therefore conflict and scandal arises, to avoid
this it has been established from time immemorial that the abp. of
Canterbury, by the Prerogative of the church of Canterbury, should grant
probate of the testaments of all persons having at the time of their
death goods and debts in various dioceses of the province, and this
custom is still observed at the present time. The pope, realising that
this custom was introduced to avoid conflict and to facilitate the
execution of the wishes of the deceased, and considering the status
of the church of Canterbury, over which John cardinal priest of
St Anastasia is by apostolic concession and dispensation set, by reason
of which the abp. has from the foundation of the church been primate
over the whole realm of England and legatus natus, approves, motu
propria and not at the instance of the cardinal or any person acting
on his behalf, the foresaid Prerogative and custom, and confirms it by
the protection of these presents, supplying all defects of law or fact
which may have occurred, and decreeing that this custom should be
observed as inviolable in perpetuity. Notwithstanding apostolic,
legatine, provincial and conciliar decrees to the contrary. St Peter's
Rome, 1 March 1495[1].

[1. The bull is dated anno incarnationis dominice millesimo
quadringentesimo nonagesimo quinto kal. Martii (1496) pontificatus

(1495). 1495 is far more likely than 1496.]

205   Bull of Pope Alexander VI confirming the sede vacante jurisdiction
of the abp. of Canterbury. The pope has recently received a petition
on behalf of John, cardinal priest of St Anastasia and abp. of
Canterbury, stating that although from time immemorial the abps. of
Canterbury have been in peaceful possession of the exercise of all
ordinary and ecclesiastical jurisdiction in all cathedral churches
within the province of Canterbury during times of vacancy, and have
been in receipt of all tithes and spiritual revenues proceeding from
the said churches during such vacancies, just as were the bps. of
those churches while they were alive and presided over them,
nevertheless, because it is not possible to demonstrate these rights
except by their continual possession, the abp. fears that in the future
he and his successors will be contraverted in this matter, wherefore
supplication is made on the abp.'s behalf that, in order that this
custom may be maintained, the pope should fortify it by apostolic
confirmation and otherwise provide for its maintenance. The pope
therefore, considering the status of the church of Canterbury etc.[as
in no.204], and that, as the cardinal asserts, the foresaid custom
has been observed since the Incarnation of Our Lord, approves and
confirms this custom by these presents, supplying all defects of law
or of fact which may have occurred, and decreeing that this custom
should be observed as inviolable in perpetuity. Notwithstanding
apostolic, legatine, provincial and conciliar decrees to the contrary.
St Peter's Rome, 4 Oct. 1494.

206   [fo.219] Bull of Pope Alexander VI confirming the sede vacante
jurisdiction of the abp. of Canterbury, with special reference to the
receipt of revenues. Recitation of the customary rights of sede
vacante jurisdiction [as in no.205]. During vacancies, the abp. is
in possession of all the tithes and spiritual revenues of the said
churches, even of churches united and annexed to the episcopal mensa,
and of the right of conferring benefices, just as the bps. while they
were alive and presided over their churches, but it is not possible
to demonstrate these rights except by their continuous possession.
Wherefore the pope, considering the status of the church of Canterbury
[as in no.204], and that the abps. exercise great care in the foresaid
churches and dioceses and incur great expense by their labours in
visitation and the exercise of jurisdiction, and that he should receive
the profit who bears the burden, motu propria, etc., approves and
confirms this custom by these presents, etc. [as no.205]. St Peter's
Rome, 1 March 1495[1].

    [1. See no.204, n.1.]

207   Indult of Pope Alexander VI to the cardinal abp., allowing him to
dispose freely of all his goods, including the issue of his churches,
after due restitution of debts and reparation for loss or damage
sustained by any church as a result of the guilt or negligence of the
cardinal abp. or his proctors. St Peter's Rome, 4 Oct. 1494.

208 [fo.219v] Indult of Pope Alexander VI to the cardinal abp., in response to his petition that the pope might dispense him from the customary oath which he swore at the time of his translation to the see of Canterbury to undertake in person or by deputy regular visits ad limina apostolorum. The pope, wishing to relieve him and his church of the expense, labour and burdens which arise from this obligation, grants that the abp. is freed for his lifetime from the obligation to visit the threshold of the apostles, unless he is bound to come there for some other reason. Notwithstanding etc. St Peter's Rome, 4 Oct. 1494.

209 Indult of Pope Alexander VI to the cardinal abp. The pope motu proprio, etc., concedes to him the faculty to grant by canonical collation all dignities, prebends and other ecclesiastical benefices with or without cure which are in his provision, presentation or otherwise at his disposal by reason of his title, jointly or singly as they successively fall vacant in any month, to any suitable persons, however many and whatever kind of ecclesiastical benefices they hold or expect, and to dispose freely, in person or by his vicar or proctor, of all houses, possessions, fees, and all other goods, rights and revenues pertaining to the same title, disregarding general or specific reservations of benefices by the apostolic see in the past or in the future, as he might do were he personally resident in the court of Rome. The pope hereby declares void any witting or unwitting act by any person in contravention of this faculty. Notwithstanding etc. St Peter's Rome, 4 March 1495.

210 Certificate of Raphael, cardinal deacon of St George ad Velum Aureum, papal chamberlain, that since John abp. of Canterbury is bound to visit the apostolic see or the threshold of the apostles every three years while the court of Rome is south of the Alps, on this day he so visited the apostolic see with due honour and reverence, in the person of his specially deputed proctor Hugh Spaldyng, priest, for one triennium beginning on 6 October 1486; but he made no payment of servitia to the apostolic camera on account of this visit. Sealed with the chamberlain's seal of office. Rome, 18 March 1491.

211 [fo.220] Mandate of Pope Alexander VI to the abp. of Canterbury and the bp. of Durham (Dunelmen'). The pope has learned from the letters of King Henry VII and from the reports of his orators at the curia that Anselm, once abp. of Canterbury, lived such a holy life that after his death the Almighty performed many miracles by his merits and intercession, and he was held by Christians in England and neighbouring lands to be a saint. The king and his subjects are anxious that Anselm's name should be added to the catalogue of saints, and the king has petitioned the pope accordingly. Therefore the pope, following the example of his predecessor Innocent VIII, who issued a similar commission, orders the abp. and the bp., together and in person, to enquire diligently into the life and miracles of Anselm and as speedily as possible to send their findings, recorded by notaries public, to the pope. St Peter's Rome, 4 Oct. 1494.

[Printed: Wilkins, iii, 641.]

212   Mandate of Pope Alexander VI addressed to the abbot of Faversham and the prior of St Martin's Dover (<u>Dovoria</u>). The abp. of Canterbury has informed the pope that the parish church of Folkestone (<u>Folkeston'</u>) has long been annexed to and incorporated in the Benedictine priory, and is served by one perpetual vicar. Through the union it suffers great losses in spirituals and temporals, and because of the multitude of parishioners one vicar cannot easily support the burden of the cure, and unless a speedy remedy is provided, the parish church is certain to suffer even greater losses, wherefore the cardinal abp. has supplicated that the union be dissolved and the church restored to its former status. The pope therefore orders the abbot and the prior, or one of them, to summon the prior of Folkestone and others who should be summoned, and if the foregoing appears to be true, to dissolve by papal authority the union, annexation and incorporation, to separate the parish church from the priory and to restore it to its former status. If they do this, they shall ordain that the church should henceforth be served by a perpetual vicar and three other priests, assigning suitable portions of the revenues to each of them, the vicar having the greater portion, and shall not allow the vicar and priests to be molested by the prior or any other person. They are to enforce their decision by ecclesiastical censures, <u>appellatione remota</u>. Notwithstanding the foregoing and apostolic, legatine, provincial and conciliar decrees to the contrary, and notwithstanding any indult to the prior or any other person that they may not be interdicted, suspended or excommunicated by apostolic letters not making express and verbatim reference to that indult. St Peter's Rome, 4 Oct. 1494.

213   [<u>fo.220v</u>] Bull of Pope Alexander VI confirming the testamentary jurisdiction of the abp. of Canterbury, and during vacancies of the archiepiscopal see of the prior and convent of Christ Church. Recitation of the reasons for the Prerogative jurisdiction of the church of Canterbury in matters of probate [as no. 205], which is exercised by the abp., and during vacancies by the prior and conv. Papal confirmation of the testamentary Prerogative of the church of Canterbury. And for better protection (<u>potiori pro cautela</u>) the pope concedes and elaborates by his will, knowledge and plenitude of power the right or Prerogative of proving, approving and enregistering such testaments, and of doing all else in the above form, to be exercised by John cardinal abp. of Canterbury, and in the vacancy of the see by the prior and conv., declaring void any attempt against the Prerogative, witting or unwitting, by any authority. Notwithstanding apostolic, legatine, provincial and conciliar decrees to the contrary. St Peter's Rome, 4 Oct. 1494.

[Printed: Wilkins, iii, 641-2.]

214   [fo.221] Mandate of Pope Alexander VI to the abbots of St Augustine's
Canterbury, St Peter's Westminster and St Albans, reciting the
foregoing bull [no.213], and ordering them, when so required by the
abp. of Canterbury, or in the vacancy of the see by the prior and
conv. of Christ Church, solemnly to publish this bull and enforce the
observation of its provisions by apostolic authority, not allowing
the abp. or the prior and conv. to be molested by any person in this
matter, and compelling contradictors or rebels, of whatever rank or
dignity, by ecclesiastical censures and other suitable legal remedies,
appellatione postposita, extending even to the invocation of the
secular arm. Notwithstanding the above, or the constitution of Pope
Boniface VIII relating to judges outside their own dioc., or any
indult relating to interdict, etc. [as no.199], or any other apostolic
privileges, indulgences and letters. St Peter's Rome, 4 Oct. 1494.

    [Printed: Wilkins, iii, 642-3.]

215   [fo.221v] Bull of Pope Alexander VI confirming the sede vacante
jurisdiction of the abp. of Canterbury. Recitation of the rights of
sede vacante jurisdiction and the receipt of revenues, including those
of churches appropriated to the episcopal mensa [as no.206]. Papal
confirmation of these rights. And for better protection (potiori pro
cautela) the pope concedes and elaborates by his will, knowledge and
plenitude of power this Prerogative jurisdiction to be exercised by
John, cardinal abp., and by his successors in the see of Canterbury,
declaring void any attempt against the Prerogative, witting or
unwitting, by any authority. St Peter's Rome, 4 Oct. 1494.

    [Printed: Wilkins, iii, 643.]

216   [fo.222] Mandate of Pope Alexander VI to the abbots of St Augustine's
Canterbury, St Peter's Westminster and St Albans, ordering them to
execute no.215 when so required [form as no.214]. St Peter's Rome,
4 Oct. 1494.

217   [fo.222v] Bull of Pope Alexander VI confirming the sede vacante
jurisdiction of the church of Canterbury [as no.215] with specific
mention of the identical rights of the prior and conv. of Christ Church
during vacancies of the see of Canterbury. St Peter's Rome, 4 Oct.
1494.

  Certification by Mr John Barett, notary public, of his collation of
this transcript with the original bull.

218   [fo.223] Mandate of Pope Alexander VI to the abbots of St Augustine's
Canterbury, St Peter's Westminster and St Albans, ordering them to
execute no.217 when so required [form as no.214]. St Peter's Rome,
4 Oct. 1494.

  Certification by Mr John Barett, notary public, of his collation of this transcript with the original mandate.

219 [fo.223v] Bull of Pope Alexander VI confirming the testamentary
Prerogative of the church of Canterbury [as no.213], conceded to John
the present abp., his successors in the see, and in the vacancy of
the see to the prior and conv. of Christ Church. St Peter's Rome,
4 Oct. 1494.

220 [fo.224] Mandate of Pope Alexander VI to the abbots of St Augustine's
Canterbury, St Peter's Westminster and St Albans, ordering them to
execute no.219 when so required [form as no.214]. St Peter's Rome,
4 Oct. 1494.

221 Final decision in the case between the abp. of Canterbury and the
prior and conv. of Winchester (Winton')[see nos 223-66]. The pope has
learned that the prior and conv. of Winchester, O.S.B., claim that
during a vacancy of the see spiritual jurisdiction and the tithes of
the churches of East Meon (Eastmeanes) and Hambledon (Halmeldon),
which are annexed in perpetuity to the episcopal mensa, pertain to
them. The cardinal abp. of Canterbury, however, claims that the care
and custody of the churches and receipt of the tithes pertain to him
and the church of Canterbury, by ancient and hitherto inviolate custom.
When the see became vacant by the death of Bp. Peter Courtenay, he
inhibited the prior and conv. of Winchester, on pain of excommunication
and other ecclesiastical penalties, from infringement of these rights.
The prior and conv. claim that the abp. has denied them justice, and
has imposed silence on them so that they should not dare to speak of
their rights, and therefore they have repeatedly appealed to the
apostolic see against the denial of justice, the imposition of silence
and other alleged tyrannical actions. At the instance of the prior
and conv., the pope committed the case concerning the nullity of any
attempted innovations, together with the main case, to Anthony bp. of
Castellimare (Castellimaris), an Auditor of the Sacred Palace,
notwithstanding that the case had not legitimately devolved to the
apostolic see nor should by legal necessity be conducted at the court
of Rome. After the case had proceeded some way, but had not been
concluded, and after letters remissory had been despatched to judges
in partibus to gather the necessary evidence, the pope, wishing to
spare the litigants expense and inconvenience, recalled the case to
himself and delegated it to the bps. of Durham and Bath and Wells and
the abbots of Westminster, Waltham Holy Cross and Bermondsey, jointly
or singly to hear the evidence of witnesses produced before them by
virtue of the letters remissory, and to hear and terminate the case,
appellatione remota. The abbot of Bermondsey proceeded by virtue of
this commission, and promulgated definitive sentence in favour of
the abp., awarding expenses against the prior and conv., and, because
the latter would not obey this sentence, he excommunicated them and
repeatedly aggravated the sentence. The prior and conv. of Winchester
once more appealed to Rome, claiming to be wrongfully oppressed by

68

this sentence, and the pope committed the cases of this later appeal,of the nullity of the attempted innovations and of the main issue to Anthony bp. of Castellimare. When Matthew bp. of Nocera (Nucerin'), another Auditor of the Sacred Palace, acting in place of Bp. Anthony, who was then absent from the curia, had proceeded some way in the case but not terminated it, the pope recalled the case to himself and committed it to John, cardinal priest of Santa Maria Transtiber (in Transtiberim). The cardinal heard several proctors of the two parties, and diligently informed himself of the circumstances and merits of the case, which he subsequently referred to the pope, who, wishing to terminate the case, motu proprio and not at the petition of either party, recalled the case to himself and entirely extinguished the conflict, except for the matter of expenses, which he remitted to John cardinal priest of Santa Maria Transtiber.The pope absolved the prior and conv., their advocates and proctors and any others, from any sentence, censure or penalty incurred as a result of this case, relaxed sentence of interdict which might have been imposed on the church of Winchester or any other church, imposed silence on the parties, and dispensed those who had celebrated the divine office while bound by these sentences. Non obstantibus etc. St Peter's Rome, 14 July 1499.

222 [fo.225] Notification by John cardinal priest of Santa Maria Transtiber to all ecclesiastical persons in the diocese of Winchester and elsewhere. When the pope earlier committed to him the case between the abp. of Canterbury and the prior and conv. of Winchester concerning spiritual jurisdiction and the tithes of East Meon (Estmen') and Hambledon (Hameldon'), which had already been heard by various judges and auditors at Rome and in partibus, he frequently heard the prior and the proctors of the abp. and the prior and conv., and then, considering the gravity of the case, he referred to the pope a full account, including the merits of the case, whereupon the pope recalled the case to himself in order to extinguish the conflict and impose silence, but committed the assessment of expenses to the cardinal. Therefore, sitting judicially in the small hall of his accustomed residence in the apostolic palace, he assessed the expenses, with the consent of the prior and the proctors, at 400 marks sterling, which is 1200 ducats auri de camera. The prior agreed, for himself and the conv., to pay 100 marks at Easter, 100 at All Saints and the remainder the following Easter, on pain of excommunication and other ecclesiastical penalties, extending to the invocation of the secular arm. The three instalments are to be paid to the abp. or his proctor at his accustomed place of residence, on pain of a fine of 3000 ducats payable to the abp. As better security for payment, the prior took upon himself the obligations of principal in meliori forma camere, and, in the event of non-payment, expressed himself willing to incur excommunication, and other ecclesiastical penalties. The cardinal orders the recipients of these letters, after expiry of the due terms for payment, and when so required by the provision of these letters, to announce publicly the excommunication of the prior, and to continue so to do until otherwise instructed by the cardinal or by a superior authority,

informing the cardinal of the action they have taken. The prior, on
behalf of his chapter, swore before the notary public subscribing this
document and before witnesses, to observe these conditions, and as
security, on behalf of himself, his chapter and his successors, he
pledged all his movable and immovable goods, and submitted by a
solemn covenant to the jurisdiction of the Court of Causes of the
apostolic <u>camera</u> and of any auditor, <u>locumtenens</u> or commissary of the
same, and of all other ecclesiastical or secular courts where this
public instrument might be produced, renouncing all forms of exemption
and of subterfuge. For better security, the prior named as his
proctors Nicholas de Parma, Thomas Regis, Alexander de Bononia, James
de Fidelibus and Bernard Mokarum, proctors in the court of Rome, and
John Desiderii, Francis de Pycia and Ducius de Pycia, notaries of the
Court of Causes of the apostolic <u>camera</u>, and all other proctors or
notaries of other courts, to appear at any time and place to
acknowledge on behalf of the prior and conv. all that is contained
in this instrument and accept any sentence. He swore that anything
done by them would be confirmed by him, and released such proctors
from any obligation entailed by their actions. Notarial exemplification
by Adrian de Caprinis, clerk of Viterbo (<u>Viterbien'</u>) dioc., notary
public and secretary to the cardinal, in the presence of Jeremy bishop
of Assisi (<u>Assisien'</u>) and Silvester bishop of Worcester (<u>Wigorn'</u>),and
of John de Cremona, clerk of Segovia (<u>Segobien'</u>) dioc., and Didacus
del Serro, clerk of Seville (<u>Ispalen'</u>) dioc. Rome, 4 July 1499.

223 PROCEEDINGS IN THE CASE BETWEEN THE PRIOR AND CONVENT OF THE CATHEDRAL
CHURCH OF WINCHESTER AND THE ARCHBISHOP OF CANTERBURY CONCERNING THE
SPIRITUAL REVENUES OF THE CHURCHES OF EAST MEON AND HAMBLEDON, WHICH
ARE APPROPRIATED TO THE EPISCOPAL <u>MENSA</u>, DURING THE VACANCY OF THE SEE.

[<u>fo.227</u>] Mandate of Mr Anthony Flores, J.U.D., protonotary of the
apostolic see, Auditor of Causes in the Apostolic Palace, referendary
and chaplain of the pope, to all ecclesiastical persons in the city
and dioc. of Canterbury and elsewhere. The pope has conveyed to
Mr Flores the following supplication of the prior and conv. of
Winchester, in which they complain that, contrary to the privileges
of their church and to long-established custom, the abp. of Canterbury,
during the recent vacancy of the see, exercised spiritual jurisdiction
in, and received the spiritual revenues of, the parishes of East Meon
(<u>Estmens</u>) and Hambledon (<u>Hamyden</u>). Despite a previous appeal lodged
against him, the abp. still maintains that these rights pertain to his
see, and enforces them by spiritual and temporal censures, and he has
ordered the sequestration of the tithes of these parishes. Due to
the immense power of the abp. in England, the prior and conv. have
appealed to the pope in the following terms, supplicating that the
case might be assigned to an Auditor of the Apostolic Palace:

Blessed Father, although when the see of Winchester is vacant by the
death of the bp. or otherwise, according to the foundation of the
church and by royal ordinance and apostolic confirmation, custody of
the spiritualities and receipt of the tithes of the parish churches of

East Meon and Hambledon has pertained from time immemorial to the prior
and chapter of Winchester, and they have been and are today in
peaceful possession of these rights which have been violated only by
this present molestation, and the abps. of Canterbury have permitted
and consented to this, either tacitly or expressly, nevertheless,
despite the appeal of the prior and conv. to the apostolic see against
certain injuries threatened by the present abp. and his officials,
the abp., who was aware of this appeal, has falsely asserted that the
custody of the spiritualities and right to the tithes of these parishes
pertained and pertains to him and his successors during vacancies of
the see, and daily adding injury to injury, when the see was recently
vacant following the death of Bp. Peter Courtenay, he warned the
appellants, under threat of spiritual and temporal penalties, that
they should not intrude in this matter and ordered the sequestration
of the tithes, which he eventually received, and although the prior
and conv. appealed frequently to him to render them justice, this he
refused to do, but rather imposed upon them perpetual silence under
threat of the most dire penalties, to the grave prejudice of the
appellants and their successors. Therefore the prior and conv. have
appealed to the apostolic see as the most sure refuge for the
oppressed against the forestated and many other injuries inflicted
upon them by the abp., as more fully specified in their previous
appeal, which can scarcely be remedied by appeal against his sentence.
Since it is notorious that the abp. is primate in the kingdom, and
mighty in word and deed, and that nobody can be found who would dare
proceed and pronounce against him, and since the cause concerns a
matter of great prejudice to the spiritual rights of the church of
Winchester, supplication is made to the pope that he should commit the
causes of the foresaid appeals, and of the nullity of any attempts and
innovations, together with the principal matter, to an Auditor of the
Apostolic Palace, who should hear and terminate these causes, with
power to cite the abp. and all others involved, publicly, by edict in
the court of Rome and outside, having determined summarily that there
is no safe access to them, and with power to issue public inhibition under
threat of ecclesiastical censures and penalties; and since this case
has perhaps not legitimately devolved to the court of Rome and should
not by its nature and legal necessity be conducted and terminated
there, with the clause apostolic constitutions and ordinances to the
contrary notwithstanding.

At the bottom of the schedule was written in a different hand: Let
Mr Anthony Flores hear the case, and having summarily satisfied himself
as to lack of safe access, let him issue citation and inhibition by
edict as requested, and let him do justice. Below this, on the bottom
margin in a third hand, was written: The pope approves. John,
cardinal of Alessandria (Alexandrinus).

After the receipt of this commission, Mr Flores was requested on
behalf of the prior and conv. to issue a citation against the cardinal
abp. and others involved. Considering this request to be just, he
therefore orders all who may receive this mandate that within six days
(two days for the first, two for the second and two for the third and
peremptory warning) they shall issue a citation against the abp. and

all other persons named to them by the prior and conv. of Winchester.
They should be cited in person if possible, otherwise at the
archiepiscopal palace and the usual residences of the others, and
citations should be posted also in the metropolitan church of
Canterbury and the parish churches of the others, or at least in other
churches and public places, so that they may not claim to be ignorant
of the citation. They are to appear on the seventieth day after
citation or the next judicial day thereafter, in Rome or wherever the
pope may be, in the Court of Audience before Mr Flores or any other
judge assigned to the case, either in person or by suitable proctors,
with all the documents pertaining to the case, so that a definitive
judgement may be delivered. The case will be heard whether or not
they appear. While the case is pending no further action is to be
taken in the matters with which it is concerned. Those issuing the
citation should also, if so requested by the prior and conv., inhibit
the abp. from any action in contempt of the jurisdiction of the
apostolic see or prejudicial to the rights of the prior and conv.,
either personally or through his agents, publicly or secretly, the abp.
on pain of interdict of entry to his church, his Official General and
others on pain of excommunication. If such action is taken by the abp.
it will be declared null. Mr Flores or his deputy is to be certified
of the delivery of the citation. Absolution from any sentence of
excommunication is reserved to Mr Flores or a superior authority.
Witnessed by Mr John Coricio and Mr Jerome Datell, notaries public,
clerks of Trier[1] and Bamberg (Bambergen') diocs. Notarial
exemplification by Michael Sheel, notary public of Wurzburg
(Habipolen') dioc., on behalf of Everard Kadmore, canon of St Stephen's
Bamberg. Court of the Apostolic Palace, Rome, 16 May 1494.

[1. MS: Ternoten'; cf. no.228, Treveren'.]

224 [fo.228] Public instrument notifying the appointment by the abp. as
proctors to represent him, in matters concerning him, the church of
Canterbury and the Prerogative, at the court of Rome, of Adrian
Castellesi, protonotary of the apostolic see, Thomas Routhale, Decr.D.,
William Robynson, Decr.D., John de Gerona, clerk of the apostolic
camera, Hugh Spaldyng, warden of the hospice of St Thomas the Martyr
at Rome, and John Laurencii, Decr.D., clerk of Tortosa (Dertusen')
dioc. Lambeth, 3 Dec. 1494.

225 ACCOUNT DESPATCHED TO MR ANTHONY FLORES OF THE PROCEEDINGS BEFORE
MR THOMAS HUTTON, DECR.D., ARCHDEACON OF LINCOLN AND EXECUTOR, AT
THE REQUEST OF THE ARCHBISHOP OF CANTERBURY, OF LETTERS COMPULSORY
FOR THE PRODUCTION OF DOCUMENTS RELEVANT TO THE DISPUTE BETWEEN THE
ARCHBISHOP AND THE PRIOR AND CONVENT OF WINCHESTER.

On 16 Nov. 1495, in the Long Chapel of St Paul's [cath.] London, and
in the presence of Mr William Imbroke and Mr Thomas Chamberleyn,
notaries public and scribes of Mr Hutton's acts, Mr William Falke and
Mr John Coplande, notaries public, and Mr Gregory Lynn, M.A.,

Mr Hutton was approached by Mr John Reed, proctor of the Court of Canterbury and the abp.'s proctor, who produced his letters of proxy.

226   [fo.228v] Appointment by the abp. of Mr John Reed as his proctor, to represent him before any judge in all business concerning his own status and the liberties and Prerogative of the church of Canterbury, with special reference to a search for relevant documents and the acquisition of transcripts. Lambeth, 2 Nov. 1495.

227   [fo.229] Mr Reed requested Mr Hutton to execute the letters compulsory issued by Mr Flores [see no.228], which he did, appointing as his scribes Mr Imbroke and Mr Chamberleyn. Mr Reed stated that there were documents necessary for the statement of the abp.'s case in the registry of the Prerogative at Lambeth, in the custody of Mr Hugh Peyntwyn, Commissary General of the abp. and his Prerogative, and Mr John Barett, notary public and registrar of the Prerogative. He requested that Mr Hutton should go to the registry, order the production of the documents, and cite the prior and conv. of Winchester to be present to witness the production of documents and the examination of witnesses. Mr Hutton declared that he would go there on 2 Dec., and appointed Mr William Potkyn, notary public, to deliver the relevant citations.

228   [fo.229v] Mandate of Mr Thomas Hutton addressed to Mr William Potkyn and all ecclesiastical persons in the dioc. of Winchester and elsewhere, rehearsing letters compulsory of Mr Anthony Flores, sealed with his round seal in a small wooden box attached by red cord, in the manner of the court of Rome, whose tenor is thus:

Mandate of Mr Anthony Flores addressed to all ecclesiastical persons in the dioc. of Canterbury and elsewhere, reciting his authority for proceeding in this case [as no.223]. Proceedings have been conducted at Rome between the proctors of the parties, but the case has not been brought to a conclusion. Therefore, in the absence of Mr Bartholomew de Perusio, proctor of the monks of Winchester, who had been cited and whom Mr John Laurencii the abp.'s proctor accused of contumacy for his non-appearance, Mr Laurencii stated that various ecclesiastical persons in the dioc. of Canterbury and elsewhere had in their archives documents relevant to this case, and requested the issue of letters compulsory for use outside the court of Rome. Mr Flores issued such letters [in the form of no.203]. Dated at the residence of Mr Flores in Rome, Monday 17 Aug. 1495, in the presence of John Coricio of Trier (Treveren') dioc. and Magnus de Haslach of Bamberg (Bambergen') dioc., notaries public and his scribes. Notarial exemplification by Michael Sheel of Wurzburg (Herbrolen') dioc., acting on behalf of Everard Kadmer, prior of St Bangolf at Bamberg.

Having received these letters from Mr Reed and having appointed Mr Potkyn to deliver citations, Mr Hutton now orders the recipients of this mandate, and Mr Potkyn in particular, to cite Mr Peyntwyn and

Mr Barett to appear at 10 a.m. on 2 December and to produce the
relevant documents, and to cite the prior and conv. of Winchester,
in person if possible, or by affixing citations to the doors of their
church and chapter house, to be present in person or by their proctor,
if they consider that the matter concerns them. Whoever executes this
mandate is to certify Mr Hutton. Sealed with the seal of Mr Richard
Lychfeld, archd. of Middlesex, as Mr Hutton's seal is not to hand.
Witnessed by Mr Falke, Mr Copland and Mr Lynn. Notarial
exemplification and confirmation of the validity of the interlineation
in the original by Mr Imbroke and Mr Chamberleyn. St Paul's London,
16 Nov. 1495.

229 [fo.231v] On 2 Dec. 1495 at 10 a.m. in the registry at Lambeth,
Mr Potkyn appeared before Mr Hutton and announced that he had cited
Mr Peyntwyn and Mr Barett on 17 Nov. in Peyntwyn's chamber at Lambeth,
and the conv. of Winchester on the morning of 20 Nov. in their chapter
house. The prior of Winchester had avoided personal citation, despite
Potkyn's efforts, therefore on the afternoon of 20 Nov. he had affixed
the citation to the cathedral doors, replacing it shortly by a
notarialized copy, and it was read by some monks in his presence, and
so probably came to the notice of the prior. There appeared Mr Reed,
and William Manwood monk of Winchester, who presented letters of
proxy for the prior and conv., dated 29 Nov. 1495. Mr Peyntwyn and
Mr Barett, having been cited, declared themselves ready to obey the
mandate. Mr Reed again exhibited his letters of proxy from the abp.
Mr Hutton then required the notaries public to swear that they would
record faithfully the proceedings. At Mr Reed's request and Mr
Hutton's instruction, Mr Peyntwyn and Mr Barett produced six ancient
volumes, containing records of the acta of various abps. which were
relevant to the case, and Mr Reed exhibited these as evidence
supporting the case of the abp. against the prior and conv. of
Winchester. Mr Hutton ordered that these books should be signed by
Mr Imbroke and Mr Chamberleyn, and also by William Manwood.

230 [fo.232] Extracts from the register of Abp. John Pecham:

i) Commission to Mr Adam de Hales to act as Official in Winchester
dioc. sede vacante, since the abp. wished to recall to his own
presence Mr Richard de Ferynges, whom he had previously appointed.
Tachbrook (Tachebrok'), Wa., 26 Feb. 1280.

[Printed: Reg. Ep. Peckham, i, 98; Churchill, ii, 81.]

ii) [fo.232v] Revocation of the commission to Mr Adam de Hales as
Official in Winchester dioc. sede vacante. Slindon (Slyndon), Sx.,
23 May 1282.

[Printed: Reg. Ep. Peckham, i, 362-3.]

iii) Commission to Mr Robert de Lacy to act as Official in Winchester dioc. <u>sede vacante.</u> Slindon, Sx., 23 May 1282.

[Printed: <u>Reg. Pecham</u>, ii, 43; Churchill, ii, 81.]

iv) Notification to the prior and conv. of Winchester and all persons within the dioc. of the appointment of Mr Robert de Lacy as Official <u>sede vacante</u>. Slindon, Sx., 23 May 1282.

[Printed: <u>Reg. Pecham</u>, ii, 43.]

v) Absolution of Adam, the prior, and William de Basingstoke, monk of Winchester from the sentence of excommunication imposed by the abp.'s commissaries. Wingham (<u>Wengeham</u>), 31 July 1282.

[Printed: <u>Reg. Pecham</u>, i, 188.]

vi) Request by the proctor of certain monks of Winchester for their absolution from sentence of excommunication, which was granted by the abp. Maidstone (<u>Maydenestane</u>), 31 Aug. 1282.

[Printed: <u>Reg. Pecham</u>, i, 188–90.]

231   [fo.233] Extracts from the register of Abp. Robert Winchelsey.

i) Citation of the prior and conv. of Winchester to submit to visitation by the abp. during the vacancy of the see. 6 Dec. 1304.

[Printed: <u>Reg. Winchelsey</u>, i, 487.]

ii) Mandate to the abp.'s Official in Winchester dioc. <u>sede vacante</u> to cite any person opposing the election of Henry de Merewell as bp. of Winchester to appear before the abp. 6 Feb. 1305.

[Printed: <u>Reg. Winchelsey</u>, i, 796–7.]

iii) Letter to King Edward I, requesting him to restore the temporalities of the see of Winchester to the bp. elect. [Undated.]

[Printed: <u>Reg. Winchelsey</u>, i, 797–8.]

232   Extracts from the register of Abp. Walter Reynolds.

i) Commission to Mr Peter Polayne and Mr J. de Hoghton to visit the religious houses of Winchester dioc. <u>sede vacante</u>, with reservation to the abp. of visitation of Merton (<u>Merten'</u>) and St Mary Overy at Southwark (<u>Suthwerck</u>) and of deposition from any dignities. Cheshunt (<u>Chesthunte</u>), Hrt., 19 July 1316. [Reg. Reynolds, fo.117v.]

ii) Commission to Mr Andrew de Brug, Mr Peter Poleyne, Mr J. de Hoghton and Mr W. de Derby, or any two of them, to visit the Cistercian nunnery of Wintney (Winteneye) during the vacancy of the see of Winchester. Thorley (Thorele iuxta Ware), Hrt., 28 July 1316. [Reg. Reynolds, fo.117v.]

iii) Commission to Mr Peter Poleyn to act as Official in Winchester dioc. sede vacante. Sleaford (Sleford), Li., 28 July 1316.

[Printed: Churchill, ii, 84.]

iv) Acquittance of Mr Peter Poleyn, Official in Winchester dioc. sede vacante, and Gilbert de Secheford, abp.'s clerk and his registrar. They account for £38 0s 10d, their expenses are £5 6s 10d, and £32 14s 3d is paid into the abp.'s wardrobe and received by John de London, clerk of the archiepiscopal camera. Lambeth, 16 Oct. 1316. [Reg. Reynolds, fo.178v.]

v) [fo.233v] Mandate to Mr Peter Poleyn, Official in Winchester dioc. sede vacante. The prior and conv. have informed the abp. that they have elected John de Sandale, Chancellor of the king of England, as their bp. Because it is not possible to confirm this election without the issue of the summons or proclamation required by law, the Official is to cite any who wish to contest this election to appear before the abp. on the first judgement day after the feast of the Exaltation of the Holy Cross to show reason for their objection. Nettleham (Netleham), Li., 6 Aug. 1316. [Reg. Reynolds, fo.90v.]

vi) Commission to Mr Gilbert de Myddleton, Official of the Court of Canterbury, to appoint a suitable person to administer Winchester dioc. during the vacancy of the see following the death of Bp. John de Sandale. Barlings (Barlyng), Li., 13 Nov. 1319. [Reg. Reynolds, fo.89.]

vii) Commission to Mr Gilbert de Middleton, Official of the Court of Canterbury, to Mr Robert de Wamberg, Commissary General of the Official of the late bp. of Winchester, to administer the dioc. during the vacancy of the see. Wycombe, Lei., 23 Nov. 1319. [Reg. Reynolds, fo.89.]

viii) Commission to Mr Robert de Wamberg to institute and induct to benefices valued at less than 30 marks, having made suitable enquiries. St Neot's (Sanctum Neotum), Hu., 13 Jan. 1320. [Reg. Reynolds, fo.89.]

ix) Commission to Mr John de Badeslee to administer Winchester dioc.

sede vacante. Mortlake (Mortelake), Sy., 26 Apr. 1323. [Reg. Reynolds, fo.130v.]

x) Commission to the Official of Winchester dioc. sede vacante, because the abp. is prevented by urgent business concerning the welfare of the realm and church in England, to visit monasteries, colleges and hospitals in the dioc., deposition from dignities being reserved to the abp. Cheshunt (Chestehunte), Hrt., 19 July 1316. [Reg. Reynolds, fo.118v.]

xi) Commission to Mr John de Hoghton, Official in Winchester dioc. sede vacante, to enquire into the status of all ecclesiastical persons who retain benefices against the common law of the church. He is to cite all such persons to show by what right they hold such benefices, copies of their statements are to be made, and any doubtful cases are to be referred to the abp. or his commissaries in the parish church of Lambeth on the first judgement day after the feast of the Exhaltation of the Holy Cross. Navenby, Li., 28 July 1316. [Reg. Reynolds, fo.117v.]

xii) [fo.234] Commission to Mr P. Poleyn, Official in Winchester dioc. sede vacante, to visit religious houses, colleges and hospitals in the dioc. Navenby, Li., 28 July 1316. [Reg. Reynolds, fo.118.]

xiii) To Mr P. Poleyn and Mr J. de Hoghton. With reference to the previous commission to visit religious houses sent by the hand of the abp.'s clerk Gilbert de Secheford, because of the pressure of business the abp. did not express any intention concerning him. He is to assist them as registrar and notary, in which function he is expert. Navenby, Li., 28 July 1316. [Reg. Reynolds, fo.117v.]

xiv) The abp. is horrified to hear of the opposition of the prior and conv. of Winchester to his proposed visitation. This is not a novelty, for during a vacancy of the see the abp. conducts such a visitation by his diocesan, rather than his metropolitan authority. As he is occupied by the grave dangers to the realm caused by the Scots, he intends to visit the cathedral priory through his commissaries. 23 Aug., probably 1316[1]. [Reg. Reynolds, fo.118v.]

  [1. This document is grouped with others concerning the 1316 vacancy, and in 1320 and 1323 a truce with the Scots was in force. This is the crucial document in the archiepiscopal case. The exercise of sede vacante jurisdiction in the diocese as a whole was not contested, merely jurisdiction within parishes attached to the episcopal mensa. Reynold's assertion that auctoritate diocesana non metropolica fungimur in hac parte might logically be extended to embrace receipt of all the revenues of the episcopal mensa.]

xv) Undated mandate to the prior and conv. of Winchester
invalidating any conventicles or oaths taken to render his visitation
ineffective. None are to conceal the truth, on pain of
excommunication, and none shall suffer subsequent persecution from
his brethren for what he has revealed. [Reg. Reynolds, fo.81.]

xvi) Undated mandate to the prior and conv. of Winchester not to
impede the course of visitation, on pain of excommunication, with
absolution reserved to the abp. himself. [Reg. Reynolds, fo.81v.]

xvii) Commission to Mr J. de Badesley, Official in Winchester dioc.
sede vacante, to examine the election of Br Walter de Wolhop, prior
elect of Mottisfont, and to confirm or invalidate the election as
appropriate. Otford (Otteford), 30 Aug. 1323. [Reg. Reynolds, fo.131.]

233 [fo.234v] The fourth of the six books is commonly known as le Calfys
Skynne, containing acta of various abps. Its incipit is Extracta
diversorum registrorum dominorum archiepiscoporum super iuribus et
consuetudinibus ecclesie Cant' predicte etc. The extract produced is:
In vacancies of the see of Winchester the abp. will depute his
Official there, who for the duration of the vacancy will take
cognisance of all causes moved or to be moved, saving all other powers
of the ordinary to the abp. (salva eidem archiepiscopo omni alia
ordinaria potestate), as is contained in all the registers.
[Registrum Album, fo.16v.]

234 Extracts from the register of Abp. Simon Langham.

i) Mandate of John Beautre, keeper of the spirituality of Winchester
dioc. in the vacancy following the death of Bp. William of Edyndon,
to the rural dean of Andover (Andevere) to issue citations for
visitation. [Nov. 1366.]

   [Printed: Reg. Langham, pp.245-6.]

ii) Bull of Pope Urban V appointing William de Wykeham as
administrator of the bishopric of Winchester during the vacancy of
the see. Avignon, 11 Dec. 1366.

   [Printed: Reg. Langham, pp.242-3.]

iii) [fo.235] Mandate for the restitution of the temporalities of
the bishopric of Winchester to William de Wykeham. Lambeth, 22 Feb.
1367.

   [Printed: Reg. Langham, p.244.]

iv) Delivery, by John Beautre, of custody of the spiritualities to John de Wormenhale, commissary of William de Wykeham. Winchester, 8 March 1367.

[Printed: Reg. Langham, pp.258-9.]

v) Acquittance of John Beautre for the sum of £41 1s, being the revenues of the see of Winchester sede vacante. Lambeth, 1 May 1367.

[Printed: Reg. Langham, p.260.]

vi) Confirmation and consecration of William de Wykeham as bp. of Winchester, together with his profession of obedience to the abp. London, 10 Oct. 1367.

[Printed: Reg. Langham, pp.264-5.]

235 [fo.235v] Extracts from the register of Abp. Thomas Arundel, concerning the vacancy of the see of Winchester following the death of Bp. William de Wykeham.

i) Commission to Mr John Maydenhith, B.C.L., dean of the cathedral church of Chichester, to administer Winchester dioc. sede vacante. Coventry, 6 Oct. 1404. [Reg. Arundel, i, fo.499.]

ii) [fo.236] Short formal account of the visitation by Mr Maydenhith of the cathedral priory of Winchester, the citation being dated at Chichester on 7 Oct., the certificate 12 Oct. The visitation was conducted without resistance and the prior, Thomas Nevyle, appeared in person, promised canonical obedience and displayed sufficient title. Winchester, 17 Oct. 1404. [Reg. Arundel, i, fo.499v.]

iii) Mandate to Mr John Maydenhith to deliver the spiritualities and the muniments of the see of Winchester to Henry Beaufort, translated by Pope Innocent VII from the see of Lincoln. The mandate was received in the cathedral church of Winchester on 22 March, and by virtue of it Mr Maydenhith ceased to exercise his jurisdiction in spirituals. Lambeth, 18 March 1405. [Reg. Arundel, i, fo.517.]

iv) Profession of obedience made by Henry Beauford [Beaufort] on his translation from the see of Lincoln to that of Winchester, in the presence of Richard, bp. of Worcester, John Beaufort, earl of Somerset, Thomas Langley, Chancellor of England, and Nicholas Bubwith, Keeper of the Privy Seal. The abp. thereupon released to him the spiritualities of the see, and ordered Mr Maydenhith to hand over the seals and registers. The bp. of Winchester's palace in London, 18 March 1405. [Reg. Arundel, i, fo.28v.]

236   [fo.236v] After the exhibition of these six volumes, Mr Reed set out
to demonstrate the status of the registry and the validity of the
documents preserved there, and produced as witnesses Mr John Belle,
Mr Thomas Ford, Mr John Emlyn and Mr John Sheffeld, and William Maryner,
literate, and asked that they should be examined under oath by
Mr Hutton, who agreed, and ordered them to testify according to the
truth. He also instructed Mr Peyntwyn and Mr Barett that before 14
Dec. they should transcribe the relevant documents in a form
admissable in a court of law, and deliver them to the abp. or his
proctor in the Long Chapel at St Paul's, to which place at 10 a.m. on
14 Dec. he adjourned these proceedings. Since William Manwood was
authorised to act for the prior and conv. of Winchester only on 2 Dec.,
Mr Hutton issued a citation to the prior and conv. for 14 Dec., which
was drawn up by Mr Imbroke and Mr Chamberleyn and sealed with the
seal of the archd. of Lincoln. A commission was issued to Mr Potkyn
and all ecclesiastical persons in the diocese of Winchester to
deliver this citation to the prior and conv. of Winchester, of the
Order of St Augustine [sic]. The whole proceedings of 2 Dec. were
witnessed by Mr Gregory Lynn, M.A., and Mr William Falke and Mr John
Copland, notaries public of London, especially summoned as witnesses.
Notarial attestation by Mr Imbroke and Mr Chamberleyn. Witnesses
were to be examined in the Long Chapel of St Paul's on 12 and 13 Dec.

237   [fo.237v] John Bell, born in the city of London, notary public by
apostolic authority, aged over fifty-nine and of free birth, stated
that the registry was that of the Prerogative of the church of
Canterbury and of the present cardinal abp. He had known the present
registry for about twenty-four years; before that it was sited opposite
the janitor's dwelling in the new gatehouse, where it had been for
many years. He knew this because for the past forty years he had been
one of the registrar's clerks, together with Mr Thomas Ford, and he
had enregistered some of the acta and proceedings conducted before
Abp. Bourgchier and his Commissaries of the Prerogative. He had often
examined the volumes which had been produced, had used at least the
majority of them, and had conducted searches in them for many people
who came to the registry for that purpose. Absolute trust might be
placed in the entries in them as public and authentic writings, kept
and found in public places. He had known as registrars first
Mr Robert Growte, then Mr Roger Malmysbury, then Mr John Bele, and the
present registrar Mr John Barett.

238   John Emlyn, of the city of London, notary public by apostolic
authority, aged over sixty-one and of free birth, had known the
present registry well for over twenty years, and before that the
registry in a low chamber opposite the janitor's dwelling in the new
gate. In both locations it had been, and still was, a place of
common resort for persons of the province of Canterbury searching for
documents kept there. The greatest trust might be placed in
documents emanating from it. This he knew because he had often
conducted searches in the books there, and especially in the volumes

in question. The registry was considered a public place, and frequent recourse was made to it for documents. He had known as registrars Malmysbury, Bele and Barett.

239   John Sheffeld, notary public by apostolic authority, dwelling in the city of London, aged over forty-four and of free birth, gave similar testimony. This he knew from personal acquaintance over twenty years, and because for thirteen years continuously he had been an assistant to Mr Thomas Winterborn, Commissary of the Prerogative under Abp. Bourgchier, in whose chamber he had seen the books in question when they were brought from the registry for scrutiny.

240   [fo.238] William Maryner, citizen of the city of London, aged over fifty and of free birth, testified that the present registry was situated on the right hand side within the entrance to the manor of Lambeth; before that it was in a low chamber on the left of the entrance opposite the janitor's dwelling newly constructed there. Otherwise he testified as the previous witnesses. He knew this because he had often been there when various persons had requested the registrar to provide copies of documents. He had known as registrars Malmysbury, Beele and Barett.

241   Thomas Forde, of Lambeth in Winchester dioc., notary public by papal and imperial authority, aged over sixty-four and of free status, testified that he had known the present registry as the normal registry of the Prerogative for over sixteen years; before that it was situated in a low chamber near the gate, where a new tower was at present being built by the cardinal abp. Otherwise he testified as the other witnesses. He knew this because for the greater part of forty years he had worked as clerk to the registrars, and in particular under the direction of Mr Roger Malmysbury he had copied many documents from the volumes now exhibited. He had known as registrars Malmysbury, Beele and Barett.

242   On 14 Dec. at 10 a.m. in the Long Chapel of St Paul's, Mr Potkyn announced and swore that on 6 Dec. he had personally cited the prior of Winchester in the cathedral and the conv. in the chapter house. At Mr Reed's request, Mr Hutton ordered the prior and conv. to be summoned, and William Manwood appeared, bearing another letter of proxy sealed in red wax with the common seal of the prior and conv., dated 10 Dec. He requested that it should be noted in the records of the process that the conv. of Winchester was of the Order of St Benedict, not of St Augustine [cf. no.236].

243   [fo.238v] Mr John Barett produced a quire of parchment recently found in the registry since the scrutiny ordered by Mr Hutton, which related to the vacancy of the see of Winchester following the death of Bp.

Peter Courtenay, from 22 Sept. 1492. The extracts produced were:

i) Commission to Mr Robert Sherborne and Mr Michael Clive to administer Winchester dioc. sede vacante. Lambeth, 20 Oct. 1492. [vol. ii, no.77.]

ii) [fo.239] Mandate to Mr Sherborne and Mr Clive for the release of the spiritualities of the see of Winchester to Thomas Langton, translated from the see of Salisbury, with reservation to the abp. and his ministers of the correction of faults discovered during visitation and the collection of spiritual revenues due to the abp. by reason of the vacancy. Lambeth, 24 June 1493.

244   [fo.239v] Mr Hutton then ordered the transcripts of all these documents to be collated with the copies in the registers by the notaries public, and this they did, Mr Imbroke reading aloud the transcripts, Mr Chamberleyn and Mr Barett along with William Manwood checking by reading the registers. As this process could not be finished by noon, proceedings were adjourned to 2 p.m., and when they were still not finished, a further adjournment was made to 2 p.m. on 16 Dec.

245   On 16 Dec. Mr Hutton declared the transcripts to be faithful copies. Mr Peyntwyn and Mr Barett stated that despite Mr Hutton's monition, they had been unable to draw up an account of the proceedings to deliver to the abp.'s proctor for conveyance to Rome, because of their occupation with the business of Convocation, presently meeting at St Paul's. Mr Hutton ordered that they should hand over such an account ready for sealing on 18 Jan. at 10 a.m. in the same place.

246   [fo.240] On 18 Jan. 1496 Mr Hutton ordered the prior and conv. of Winchester to be summoned, and when they failed to appear, Mr Reed accused them of contumacy and demanded that the case should proceed in their absence, to which Mr Hutton assented. Mr Peyntwyn and Mr Barett produced an account of the proceedings to be subscribed by Mr Hutton and the notaries and sealed. The document was handed to Mr Reed, acting on the abp.'s behalf, in the presence of Mr Gregory Lynn, M.A., and Mr John Copland, notary public. The whole proceedings were drawn up in the form of a public instrument, sealed with the seal of the archd. of Lincoln.

247   ACCOUNT OF PROCEEDINGS DESPATCHED TO JOHN, ABBOT OF ST SAVIOUR'S BERMONDSEY, JUDGE DELEGATE COMMISSIONED JOINTLY AND SEVERALLY WITH THE BISHOPS OF DURHAM AND BATH AND WELLS AND THE ABBOTS OF WESTMINSTER, WALTHAM HOLY CROSS AND ST AUGUSTINE'S CANTERBURY, OF THE PROCEEDINGS CONDUCTED BEFORE RICHARD HALL, ABBOT OF HYDE, JOHN ABBOT OF ST AUGUSTINE'S CANTERBURY, AND THOMAS OKE ABBOT OF TITCHFIELD, JUDGES, COMMISSARIES OR EXECUTORS SPECIALLY DEPUTED IN THE MATTERS MENTIONED BELOW BY MR ANTHONY FLORES, BISHOP-ELECT OF CASTELLIMARE, REFERENDARY OF THE POPE AND ONE OF THE AUDITORS OF THE SACRED PALACE.

[fo.240v] On Monday 8 Aug. 1497, in the parish church of Holy Cross at Southampton (Hamptuna), the abbots of Hyde (Hida), St Augustine's Canterbury and Titchfield (Tichefelde) received from William Manwood, monk of Winchester, a commission from Mr Anthony Flores, sealed with his small seal, together with a rotulus remissorius attached to it by red cord. This was done in the presence of Mr William Imbroke, Mr James Vaghan and Mr John Richardson, notaries public by apostolic authority, and of Peter Essart, literate, of the dioc. of York and Coutances, specially summoned as witnesses. The abbots agreed to execute the commission, and appointed as their scribes Mr Imbroke and Mr Vaghan. Manwood then presented another commission from Matthew de Ubaldis, addressed to the abbots of Hyde and Titchfield only. Mr Imbroke read aloud both commissions. Manwood presented his letters of proxy from the prior and conv. of Winchester.

248 [fo.241] Commission to Thomas Gyan, Richard Lacy, William Manwood and Thomas Knyght, monks of Winchester, and to Mr John Lovyer, B.C.L., and Mr James Vaghan, B.C.L., to act as proctors of the prior and conv. in their dispute with the abp. of Canterbury. 3 Aug. 1497.

249 Manwood then protested that, notwithstanding the presence of the abbot of St Augustine's and the request made to him elsewhere by Br Thomas Knyght to execute the first commission, if the abbot could not or would not so execute it, he intended to utilise the second commission. At his urgent request, the abbots of Hyde and Titchfield assumed the task of executing this second commission. There then appeared Mr John Reed, who presented the abp.'s letter of proxy dated at Lambeth on 4 July 1497, and he protested in the abp.'s name the nullity of Manwood's actions before the abbots of Hyde, Titchfield and St Augustine's. Before the abbots of Hyde and Titchfield, sitting judicially, the abbot of St Augustine's protested publicly that he should receive the requisite expenses. Manwood then requested that the roll attached to the first commission should be opened, to which the abbot of Hyde, with the consent of the abbots of Titchfield and St Augustine's agreed, and he instructed Manwood to produce witnesses and any muniments which he needed to support the monks' case on 20 Oct. in the church of Holy Cross. Mr Reed and Manwood repeated their respective protestations.

250 [fo.241v] On 20 Oct. 1497 in the church of Holy Cross, Southampton, Mr Elys Ruthyn, J.U.B., and Mr John Lovyer, B.C.L., proctors of the prior and conv. of Winchester, appeared before the abbots of Hyde and Titchfield, sitting judicially in the presence of the forementioned notaries. Mr Ruthyn presented a letter of proxy, superceding previous proxies, appointing William Manwood and Thomas Knyght, monks, Mr Lovyer and Mr Ruthyn, and Stephen Semer, literate, dated 19 Oct. 1497. The judges then appointed Simon Bingham, literate, of the parish of St Michael, Southampton, as their apparitor. The monks' proctors requested that the abp. or his proctor should be summoned, and this

the apparitor did three times in a loud voice. Notwithstanding the absence of the abp. or his proctor, and with the reservation to them of the right to object to any witness, the monks' proctors were granted leave to produce witnesses, and produced Thomas Holden, Thomas att Hasill, Richard Hether, William Bulbeke, William Weston, John Raustowe and Richard Stympe, parishioners of East Meon, and William Fleshmonger and John Wyndar, parishioners of Hambledon, who were admitted and swore an oath upon the Gospels. The judges required the proctors to produce their witnesses and documentary evidence on the following Friday. Mr Ruthyn stated that Mr Michael Clefe, Decr.D., warden of the new college at Winchester, was an essential witness, but because of old age and ill health a journey to Southampton would endanger his life. Therefore the judges agreed to hear his testimony on the morning of Thursday 26 Oct., either in the cathedral or in Fromond's Chapel at Winchester College.

251 [fo.242v] On Friday 27 Oct. Mr Ruthyn and Mr Lovyer appeared before the abbots of Hyde and Titchfield and produced a document sealed with the seal of Richard bp. of Ross (Rossen'), and subscribed by Nicholas Consell, clerk of the dioc. of Bath and Wells and notary public by apostolic authority. At their request the judges ordered that it should be transcribed and exemplified by the notaries and included in the records of these proceedings.

252 Inspeximus by Richard bp. of Ross, Mr Thomas Forest, B.C.L., warden of the hospital of St Cross, Winchester, and Mr John Langthorn, Decr.B., guardians of the spiritualities and vicars general of the abp. in Winchester dioc. sede vacante, of the following documents:

i) Documents produced by Richard de Caune, monk of Winchester and proctor of the prior and conv., before Mr Henry de Derby, Commissary General of the administrators of the archbishopric of Canterbury specially deputed by the pope, in the presence of Mr William de Maldon, Mr William le Dorturer, Mr Richard Scotus and Mr John de Walkerne, notaries public, and others. The Commissary General instructed Mr William de Maldon to exemplify these documents, which were free from any taint of suspicion, in public form.

a) Resignation by Ralph de Staneford, r. of Wootton St Lawrence (Wotton'), Ha., of his church into the hands of John bp. of Winchester. Sealed, in red wax, with his seal, and, as it is unknown to many men, also with the seal of the archd. of Dorset. Southwark (Sowthwerke), Sy., 16 May 1299.

b) Grant by John bp. of Winchester to the prior and conv. of Winchester, because of his affection for them and their hardships, of the advowson of the church of Wootton St Lawrence, with the other rights possessed by him in that church. Sealed with green wax. Marwell (Merewell), Ha., 20 Apr. 1299.

[Printed: Reg. Pontissara, p.83.]

c)   [fo.243] Appropriation by Bp. John of the church of Wootton St Lawrence (Woton') to the prior and conv. of Winchester. Sealed with green wax. Marwell (Morewelle), Ha., 26 Apr. 1299

  [Printed: Reg. Pontissara, p.81.]

d)   Inspeximus and confirmation by King Edward I of the grant by Bp. John of the advowson of the church of Wootton St Lawrence to the prior and conv. of Winchester. Sealed with green wax. Stepney (Stevenheth), Mx., 20 May 1299.

e)   Institution of the prior and conv. of Winchester as rectors of Wootton St Lawrence. Sealed with green wax. Southwark (Southwerk'), Sy., 23 May 1299.

  [Printed: Reg. Pontissara, p.85.]

f)   Mandate of Bp. John to Henry Sympligham, canon of Wherwell, to induct the prior and conv. of Winchester, in the person of Br Roger de Entingeham their proctor, to the church of Wootton St Lawrence. Sealed with green wax. Southwark, Sy., 1299.

  [Printed: Reg. Pontissara, p.85.]

g)   Certificate by Henry de Sympligham of the bp.'s mandate to induct. Sealed with green wax. Wootton St Lawrence, Ha., 24 May 1299.

h)   [fo.243v] Confirmation by Bp. John of the rights of the prior and conv. of Winchester in Littleton (Littelton), Ha., and other churches. Sealed with green wax. Winchester, 5 July 1289.

  [Printed: Reg. Pontissara, p.437.]

  Notarial exemplification by Mr William de Maldon and Mr William, son of William le Dorturer, notaries public by authority of the pope and the prefect of the Holy City, and Mr John de Walkerne of Winchester dioc. and Mr Richard Welythwode, son of Adam of York, notaries public by imperial authority. St Mary Aldermary, London, 16 Dec. 1306.

ii)   Grant by King Edward III, at the request of John Stratford bp. of Winchester, to the prior and conv. of custody during the vacancy of the see of the churches of East Meon and Hambledon, previously exercised by the keepers of the temporalities appointed by the crown. Westminster, 6 Feb. 1331.

  [Calendared: CPR 1330–34, p.73.]

iii)   Confirmation by Pope John XXII that the prior and conv. of Winchester shall during vacancies of the see be guardians of the

85

churches of East Meon and Hambledon, in place of Robert de Wells and his fellow lay keepers of the temporalities appointed during the last vacancy. Avignon, 31 Oct. 1333.

[Calendared: CPL 1305–42, p.397.]

iv) [fo.244] Confirmation by Bp. Henry of Blois to the prior and conv. of Winchester, for the better performance of divine service, of all the dignities, liberties, customs, fees and services of the manorial tenants, allowing them the homage of the tenants and giving the prior full powers of administration within and outside the cloister, and confirming also the patronage of all their churches as they held them when he became bp., with the threat of spiritual penalties against those who infringe this confirmation. 6 Jan. 1172.

[Printed: Reg. Pontissara, p.624.]

To the transcript of these documents the keepers of the spiritualities affixed their seals. Notarial exemplification by Nicholas Consell, clerk of Bath and Wells dioc., notary public by apostolic authority. Winchester, 6 May 1447.

253 [fo.244v] After the exhibition of this evidence, Mr Ruthyn and Mr Lovier produced Mr Chipman, M.A., v. of East Meon, and requested that he be admitted as a witness, notwithstanding the absence of the abp. or his proctor. When the judges agreed, he swore to testify truthfully. The judges then ordered their scribes to compile a record of the proceedings before the feast of St Hilary for transmission to Rome; they instructed the monks' proctors to produce any other documentary evidence they wished on 30 Nov., when they would appoint a messenger to convey the record of these proceedings to Rome. Proceedings were then adjourned to 30 Nov., but before they rose, Thomas Elcok, literate, presented a letter of proxy from the abbot of St Augustine's Canterbury.

254 Appointment of Mr John Richardson, B.C.L., John Walshe of Southampton (Hampton), Thomas Elcok and Peter Essarde, literates, jointly and severally, as proctors of the abbot of St Augustine's Canterbury, with power to exhibit before the abbots of Hyde and Titchfield an instrument protestatory or excusatory, and to notify the abbots and the prior and conv. of Winchester that the abbot of St Augustine's was prepared to execute the forementioned commission or any other, provided that he was duly requested so to do by one of the parties, and of doing all else necessary or desirable in this matter that the abbot might do himself if present. Chapter House of St Augustine's Canterbury, 17 Oct. 1497.

255 [fo.245] Protestation of John, abbot of St Augustine's, relating how he had been requested by Br Thomas Knyght, proctor of the prior and

conv. of Winchester, to execute letters remissory addressed by Mr Anthony Flores to himself and the abbots of Waltham (Walteham) Holy Cross, Hyde (Hyda) and Titchfield (Tichefeld'). Although the request was not made in due manner and form, he went at the specified time to the church of Holy Cross at Southampton, not without great trouble and expense, as it is one hundred and twenty miles from his normal residence. There, with the abbots of Hyde and Titchfield, he assumed the task of executing these letters. After proceedings had commenced, Br William Manwood, the monks' proctor, produced another commission addressed to the three abbots by Matthew de Ubaldis de Parisio, an Auditor of the Apostolic Palace, deputed in place of Mr Flores, and then asked the abbots of Hyde and Titchfield to execute these letters, looking scornfully at the abbot of St Augustine's and objecting to him. The abbots of Hyde and Titchfield, at Manwood's petition, assumed unilaterally the task of execution, scorning their colleague, failing to fulfil the terms of the letters, notwithstanding that all three had assumed together the task of executing the letters of Mr Flores and that the abbot of St Augustine's declared himself ready to fulfil either commission, if he was so requested on behalf of the monks of Winchester, and if expenses and money for his travel were provided, as indeed he is still prepared to do. He wishes to have all the proceedings at Southampton on 28 Aug. recorded, insofar as they serve to exonerate him. He had incurred great trouble and expense at the petition of Br Thomas Knyght, and for his expenses he has received no satisfaction. Despite repeated requests, the prior and conv. of Winchester have refused to pay, asserting that, whether or not he had come to Southampton, the letters would have been executed. Furthermore, Br William Manwood insultingly refused to request the abbot to execute the second commission, and the abbots of Hyde and Titchfield ignored him and did not attend to the conditions contained in the commission. For these reasons, and not for any other, the abbot of St Augustine's has refused to proceed further at the present time, protesting that he was and is fully prepared to obey this and any other apostolic mandate, if the party or parties with an interest in the case wished to approach him. Witnessed by Mr John Williamson, Decr.B., Mr Edward Honynden, B.C.L., Thomas Clifford, generosus, and John Ker, literate, of Canterbury, Coventry and Lichfield and London dioc., specially summoned as witnesses. Notarial exemplification by John Richardson, clerk of York dioc., notary public by apostolic authority. St Andrew's chapel, commonly called the abbot's chapel, at St Augustine's Canterbury, 17 Oct. 1497.

256 [fo.245v] Further to the exhibition of this public instrument, Thomas Elcok his proctor stated verbally that, had the abbot of St Augustine's been asked, either by his colleagues or by a party in the case, and if he had received the requisite expenses, he would have been present there with his colleagues for the execution of the commissions.

257 On 30 Nov. at 9 a.m. in the church of Holy Cross, Southampton, William Manwood presented to the judges a certain Christopher de Barnererio, literate, who was commissioned under oath to take an account of this

process to Rome. The judges instructed the prior and conv. to appear
before Mr Flores or another auditor deputed in his place on the feast
of St John the Baptist to hear a just verdict. This was done,
notwithstanding the absence of the abp. or his proctor, in the presence
of Mr James Vaughan, notary public, and scribe of the judges, Mr
Bernard Holden, M.A., and Mr William Nicholson of the dioc. of Durham,
notary public, specially summoned as witnesses, and in the absence of
Mr William Imbroke.

[In the ms. the questions and articles to be put to the witnesses
produced by the prior and conv. of Winchester (no.258) are
punctuated by the answers given by Richard Hether, the first
witness (no.259), and the testimony of the other witnesses (nos.
260-66) is related to the questions put to Hether. For the sake
of clarity, it has seemed better here to isolate the questions
which were put to all witnesses.]

258   EXAMINATION OF THE WITNESSES SUMMONED BY THE PRIOR AND CONVENT OF
WINCHESTER, ACCORDING TO THE ARTICLES OF A ROTULUS REMISSORIUS
DESPATCHED BY MR ANTHONY FLORES, CONDUCTED SECRETLY AND INDIVIDUALLY.
THAT OF RICHARD HETHER WAS BEGUN BEFORE THE ABBOT OF HYDE AT HYDE ON
22 OCTOBER, AND COMPLETED BY MR IMBROKE AND MR VAUGHAN IN THE
CATHEDRAL ON 23 OCTOBER. THE OTHER LAYMEN WERE EXAMINED IN THE
CATHEDRAL ON 23, 24 and 25 OCTOBER, AND MR WILLIAM CHIPNAM, M.A., IN
THE PARLOUR OF JAMES MIRYK'S HOUSE IN THE PARISH OF HOLY CROSS ON
28 OCTOBER.

[fo.246] Rotulus remissorius containing questions proposed by the
abp.'s proctor to be put on behalf of the abp. of Canterbury to those
witnesses produced in the locality by the prior and conv. of
Winchester. Each of the witnesses should be reminded, as they take
the oath, of the sacred nature of the oath, that the bearer of false
witness denies God, offends his neighbour and damns his own soul, and
that if a man gives false testimony, it stands to the credit of his
opponent, and he will be punished as a perjurer. Then the following
questions shall be put to each witness.

i and ii) The witness should be asked his name and surname, the name
of his father, from what locality he comes, his age, the extent of
his possessions, and at whose charge and cost he lives.

iii and iv) In which diocese he was born, and where he has lived
hitherto. He must state clearly whether he is beneficed of the church
of Winchester, or salaried by the chapter by virtue of any office,
whether he is lay, clerk or religious of any order, and if the last,
in which house he is professed, and he should produce any license to
be outside the cloister.

v) Whether he has seen the articles on which he is to be examined and
knows their content, and by whom he has been instructed as to what he

should depose.

vi) Whether he has ever been in the locality of the churches in
dispute. If so, he should be asked their names, their situation,
whether in the city or not, their distance one from another, and
whether he has ever been there. If not, he should be asked how he
can know anything of the matters contained in the articles.

vii) Whether he has ever known any of the priors of Winchester. If
so, he should be asked their names, and when and where he became
acquainted with them. And similarly, did he know any of the bps. of
Winchester. If not, he should be asked how he can know anything of
this matter.

viii) Whether he has ever known the church of Winchester deprived of
her bp. during a vacancy. If so, he should be asked by whose death
the vacancy occurred, who then administered the church, and under
whose metropolitical authority the church of Winchester is constituted.

ix) Whether he has ever been in the province of Canterbury, and
whether, when churches of that province were vacant after the death
of a bp., the abp. normally governed and administered those churches,
exercising the totality of episcopal jurisdiction and receiving during
the vacancy the payments, issues and tithes pertaining, sede plena, to
the bp.

x) Whether he knows the prior of Winchester, and whether he is his
kinsman by blood or marriage, or a friend or well-wisher to the prior
or to any of the monks; and whether he is hostile to the abp. of
Canterbury, or has received any offence or injury at the hands of the
abp. or his officials.

xi) Whether any promise or incentive has influenced him in this case.

xii) Whether he hopes to obtain any advantage or to avoid any
inconvenience by the victory of the prior and conv., and which party
he wishes to win the case. If he replies 'the party with right on its
side', he should be asked which party he wishes to obtain its rights.

There should then be read to the witness the following propositions
and articles, particularly the first three, and if he states that they
are true, he should be asked how he knows this, and whether he has
ever been in the churches and chapels in question. If he answers in
the affirmative, he should be asked where they are located, their
distance from each other, and who is accustomed to administer them
and receive the revenues, and whether they have their own rectors or
are occupied by someone other than their own rectors.

There follow the articles proposed by the prior and conv.

of Winchester, on which the witnesses in the locality should be
examined. In order to demonstrate clearly the legitimate right of
the prior and conv., the lack of any right by the cardinal abp.
and his undue harassment of the prior and conv., the proctor of the
monks advances the following propositions and articles, to each of
which it should suffice for the witness to reply under oath <u>credo</u> or
<u>non credo</u>. If the articles are denied, he seeks that he and his
principals be allowed to prove their truth in the court of Rome, not
however committing himself to superfluous proof.

xiii) Art. i) If necessary, he will prove that for a hundred years
and more, from time immemorial, the cathedral church of Winchester,
O.S.B., was, and is today, eminent and famous, with a bp. at its head,
and the prior and conv. constituting the chapter. It is a dioc. of
wide extent, distinct and separate from other dioc., and has other
rights and distinctions.

Art. ii) From that time onwards there were among the other parish
churches of the dioc., as there are today, two parish churches, East
Meon (<u>Estmeane</u>) and Hambledon (<u>Hameldon</u>), which have extensive
parishes with many parishioners, cemeteries, baptismal fonts, and
other rights and privileges demonstrating them to be parish churches.

Art. iii) From that time onwards there were, among other chapels in
the foresaid parishes, the chapels of Wroxfield (<u>Groxolos</u>), Steep
(<u>Stupe</u>) and Westbury (<u>Exere</u>).

xiv) Art. iv) From that time onwards the forementioned churches with
their chapels have been perpetually united, annexed and incorporated
with the cathedral church of Winchester, and are possessed by the bp.
of Winchester or in his name, and this is public knowledge.

Art. v) From that time onwards the forementioned chapels were
perpetually united, annexed and incorporated with the said parish
churches, and as such were possessed by the bp. of Winchester or in
his name, and this is public knowledge.

Art. vi) All the above was and is manifestly true, and a matter of
public knowledge.

   After these articles have been put to the witness, the abp.'s
proctor requests that if he says they are true, he should be asked
whether he has seen the annexations, whether they were several or one,
by whom they were authorised, whether by papal or episcopal authority,
and he should state the name of the pope or bp. who had authorised the
unions, and whether they were for a term or in perpetuity.

xv) Art. vii) From that time onwards, by right and by custom and by
the ordinance of the kings of England confirmed by the apostolic see,

the custody of the spiritualities and the tithes and of the foresaid churches perpetually annexed to the episcopal _mensa_ pertained, _sede vacante_, to the prior and conv., and this is public knowledge.

Art. viii) From that time onwards the prior and conv. have, during a vacancy of the see, had custody of the spiritualities and received all the tithes of those parish churches, and have exercised these rights quietly and pacifically until the present dispute. It is acknowledged throughout the locality that they are entitled to exercise these rights.

After these articles have been put to the witness, the abp.'s proctor requests that if he says they are true, he should be asked the source of his knowledge, and whether he has seen these ordinances and confirmations, which king ordained this and when, and where and why he saw these documents, and what is their content.

xvi) The witness should be asked whether he has known any bp. of Winchester, and whether he has ever seen the see vacant; if he replies in the affirmative, he should be asked how many times and by whose death, how long the vacancy lasted, who held the custody of the forementioned parish churches and received their fruits and tithes, whether he himself was present and saw this, or heard it from others, and if from others, he should be asked where, when and from whom he heard it.

xviii) [_sic_] He should be asked whether the bp. [_sic_] of Canterbury, during the vacancy of the church of Winchester, has been accustomed to exercise the custody of that church and to receive all fruits and tithes pertaining in any manner to the bp. If he replies in the negative, he should be asked if the abp. might not have received them without the knowledge of the witness.

xix) Art. ix) For the clarification of the previous articles, the monks' proctor intends to prove that from 1334 and the translation of Bp. John Stearford[1] to the church of Canterbury up till the present vacancy, the prior and conv. had the custody of the forementioned churches, and received the tithes, publicly and openly.

[1. Bp. John Stratford, 1323-33.]

Art. x) That the same has been true from 1345 and the vacancy caused by the death of Bp. Adam [Orleton].

Art. xi) That the same has been true from 1366 and 1404, and the vacancies caused by the deaths of William Edincten[1] and William Vican[2].

[1. Bishop William Edington, 1346-66.
 2. Bishop William of Wykeham, 1367-1404.]

91

Art. xii) That the same has been true from 1467 [sic, recte 1447] and
1486 and the vacancies caused by the deaths of Henry Beauforde
[Beaufort] and William Waynflete.

Art. xiii) That all the foregoing is true, and is manifest public
knowledge.

After these articles have been put to the witness, the abp.'s
proctor requests that if he says they are true, he should be asked
how he knows, and whether he was present at the events mentioned and
knows the persons named. If he replies in the negative, he should
be asked how then he can know of these matters.

xx) Art. xiv) When the see of Winchester was last vacant in 1492
following the death of Bp. Peter, the abp. of Canterbury by force
and usurpation, unjustly and contrary to right, prevented the prior
and conv. from exercising their right to administer the spiritualities
and to collect the tithes of the foresaid churches, and openly
harassed them, or caused them to be harassed.

Art. xv) That all the foregoing is true, and manifest public
knowledge.

After these articles have been put to the witness, the abp.'s
proctor requests that he be asked whether he knew Bp. Peter, where
and when he died, and what the abp. did after his death.

xxi) The witness should be asked whether the prior and conv. of
Winchester were in possession of these rights, and if he replies in
the affirmative, he should be asked what he has seen them do, and to
what effect they could be said to be in possession. He should be
asked by whom he had seen such things done, and how he knew such a
person was acting for the prior and conv., and whether he had seen
his letters of proxy, if they were special or general, their date,
and by which notary public were they subscribed.

259   Richard Hether, agricultor, lived at East Meon from birth until he
was twenty-two, then for three years with Thomas att Hasill at
Privett (Pryvett), Ha., and then for thirty years or more at Woodland
(Wodlond'), a hamlet in the parish of East Meon, to where he then
returned and lived for thirty years. He is aged over eighty, is
illiterate and of free status. He has known the priory of St Swithun
from his youth, but of the present monks he knows only the treasurer,
and he does not know the abp. He is the son of Thomas Hether deceased,
of East Meon, his goods are worth hardly twenty shillings, and he
lives at the charge of Thomas Pynk of East Meon, his son-in-law. He
receives no salary from the church of Winchester, and has not seen
the articles. He is a parishioner of East Meon, and has often been in
Hambledon church; both churches are in the dioc. of Winchester and the

province of Canterbury, and there is a mile between them. He has not
known any prior, but has known Bps. Beauford [Beaufort], Waynflete and
Courtenay, all of whom he has seen at East Meon. He has seen three
vacancies, after the deaths of Bps. Beauford, Waynflete and Courtenay,
but does not know how long the vacancies lasted or who administered
the church of Winchester in the interim, but it is commonly said that
the church of Winchester exists under the metropolitan church of
Canterbury. He has lived in the province of Canterbury from his youth,
but does not know how to reply to the other matters in qu. ix. He is
not related to the prior of Winchester, is no more well disposed to
him than to any other Christian, and he feels no hostility to the abp.
from whom he has received no injury. He hopes to gain nothing from the
victory of the prior and conv., and is indifferent between the parties.
Replying to qu. xiii, he states that articles i, ii and ii are true,
and he knows this because it is common knowledge. He has been in the
churches in dispute, and in other churches in the dioc., and these
churches have the common distinguishing marks of parish churches, and he
has also been in the three chapels in the parish of East Meon. East
Meon is fourteen miles from the cathedral and two miles from Hamb edon.
Wroxfield (Wroxfeld) is two miles from East Meon church, four miles
from Hambledon and fourteen miles from the cathedral. Steep (Stepe),
is two and a half miles from East Meon, four miles from Hambledon, and
fourteen and a half miles from the cathedral. Westbury is one mile
from East Meon, about three miles from Hambledon and twelve or
thirteen miles from the cathedral. Hambledon is about sixteen miles
from Winchester, Wroxfield is one mile from Steep and three 'long
miles' from Westbury. Steep is three miles from Westbury. The churches
of East Meon and Hambledon are administered by the bp. of Winchester,
to whom they are appropriated, and the cure of souls is committed to
vicars. Both the churches and the chapels are under the jurisdiction
of the bp., to whom pertains the power of visitation and the correction
of delinquents. The fruits and tithes are received and administered
by the bp. and the vicars. The vicar of East Meon maintains the
chaplains of the foresaid chapels, but the witness does not know which
fruits and tithes belong to the bp. and which to the vicars. Replying
to qu. xiv, he states that articles iv, v and vi are true, and when
asked how he knows, states that it is common knowledge that the bp. is
set over the vicars and each year receives certain spiritual revenues
from the churches. He does not know if there was one act of annexation
or more, nor by what authority the churches were appropriated to the
bp. Replying to qu. xv, he states that according to the common opinion
of the parishioners of East Meon and of many others in the dioc., whose
names he cannot recall, articles vii and viii are true. When the see
was vacant after Bp. Beauford's death, around the feast of the
Assumption of the B.V.M. he saw a man with a bushel (buta) of tithed
sheaves which he said that he was taking to the church barn at East
Meon, for the use of the prior and conv., he believed, but he cannot
remember the man's name or from whose corn the sheaves came. He had
seen the church of Winchester vacant following the deaths of Bps.
Beauford, Waynflete and Courtenay, but how long the vacancies lasted
and who exercised custody of the spiritualities he does not know, nor
who received the fruits and tithes, except as he has testified, and

except that he has heard many people, whose names he cannot recall, say that all the fruits and tithes of the churches in dispute belong to the prior and chapter during vacancies. He does not know that the abp. administered the dioc. or received the fruits and tithes pertaining to the bp. while he lived, but the abp. could have done all this without the knowledge of the witness. Replying to qu. xix, he can provide no testimony beyond what he has already said. He knew the lord Peter Courtenay when he was alive, but cannot testify to the place or precise time of his death, and he does not recall what the abp. did when he died. All the testimony he has given is true and is common knowledge. To qu. xxi he replies as he has above, and can offer no further testimony.

260 [fo.247v] John Raustowe, <u>agricultor</u>, has lived in the parish of East Meon for more than seventy-two years, and before that he lived at Hambledon, where he was born. He is aged over eighty, is illiterate and of free status. He does not know the prior and conv. He is the son of John Raustow deceased, of Hambledon, has goods to the value of £20 and lives at his own charge. He does not hold office or receive a salary from the prior and conv., and has not seen the articles. He has frequently been in the parishes in dispute, and the churches are three miles distant from each other. He has not known any prior of Winchester, but has known four bps., Beauford, Waynflete, Courtenay and Thomas Langton, and has witnessed three vacancies, following the deaths of Beauford, Waynflete and Courtenay, but he does not know how long they lasted or who governed the church of Winchester in the interim, but he does say that the church of Winchester exists under the metropolitan church of Canterbury. To qu. ix he replies that he lives within the province of Canterbury, but he can answer no further. He does not know the prior, is not related to him or any of the monks, he is no better disposed to one party in the case than to the other, and has received no injury or offence from the abp. or his officials. No promise or incentive has been offered, and he has no interest in which party wins the case. Replying to qu. xiii, he states that articles i, ii and iii are true, and asked how he knows, he states that he has seen four bps. of Winchester, and that the church of Winchester is the mother church and cathedral of the dioc. He has been in the two churches in question and has seen the distinguishing marks of a parish church (<u>insignia parochialia</u>) – beautiful churches with cemeteries, baptismal fonts, choirs, chancels, and the other marks of a parish church. He knows also the chapels of Wroxfield, Steep and Westbury annexed to East Meon, whose chaplains are under the direction of the vicar. The fruits of these churches and chapels are at the disposal of the bp., to whom they are appropriated, and of the vicars, who receive some of the fruits and tithes as their portion, as they exercise the cure of souls. Replying to qu. xiv, he states that articles iv, v and vi are also true. He knows this because he has been accustomed every year to collect for the bp. the tithe of sheaves from the parishes and farmers of East Meon and Hambledon, and to take them to the bp.'s barns in the parishes, and sometimes he has seen the bp. retain these tithes in his own hands.

It is common knowledge in the locality that these churches and chapels
are annexed to the episcopal mensa. He has never seen the act of
annexation and does not know by whose authority it was executed.
Replying to qu. xv and articles vii and viii, he states that it is
commonly believed that the right of receiving the fruits and tithes
pertains to the prior and conv. during a vacancy, but he cannot speak
of the spiritual jurisdiction. In the vacancies following the deaths
of Bps. Beauford and Waynflete the prior and conv. received the tithe
of sheaves and the other tithes of East Meon, but he cannot say what
happened at Hambledon, nor does he know from whom the prior and conv.
received those tithes, or whether they were paid in cash or in kind.
He has seen neither royal grant nor apostolic confirmation. He has
seen the church of Winchester vacant three times, but cannot state
the length of any of the vacancies, or who exercised the cure and
custody of the churches. As to the tithes, he replies as before, but
has never been present when they were rendered to the prior and conv.,
although he has heard it said by the majority of the parishioners of
East Meon that the prior and conv. do receive the tithes sede vacante;
he does not however know by whom they are paid, nor can he remember
the names of those who told him this. He has no knowledge of the abp.
exercising any jurisdiction or receiving the spiritual revenues during
a vacancy, but admits that he could have done so without his knowledge.
Replying to qu. xix, he can say nothing about articles ix, x and xi,
but xii is true, for reasons he has already specified. As to qu. xx
and articles xiv and xv, he can reply only from what he has heard, as
this is common knowledge. He knew Peter Courtenay, but does not know
the place or date of his death, and as for what the abp. did on his
death, he can only testify according to what he has heard from the
parishioners of East Meon. To qu. xxi he replies as he has testified
above.

261   [fo.248v] Thomas att Hasill has lived in the parish of East Meon from
his youth. He is aged over sixty and of free status. He has known
the prior of Winchester for six years and one of the monks for a month
or more, but does not know the abp. He is the son of Richard att
Hasill deceased, of East Meon, his goods are worth hardly ten marks,
and he lives at his own charge. He receives no salary from the church
of Winchester, and has not seen the articles. At various times he has
been in the churches of East Meon and Hambledon, which are three miles
apart. Over about fifty years he has known one prior called Marlborow
and the present prior, but not any other; he has known four bps.,
Beauford, Waynflete, Courtenay and Langton, and has seen three vacancies
but does not really know how long they lasted or when they began,
because it was not a matter that greatly concerned him. He does not
know who governed the church and dioc. of Winchester during vacancies;
it exists under the metropolitan church of Canterbury, but whether the
abp. did or ought to administer the church sede vacante he did not
know until after the death of Bp. Courtenay, when the abp.'s officers
took over the administration (intromiserunt se cum gubernatione) of
the church and dioc. He has lived in the province of Canterbury from
his youth. He knows the present prior, but is not related to him nor

better disposed to him than to all Christians, and he is not hostile to the abp. and has not received any injury from him. He is not partial, and no incentive has been offered him. Replying to qu. xiii, he states that articles i, ii and iii are true, and this is common knowledge. He has been in the cathedral church, the two parish churches in dispute and the three chapels of East Meon; they are in the dioc. of Winchester, but he does not know the distances between them. The churches and chapels are administered by the bp. as rector, and by vicars. The vicar of East Meon maintains stipendiaries in the chapels, and the bp. and the vicars receive the fruits and tithes of the churches. Replying to qu. xiv, he believes articles iv, v and vi to be true, because this is the common opinion. He has not seen the act of annexation, and does not know if there was one or more, or whether it was temporary or permanent. Replying to qu. xv, he believes articles vii and viii to be true, because he has never heard to the contrary, and after the deaths of Bps. Beauford and Waynflete the prior and conv. received all the bp.'s tithes from these churches and chapels for the duration of the vacancy, but he does not know if they took them in cash or in kind, or who collected them on their behalf. He has not seen any grant or confirmation by which the prior and conv. receive these tithes. To qu. xvi and xvii he replies as above; he does not believe that the abp. or his Official exercised custody or collected the tithes, but they could have done this everywhere except in the parish where he resides. If they did so there, he would have known of it, since he has known the parish for sixty years and has never heard of such things, and neither had his father, who had known the parish for as long. To qu. xix and xx and articles ix–xv, he replies as above; his previous testimony is true, but he cannot say what is public knowledge. To qu. xxi he replies as above.

262   [fo.249] William Weston, butcher, was born in East Meon and has lived there from his youth. He is aged about sixty, is literate and of free status. He is the natural son of John Weston of East Meon, has goods worth about four marks and lives by his own industry. He does not know the present prior, but does know two of the monks. He does not know the abp. He receives no salary from the church of Winchester, and has not seen the articles. He has been in the churches in dispute, and as to distances between them agrees with the first witness. He has not known any of the priors, but has known Bps. Waynflete, Courtenay and Langton. He has seen two vacancies, following the deaths of Waynflete and Courtenay, but does not know when they began or their duration. He does not know who exercises jurisdiction during vacancies, but says that the abp. of Canterbury is the chief (principalior) among all the bps. of England, and therefore believes that he is metropolitan and that the church of Winchester exists under the metropolitan church of Canterbury; but the other propositions in qu. ix he denies. He is not the kinsman or friend of the prior or any monk, nor is he hostile to the abp., from whom he has received no injury. He is not partial, and no incentive has been offered him. His testimony is in accordance with that of the other witnesses. After the death of Waynflete, the tithe of sheaves from East Meon was placed in

a barn there, as it was before the bp.'s death. A monk, of whose name
he is uncertain, came from Winchester and in the name of the prior and
conv. sealed the doors of the barns at East Meon, Wroxfield and Steep
in which the tithes were stored; this he saw himself. Later he saw
the same monk reach an agreement with Simon Bee of East Meon for the
sale of those sheaves on behalf of the prior and conv., and he believes
that Simon sold the sheaves and gave the money to this same monk, but
he does not know the sum of money. During this vacancy, moreover, he
saw this same monk hold a court, and his own father made fine of 5s
with the monk for ten acres of arable and a dwelling belonging to the
church of East Meon, while Simon Bee made fine of 10s for a cottage
which he held of the same church, John Goss made fine of 3s 4d for ten
acres, and John Bull made fine for ten acres. He cannot testify as to
what happened at Hambledon, nor as regards the exercise of <u>sede vacante</u>
jurisdiction. All that he has testified is true and common knowledge,
but he cannot testify as to what was done by the abp. after Bp.
Courtenay's death. He has not seen any grant or confirmation relating
to the rights of the prior and conv. during vacancies, but says that
the abp. cannot have exercised custody or collected the tithes at
East Meon, because he would know, but he could have done this
elsewhere. In reply to qu. xxi he can say no more, except that he has
not seen any mandate or proxy.

263 William Bulbek, <u>agricultor</u>, has lived at East Meon for more than forty
years, and before that at Froyle (<u>Froell'</u>), Ha., where he was born.
He is aged over sixty, is of free status, being the natural son of
John Bulbek of Froyle, has goods and chattels worth at least £40,
lives at his own charge, and is a tenant of the prior and conv. for
lands for which he pays an annual rent of 10s. He has known the
prior and some of the monks for about seven years, especially the
<u>camerarius</u>, to whom he pays his rent, but does not know the abp. He
has been in the churches of Hambledon and East Meon, which are about
three miles distant from each other in the dioc. of Winchester. He
has known only the present prior, but has known Bps. Waynflete,
Courtenay and Langton. He has seen the vacancies following the deaths
of Waynflete and Courtenay, but does not know when they began or their
duration, although he recalls that the see was vacant in the autumn.
To qu. ix he can reply only as he has already testified, and his
reply to qu. x is in accordance with that of the other witnesses. No
promise or incentive has influenced him in this matter. Replying to
qu. xii he agrees with the other witnesses, and testifies that in the
autumn following Waynflete's death a monk, who is now subprior, came
from Winchester and in the name of the prior and conv. admonished the
parishioners of East Meon to divide the tithed sheaves from their own,
since the tithes now belonged to the prior and conv. because of the
vacancy. At his command many of the parishioners divided their
sheaves and the monk had the tithed sheaves placed in the barn for the
use of the prior and conv., he believes, for if anyone else had
received them the parishioners would have heard of it, but as far as
they know the prior and conv. received the tithes of the church and
the chapels peacefully and without disturbance on that occasion and
during other vacancies, except after the death of Bp. Courtenay, when

97

a certain Mr Robert Shirborne, acting in the name of the present abp., held the tithes and all other ecclesiastical dues during the vacancy. This he heard from William Flesshmonger, who told him that he had paid money to Mr Shirborne for his tithes. He cannot say more than this, except that this is common knowledge. Replying to the other questions he agrees with the previous witnesses, but says that the abp. could have visited and done the other things specified without his knowledge.

264 [fo.249v] Thomas Holden, agricultor, has lived for more than fifty years at East Meon, and before that from his youth at Farnham, Sy., where he was born. He is aged over sixty-nine, is literate and of free status, the natural son of William Holden deceased, of Farnham, has goods worth £20 and lives at his own charge. He has known the present prior and some of the monks for twenty years, but does not know the abp. Replying to qu. vi-xii, he agrees in general with Thomas att Hasill, and in addition testifies that after the death of Bp. Beauford the officials of the prior and conv. held a court for the lands and tenements pertaining to the spiritualities of the church of East Meon, and he himself saw Simon Bee and John Weston make fine for lands pertaining to the church of East Meon and to the bp. when he was alive. This court was held within a few days of Beauford's death, a little after Easter, and he died, he recalls, in Easter week some fifty years ago. At the same time the officials sold the fruits and tithes in the barn, and had the doors of the tithe barns at East Meon, Steep and Wroxfield sealed. The witness asked John Hovar, whose daughter he subsequently married, why the prior and conv. had sold him the tithes, and he replied that from time immemorial during a vacancy the monks had received the tithes and other spiritual revenues of East Meon and its chapels. The prior and conv. did likewise after the death of Bp. Wayneflete, and on that occasion the witness was present in a court and saw John Davy of Steep make fine with the officials of the prior and conv. for lands held of the church and of the bp. while he lived. The monks, for the duration of this vacancy, received the tithe of sheaves, some of which were in the barn before the bp.'s death, and some still in the fields. He can testify no further, except to say that after Bp. Courtenay's death Richard Cager of East Meon collected the tithes and revenues of the church and chapels and paid them to Mr Robert Shirborne, the abp.'s commissary, after Shirborne had sworn that if the rights of the prior and conv. were maintained he would save him harmless and would restore to the monks the value of these tithes and revenues, but their value the witness cannot now remember. All that he has testified is true and common knowledge. Replying to the other questions, he agrees with the previous witnesses.

265 Richard Stympe, agricultor, natural son of Thomas Stympe deceased, of West Dean (Westden), Sx., has lived for more than thirty years at East Meon, and before that at Findon (Fyndon), Sx., where he was born. He is aged over fifty-five, is literate and of free status, has goods worth at least £20 and lives at his own charge, is a tenant of the

prior and conv., paying 12s rent, and also receives from them an annual
fee of 40s for the collection of rents with an annual value of £40. He
knows the present prior and some of the monks, and knows the abp. well
by sight. He is also a tenant of the bp. of Winchester, and has at
farm certain revenues of the church of East Meon, for which he pays the
bishop £8 8s 4d per annum. He has known Bps. Wayneflete, Courtenay
and Langton, and has seen two vacancies, after the deaths of Wayneflete
and Courtenay, but he does not know when they began or their duration,
or who administered the church sede vacante, until after Courtenay's
death, when Mr Shirborne administered the see in the abp.'s name. When
examined on the various questions and articles, he agrees with Thomas
Holden, except that he does not know the names of those who made fine
after Wayneflete's death, nor when he died, nor does he know of the
sealing of the barns. He testifies also that after Courtenay's death
the subprior held a court and warned the farmers that they should pay
money to no persons save the prior and conv. Afterwards there arrived
John Gossage, Mr Shirborne's servant, with Mr John Wyett, and they
held a court in the abp.'s name, and here Gossage exhibited a citation
and warned Richard Cager, rent collector for certain of the rectory
tenements, to appear in person before the abp. because he would not
pay Gossage what he had collected. Frightened by this citation, Cager
followed Gossage to Alton (Aulton), a distance of eight miles, and
there made payment to him, and the other farmers also paid because of
fear of citation. The witness himself paid £8 8s 4d, not through fear,
but because he obtained a bond, dated 10 Nov. 1492[1], which he now
exhibits, which acknowledges receipt of this sum on the abp.'s behalf,
and binds John Gossage to discharge the witness of this sum before the
prior and conv., otherwise to recompense him in full. He also testifies
that, after Bp. Courtenay's death, Richard Pynk made fine of 3s 4d with
the subprior for his cottage and ten acres, and afterwards made similar
fine with Gossage, who threatened to evict him if he would not pay.
Otherwise he replies as the other witnesses, but also states that he
was at Taunton when the see of Bath and Wells was vacant and Mr
Shirborne was vicar general in spirituals for the abp., and because of
this Shirborne believed that he had the same jurisdiction in other
dioceses of the province as he had there.

[1. MS: the ix^th yere of Kyng Henry vii^th (1493), but the vacancy
was then over.]

266 [fo.250] William Flesshmonger, agricultor, has lived at Hambledon for
more than twenty-five years, and before that at Southwick (Suthwyk),
Ha., for about twenty-three years. He is aged about sixty, of free
status, the son of Richard Flesshmonger deceased, of Preston Candover,
Ha. He is a tenant of the bp. of Winchester and was farmer of
Hambledon rectory at the time of the dispute and for a long time before.
He has moveable goods worth at least £40 and immoveable goods to the
value of 40s per annum, lives at his own charge by his industry, and
is in receipt of no salary from the prior and conv. nor beneficed by
them. He has not seen the articles nor discussed with anyone what
deposition he should make. He has often been in the churches of
Hambledon and East Meon; the latter has three chapels, but he cannot
name them; one church is three miles from the other. He has known the

present prior for twenty years, and has known Bps. Wayneflete, Courtenay and Langton, but does not know the abp. He has seen the church of Winchester vacant after the deaths of Waynflete and Courtenay, but does not know when the vacancies began, their duration or who administered the see, or was accustomed so to do. After Bp. Courtenay's death, however, Mr Robert Shirborne governed the church in the abp.'s name, and he believes that he exercised all jurisdiction and received all the spiritual revenues. Otherwise he agrees with the previous witnesses. He states that after Bp. Wayneflete's death, about eleven years ago, a monk who is now subprior came to Hambledon and in the name of the prior and conv. enquired from the witness who held the farm of the tithe of sheaves for that year, and he replied that he farmed the tithes. The monk then said to him, 'You do know that the fruits of this church belong to the prior and conv. when the see is vacant?', to which he replied immediately, 'I have mixed the tithed sheaves with my own grain, so I cannot separate them.' The monk then said, 'See that the money for them is paid, and if you are not honest, I shall seal the doors of the barn.' Agreement was reached around the feast of St Andrew [30 November] after Wayneflete's death; the witness paid the prior and conv. the receipts for all the fruits collected by him up to then, some of which were in the barn before the bp.'s death, and some placed there afterwards. The total was £24, and this arrangement was not challenged. After Bp. Courtenay's death, however, Mr Shirborne sent his servant John Gossage to the witness to collect the money, which he refused to pay because he believed that the prior and conv. should hold these revenues, as before. Mr Shirborne then summoned him to the hospital of St Cross at Winchester. When he arrived, Shirborne and the subprior were both there, and a discussion ensued. Mr Shirborne warned the witness that he would have to appear before the abp. within three days, and through fear of this he gave Shirborne an obligation binding himself to payment for the tithe of sheaves for the duration of the vacancy. This obligation was discharged by the payment of £24 to John Gossage. Mr Shirborne then bound himself, by an obligation dated 21 Apr. 1493, to pay to William Flesshmonger at the following Michaelmas £30. The condition of this obligation, specified in a bill dated 29 May 1493, was that it should be void if Mr Shirborne saved Flesshmonger harmless before the prior and conv. of Winchester, otherwise full payment would be made by next Christmas.

[The transcript of the testimony ends at this point.]

COMMISSIONS FOR THE ADMINISTRATION OF THE ESTATES OF INTESTATES WITHIN THE PROVINCE OF CANTERBURY, ISSUED BY THE AUTHORITY OF THE ARCHBISHOP, FROM 9 DECEMBER 1486, THE FIRST YEAR OF HIS TRANSLATION.

> [Note: for full discussion of the archbishop's testamentary jurisdiction, see E.F. Jacob, Reg. Chichele, ii, Introduction, and I.J. Churchill, Canterbury Administration, i, chapter ix.]

267   [fo.251] Commission to Thomas Ayloffe of Sudbury, Sf., to administer the goods of Edmund Ayloffe of Sudbury, whose executors Thomas Ayloffe, John Roberd and Eleanor Ayloffe have refused to act. Inv. by 1 May. Lambeth, 7 Jan. 1497.

268   Commission to James Cokett, natural brother of John Cokett of Barrington (Beryngton), Ca., who has died intestate, to administer his goods. Inv. by 3 May. Lambeth, 7 Jan. 1487.

269   Commission to Alice, widow of Richard Playston of Godstone (Godston), Sy., intestate, to administer his goods. Inv. by 24 June. Lambeth, 11 May 1487.

270   [fo.251v] Commission to John Blagge, chaplain, in the person of his proctor Mr Nicholas Trappe, notary public, to administer the goods of Mr John Ryche, clerk, whose executors have died before the completion of their administration. Inv. by 1 Aug., to be presented by his proctor. Lambeth, 21 May 1487.

271   Commission to Gervase Hoorne, esq., to administer the goods of John Spycer of Canterbury dioc., intestate. Inv. by 1 Aug. Lambeth, 12 June 1487.

272   Commission to Nicholas Wynnesbury and Thomas Wolshawe of Coventry (Coven'), Wa., to administer the goods of Thomas Hadley of Coventry, whose widow and executrix Elizabeth has refused to act. Inv. by 29 Sept. Lambeth, 10 July 2487.

273   Commission to William Boly, citizen of London, to administer the goods of Robert Lenster of London, whose executors have refused to act. Inv. by 29 Sept. Lambeth, 12 July 1487.

274   Commission to Thomas Bury of Bristol (Bristoll') and Thomas Keamys of Shirehampton (Shirenhampton), Gl., in the person of their proctor John Withipoll, literate, to administer the goods of Humphrey Fox of

Bristol, intestate. Inv. by 29 Sept. Lambeth, 8 Aug. 1487.

275 Commission to Mr Walter Moryce, Decr.B., and John Withipoll senior of Bristol (<u>Bristoll</u>') to administer the goods of John Langriche, late master of the hospital of St Mark in Bristol, whose executors have refused to act. Inv. by 1 Nov. Mortlake, 7 Sept. 1487.

276 Commission to Richard Greseley to administer the goods of his father Sir John Greseley, kt., of Drakelow (<u>Drakelowe</u>), Db., intestate. Inv. by 10 Nov. Lambeth, 4 Oct. 1487.

277 [fo.252] Commission to James Yerford, mercer and citizen of London, to administer the goods of Pax Yerford of London. Inv. by 10 Nov. Lambeth, 4 Oct. 1487.

278 Commission to Henry, prior of Lanthony (<u>Lanthon' iuxta Gloucestr'</u>), to administer the goods of Br John Haywarde, canon of Lanthony, intestate. Inv. by 25 Nov. Lambeth, 16 Oct. 1487.

279 Commission to William Maryner and Simon Hoggan of London to administer the goods of John Colrede of the parish of St Edmund in the city of London, intestate. Inv. by 30 Nov. Lambeth, 27 Oct. 1487.

280 Commission to John Sibill of London to administer the goods of Walter James of the parish of St Martin by Ludgate, London. Lambeth, 8 Nov. 1487.

281 Commission to Sybil, widow of Walter James of Southampton, to administer his goods. Inv. by 21 Dec. Lambeth, 8 Nov. 1487.

282 Commission to Laurence Spencer of <u>Moreton Magna</u>, He., to administer the goods of George Spencer of <u>Knaptofte</u>, Coventry and Lichfield dioc., intestate. Inv. by 13 Jan. 1488. Lambeth, 10 Nov. 1487.

283 Commission to John Ewen and Robert Webster of Reach (<u>Riche</u>), Ca., to administer the goods of William Growght of Reach (<u>Rich</u>), intestate. Inv. by 13 Jan. 1488. Lambeth, 24 Nov. 1487.

284 Commission to John Peeke, esq., and William Tailard, esq., to administer the goods of Sir Richard Enderby, kt., of Biggleswade (<u>Bikkylyswade</u>), Bd., intestate. Inv. by 25 March 1488. Lambeth, 29 Nov. 1487.

285 [fo.252v] Commission to Walter Wheler to administer the goods of Robert Forster of London. Inv. by 13 Jan. 1488. Lambeth, 5 Dec. 1487.

286 Commission to Thomas, earl of Arundel, to administer the goods of William, late earl, his father, of Chichester dioc., intestate. Inv. by 1 March 1488. Lambeth, 15 Dec. 1487.

287 Commission to John Nancothon, of the parish of St Swithin in London, to administer the goods of Simon Bartelott alias Amynewe of Salisbury (Sarum), Wlt., intestate. Inv. by 1 March 1488. Lambeth, 21 Dec. 1487.

288 Commission to William Donyngton of Dean (Dene), Bd. or Ox., Lincoln dioc., to administer the goods of John Benett, chaplain, of Dean, intestate. Inv. by 6 Apr. Lambeth, 25 Jan. 1488.

289 Commission to Agnes, widow of Thomas Marshe of London, intestate, to administer his goods. Inv. by 6 Apr. Lambeth, 31 Jan. 1488.

290 Commission to John Hill of Farnham (Farneham), Sy., to administer the goods of Christopher Brounebrede alias Aubre of Farnham. Inv. by 6 Apr. Lambeth, 6 Feb. 1488.

291 Commission to John Horsley, of the parish of St Martin in the Fields near Charing Cross, to administer the goods of William Worme, of the parish of St Clement without Temple Bar, London, intestate. Inv. by 6 Apr. Lambeth, 13 Feb. 1488.

292 [fo.253] Commission to William Mosden of Wittersham (Witersam), Kent to administer the goods of James Mapulsden of Wittersham, intestate. Inv. by 6 Apr. Maidstone, 22 Jan. 1488.

293 Commission to Roger Feytzherbert of Perry Barr (Pery), St., to administer the goods of his father, Nicholas Feytzherbert of Norbury, St., intestate. Inv. by 6 Apr. Lambeth, 13 Feb. 1488.

294 Commission to Mr Thomas Warner, clerk, to administer the goods of John Penhalse of Oxford University, intestate. Inv. by 1 May. Lambeth, 20 March 1488.

295 Commission to Henry Page, generosus, of the city of London, to administer the goods of John Watnoo of the city of London, intestate. Inv. by 15 May. Lambeth, 21 March 1488.

296 Commission to Richard Poley to administer the goods of his father
John Poley, generosus, of Wormingford (Wormyngforde), Ess., intestate.
Inv. by 24 June. Lambeth, 26 Apr. 1488.

297 Commission to Thomas Bowthe of Westminster (Westm') and John Pyke of
the city of London to administer the goods of Robert Lynton, anchorite,
of the parish of All Hallows London Wall, intestate. Inv. by 1 June.
Lambeth, 10 May 1488.

298 Commission to Mr Henry Sutton and Walter Hayles, clerks, and to John
Fitzjames, Henry Burnell and William Maryner, to administer the goods
of Thomas Beauchamp, esq., of Egham, Sy., intestate. Inv. by 24 June.
Lambeth, 12 May 1488.

299 [fo.253v] Commission to Robert Fenne, generosus, of Salisbury, Wlt.,
to administer the goods of Henry Trenniell and Margery his wife of
Urchfont (Orchfounte), Wlt. Inv. by 1 Aug. Lambeth, 20 May 1488.

300 Commission to Robert Vincent, servienti domini de le marquis[1], to
administer the goods of Edmund Edy of Langton [unid.], Lincoln dioc.,
intestate. Inv. by 1 Aug. Lambeth, 21 June 1488.

   [1. Thomas Grey, marquis of Dorset.]

301 Commission to Margery, widow of the deceased, and to Humphrey Cotes,
generosus, to administer the goods of Thomas Hawes of Stony Stratford
(Stony Stratforde), Bk., intestate. Inv. by 1 Aug. Lambeth, 21 June
1488.

302 Commission to James Holme and John Holbeme of Doddiscombleigh
(Doddescome Lye), De., to administer the goods of Christopher Holbeme
of Grays Inn in Holborn. Inv. by 24 Aug. Lambeth, 23 June 1488.

303 Commission to Thomas Warner of Stanmore (Stammer Magna), Mx., to
administer the goods of John Warner, intestate. Inv. by 1 Aug.
Lambeth, 30 June 1488.

304 Commission to Margery, widow of the deceased, and to John Keamys to
administer the goods of John Southougbi of Bristol (Bristoll').
Inv. by 24 Aug. Lambeth, 19 July 1488.

305 [fo.254] Commission to Richard Price and Alice Price, lately widow of
the deceased, to administer the goods of William Tavernere of London
dioc., intestate. Inv. by 6 Oct. Lambeth, 29 July 1488.

306   Commission to John Vaughan, canon, and William Paynell, chaplain, to administer the goods of Thomas Pawlett, r. of Wotton, Lincoln dioc., intestate. Inv. by 6 Oct. Lambeth, 4 Aug. 1488.

307   Commission to John Winto, chaplain, and William Cooke of Norwich (Norwici), to administer the goods of Walter Cooke, chaplain, of Norwich dioc., intestate. Inv. by 1 Nov. Lambeth, 3 Sept. 1488.

308   Commission to Simon Hunbolde of Hartley Westpall (Hartley Waspall), Ha., Winchester dioc., to administer the goods of John Wigley of Sherfield (Shirfelde), Ha., intestate. Inv. by 10 Nov. Lambeth, 4 Sept. 1488.

309   Commission to Matilda and John, widow and son of the deceased, to administer the goods of John Bircholde senior, of the parish of St Sepulchre, London, intestate. Inv. by 1 Nov. Lambeth, 5 Sept. 1488.

310   Commission to Margaret, widow of the deceased, to administer the goods of Henry Dawncy of King's Lynn (Lenn Episcopi), Nf., intestate. Inv. by 25 Dec. Lambeth, 19 Sept. 1488.

311   Commission to John Tailor to administer the goods of Thomas Hokty of Norwich dioc., intestate. Inv. by 25 Dec. Lambeth, 23 Sept. 1488.

312   [fo.254v] Commission to John Grousmouth alias Draper, of the city of Hereford, to administer the goods of John Bynnor of Hereford, intestate. Inv. by 25 Dec. Lambeth, 14 Oct. 1488.

313   Commission to John Bolley, of the parish of St Martin by Ludgate, son of the deceased, to administer the goods of Gertrude Bolley of the city of London. Inv. by 25 Dec. Lambeth, 17 Oct. 1488.

314   Commission to John Gardynere and Thomas Garston of Beaconsfield (Bekennefeld), Bk., to administer the goods of John Gardener of Lincoln dioc., intestate. Inv. by 25 Dec. Lambeth, 22 Oct. 1488.

315   Commission to Thomas Garthe, esq., of the city of London, to administer the goods of Sir John Woode, kt., of the same city, intestate. Inv. by 2 Feb. 1489. Lambeth, 15 Nov. 1488.

316   Commission to Agnes, widow of the deceased, and to Peter Bekett, chaplain of the city of London, to administer the goods of Patrick Rocheford, of the same city. Inv. by 2 Feb. 1489. Lambeth, 15 Nov. 1488.

317   Commission to Richard Pole, son of the deceased, to administer the goods of John Pole of Wilton, Wlt., Salisbury dioc., intestate. Inv. by 2 Feb. 1489. Lambeth, 21 Nov. 1488.

318   Commission to John Sigar, chaplain, of Lincoln dioc., to administer the goods of Stephen Sygar, of the same dioc. Inv. by 2 Feb. 1489. Lambeth, 28 Nov. 1488.

319   [fo.255] Commission to Robert Norman of Bromham (Brumham), Wlt., and Thomas Norman of Sherborne (Shirborne), Do., to administer the goods of John Storke of Shaftesbury (Shaffesbury), Do., intestate. Lambeth, 13 Dec. 1488.

320   Commission to Robert Furnes and Beatrice his wife, lately widow of the deceased, to administer the goods of John Cant of Wisbech (Wisebich), Ca., intestate. Inv. by 19 Apr. Lambeth, 7 Jan. 1489.

321   Commission to Mr Richard Estmonde, S.T.P., to administer the goods of Margaret Doo of Lincoln dioc., intestate. Inv. by 19 Apr. Lambeth, 16 Jan. 1489.

322   Commission to William and Richard Awbrey, sons of the deceased, to administer the goods of William Awbrey of Iver (Evere), Bk., intestate. Inv. by 1 March. Lambeth, 17 Jan. 1489.

323   Commission to John Warde of Southampton to administer the goods of John Walker of the same town, intestate. Inv. by 25 March. Lambeth, 23 Jan. 1489.

324   Commission to Thomas Gerveys of Rochester (Roffens'), Kent, to administer the goods of Thomas Gerveys of the same city, intestate. Inv. by 2 Feb. Lambeth, 23 Jan. 1489.

325   [fo.255v] Identical entry to no.323, except dated Lambeth, 31 Jan. 1489.

326   Commission to Sir Roger Luknor, kt., son of the deceased, Mr Robert Shirborne, Richard Lukenor junior and Roger Lukenor, generosus, to administer the goods of Sir Thomas Lukenor, kt., of Broadhurst

(Brodehirst), Sx., intestate. Inv. by 19 Apr. Lambeth, 10 Feb. 1489.

327 Commission to John and Robert Beverley of the city of London to administer the goods of William Chapman of Stevenage, Hrt., intestate. Inv. by 7 June. Lambeth, 7 March 1489.

328 Commission to Mr William Goode to administer the goods of Mr Richard Newbrigge, v. of Farnham (Farneham), Sy. Inv. by 7 June. Lambeth, 29 March 1489.

329 Commission to Mr Thomas Sutton to administer the goods of John Sutton, of the parish of All Saints, South Lynn (South Lyn'), Nf., intestate. Inv. by 14 Sept. Lambeth, 29 March 1489.

330 Commission to John Abbats, chaplain of Northmoor (More), Ox., to administer the goods of William Yate, v. of Clifton, He., intestate. Inv. by 7 June. Lambeth, 31 May [sic] 1489.

331 Commission to Robert Vincent, servienti domini de le Marques,[1] to administer the goods of John Pluchett, chaplain, of Wilton, Wlt. Lambeth, 31 March 1489.

    [1. See no. 300.]

332 [fo.256] Commission to Richard Hurst, chaplain, to administer the goods of Robert Hurst of Horsham (Horseham), Sx. Inv. by 1 May. Lambeth, 2 Apr. 1489.

333 Commission to the Lady Eleanor Manyngham alias Hungerford, daughter of the deceased, to administer the goods of Anne Molence, widow, intestate, because her pretended testament was not exhibited by John Hampden and John Chambre, chaplain, the executors named in the testament, and was not proved. Inv. by 7 June. Lambeth, 2 May 1489.

334 Commission to Mr William Cockys, clerk, of the city of London, in the person of his proctor Robert Mannyng, chaplain, to administer the goods of John Peryn, chaplain, of Sudborough (Sudburg), Np., Lincoln dioc. Inv. by Trinity Sunday. Canterbury, 20 Apr. 1490 [sic].

335 Commission to Edmund Bowsy and John Tailour of King's Lynn (Leen Episcopi), Nf., to administer the goods of Catherine Smith of the same town. Inv. by 14 June. Lambeth, 2 May 1489.

336   Commission to Nicholas Kirkeby and Catherine Unton of London to administer the goods of Thomas Unton of the city of London. Inv. by 14 June. Lambeth, 16 May 1489.

337   Commission to Robert Atherton, of the parish of St Botolph Aldersgate, to administer the goods of Henry Sewall of the city of London. Inv. by 24 June. Lambeth, 16 May 1489.

338   Commission to Henry Hodingfellys, esq., lately of Stepney (Stevenhithe), Mx., to administer the goods of Morgan Botiller and Alice his wife, of London dioc. Inv. by 1 Aug. Lambeth, 16 May 1489.

339   [fo.256v] Commission to Richard Corpusty of Norwich and John Purdy, chaplain, of Norwich, to administer the goods of Nicholas Purdy, chaplain, of Aylsham (Aylesham), Nf., intestate. Inv. by Feast of the Relics [sic]. Lambeth, 12 July 1489.

340   Commission to John Massay, Henry Shotforde and William Ramesey of the city of London to administer the goods of Robert Carleton of the same city, intestate. Lambeth, 1 June 1489.

341   Commission to Hugh Colstenestoke to administer the goods of Lawrence Wareham. Lambeth, 1 June 1489.

342   Commission to Roger Morton of Haliwell (Halywell), Mx., to administer the goods of Cecily Morton of Crayford (Crayforde), Kent. Inv. by 1 Nov. Lambeth, 3 Aug. 1489.

343   Commission to Mary, widow of the deceased, to administer the goods of Nicholas Isaak of the city of London, intestate. Inv. by 29 Sept. Lambeth, 22 Aug. 1489.

344   Commission to Richard Sangwen to administer the goods of Walter Bruyn of the city of London. Inv. by 1 Nov. Lambeth, 29 Sept. 1489.

345   Commission to dominus William Cole and William Maryner to administer the goods of Elizabeth Bastard of Norwich dioc., intestate. Inv. by 11 Nov. Lambeth, 1 Oct. 1489.

346 [vol.ii, fo.122] <u>Inspeximus</u> by Thomas Brouns, Chancellor and Auditor of Causes of Abp. Henry Chichele, at the request of Richard Godyn, priestly scholar of the College of the Holy Trinity, Bredgar (<u>Bredgare</u>), of letters of King Richard II, sealed with green wax attached with silken thread, and of the foundation or ordination of the college by Mr. Robert Bradgare, sealed with his seal in red wax, and confirmed by Abp. Thomas Arundel and the prior and conv. of Christ Church, Canterbury. As he did not have duplicates of these, which for the welfare of the college he might need to exhibit in distant places, he requested Mr. Brouns to inspect them, and if he found them authentic, to order their exemplification by a notary public.

i)   Royal licence for the foundation, dated at Windsor Castle, 19 July 1392.[1]

ii)   Second foundation charter of Robert de Bradgare, dated at Leeds, 12 Aug. 1398.[2] Notarial testification by John Burbach, clerk of Canterbury diocese, notary public by apostolic authority.

iii) Confirmation by Thomas Arundel, abp. of Canterbury, dated at Canterbury, 8 July 1399.

iv) Confirmation by Prior Thomas and the conv. of Christ Church, Canterbury, dated at Canterbury, 8 July 1399.

v)   In accordance with the power reserved to him in the original statutes of 7 April 1393[3], Robert de Bradgare amends and amplifies the statutes of the college. It shall be governed in perpetuity by a secular clerk in priestly orders, and by two clerk scholars, one of whom shall be a priest. The election and presentation of the chaplain and the priestly scholar and the appointment of the non-priestly scholar shall pertain to Robert Bradgare and Thomas Jeakyn, clerks, and John atte Wyse, the founders, and after their decease, to the two other members of the foundation. The electors of the chaplain shall within forty days choose a suitable man and present him to the ordinary for institution, after which a mandate shall be addressed to the scholars to induct him into corporal possession. Before his induction, the chaplain shall swear the following oath: I, M., chaplain of the College of the Holy Trinity at Bredgar in the dioc. of Canterbury, swear by these Holy Gospels that henceforth with all my strength I will be faithful to the college and will personally reside therein. I will conserve the ordinances of the college made by Robert de Bradgare, clerk of Canterbury dioc., and the rights and liberties of the college, and I will reveal its counsel to no man to the injury of the college or of the scholars. So help me God and these Holy Gospels.

The electors of the priestly scholar shall within forty days choose a suitable man and present him to the ordinary, and before induction he shall swear a similar oath. The electors of the non-priestly scholar shall within twenty days appoint a suitable man, who before his induction shall also swear a similar oath.

The chaplain and scholars shall be subject to the abp., and, sede vacante, to the prior and conv. of Christ Church, Canterbury. The scholars shall be obedient to the chaplain in all his licit and canonical commands. Neither the chaplain nor the scholars shall hold any benefice, etc., by which their personal residence or performance of divine office might be impeded. One of the three members of the foundation shall in perpetuity be chosen from the consanguinity or affinity of Robert de Bradgare. The scholars should first learn to read and sing well, and then learn grammar, until they can compose perfectly six metrical verses from the material prescribed for them by the chaplain. The chaplain and the priestly scholar shall each day in Bredgar church say Matins, Prime, Tierce, Sext, None and Compline, and shall celebrate Mass together, unless one of them is prevented by a reasonable cause. Whenever they so wish they shall say Matins of St Mary, Placebo, Dirige, Vespers and Compline, and on each of the six week-days the seven penitential psalms with the litany according to the use of Sarum. As long as Robert de Bradgare is alive, they shall celebrate Mass and other divine offices whenever and for whomsoever he wishes. On each of the principal feast days and on Sundays the chaplain and scholars, vested in surplices, shall celebrate Matins, high Mass and both Vespers for the welfare of Prior Thomas Chilinden and the chapter of Canterbury, Mr. Adam Mooteron, archd. of Canterbury and their successors, and for the founders, the parishioners of Bredgar and all their benefactors, and for the souls of Simon de Soutbiria and William Courtnay, formerly abps., of Robert Stratton, Auditor of Causes in the Sacred Palace, of Roger Bygood, chaplain, Robert de Bradgare, Gilbert de Swanton, John and his sister Joan le Man, their wives, relatives and children, and of all the faithful departed.

The non-priestly scholar shall be appointed for a term until the completion of his nineteenth year, and shall receive each week for his commons 8½d, and he shall recite the psalm De profundis with the versicles Requiem eternam, Deus cuius miseratione, Miserere and Omnium sanctorum intercessionibus. If, however, in the first four months of his twentieth year he takes subdeacon's orders, he may remain a scholar until the end of his twenty-fifth year, and he shall then receive each week for his commons 10d, and shall in addition each week say Placebo and Dirige, with the forementioned prayers for the souls specified above. In this period when he is aged between twenty and twenty-five, he shall work at the harvest for nine weeks each year, and shall receive a stipend for this work in addition to his commons, but the divine office is not thereby to be impeded.

The chaplains and scholars shall live together and eat and sleep in the college, and if they ever fail to do so, they shall forfeit the revenue of their benefice for one month, unless there is reasonable excuse, which is to be determined by the chaplain.

The chaplain shall have for his wages, and for the provision of lights, vestments and other necessities, twelve marks per annum and the proceeds of the dovecote in the college, together with an acre of wood each year from the woodland called Le Ride. For his dwelling he shall have the high chambers with the cellars to the north of the hall of the college, and he shall have the copse to the east of the hall with the hay, pears and apples growing there.

The priestly scholar shall each year receive twelve marks from the goods of the college, that is, forty shillings at each quarter. The two scholars shall have for their dwelling the high south chamber of the college, with the western cellar beneath it, and the building between the kitchen and the dovecote, with free access thereto.

Each of the three members of the foundation shall each year before Christmas plant three apple trees in the garden of Thernstede, and for this labour the chaplain shall each year receive eight bushels of the best apples, the priestly scholar six bushels and the non-priestly scholar four bushels. So that they shall not be unmindful of the benefits which they have received, each of them shall before their death give a jewel worth forty shillings, or forty shillings in money, to the college. They shall have a chapel in which they may celebrate Mass and other divine offices whenever they wish. The books, vestments and vessels of the college shall not be used outside the college. The chaplain and scholars shall pay the relief and heriot of the court of Hollingbourne due for the tenement of Thornstede from their own goods, not those of the college. The wood from fifty acres of woodland in Hollingbourne (Holyngborn) and Hucking (Huckinge), to the north of the hills of Hollingbourne, shall be felled, with the consent of the scholars, and the profits used for the repair of the college buildings, and for no other purpose. If the chaplain does not maintain the buildings, after he has quit his office he shall be bound to effect repairs at his own expense.

The chaplain and scholars shall continually wear outer garments of russet or black cloth, reaching to mid-thigh, unless for some reasonable cause it is decided otherwise. When stipends have been paid and all other obligations on the college discharged, the chaplain shall draw up an inventory and account of the residue of the proceeds, including receipts for any periods of vacancy in the chaplaincy or scholarships, and he shall render a faithful account to the scholars. The inventory, with the residue of the receipts, shall be placed in a common chest to be used by the chaplain, with the consent of the scholars, for the necessities of the college. This chest shall have three keys, one to be held by each member of the foundation.

In witness of which John atte Vyse, one of the founders, set his seal, as Robert de Bradgare was forestalled from so doing by his death. Dated at Robert de Bradgare's house at Wingham, in the presence of Mr. John Puchelle of Canterbury dioc. and dominus William Boteler of Lichfield dioc., 6 Sept. 1409.

vi)   Confirmation by Thomas Arundel, abp. of Canterbury, dated at Lambeth, 10 Feb. 1410.

vii)   Confirmation by Prior John and the chapter of Canterbury in their chapter house, March 1410.

111

Exemplification of all the foregoing by Mr. Thomas Brouns, who
ordered John Boold, notary public, to draw up these documents in the
form of a public instrument sealed with the seal of Henry abp. of
Canterbury, in the presence of Thomas Creme, esq., of Norwich dioc.,
Thomas Lyllisden, clerk of Canterbury dioc., and John Penwortham,
clerk of Coventry and Lichfield dioc. Notarial exemplification by
John Boolde, clerk of Canterbury dioc., scribe of the acts to
Mr. Brouns in the Court of Audience. Lambeth, 20 Oct. 1430.

[1. CPR 1391-96, p.122.
2. Monasticon, vi (pt iii), 1391-3.
3. Literae Cantuarienses, iii, 15-21.]

INSTITUTIONS, EXCHANGES AND OTHER BUSINESS RELATING TO BENEFICES IN THE DIOCESE OF CANTERBURY, THE ARCHBISHOP'S PECULIAR JURISDICTION AND VACANT SEES, 1487–89.

[Note: the procedure for institution to benefices is fully discussed by E.F. Jacob, Reg. Chichele, i, lxxii–lxxiv.

Unless otherwise stated, all benefices are in the diocese of Canterbury and the county of Kent, and mandates for induction were directed to the archdeacon of Canterbury or his Official.]

347   [fo.128]   Inst. of William Smyth, chaplain, to church of Ruckinge (Rokyng), vac. by res. of William Chaunceler, in the abp.'s collation. Lambeth, 13 Jan. 1487.

348   Inst. of John Dynham, chaplain, to church of Hareway, Thérouanne dioc., vac. by res. of Mr William Shaldoo. P. the king. I. the rs. and chaplains of the Calais jurisdiction.   27 Jan. 1487.

349   Inst. of Theobald Offargall, chaplain, to vic. of Alkham (Alkeham), vac. by res. of Stephen Wylles. P. abbot and conv. of St. Radegund. 7 Feb. 1487.

350   Inst. of John German, chaplain, as one of the two chaplains of the chantry at the altar of St. Nicholas in the church of St. Dunstan-without-the-walls, Canterbury, vac. by d. of Thomas Careys. P. John Rooper, esq. Lambeth, 10 Feb. 1487.

351   [fo.128v]   Inst. of Robert Motton, chaplain, to church of Lower Hardres (Nether Hardys), in the abp.'s collation on this occasion by devolution, according to the decrees of the Lateran Council. Lambeth, 6 Feb. 1487.

352   Inst. of John Norman, chaplain, to church of St. Nicholas, Weybridge (Weybrigge), Sy., in Winchester dioc., vac. by d. of John Lightfoote. P. Mr. John Cooke, clerk. I. archd. of Surrey.   Lambeth, 15 Feb. 1487.

353   Inst. of Thomas Hilp, chaplain of Bath and Wells dioc., to vic. of Lenham (Leenham), vac. by d. of John Hunden, bp. in the Universal Church. P. abbot and conv. of St. Augustine, Canterbury.   Lambeth, 15 Feb. 1487.

354   Presentation to the abp. by Peter, bp. of Exeter and elect of Winchester, by virtue of the concession to him by the king of the temporalities of the see of Winchester, of Mr. William Smith to the

archdeaconry of Winchester, vac. by the consecration of Mr. Robert
Morton as bp. of Worcester. Palace of the bp. of Exeter in London,
22 Feb. 1487.

[fo.129 lacking]

355   [fo.130] Inst. of Mr. William Smyth to the archdeaconry of Winchester,
      vacant by the consecration of Mr. Robert Morton. P. Peter, bp. of
      Exeter [as in no. 354]. I. prior of St.Swithun's, Winchester or his
      deputy, to induct Mr. Smyth either in person or by his proctor.
      Lambeth, 24 Feb. 1487

356   Inst. of Mr. William Smyth, clerk, to the canonry and prebend of
      Wherwell (Wherewell), in the conventual church of Wherwell, Ha.,
      Winchester dioc., vac. by res. of Mr. Robert Morton, D.C.L. P.
      abbess and conv. of Wherwell. I. archd. of Winchester, to induct
      Mr. Smyth either in person or by his proctor. Lambeth, 24 Feb. 1487.

357   Exchange between Mr. Adam Redeshefe, r. of St. Martin, Campe, Thérouanne
      dioc., and Richard Newport, r. of St. Mary Magdalen, Offekerque
      (Hofkyrk), Thérouanne dioc. P. the king. I. commissary of the Calais
      jurisdiction or his deputy. 24 Feb. 1487.

358   Inst. of Christopher Porter, chaplain, to church of Boughton Malherbe
      (Bogton Maleherbe), vac. by d. of Philip Walsh. P. Reginald Sondes,
      generosus. Lambeth, 17 March 1487.

359   Inst. of Oliver Chapman, chaplain, to vic. of St. Margaret at Cliffe
      (Clyff iuxta Dovorr'), vac. by res. of Thomas Nudery. P. prior and
      conv. of St. Martin, Dover. I. Commissary General of Canterbury.
      Lambeth, 22 March 1487.

360   [fo.130v] Inst. of Thomas Harryson, chaplain, to vic. of Chertsey
      (Chertesey), Sy., Winchester dioc., vac. by res. of Thomas Alkok. P.
      abbot and conv. of Chertsey. I. archd. of Surrey. Croydon, 23 March
      1487.

361   Inst. of John Ley, priest, to vic. of Tooting (Totyng), Sy.,
      Winchester dioc., vac. by d. of John Newton. P. prior and conv. of
      St. Mary Overy, Southwark. I. archd. of Surrey. Croydon, 24 March
      1487.

362   Inst. of William Stanes, chaplain, to church of Ockley (Okeley), Sy.,

Winchester dioc., vac. by res. of Mr. Thomas Burteswyll. P. Richard Culpeper and Margaret his wife, and Nicholas Culpeper and Elizabeth his wife, of Chichester dioc. I. archd. of Surrey. 17 March 1487.

363   Inst. of Robert Bilton, priest, to church of Shadoxhurst, vac. by d. of John Blake. P. minister and conv. of Moatenden (Motynden). Lambeth, 13 June 1487.

364   Inst. of John Hervy, Decr. B., to church of St. Michael Crooked Lane in the dy. of Arches, in the apb.'s collation, vac. by d. of Mr. Simon Baxter. I. dean of Arches. Lambeth, 2 June 1487.

365   Inst. of Henry Ediall, chaplain, to church of Saltwood (Saltwoode), in the abp.'s collation, vac. by d. of Mr. John Peese, D.C.L. I. Commissary General of Canterbury or his vicegerent. Lambeth, 16 June 1487.

366   [fo.131] Inst. of Thomas Foster, chaplain, in the person of his proctor Thomas Colman, notary public, to vic. of Petham, vac. by d. of Richard Tanner. P. abbot and conv. of St. Osyth. Lambeth, 9 June 1487.

367   Inst. of Alexander Crowmer, clerk, to free chapel of Radfield (Rodefeld), vac. by d. of Peter Dyngley. P. Richard Lovelasse, generosus. Lambeth, 19 July 1487.

368   Inst. of William Cornell, chaplain, to church of Wormshill (Wormeshill) vac. by d. of James Tiknes. P. Juliana Seintnycoles, widow. 20 July 1487.

369   Inst. of Giles Banes, chaplain, to church of Halstead (Halstede), in Shoreham dy. and the abp.'s immediate jurisdiction, vac. by d. of last incumbent. I. dean of Shoreham. 27 July 1487.

370   Inst. of Miles Chapman, chaplain, to church of Knowlton (Knolton), vac. by d. of Br. Stephen Bekley. P. Br. Robert Egilsfeld, preceptor of Beverley and locumtenens of John Weston, prior provincial of the Hospital of St. John of Jerusalem in England. Lambeth, 30 July 1487.

371   Inst. of Mr. John Cosshon, M.A., in the person of his proctor Mr. Henry Ediall, to church of St. Alphege, Canterbury, in the abp.'s collation. I. Commissary General of Canterbury. Mortlake, 1 Sept. 1487.

372   Inst. of Br. Ingram Fraunces, lately abbot of St. Radegund, to vic.
       of Postling (Postlyng), vac. by d. of Thomas Kyrbither. P. abbot and
       conv. of St. Radegund. Lambeth, 27 Aug. 1487.

373   [fo.131v] Inst. of Br. Robert Johnson, canon, upon the exhibition of
       a legitimate dispensation, to vic. of River (Riperia), vac. by d. of
       Br. James Bradford, canon. P. abbot and conv. of St. Radegund.
       Lambeth, 28 Aug. 1487.

374   Inst. of Thomas Hilp, chaplain of Bath and Wells dioc., to church of
       Snave (Snaves), vac. by d. of Peter Dingley. P. abbot and conv. of
       St. Augustine, Canterbury. Lambeth, 17 Aug. 1487.

375   Inst. of William Petyte, chaplain, to vic. of Milton (Middelton), vac.
       by d. of Peter Dingley. P. abbot and conv. of St. Augustine,
       Canterbury. Lambeth, 17 Aug. 1487.

376   Inst. of Mr. Thomas Lyndeley, S.T.P., to church of Chiddingstone
       (Chedingston), in Shoreham dy. and the abp.'s immediate jurisdiction
       and collation, vac. by d. of Mr. John Woode. I. dean of Shoreham.
       Lambeth, 17 Sept. 1487.

377   Inst. of Mr. Thomas Cooke,D.C.L., to church of Lyminge (Lemynge), vac.
       by d. of Mr. John Peese, D.C.L., in the abp.'s collation. I.
       Commissary General of Canterbury. Lambeth, 26 Sept. 1487.

378   Inst. of Mr. Thomas Frende, J.U.B., as warden or master of the College
       of the Blessed Virgin, SS Thomas of Canterbury and Edward the
       Confessor at Higham Ferrers, Np., vac. by d. of William Bryan, and in
       the abp.'s collation according to the statutes of the college,
       together with his nomination by the abp. to the dean and chapter of
       the collegiate church of Newark, Leicester (novi collegii Leicestr'),
       that they should present him to the bp. of Lincoln as v. of the
       parish church of Higham Ferrers. Mandate to the submaster, or, in
       his absence, one of the permanent fellows, to induct. Lambeth,
       8 Oct. 1487.

379   [fo.132] Inst. of John Wylson, chaplain, to church of Wichling
       (Wychelinge), vac. by res. of Ralph Harington. P. Thomas Adam.
       Lambeth, 11 Oct. 1487.

380   Inst. of William Huett, chaplain, to church of Pluckley (Plukley),
       vac. by res. of Henry Edyall, in the abp.'s collation. Lambeth,
       15 Oct. 1487.

381 Inst. of Mr. John Warde, clerk, to vic. of St. Mary Bredin (Bredden),
Canterbury, vac. by d. of Robert Flete. P. prioress and conv. of
St. Sepulchre, Canterbury. Lambeth, 2 Nov. 1487.

382 Inst. of William Marshall, chaplain, to vic. of Appledore (Appuldur'),
with the dependent chapel of Ebony (Ebney), vac. by d. of Richard
Multon. P. prior and conv. of St. Martin, Dover (Dovorr'). Imposition
of an oath to pay an annual pension of 40s to Br. Robert Overton,
lately vicar. Lambeth, 6 Nov. 1487.

383 Inst. of Robert Harrys, chaplain, to vic. of Thornham (Thorneham),
vac. by res. of John Pratt. P. prior and conv. of St. Mary Magdalen,
Combwell (Combewell). Lambeth, 10 Nov. 1487.

384 [fo.132v] Inst. of Thomas Hemiot, chaplain, to church of Hervelinghen
(Helveryngham), Thérouanne dioc., vac. by d. of William Richemond.
P. the king. I. commissary of the Calais jurisdiction. Lambeth,
14 Nov. 1487.

385 Inst. of Peter Coltherst, chaplain. to church of Brook (Brooke), vac.
by res. of Mr. William Knyght. P. prior and conv. of Christ Church,
Canterbury. Lambeth, 14 Nov. 1487.

386 Inst. of John Colynys, chaplain, to church of St. Peter, Canterbury,
vac. by res. of John Androsone. P. prior and conv. of Christ Church,
Canterbury. Lambeth, 16 Nov. 1487.

387 Inst. of John Cabell, chaplain, to vic. of Wadhurst (Wadehurst), Sx.,
in South Malling deanery and the abp.'s immediate jurisdiction and
collation, vac. by d. of last incumbent. I. dean of South Malling.
Lambeth, 16 Nov. 1487.

388 Nomination by the abp. to the abbot and conv. of St. Saviour,
Bermondsey (Barmondesey), of Mr. William Shaldoo, S.T.B., and
Mr. Robert Shyrborn, M.A., one of whom is to be presented to the
abp. as v. of Croydon, Sy., vac. by res. of Mr. Henry Carpenter,
J.U.B. Lambeth, 17 Nov. 1487.

389 Presentation by Abbot John and the conv. of Bermondsey, according to
the composition drawn up between the abbey and William Courtenay,
abp. of Canterbury, on the occasion of the appropriation of Croydon
church[1], of Mr. William Shaldoo, S.T.B., as v. of Croydon. Before
his induction, he is to take an oath of obedience to the abbot and
conv. as rectors, as specified in the composition. Bermondsey,

21 Nov. 1487.

[1. Reg Courtenay, fo.182.]

390 [fo.133] Inst. of Mr. William Shaldoo, S.T.B., to vic. of Croydon [as in no.389]. I. William Barker, Official of the archd. of Surrey, or the parochial chaplain of Croydon. Lambeth, 3 Dec. 1487.

391 Inst. of John Bostone, chaplain, to the vic. of Lenham, vac. by res. of Thomas Hilpp. P. abbot and conv. of St. Augustine, Canterbury. Lambeth, 18 Dec. 1487.

392 Inst. of Mr. Robert Holer, M.A., to perpetual chantry at the altar of St. Nicholas in Croydon church, vac. by d. of Robert Dady. P. Elizabeth Welden, widow. I. dean of Croydon or his vicegerent. Lambeth, 9 Feb. 1488.

393 Inst. of Thomas Strangways, chaplain, to church of Denton, vac. by res. of John Boston. P. William Mauleverer, esq., and Joan his wife, widow of Thomas Peyton, esq. Lambeth, 17 Feb. 1488.

394 [fo.133v] Inst. of John Terry, chaplain, to church of Peuplingues (Pitham), Thérouanne dioc., vac. by d. of Thomas Marten. P. the king. I. commissary of the Calais jurisdiction. Lambeth, 16 Feb. 1488.

395 Inst. of Thomas Middilton, chaplain, to vic. of St. Margaret at Cliffe (Clyffe iuxta Dovorr'), vac. by d. of Oliver Chapman. P. prior and conv. of St. Martin, Dover. I. Commissary General of Canterbury. Lambeth, 26 Feb. 1488.

396 Inst. of John Lawnde, chaplain, to vic. of Elmstead (Elmstede), vac. by d. of John Ede. P. prior and conv. of St. Gregory, Canterbury. 3 Jan. 1488.

397 Inst. of Mr. Humphrey Hawardyn, D.C.L., to church of Shoreham with the dependent chapel of Otford, in Shoreham dy. and the abp.'s immediate jurisdiction and collation, vac. by d. of Mr. Thomas Hoope, D.C.L. I. dean of Shoreham. Lambeth, 4 March 1488.

398 Inst. of Thomas Hustwayte, chaplain, to church of Oye, Thérouanne dioc., vac. by res. of Thomas Wyrell. P. the king. I. commissary of the Calais jurisdiction. Lambeth, 24 March 1488.

399 Inst. of Thomas Bote, chaplain, to vic. of East Peckham (Estpekham), in Shoreham dy., vac. by res. of Br. Thomas Somerham alias Story. P. Mr. Thomas Downe, r. of East Peckham. I. dean of Shoreham. Lambeth, 2 May 1488.

400 Inst. of Robert Lasynby, chaplain, to vic. or portion of the chapel of St. Peter, Isle of Thanet (insula de Thaneto), annexed to the parish church of Minster (Mynstre), vac. by d. of Richard Martyn. P. abbot and conv. of St. Augustine, Canterbury. Lambeth, 7 June 1488.

401 [fo.134] Inst. of Mr. John Ashton alias Catt, Decr. B., to vic. of Gillingham (Gillyngham), in Shoreham dy., vac. by res. of John Lawe. P. prioress and conv. of SS Mary and Sexburga in Sheppey. I. dean of Shoreham. Lambeth, 10 June 1488 [cf. no. 405].

402 Inst. of Simon Wilkes, chaplain, to church of St. Peter, Dover, vac. by res. of Richard Colfox. P. prior and conv. of St. Martin, Dover. I. Commissary General of Canterbury. Lambeth, 31 March 1497 [sic in MS].

403 Inst. of Richard Ludwhich, chaplain, as one of two chaplains of Arundelles Chauntry in the nave of Christ Church, Canterbury, vac. by d. of William Pope. P. prior and chapter of Christ Church. I. prior of Christ Church. Lambeth, 1 Apr. 1487 [sic in MS].

404 Inst. of Robert Harsett to church of Newington by Lambeth (Newenton), Sy., in the abp.'s immediate jurisdiction and collation, vac. by res. of Nicholas Morton. I. dean of Croydon. Lambeth, 12 June 1488.

405 Inst. of John Lawe, priest, to church of Teynham (Tenham), vac. by res. of John Asshton alias Catt. P. Mr. John Bourgchier, archd. of Canterbury. Lambeth, 9 June 1488 [cf. no. 401].

406 Exchange between Mr. John Hervy, Decr. B., r. of St. Michael Crooked Lane, in the abp.'s immediate jurisdiction, and Mr. Nicholas Bulfynch, Decr. B., r. of Ickham (Ikham), both benefices in the abp.'s collation. I. Commissary General of Canterbury and dean of Arches. 23 June 1488.

407 [fo.134v] Inst. of John Raby, chaplain, to vic. of Grain (Grene), vac. by res. of Thomas Elys, chaplain. P. prioress and conv. of SS Mary and Sexburga in Sheppey (Shepey). I. dean of Shoreham. Lambeth, 22 May 1488.

408   Inst. of Mr. John Argentyn, clerk, to church of St. Vedast, in the abp.'s immediate jurisdiction and collation, vac. by d. of Mr. Skyby. I. dean of Arches. Lambeth, 22 July 1488.

409   Inst. of Mr. William Shaldoo, S.T.B., to church of Guisnes (Guysnes), Thérouanne dioc., vac. by res. of Mr. Richard Hatton, D.C.L. P. the king. I. rs. and chaplains of the Calais jurisdiction. Lambeth, 2 July 1488.

410   Inst. of Mr. Ralph Dalton, M.A., to church of Snargate (Snergate), vac. by res. of Richard Weston, in the abp.'s collation. Lambeth, 12 July 1488.

411   Inst. of John Porsmouth, chaplain, in the person of his proctor William Waugham, literate, to church of Hareway (Herwey), Thérouanne dioc., vac. by res. of John Dynham. P. the king. I. Mr. William Shaldoo, commissary of the Calais jurisdiction. Lambeth, 11 July 1488.

412   [fo.135] Inst. of Nicholas Erle, chaplain, to church of Wormshill (Wormeshill), vac. by d. of William Cornewell, priest. P. Roger Seint Nicholas, generosus. Lambeth, 19 July 1488.

413   Inst. of Robert Beverley, chaplain, to vic. of West Hythe (Westhith), vac. by res. of Thomas George, chaplain. P. Mr. John Bourgchier, archd. of Canterbury. Lambeth, 30 July 1488.

414   Inst. of Roger Wilkys, chaplain, to church of Hames (Hammeswell), Thérouanne dioc., vac. by res. of William Hewett, chaplain. P. the king. I. commissary of the Calais jurisdiction. Lambeth, 9 Oct. 1488.

415   Inst. of Mr. William Pett, Decr.B., to church of Brasted (Brastede), in the abp.'s immediate jurisdiction [Shoreham deanery] and collation, vac. by res. of Mr. Robert Pemberton, Decr. B. An annual pension of £4 is to be paid to the retiring incumbent, as detailed below. Lambeth, 20 Oct. 1488.

416   Details of the pension granted to Mr. Robert Pemberton, who has long ministered well to his flock, but now because of physical weakness and the onset of various ailments is unable to minister effectively and therefore for the good of his parishioners prefers to resign. He has resigned the church of Brasted into the hands of the abp., praying that, as he has no other means of livelihood, he may be assigned an annual pension. Therefore, in order that he does not have to beg,

which would not only be an uncertain means of livelihood, but would
be a disgrace to the priesthood and a reproach to the pastoral
ministry of his ordinary, the abp. assigns to him an annual pension
of £4, payable by the r. of Brasted in equal portions at Michaelmas
and Easter to Pemberton or his assigns at the church of St. Michael
Bishopsgate, the first payment to be made the following Easter.
After those with an interest had been summoned, Mr. Pett consented
and swore to observe this provision, and a similar obligation was
imposed on any of his successors for as long as Pemberton might live,
under penalty of a fine of £10 if any payment was over a month
overdue, half to be disposed in alms by the abp. and half to be paid
to Pemberton. If, however, Pemberton should accept any benefice
with cure, lesser dignity or canonry of any value, or any benefice
without cure to the value of thirteen marks, then the church of
Brasted and its rs. should be exonerated from the payment of such a
pension. Lambeth, 20 Oct. 1488.

417   [fo.135v] Inst. of Mr. Thomas Cottebery, clerk, in the person of his
proctor Mr. John Beele, notary public, to the chantry of St. Nicholas
of Harbledown (Herbal Downe), vac. by res. of Robert Beke. P.
Mr. John Bourgchier, archd. of Canterbury. Lambeth, 27 Oct. 1488.

418   Inst. of John Raby, chaplain, to vic. of St. Martin, Eynsford
(Aynesford), in the abp.'s immediate jurisdiction, vac. by res. of
Mr. Robert Beke. P. Mr. John Haynes, r. of Eynsford. I. dean of
Shoreham. Lambeth, 8 Nov. 1488.

419   [fo.136] Inst. of Andrew Crage, chaplain, to vic. of Grain (Greane)
in the abp.'s immediate jurisdiction, vac. by res. of John Raby. P.
prioress and conv. of SS Mary and Sexburga in Sheppey. I. dean of
Shoreham. Lambeth, 8 Nov. 1488.

420   Inst. of John Clerk, priest, to vic. of Newington near Hythe
(Newenton iuxta Heth), vac. by res. of Mr. Brian Coltherst. P.
Mr. Nicholas Wright the warden and the fellows of the College of SS
Gregory and Martin, Wye. Lambeth, 6 Nov. 1488.

421   Inst. of John Smyth, chaplain, to the chantry of St. Mary in Bocking
(Bokkyng) church, Ess., in the abp.'s immediate jurisdiction, vac.
by res. of John Sawle, chaplain. P. Thomas Fenys, esq. I. dean
of Bocking. Knole, 21 Nov. 1488.

422   Inst. of Richard Idon, chaplain, to the office of penitentiary in
South Malling (Southmallyng) dy., with the church of Stanmer, Sx.,
annexed to that office, in the abp.'s immediate jurisdiction and
collation. I. dean of Shoreham [sic]. Lambeth, 15 Nov. 1488.

423 Inst. of Richard Cooke, chaplain, to church of Chiddingstone
(Chedyngston'), in the abp.'s immediate jurisdiction and collation,
vac. by res. of Mr. Thomas Lyndley, S.T.P. I. dean of Shoreham.
Lambeth, 4 Dec. 1488.

424 [fo.136v] Inst. of Mr. Thomas Lynley, S.T.P., to church of St. Michael,
Paternoster Royal (in Riola), in the abp.'s immediate jurisdiction,
vac. by the inst. of Mr. Robert Smyth to church of Wath in the archdeaconry of Richmond. P. prior and conv. of Christ Church, Canterbury,
at the nomination of the warden of the Mercers' Company, according to
the composition between them[1]. I. dean of Arches. Lambeth, 2 Dec.
1488.

    [1. The church of St. Michael, Paternoster Royal, was held in
    conjunction with the mastership of Whittington College. Normally
    the chaplains selected one of their number for presentation to
    the wardens of the Mercers' Company, who formally appointed the
    master. The wardens of the Mercers' Company then nominated this
    man to the prior and conv. of Christ Church, who were patrons of
    the rectory; see VCH London, i, 578-80.]

425 Inst. of Mr. Matthew Knyveton, M.A., to vic. of Ospringe, vac. by
res. of Richard Wredilsforth. P. Thomas Asshby, master of Ospringe
hospital. Lambeth, 24 Nov. 1488.

426 Inst. of William Cretyng, clerk, to church of St. Mary, Calais,
Thérouanne dioc., vac. by d. of Mr. Thomas Smyth. P. the king. I.
commissary of the Calais jurisdiction. Lambeth, 12 Jan. 1489.

427 Inst. of Richard Acastre, chaplain, to church of St. James, Dover,
vac. by res. of William Riall. P. prior and conv. of St. Martin,
Dover. I. Commissary General of Canterbury. Lambeth, 24 March
1489.

428 Inst. of John Elliott, chaplain, to vic. of East Peckham (Est Pekham),
in the abp.'s immediate jurisdiction, vac. by res. of Thomas Kerver.
P. Mr. Thomas Downe, r. of East Peckham. I. dean of Shoreham.
Lambeth, 7 Feb. 1489.

429 Commission to the bp. of London to examine the proposed exchange
between Robert Grenehode, chaplain of the free chapel of Sheering
(Sheryng), Ess., and John Dynham, r. of Hareway (Harwey), Thérouanne
dioc. 16 Feb. 1488 [sic in MS].

430 Inst. of Mr. Robert Myddleton, D.C.L., to church of St. Dionis

Backchurch (<u>Sancti Dionisii</u> civitatis <u>London</u>'), in the abp.'s immediate
jurisdiction and collation[1], vac. by res. of Mr. Thomas Greteham,
Decr. B. Imposition of an oath to pay to the retiring incumbent an
annual pension to be determined by the abp. I. dean of Arches.
Lambeth, 14 Feb. 1489.

[1. <u>Sic</u> in MS. This church was normally in the gift of the prior
and conv. of Christ Church Canterbury.]

[Note: all ordinands are from Canterbury diocese, unless otherwise stated.]

431 [fo.137] Ordinations celebrated by Richard Martyn, bp. in the Universal Church, by the authority of the abp., in the cathedral church of Canterbury on 1 March 1488.

a. Accolites

John Clerk, to t. of priory of St. Mary Magdalen, Tonbridge (Tunbrigge), Rochester dioc.
Richard Fayting, B.A., of Worcester dioc., by l. d., to t. of Osney abbey, Lincoln dioc.
Thomas Hanselape, William Yorke, ms. of Dover priory.

b. Subdeacons

Br. Edmund Feversham, can. of St. Gregory's, Canterbury.
Henry Newchirch, William Sandwiche, ms. of Boxley (Boxle).

c. Deacons

Stephen Wikham, to t. of St. Gregory's priory, Canterbury.
William Chevenyng, to t. of St. Saviour's, Bermondsey, Winchester dioc.
Alexander Smerden, m. of Boxley.
Thomas Foche, to t. of St. Radegund's abbey.

d. Priest

Br. Thomas Nawte, O.P. of Canterbury.

432 Ordinations celebrated by John abp. of Canterbury in the cathedral church of Canterbury on 5 April 1488, Holy Saturday[1].

a. [fo.137v] Accolites

John Goodhewe
John Ramsey
John Dunster, Christopher Mynster, Richard Somerfield, William Hawkherst, Thomas Maydeston, ms. of St. Augustine, Canterbury.

b. Subdeacons

Fayting, Clerk [as in no.431a].

c. Priests

Chevenyng, Foche [as in no.431c].
Thomas Hooke, of Bangor dioc., by l. d., to t. of hospital of St. John
    the Evangelist, Cambridge (Cantebr'), Ely dioc.
William Holyngborn, m. of St. Augustine, Canterbury.
Br. William Kyrkby, can. of St. Radegund's abbey.

    [1. MS: quarto die Aprilis. Holy Saturday in 1488 fell on 5 Apr.
    (Handbook of Dates, p.159).]

433 Ordinations celebrated by Richard Martyn, bp. in the Universal Church,
by the authority of the abp., in the cathedral church of Canterbury
on 14 Apr. 1487, Holy Saturday[1].

a. Accolites

Nawte [as in no.431d]; Br. Nicholas Dolfyn, O.P. of Canterbury.
John Smyth, of Worcester dioc.

b. Subdeacons

Br. John Boparc, O.F.M. of Canterbury.
Br. Roger Beyveley, Br. George London, O.E.S.A. of Canterbury.
Br. William Holyngborn, can. of Leeds.
William Aisshmynton, to t. of St. Sepulchre's priory, Canterbury.
Nicholas Crosse, of Lincoln dioc., by l. d., to t. of Haliwell priory,
    London dioc.

c. [fo.138] Deacons

Br. John Mortymer, O.F.M. of Canterbury.
Thomas Colley, to t. of St. Mary's hospital, Dover.
Br. Thomas Hariettsham, can. of Leeds.
Br. Thomas Saunder, of the Trinitarian house of Moatenden (Motynden).
Henry Legh, m. of Faversham.
Geoffrey Wellys, to t. of St. Sepulchre's priory, Canterbury.

d. Priests

Thomas Valance, m. of St. Augustine, Canterbury.
Br. John Hebbing, of St. Mary's hospital, Dover.

William Pette, to t. of hospital of St. John the Evangelist, Cambridge.
Br. John Gooldstone, Br. Robert Betterysden, cans. of Leeds.
Alexander Dynes, of Lincoln dioc., to t. of St. Giles's priory,
    Barnwell, Ely dioc.
John Clement, Thomas Farlegh, ms. of Christ Church, Canterbury.
Robert London, Richard Pevensey, ms. of Faversham.
Thomas Brand, to t. of St. Mary's hospital, Dover.
William Cowper, to t. of St. Gregory's priory, Canterbury.

> [1. MS: A.D. millesimo CCCC octuagesimo octavo, but Holy Saturday
> fell on 14 Apr. in 1487 (Handbook of Dates, p.159). This date is
> confirmed by the ordination of Nawte as accolite, and as priest
> in no.431d.]

434 Ordinations celebrated by Richard Martyn, bp. in the Universal Church,
by the authority of the abp., in the parish church of Croydon within
the immediate jurisdiction of the church of Canterbury, on 9 June
1487[1].

a. Accolite

Walter Gaynesford, of Winchester dioc.

b. Subdeacon

Br. Robert Dauson, O.E.S.A. of London.

c. Deacons

Asshmynton [as in no.433b].
Br. William Frere, O.E.S.A. of London.

d. [fo.138v] Priests

Colley, Lee [cf. Legh, as in no.433c].
William Harnehill, to t. of St. Gregory's priory, Canterbury.
Br. Gerard Matheu, O.E.S.A. of London.

> [1. MS: A.D. millesimo CCCC octuagesimo octavo, with octavo
> written over erasure. Ember Saturday following Pentecost fell on
> 9 June in 1487 and 1498. Since Asshmynton, who had been ordained
> subdeacon on 14 April 1487, was now ordained deacon, 1487 is
> almost certainly correct.]

435 Ordinations celebrated by Richard Martyn, bp. in the Universal Church,
by the authority of the abp., in the cathedral church of Canterbury on
22 Sept. 1487[1].

a. Accolites

William Chevenyng.
Thomas Foche.
Sandwich, Newchirch [as in no.431b].
Faversham [as in no.431b]; Br. Walter Caunterbury, can. of St. Gregory,
    Canterbury.

b. Subdeacons

Nawte [as in no.431d].
Smerden [as in no.431c].

c. Deacons

Br. John Ware, O.F.M. of Canterbury.
Nicholas Crofte, of Lincoln dioc., by l. d. [cf. Crosse, in no.433b].
Kyrkby [as in no.432c]; Br. Thomas Caunterbury, can. of St. Radegund's
    abbey.

d. Priests

John Cornewell, William Dovorr, ms. of St. Martin, Dover.
Aisshmynton [as in no.433b].
Geoffrey Wellys of Croydon, in the immediate jurisdiction of the
    church of Canterbury [cf. no.433c].
Br. Thomas Hedcrone, of the Trinitarian house of Moatenden.

    [1. MS: A.D. millesimo CCCC octuagesimo (septimo struck out) octavo.
    Ember Saturday fell on 22 Sept. in 1487 and 1498. Since Nawte,
    who was ordained accolite on 14 Apr. 1487 and priest on 1 March
    1488, was now ordained subdeacon, 1487 must be correct.]

436 [fo.139] Ordinations celebrated by Richard Martyn, bp. in the
Universal Church, by the authority of the abp., in the cathedral
church of Canterbury on 20 Sept. 1488[1].

a. Accolites

David Beere Anelen', of St. Andrew's dioc. in Scotland (Scotia).
Thomas Baxster.
John Raynold.
Edmund Lambherst.
John Pevyngton, can. of Combwell (Combewell).
Henry Salmyston, Richard Teneham, Edmund Litleborn, ms. of
    St. Augustine, Canterbury.
Br. John Mascall, O.E.S.A. of Canterbury.
Br. Cornelius Middilbourgh, O.F.M. of Canterbury.

b. Subdeacons

Br. Herman Horsey, O.F.M. of Canterbury.
William Hikson, to t. of St. Gregory, Canterbury.
Henry Lucas, of Lincoln dioc., by l. d., to t. of Ospringe hospital.

c. Deacons

Br. John Horsham, Br. William Toby, O. Carm. of Sandwich.
Mynster, Somerfeld [as in no.432a].

d. Priest

Br. John Vineria, O.F.M. of Canterbury.

[1. MS: A.D. millesimo CCCCLXXXIX. Ember Saturday fell on
20 Sept. in 1488.]

437 Ordinations celebrated by Richard, bp. in the Universal Church, by
the authority of the abp., in the cathedral church of Canterbury
on 18 Sept. 1490.

a. [fo.139v] Accolites

Walter Naughe, of Meath (Miden') dioc.
John Notingham.
Richard Clyfford.
Robert Gybsonne of Orpington, in Shoreham dy.
Richard Engerst de Sudeden' [? of Sweden].
Thomas Rochestre, can. of Leeds (Ledes).

b. Subdeacons

John Sydingborn, Thomas Langle, cans. of Leeds.
Br. William Wingeham, can. of St. Radegund.

c. Deacon

Edmund Lamherst, to t. of St. Sepulchre, Canterbury.

d. Priests

Hicson [cf. Hikson, as in no.436b].
Heriettesham [as in no.433c].
Caunterbury [as in no.435c].
Feversham [as in no.431b]; Thomas Wellys, can. of St. Gregory,
    Canterbury.

438 Ordinations celebrated by John abp. of Canterbury in the cathedral church of Canterbury on 10 Apr. 1490.

a. Accolites

Henry Medewall, of Winchester dioc.
Walter Senden.
Siddingborn, Langley, Wingham [as in no.437b].

b. [fo.140] Subdeacons

John Sudbury, William Chartham, Thomas Aisshe, John Dunston, John
    Hanfeld, John Elham, ms. of Christ Church, Canterbury.
Br. Cornelius Henrici, O.F.M.
Yorke [as in no.431a].
Pevington [as in no.436a].
Caunterbury [as in no.435a]; Wellys [as in no.437c].
Lawrence Snell, can. of Bilsington.
Lamberhurst [cf. Lamherst, as in no.437c].
Br. Peter Preston, O. Carm. of Losenham (Lasnon).
William Woodeford, to t. of St. Saviour's abbey, Syon.
Br. John Marsshall, O.E.S.A.

c. Deacons

Hollingborn [as in no.433b].
Lucas, Hikson [as in no.436b].
Br. Robert Stephinson, O. Carm. of Losenham.

d. Priests

Henry Arundell, John Menys, John Antony, ms. of Christ Church,
    Canterbury.
Horsham, Toby [as in no.436c].
John Boston, can. of West Langdon.
Gerard Wiseman, O.F.M.
Hanslope [cf. Hanselape, as in no.431a].

439 Ordinations celebrated by John abp. of Canterbury in the cathedral church of Canterbury on 2 Apr. 1491, Holy Saturday.

a. Accolites

Br. Thomas Kyrkby, O.P.
Robert Holyngborn, Nicholas Clement, John Sutton, Robert Shirewood,
    Alexander Staple, John Boxwell, ms. of Christ Church, Canterbury.

John Woodell, Thomas Roose, John Pesemede,not yet with title.
John Lany, can. of Combwell.
John Sheppey, William Chilham, ms. of Faversham.
Edmund Norwiche, can. of St. Radegund's.

b. [fo.140v] Subdeacons

Salmyston, Litilborne [as in no.436a].
Rochestre [as in no.437a].
Thomas Kyrittes, of London dioc., to t. of St. Gregory, Canterbury.
Richard Dover, m. of St. Martin, Dover.
John Barkesore, to t. of Christ Church, Canterbury.

c. Deacons

Sudbury, Charteham, Aysshe [as in no.438b].
Dunster, Hawkeshurst, Maidestone [as in no.432a].
Lawrence Snell, can. of Leeds[1].
Pevyngton [as in no.436a].

d. Priests

Thomas Ikham, Roger Benett, ms. of Christ Church, Canterbury.
Mynster, Somerfeld [as in no.432a].
Langehurst [cf. Lamherst, as in no.437c].
Oliver Huddeston, can. of West Langdon.

    [1. Can. of Bilsington in nos. 438b and 440d.]

440 Ordinations celebrated by Richard, bp. in the Universal Church, by the
authority of the abp., in the cathedral church of Canterbury on
24 Sept. 1491.

a. Accolites

Thomas Worsle, O.P. of Canterbury.
Robert Debekyn, O.F.M., Matthew Pugden, O.F.M.
John Crosse, O.E.S.A., Richard Barham, O.E.S.A.
Clement Wylson, of Lincoln dioc.
Erasmus Mayo.
Arnold Burges, of the Trinitarian house of Moatenden.
Br. Stephen Garard, O.E.S.A.

b. [fo.141] Subdeacons

Br. John de Confluencia, O.P.

Norwiche, Lawny [cf. Lany], Sheppey, Chilham [as in no.439a].
Thomas Berse, to t. of St. Sepulchre, Canterbury.
David Bere, to t. of St. Gregory, Wye.
Roger Chirch.

c. Deacons

Br. Robert Weller, O.F.M.
Wyngham [as in no.437b].
Yorke [as in no.431a]; Dovorr [as in no.439b].
Caunterbury [as in no.435a].
John Barkstere, [cf. Barkesore, no.439b], to t. of St. Gregory,
    Canterbury.

d. Priests

Snell [as in no.438b].
Richard Sednor, to t. of Leeds (Ledys) priory.
Thomas Grenewiche, can. of Bayham (Begham).

441 Ordinations celebrated by John abp. of Canterbury in the cathedral
church of Canterbury on 21 Apr. 1492.

a. Accolites

Thomas Butte.
Thomas Wynfeld.
Richard Kyngiston, John Petham, Robert Thornden, John Aisshford, ms.
    of Christ Church, Canterbury.
Robert Parsalt.
Thomas Jowre, of Norwich dioc., to t. of Eye (Eey) priory.

b. Subdeacons

Worsley, Pagden [cf. Pugden], Dobkyn [cf. Debekyn] [as in no.440a].
Holyngborn, Clement, Shirwood, Sutton, Staphill [as in no.439a].
John Vaughan, of Hereford dioc., by l. d., to t. of St. Guthlac's
    priory, Hereford.

c. Deacons

Br. John de Confluencia, O.F.M.[1]
Dunston, Henfeld, Elham [as in no.438b].
Arnulf Tarry, to t. of Faversham abbey.
Sheppey [as in no.439a].

d. [fo.141v] Priests

Richard Astle, m. of Christ Church, Canterbury.
Norwiche [as in no.439a].

[1. O.P. in no.440b.]

442 Ordinations celebrated by John abp. of Canterbury in the cathedral
church of Canterbury on 6 Apr. 1493.

a. Accolites

William Springet
John Dunster, can. of West Langdon.
Thomas Egerton, can. of Leeds.
Richard Wylton, of Lincoln dioc., to t. of St. Gregory, Canterbury.
William Stevyns.
Thomas Maydeston, m. of Boxley (Boxle).
Br. William Walter, O.E.S.A., Br. Robert Sewte, O.E.S.A.

b. Subdeacons

Boxwell [as in no.439a]; Kyngiston [as in no.441a].
Thomas Wynfeld, to t. of [blank].

c. Deacons

Clement, Sutton, Staple [as in no.439a].
Clement Harding, of Salisbury dioc., by l. d., to t. of New College
    Oxford (noui collegii Winton' in Oxon')
Langley [as in no.437b]; Rochester [as in no.437a].
John Brancheley, m. of Boxley.

d. Priests

Chartham, Dunston [as in no.438b].
John Waltham, m. of Christ Church, Canterbury.
Dunster, Hawkerst, Maydeston [as in no.432a].
Walter Naughley, of Meath (Miden') dioc., by l. d., to t. of St.
    Sepulchre, Canterbury.
Sittyngborn [as in no.437b].

443 [fo.142] Ordinations celebrated by John abp. of Canterbury in the
cathedral church of Canterbury on 29 March 1494.

a. Accolites

Thomas Annselme, Adam Romney, John Appuldor, Thomas Goldwell, John
    Burne, John Dover, John Garard, John Norbury, Richard Feversham,
    William Wynchypp, ms. of Christ Church, Canterbury.
Robert Reynham, Bartholomew Lynsted, cans. of Leeds.
John Lynsey, can. of Combwell.
John Pery.

b. Subdeacons

Petham, Thorndon, Asshford [as in no.441a].
Thendham [cf. Teneham, as in no.436a].
John Notyngham, to t. of St. Gregory, Canterbury.
Egerton [as in no.442a].
William Goodwyn, of Lincoln dioc., by l. d., to t. of Revesby
    (Revisby) abbey, O. Cist.
Peter Westbrok, of Winchester dioc., by l. d., to t. of Tonbridge
    (Tunbrigg') priory.
Wilton [as in no.442a] by l. d.
Thomas Hycson, to t. of St. Gregory, Canterbury.

c. Deacons

Shirwod [as in no.439a]; Kyngston [as in no.441a].
Salmyston, Litilborn [as in no.436a].
Maydston [as in no.442a]; Richard Smardon, m. of Boxley.
Chilham [as in no.439a].

d. Priests

Mr. Hugh Pentwyn, of Norwich dioc., by l. d., to t. of his benefice.
Sudbury [as in no.438b]; Sutton [as in no.439a].
John Franklion, of Worcester dioc., by l. d., sufficiently beneficed.
Mr. Clement Hardyng, of Salisbury dioc., sufficiently dismissed by
    the privilege of New College, Oxford (Collegii Beate Marie Winton'
    in Oxonia).
Hollyngborn [as in no.433b].
William Doebull, to t. of Hagnaby (Hagneby) abbey, Lincoln dioc.

444 [fo.142v] Ordinations celebrated by John abp. of Canterbury in the
cathedral church of Canterbury on 18 Apr. 1495.

a. Accolites

William Ketyllisden.
John Harford, John Newenton, ms. of Faversham (Feversham).

Brs. John Brown, Thomas Cutner, William Cutler, Brian Henley, Herman
   William, O.F.M.

b. Subdeacons

Anselme, Romney, Appuldor, Goldwell, Borne [cf. Burne] [as in no.443a].
Mr. John Gudhew, perpetual fellow of Merton College (Collegio
   Martonio).
John Pesemeth, to t. of St. Gregory, Canterbury.

c. Deacons

Mr. Robert Honywod,B.C.L., to t. of All Souls College, Oxford.
Petham, Thornden, Assheford [as in no.441a].
Launey [cf. Lany, as in no.439a].

d. Priests

Asshe, Eleham [as in no.438b]; Clement, Staple [as in no.439a].
Mr. John Ramsey, to t. of Barnwell (Barnewell) priory, Ely dioc.
Salmyston, Litilborn [as in no.436a].
Br. Michael Benfold; Pogden [cf. Pugden] [as in no.440a].
Chilham [as in no.439a].
Br. Nicholas de Wittey.
Wilton [as in no.442a] by l. d.

445 [fo.143] Ordinations celebrated by John abp. of Canterbury in the
cathedral church of Canterbury on 2 Apr. 1496.

a. Accolites

William Gylingham, Richard Bokyngham, William Sellyng, John Wikham,
   ms. of Christ Church, Canterbury.
Roger Sondland, Robert Glassynbury, John Faram, ms. of Boxley.
Br. Richard Cook, O. Carm. of Sandwich (Sandwico).

b. Subdeacons

Dover, Garard, Feversham, Wynchepe, Reynham, Lynsted, Lynsey [as in
   no.443a].
Dunster [as in no.442a].
Robert Colyns, of Coventry and Lichfield dioc., by l. d., to t. of
   Haliwell (Holywell) priory, London dioc.
Hendley [cf. Henley], Cednor [cf. Cutnor], Brown, Hertford [cf.
   Harford], Newenton [as in no.444a].
Cook [as in no.445a].

c. [fo.143v] Deacons

Ansell [cf. Annselme], Romney, Goldwell, Berne [cf. Burne], Apuldre
   [cf. Appuldor][as in no.443a].
Egerton [as in no.442a].

d. Priests

William Hertford, m. of Christ Church, Canterbury; Henfeld [as in
   no.438b].
Holyngborn, Shirwood [as in no.439a].
Launey [cf. Lany, as in no.439a].
William Snaw, of Lincoln dioc., by l. d., to t. of hospital of
   St. Mary without Bishopsgate (Bisshopgate), London.
Pesemed [cf. Pesemeth, as in no.444b].
Mr. William Garard, to t. of St. Gregory, Canterbury.

446   Ordinations celebrated by John abp. of Canterbury in the cathedral
      church of Canterbury on 25 March 1497, Holy Saturday.

a. Accolites

William Taylor, can. of St. Gregory, Canterbury.
Br. Thomas Fraunch, O. Carm. of Sandwich.
Nicholas Cok.
Brs. John Eustas, John Hastyng, John Billyngton, O.F.M. of Canterbury.

b. Subdeacons

Gyllingham, Bokyngham, Sellyng, Wykham [as in no.445a].
Stephen Tentwarden, James Austen, John Haylsham, Thomas Milton, John
   Downe, Thomas Egerton, ms. of St. Augustine, Canterbury.
Br. John Kyng, O.P. of Canterbury.
William Launde, to t. of St. Gregory's, Canterbury.
Thomas Vincent, can. of Leeds.

c. [fo.144] Deacons

Dover, Garard, Feversham, Wynshepe, Lynsey [as in no.443a].
Thenham [cf. Teneham, as in no.436a].
Br. Theodoric Nobill, O.F.M. of Canterbury.
John Punto, can. of West Langdon.
Henley, Newyngton, Harford [as in no.444a].
Cook [as in no.445a].

135

d. Priests

Robert Asslyn, of London dioc., by l. d., to t. of Barking (Barkyng) abbey, London dioc.
John Gulson, of London dioc., by l. d., to t. of All Souls College, Oxford.
Romney [as in no.443a]; Richard Ryngeston, m. of Christ Church, Canterbury.
Worsley [as in no.440a].
Br. Nicholas Fraunces, O.F.M. of Canterbury.

447 Ordinations celebrated by John abp. of Canterbury in the cathedral church of Canterbury on 14 Apr. 1498, Holy Saturday.

a. Accolites

John Langdon, William Taylor, Christopher Eastry, Nicholas Hull, Hamo Throwle, Thomas Legh, John Crosse, Thomas Hawkerst, John Wyndisborough, ms. of Christ Church, Canterbury.
Robert Gylis, can. of St. Radegund.

b. [fo.144v] Subdeacons

Taylor [as in no.446a].
Br. Thomas Tarry, O.P. of Canterbury.

c. Deacons

Gyllingham, Sellyng, Wykham [as in no.445c].
Br. Lymmus Waley, O. Carm. of Sandwich.
Kyng, Tentwarden, Austen, Haylisham, Milton, Down, Egerton [as in no.446b].

d. Priests

Asshford [as in no.441a]; Anselme [as in no.443a].
Robert Hoton, of York diocese, by l. d., to t. of hospital of St. Thomas Acon (Sancti Thome martiris de Acon), London.
Br. John Gybson, O. Carm. of Sandwich.
Lyndesey [cf. Lynsey, as in no.443a].
Pontow [cf. Punto, as in no.446c].
Harford [as in no.444a].

448 Ordinations celebrated by John abp. of Canterbury in the cathedral church of Canterbury on 31 March 1499.

a.   <u>Accolites</u>

Thomas Launde.
Christopher Materes, to t. of Leeds priory.
Br. George Cresham, O.P. of Canterbury.
Thomas Box.
William Page.
William Bydinden, Robert Feversham, Thomas Teynham, Thomas Leynham,
    ms. of Faversham.

b.   <u>Subdeacons</u>

[The list of ordinands breaks off at this point.]

449 INSTITUTIONS, EXCHANGES AND OTHER BUSINESS RELATING TO BENEFICES IN THE DIOCESE OF CANTERBURY, THE ARCHBISHOP'S PECULIAR JURISDICTION AND VACANT SEES, FROM 10 NOVEMBER 1489.

Inst. of Mr. John Hawkyns, M.A., to church of Ruckinge (Rokinge), vac. by d. of last incumbent, in the abp.'s collation. Lambeth, 10 Nov. 1489.

450 Inst. of John Gooldston, chaplain, to church of Old Romney (Veteri Rompney), vac. by d. of John Bone. P. the king. Lambeth, 4 Dec. 1489.

451 Inst. of John Ryche, chaplain, to church of High Halden (Halden), vac. by res. of John Gooldston, in the abp.'s collation. I. Commissary General of Canterbury. Lambeth, 8 Dec. 1489.

452 Inst. of Richard Ammott, canon regular legitimately dispensed by the Apostolic See, to vic. of Seasalter (Seesalter), vac. by d. of last incumbent. P. prior and conv. of Christ Church, Canterbury. Lambeth, 31 Dec. 1489.

453 Inst. of John Caton, chaplain, to chantry of St. Mary, Herne, vac. by res. of Richard Wyreham, in the abp.'s collation. Lambeth, 4 Jan. 1490.

454 [fo.145v] Inst. of Thomas Edmondson, chaplain, to church of Otterden (Oterynden), vac. by res. of Thomas Sutton. P. John Anger, generosus. Knole, 5 Jan. 1490.

455 Inst. of Thomas Denwey, chaplain, as chaplain of the College of the Holy Trinity, Bredgar (Bradgare), founded for the soul of Robert Bradgare, vac. by d. of John Parterych. P. Alexander Crowmer, non-priestly scholar of the college. I. Alexander Crowmer. Lambeth, 8 Jan. 1490.

456 Inst. of John Kentwell, canon regular, to church of East Langdon (Estlangdon), vac. by d. of John Paston. P. abbot and conv. of St. Augustine, Canterbury. Lambeth, 25 Jan. 1490.

457 Inst. of Robert Swayne, chaplain, to church of Shadoxhurst (Shaddokesherst), vac. by death of Robert Bylton. P. minister and conv. of Moatenden. Lambeth, 26 Jan. 1490.

458 Inst. of Mr. John Warde, B.C.L., to vic. of Waltham, vac. by d. of William Folon. P. prior and conv. of St. Gregory, Canterbury. 5 May 1490.

459 [fo.146] Inst. of Mr. John Alexander, M.A., to church of Hinxhill (Henxhill), vac. by d. of last incumbent, in the abp.'s collation by devolution, according to the decree of the Lateran Council. I. Commissary General of Canterbury. Lambeth, 25 May 1490.

460 Inst. of John Fletcher to vic. of Boxley (Boxle), vac. by d. of John Munden. P. prior and conv. of Rochester. Lambeth, 12 June 1490.

461 Inst. of James Lyall, chaplain, to vic. of Bapchild (Bacchild), vac. by d. of Henry Pysok. P. Edward bp. of Chichester. Lambeth, 16 June 1490.

462 Inst. of William Beele, chaplain, to vic. of Newnham (Newenham), vac. by d. of Henry Farley. P. prioress and conv. of Davington. Lambeth, 17 June 1490.

463 Inst. of John Caton, chaplain, to vic. of Herne, vac. by res. of Mr. Richard Boneauntor, in the abp.'s collation. Imposition of oath to pay the retiring incumbent an annual pension to be determined by the abp. I. Commissary General of Canterbury. Lambeth, 2 July 1490.

464 [fo.146v] Inst. of Christopher Prentise, chaplain, to church of Hever, vac. by d. of Thomas Carteryd. P. prior and conv. of Combwell. I. archd. of Canterbury[1]. Mortlake, 5 Aug. 1490.

   [1. Probably a scribal error, since Hever was in the deanery of Shoreham.]

465 Inst. of Robert Laudevell, chaplain, to vic. of Godmersham, vac. by d. of last incumbent, in the abp.'s collation. I. Commissary General of Canterbury. 28 Aug. 1490.

466 Inst. of Thomas Grene, chaplain, to vic. of Hartlip (Hertlepp), vac. by d. of Thomas Waterladde. P. prior and conv. of Rochester. 29 Aug. 1490.

467 Inst. of Mr. Robert Stale to vic. of Westwell, vac. by d. of last incumbent, in the abp.'s collation. I. Commissary General of Canterbury. 1 Sept. 1490.

468 Inst. of Roger Squier, chaplain, to church of All Saints, Canterbury, vac. by res. of Alan Hyndemarsh. P. abbot and conv. of St. Augustine, Canterbury. Lambeth, 3 Sept. 1490.

469 Inst. of Mr. John Camberton, S.T.P., to church of Latchingdon (Lachindon), Ess., in the abp.'s immediate jurisdiction and collation, vac. by d. of last incumbent. I. dean of Bocking. Lambeth, 10 Sept. 1490.

470 [fo.147] Inst. of John Gybbys, chaplain, to church of Hastingleigh (Hastingligh), vac. by res. of William atte Woode. P. Sir Edward Ponyngis, kt. 25 Sept. 1490 [Cf. no.471.]

471 Inst. of William at Woode to church of Sevington, vac. by res. of John Gybbys. P. John Battle, esq. 28 Sept. 1490. [Cf. no.470.]

472 Inst. of Mr. Richard Spekington to vic. of Lynsted (Lynstede), vac. by d. of James Balgeswy. P. archd. of Canterbury. 17 Oct. 1490.

473 Inst. of Mr. Richard Gotinden, M.A., to vic. of Hernhill (Harnhill), vac. by d. of last incumbent, in the abp.'s collation. I. Commissary General of Canterbury. 7 Nov. 1490.

474 Inst. of Thomas Philipp alias Canton to church of Ripple (Rypill), vac. by d. of John Drake. P. the Lord Morgan, kt., guardian of John Clynton, Lord Clinton and Saye. 1 Dec. 1490.

475 Inst. of Thomas Awood, chaplain, to church of Eythorne (Eythorn), vac. by d. of Mr. John Baker. P. Sir John Gylford, kt. Knole, 7 Dec. 1490.

476 Inst. of John Saunder, chaplain, in the person of his proctor Mr. Henry Cooper, to church of Dymchurch (Demechurch), vac. by d. of William Gelytard. P. abbot and conv. of St. Augustine, Canterbury. 11 Dec. 1490.

477 [fo.147v] Inst. of Mr. Edward Payne to vic. of Hernhill (Harnehill), vac. by d. of last incumbent, in the abp.'s collation. I. Commissary General of Canterbury. Knole, 29 Dec. 1490.

478 Inst. of Richard Pereson, chaplain, to the chantry of the Holy Trinity founded for the soul of Edward the Black Prince in Christ Church,

Canterbury, vac. by d. of last incumbent, in the abp.'s collation. I. his fellow priest in the chantry. Maidstone, 29 Dec. 1490.

479   Inst. of Mr. Roger Chirch, B.C.L., to church of Kenardington (Kenarton), vac. by res. of Thomas at Wood. P. Henry Hoorne, generosus. Maidstone, 6 Jan. 1491.

480   Inst. of John Lylle, chaplain, to church of Leaveland (Leveland), vac. by res. of William FitzJohn. P. Sir Edward Ponynggis, kt. Maidstone, 3 Feb. 1491.

481   Inst. of William Adamson, chaplain, to vic. of Newington near Sittingbourne (Newenton),vac. by res. of Mr. Peter Vasor. P. abbot and conv. of Lessnes. Lambeth, 5 Feb. 1491.

482   Inst. of John Baker, chaplain, to the perpetual chantry in the parish church of Harrow-on-the-Hill (Harrowe super le Hille), Mx., vac. by d. of William Banaster, in the abp.'s immediate jurisdiction and collation by devolution, according to the decree of the Lateran Council. I. dean of Croydon. Lambeth, 7 Sept. 1491.

483   [fo.148] Inst. of William Alkok, chaplain, to church of Goodnestone (Goodneston), vac. by d. of last incumbent. P. Thomas Kempe, esq. Lambeth, 12 Feb. 1491.

484   Inst. of Robert Brownebaker, chaplain, to vic. of Eynsford, vac. by res. of John Rabye. P. Mr. John Haynes, r. of Eynsford,   Lambeth, 15 Feb. 1491.

485   Inst. of Richard Hyne, chaplain, to vic. of St. Clement, Sandwich, vac. by res. of Mr. Edward Payne. P. archd. of Canterbury. Lambeth, 16 Feb. 1491.

486   Inst. of Mr. Alexander Crowmere, M.A., to church of Tunstall, vac. by d. of last incumbent, in the abp.'s collation. I. Commissary General of Canterbury. Lambeth, 1 March 1491.

487   Inst. of Mr. Thomas Cottebury to vic. of St. Stephen, Hackington (Hakyndon), vac. by d. of Mr. Simon Hoggis. P. archd. of Canterbury. Lambeth, 24 March 1491.

488   Inst. of Richard Idon, chaplain, to church of Kingsnorth (Kyngisnorth),

vac. by res. of William Parre, on account of an exchange for the office
of penitentiary in the collegiate church of South Malling (Southmallyng),
Sx., with the church of Stanmer thereto annexed. P. abbot and conv. of
Battle. Canterbury, 28 March 1491. [Cf. no.489.]

489   [fo.148v] Inst. of William Parre to the office of penitentiary in the
collegiate church of South Malling, Sx., with the church of Stanmer
thereto annexed, in the abp.'s immediate jurisdiction and collation,
vac. by res. of Richard Idon. I. dean of South Malling. Canterbury,
29 March 1491. [Cf. no.488.]

490   Inst. of Mr. Henry Cowper, B.C.L., to church of Great Mongeham (Magna
Mungeham), vac. by d. of last incumbent, in the abp.'s collation.
12 Apr. 1491.

491   Inst. of Thomas Colley, chaplain, to the perpetual chaplaincy of the
College of the Holy Trinity, Bredgar (Bradgare), vac. by d. of Thomas
Denneway, in the abp.'s collation on this occasion, according to the
statutes and ordinance of the founders [no.346]. Because there is in
the college no scholar to whom the mandate for induction may be
directed, the mandate is sent to the Commissary General of Canterbury.
Lambeth, 15 Apr. 1491.

492   Inst. of Thomas Balfrer, chaplain, to the priestly scholarship in the
College of the Holy Trinity, Bredgar, vac. by d. of last incumbent, in
the abp.'s collation by devolution [as in no.491]. I. Thomas Colley,
chaplain of the college. Lambeth, 16 Apr. 1491.

493   [fo.149] Inst. of John Lange to church of Burstow (Burstowe), Sy., in
the abp.'s immediate jurisdiction and collation, vac. because William
Hopton, the last incumbent, has entered the Carthusian house of Sheen
(Shene) as a professed monk. I. dean of Croydon. Lambeth, 21 Apr.
1491.

494   Inst. of John Mason, chaplain, to church of Acrise, vac. by res. of
Thomas Ady. P. prior and conv. of Leeds. Lambeth, 20 Apr. 1491.

495   Inst. of John Burgele, chaplain, to vic. of Newnham (Newenham), vac. by
res. of William Beele. P. prioress and conv. of Davington. Lambeth,
30 Apr. 1491.

496   Inst. of Mr. Robert Yonge, M.A., to church of Latchingdon (Lachyndon),
Ess., in the abp.'s immediate jurisdiction and collation, vac. by res.
of Mr. John Camberton, S.T.P. I. Alexander Cooke, curate of
Latchingdon, since the dy. of Bocking is vacant. Lambeth, 3 May 1491.

497   Inst. of Mr. John Camberton, S.T.P., to church of Bocking, in the abp.'s immediate jurisdiction and collation, vac. by d. of last incumbent. I. curate of Bocking, since the dy. is vacant. Lambeth, 4 May 1491.

498   Inst. of Robert Forebas, in the person of his proctor Mr. Robert Dalton, to church of Stowting, vac. by d. of Thomas Byrde. P. Thomas Kempe, esq. Lambeth, 19 May 1491.

499   [fo.149v] Inst. of Mr. Adam Grafton, J.U.B., beloved son of the abp., in the person of his proctor John Norehand, to church of St. Dionis Backchurch, in the abp.'s immediate jurisdiction and collation by devolution, according to the decree of the Lateran Council, vac. by res. of Mr. Robert Middylton, Decr. D. Imposition of oath to pay Mr. Robert Gretham, a previous incumbent, the pension which was assigned to him by the abp. I. dean of Arches. Lambeth, 21 May 1491.

500   Inst. of Nicholas Wright, chaplain, to vic. of St. Nicholas, Isle of Thanet (insula de Thaneto), vac. by d. of Richard Johnson, in the abp.'s collation. I. Commissary General of Canterbury. Lambeth, 25 May 1491.

501   Inst. of Mr. Henry Cooper, Commissary General of Canterbury, to the prebend in the collegiate church of Wingham (Wyngham), vac. by res. of Mr. Edmund Lychefeld, in the abp.'s collation. I. master of the college or his deputy. Lambeth, 5 June 1491.

502   Inst. of Nicholas Yonge, chaplain, to church of Weston-super-Mare, So., Bath and Wells dioc., vac. by res. of Thomas Ousteby, in the abp.'s collation due to the vacancy of the see. An annual pension of ten marks is to be paid to the retiring incumbent for his lifetime, in four instalments at Michaelmas, Christmas, the Annunciation and the Nativity of St. John the Baptist, or within thirteen days of each feast. I. archd. of Wells. Lambeth, 28 July 1491.

503   Inst. of Robert Fuller, chaplain, to vic. of Brenzett (Brensett), vac. by res. of Robert Forebas. P. Mr. Nicholas Wright, the master and the fellows of the College of SS Gregory and Martin, Wye. Lambeth, 10 Aug. 1491.

504   [fo.150] Inst. of Thomas Hookes, chaplain, in the person of his proctor William Maye, literate, to church of Hastingleigh (Hastinglegh), vac. by d. of John Gybbys. P. Sir Edward Ponyngis, kt. Lambeth, 7 Sept. 1491.

505 Inst. of Christopher Lowen, chaplain, to the perpetual chantry in the chapel of St. Stephen in Selling (Sellyng iuxta Sheldewich), vac. by d. of Lewis the chaplain. P. John Norton, generosus. Lambeth, 27 Sept. 1491.

506 Inst. of William Clerk, chaplain, beloved son of the archbishop, to vic. of Bethersden (Betrysden), vac. by d. of Alexander Syday. P. prior and conv. of St. Gregory, Canterbury. Lambeth, 28 Sept. 1491.

507 Inst. of Richard Worcettor, chaplain, to the hospital of St. John the Baptist, Coventry, Coventry and Lichfield dioc., vac. by res. of Mr. Thomas Mylle, archd. of Coventry. P. the king, by virtue of the vacancy of the see. Imposition of oath to pay the retiring incumbent an annual pension of ten marks, as long as Mylle lives and Worcettor holds the benefice. I. John Whitmore, chaplain. 10 Oct. 1491.

508 Inst. of Mr. John Harall, M.A., to church of Boardfield (Bordefeld), vac. by res. of John Burgell. P. prioress and conv. of Davington. Lambeth, 27 Oct. 1491.

509 Notification to Mr. William Shaldoo, S.T.B., Commissary of the Calais jurisdiction, or his deputy, of the exchange between Mr. Adam Redsheff, dean of the college of Westbury-on-Trym (Westbury), Gl., and Mr. William Cretyng, r. of St. Mary, Calais, the exchange having been approved by the bp. of Worcester. P. the king. Mandate to induct Redsheff. Lambeth, 6 Nov. 1491.

510 [fo.150v] Inst. of Mr. Ralph Taylor, M.A., to vic. of St. Nicholas, Romney, vac. by res. of Robert Seggeford. P. warden and fellows of All Souls College, Oxford. Lambeth, 28 Nov. 1491.

511 Inst. of Thomas Parham, clerk, beloved son of the abp., to the canonry and prebend in the collegiate church of St. Chad, Shrewsbury (Salop'), vac. by death of John Englissh, in the abp.'s collation by virtue of the vacancy of the see of Coventry and Lichfield, with the reservation to Englissh of any pension due to him by any right from the canonry and prebend. I. dean of St. Chad's or his vicegerent. Lambeth, 29 Nov. 1491.

512 Inst. of Mr. Thomas Savage, J.U.D., dean of the chapel royal, beloved son of the abp., to church of Rostherne (Rosthorne), Chs., Coventry and Lichfield dioc., in the abp.'s collation sede vacante and by devolution, according to the decree of the Lateran Council. Lambeth, 15 Dec. 1491.

513   Inst. of Nicholas Spenser, chaplain, to church of Farningham (Farnyngham), in the abp.'s immediate jurisdiction and collation, vac. by d. of last incumbent. I. dean of Shoreham. Lambeth, 18 Dec. 1491.

514   [fo.151] Inst. of Mr. Henry Cowper, J.U.B., to church of Adisham (Addesham), vac. by d. of Mr. David Williams, in the abp.'s collation. I. Commissary General of Canterbury. Lambeth, 31 Dec. 1491.

515   Inst. of Mr. Richard Roberdes, Decr.B., to vic. of Preston next Faversham (Preston), vac. by d. of last incumbent, in the abp.'s collation. 3 Jan. 1492.

516   Inst. of Mr. Hugh Yonge, M.A., to church of Stonar (Stonor), vac. by res. of Mr. Andrew Benestede. P. abbot and conv. of St. Augustine, Canterbury. 14 Jan. 1492.

517   Inst. of Thomas Sampson, chaplain, to vic. of Northbourne (Northborne), vac. by d. of Thomas Langley. P. abbot and conv. of St. Augustine, Canterbury. 15 Jan. 1492.

518   Inst. of Robert Gybson, chaplain, to church of Hinxhill (Henxhill), vac. by d. of last incumbent, in the abp.'s collation. 1 Feb. 1492.

519   [fo.151v] Inst. of Mr. Richard Bromefeld, Decr.B., to canonry and prebend of Colwall (Barton Colwall) in Hereford cathedral, vac. by d. of Mr. David Hopton. P. the king, by virtue of the vacancy of the see. I. dean and chapter of Hereford. 19 Feb. 1492.

520   Inst. of John Tarry, chaplain, to church of East Lavant (Lavent), Sx., in the abp.'s immediate jurisdiction and collation, vac. by d. of Mr. Ivo Darell. I. dean of Pagham. 19 Feb. 1492.

521   Inst. of John Hony, chaplain, to church of Sevington, vac. by res. of William Atte Woode. P. John Barry, generosus. 24 Feb. 1492.

522   Inst. of Mr. John Harvy, beloved son of the abp., to church of Monks Risborough (Rysebourgh), Bk., in the abp.'s immediate jurisdiction and collation, vac. by res. of Mr. Thomas Savage. I. dean of Risborough. 24 March 1492.

523   Inst. of Thomas Bayly, chaplain, to church of Great Mongeham (Magna Moungeham), vac. by res. of Mr. Henry Cowper, in the abp.'s collation.

Palace of Canterbury, 6 Apr. 1492.

524   Inst. of Mr. John Wyllyamson. Decr.B., to vic. of Minster in Thanet (Menstre), vac. by res. of Robert Wayneflete. P. abbot and conv. of St. Augustine, Canterbury. Imposition of an oath to pay to the foresaid Robert Durant [sic] an annual pension to be determined by the archbishop, for the duration of his life. Lambeth, 16 May 1492.

525   Inst. of Adrian Castellensis, protonotary of the Apostolic See, nuncio and collector of the pope in England, to church of St. Dunstan in the East, in the abp.'s immediate jurisdiction and collation, vac. by d. of Mr. David Willyams. I. dean of Arches. Lambeth, 17 May 1492.

526   [fo.152] Inst. of John Gooldston, chaplain, to church of Ivychurch (Ivechirch), vac. by d. of Mr. Robert Sturdy, in the abp.'s collation. I. Commissary General of Canterbury. Lambeth, 16 May 1492.

527   Inst. of Mr. James Curson as one of two chaplains of the perpetual chantry founded for the soul of the Black Prince (in bassa capella subtus le Croft) in Christ Church, Canterbury, vac. by d. of Mr. Peter Maxey, in the abp.'s collation by devolution according to the statutes of the chantry[1]. I. Richard Pereson, the other chaplain. Croydon, 27 May 1492.

     [1. Curson was also presented by the crown on 5 May 1492, at Canterbury (CPR 1485-94, p.377).]

528   Inst. of Mr. Robert Sheffeld, M.A., to the canonry and prebend of Pedding (Pyddyng) in the collegiate church of Wingham (Wyngham), vac. by d. of John Ryche, in the abp.'s collation. I. provost of the college. Lambeth, 29 May 1492.

529   Inst. of Richard Martyn, bp. in the Universal Church, to church of Ickham (Ikham), vac. by res. of Mr. John Hervy, in the abp.'s collation. I. Commissary General of Canterbury. Mortlake, 31 May 1492.

530   Inst. of Mr. John Lynley, M.A., to church of Wittersham (Wyttesham), vac. by res. of Richard Martyn, in the abp.'s collation. I. Commissary General of Canterbury. Croydon, 7 June 1492.

531   Inst. of Mr. Roger Bowre, S.T.B., to church of Aldington, vac. by d. of Mr. Robert Sturdy, in the abp.'s collation. I. Commissary General of Canterbury. Croydon, 7 June 1492.

532   Inst. of Mr. Thomas Coppeland, Decr.B., to church of High Halden (Halden), vac. by d. of John Ryche, in the abp.'s collation. Croydon, 7 June 1492.

533   Inst. of Mr. John Jamys, of the royal chancery, to church of Peuplingues (Pytteham), Thérouanne dioc., vac. by res. of John Terry. P. the king. I. Commissary of the Calais jurisdiction or his deputy. Croydon, 10 June 1492.

534   [fo.152v] Inst. of Roger Wylkes, chaplain, to church of Old Romney (Veteri Romney), vac. by res. of Mr. John Jamys. P. the king. I. Commissary General of Canterbury. Croydon, 22 June 1492.

535   Inst. of Richard Saxlyngham, chaplain, to church of Hames (Hammeswell), Thérouanne dioc., vac. by res. of Roger Wylkes. P. the king. I. Commissary of the Calais jurisdiction or his deputy. Croydon, 22 June 1492.

536   Inst. of Henry Goold, chaplain, to church of Elmstone (Elneston) [in Preston hundred], vac. by d. of John Ryche. P. prioress and conv. of SS Mary and Margaret, Dartford (Dertford). Lambeth, 25 June 1492.

537   Inst. of Mr. Robert Dokett, S.T.B., as second cantarist in Arundel's Chantry in the nave of Christ Church, Canterbury, vac. by res. of Mr. James Curson, in the abp.'s collation. I. prior of Christ Church, Canterbury. Lambeth, 29 June 1492.

538   Inst. of Mr. Robert Whetely, M.A., to church of Tunstall (Dunstall), vac. by d. of Mr. Alexander Crowmere, in the abp.'s collation. I. Commissary General of Canterbury. Lambeth, 6 July 1492.

539   Inst. of Mr. Richard Walle, M.A., to church of St. Mary Magdalen, Canterbury, vac. by res. of Mr. John Cornyssh. P. abbot and conv. of St. Augustine, Canterbury. Lambeth, 12 July 1492.

540   Inst. of Mr. Walter Feld, S.T.P., in the person of his proctor John Rumpayne, clerk, to the canonry and prebend in Exeter (Exon') cathedral vac. by res. of Mr. Oliver Kinge. P. Mr. Kinge, by virtue of a royal grant[1]. I. dean of Exeter, or in absence the president of the chapter. Lambeth, 13 July 1492.

     [1. CPR 1485-94, p.389.]

541   [fo.153] Inst. of John Talbott, clerk, in the person of his proctor

Thomas Willyams, chaplain, to free chapel of Radfield (Rodevild) in the parish of Bapchild (Bakchild), vac. by d. of Alexander Crowmere. P. Richard Lovelas, esq. Lambeth, 23 Aug. 1492.

542 Inst. of Mr. Henry Medewall to church of Balinghem (Balyngham), Thérouanne dioc., vac. by d. of last incumbent. P. the king. I. Commissary of the Calais jurisdiction. Lambeth, 30 Aug. 1492.

543 Inst. of Mr. Robert Hacomblen, S.T.B., to vic. of Prescot (Prescote), La., Coventry and Lichfield dioc., vac. by d. of Mr. Richard Lincoln. P. warden and scholars of King's College, Cambridge. I. archd. of Chester. Lambeth, 30 Aug. 1492.

544 Inst. of Robert Cordemaker, chaplain, to church of St. Mary Bothaw (de Bothowe), London, in the abp.'s immediate jurisdiction, vac. by res. of Thomas Roose. P. prior and conv. of Christ Church, Canterbury. I. archd. of Canterbury [sic, recte dean of Arches]. Lambeth, 31 Aug. 1492.

545 Inst. of Mr. Thomas Pevyngton, M.A., to vic. of Orpington (Orpyngton), in the abp.'s immediate jurisdiction, vac. by d. of Robert Taylor. P. Mr. Thomas Wylkinson, r. of Orpington. I. dean of Croydon [sic, recte dean of Shoreham]. Lambeth, 18 Sept. 1492.

546 Inst. of John Fletcher, chaplain, to vic. of Marden (Merdon), vac. by d. of last incumbent. P. abbot and conv. of Lessnes. Lambeth, 25 Sept. 1492.

547 [fo.153v] Inst. of Thomas Grene, chaplain, to the perpetual chantry of St. Nicholas in the church of Croydon, in the abp.'s immediate jurisdiction, vac. by d. of Mr. Robert Hollere. P. Elizabeth Weldon. I. dean of Croydon. Lambeth, 10 Oct. 1492.

548 Inst. of Alexander Frotyngham, chaplain, to the perpetual chantry of Holy Cross in the church of St. Nicholas, Calais, vac. by res. of John Beele. P. the king. I. Commissary of the Calais jurisdiction. Lambeth, 3 Nov. 1492.

549 Inst. of Richard Bysshop, chaplain, in the person of his proctor Thomas Appylby, to the perpetual chantry in the church of Coldred (Colrede), vac. by d. of last incumbent. P. prior and conv. of St. Nicholas, Dover. I. Commissary General of Canterbury. Lambeth, 10 Nov. 1492.

550 Inst. of Mr. John Banester, Decr.B., to the canonry and prebend of Southeram (Southerham) in the collegiate church of South Malling (Southmallyng), Sx., in the abp.'s immediate jurisdiction and collation, vac. by res. of William Peyto. Imposition of oath to pay to the retiring prebendary an annual pension for the duration of his life. I. dean of the college. Lambeth, 10 Nov. 1492.

551 Inst. of Mr. Robert Yonge, M.A., to church of Cheam (Cheyham), Sy., in the abp.'s immediate jurisdiction and collation, vac. by d. of last incumbent. I. dean of Croydon. Lambeth, 11 Nov. 1492.

552 Inst. of Mr. Ralph Hanyes, Decr.B., to church of Latchingdon (Lachingdon), Ess., in the abp.'s immediate jurisdiction and collation, vac. by res. of Mr. Robert Yonge. I. dean of Bocking. Lambeth, 12 Nov. 1492.

553 Inst. of Robert Patynson, chaplain, to vic. of Orpington (Orpyngton), in the abp.'s immediate jurisdiction, vac. by res. of Mr. Thomas Pevyngton. P. r. of Orpington. I. dean of Croydon [sic, recte dean of Shoreham]. Lambeth, 12 Nov. 1492.

554 [fo.154] Inst. of Roger Wilkes, chaplain, to church of Monks Eleigh (Illegh Monachorum), Sf., in the abp.'s immediate jurisdiction and collation, vac. by d. of Thomas Haliday. I. dean of Risborough [sic, recte dean of Bocking]. 13 Nov. 1492.

555 Inst. of John Frankelyn, B.A., to church of Old Romney (Veteris Rumpney), vac. by res. of Roger Wylkes. P. the king. Lambeth, 21 Nov. 1492.

556 Inst. of Richard Wade, chaplain, to vic. of Sittingbourne (Syddingborn), vac. by res. of Mr. Thomas Davy. P. prioress and conv. of Clerkenwell. Lambeth, 7 Dec. 1492.

557 Inst. of Thomas Gouge to the perpetual chantry in the church of St. Mary, Bocking (Bokkynge), in the abp.'s immediate jurisdiction, vac. by res. of William Ripple. P. Thomas Fenys. I. dean of Bocking. Lambeth, 14 Dec. 1492.

558 Inst. of Robert Ward, chaplain, to vic. of East Farleigh (Estfarlegh), in the abp.'s immediate jurisdiction, vac. by res. of William Hildyche. P. master and brethren of the College of All Saints, Maidstone. I. dean of Shoreham. Lambeth, 20 Jan. 1493.

559   Inst. of Richard Chetham, canon regular, to free chapels of Bockingfold (Bokkingfold) and Newstead (Newstede), vac. by res. of William Corbrand. P. prior and conv. of Leeds. Lambeth, 28 Jan. 1493.

560   Inst. of Mr. John Haymer, M.A., to church of Long Ditton (Longditton), Sy., Winchester dioc., vac. by res. of Mr. Robert Yonge. P. prior and conv. of Merton. I. archd. of Surrey. Lambeth, 6 Feb. 1493.

561   [fo.154v] Inst. of Mr. Robert Yonge, M.A., to church of St. Michael, Crooked Lane (in Crokydlane), in the abp.'s immediate jurisdiction and collation, vac. by d. of Mr. Nicholas Bulfinch[1]. I. dean of Arches. Lambeth, 10 Feb. 1493.

       [1. MS: Bulfilch.]

562   Inst. of Mr. Thomas Morton, archd. of Ely, to the prebend in the collegiate church of Wingham (Wyngham), vac. by res. of Mr. Henry Cowper, in the abp.'s collation. I. provost of the college or his deputy. Canterbury, 30 March 1493.

563   Inst. of Mr. Henry Cowper to another prebend in the collegiate church of Wingham, vac. by res. of Mr. John Hervy, in the abp.'s collation. I. provost of the college or his deputy. 31 March 1493.

564   Inst. of Mr. Simon Smyth, M.A., to vic. of Charing (Charyng), vac. by d. of last incumbent, in the abp.'s collation. I. Commissary General of Canterbury. 3 Apr. 1493.

565   Inst. of Mr. James Downes, M.A., to church of Wickham (Wykham), vac. by d. of Mr. William Pydde. P. Joan Inglisthorp, widow. Lambeth, 27 Apr. 1493.

566   Inst. of John Saunders, chaplain, to the prebend in the collegiate church of Wingham vac. by res. of Mr. Thomas Alyn, in the abp.'s collation. Imposition of oath to pay the retiring prebendary an annual pension of 13s 8d for the duration of his life. I. provost of the college. Lambeth, 1 May 1493.

567   Inst. of Robert Dokett, S.T.B., to church of Chevening (Chevenyng), in the abp.'s immediate jurisdiction and collation, vac. by res. of John Potter. The retiring incumbent is to be provided with an annual pension of five marks and victuals. I. dean of Shoreham. Lambeth, 7 May 1493.

568 Inst. of Mr. Robert Curson, M.A., to church of Harbledown (Harbaldown),
vac. by d. of Henry Barradon, in the abp.'s collation. I. Commissary
general of Canterbury. Lambeth, 8 May 1493.

569 [fo.155] Inst. of John Courawgh to church of Betteshanger, vac. by d.
of Mr. William Strenger. P. Roger Lychefeld. 10 May 1493.

570 Inst. of Mr. Thomas Water as second cantarist in Arundel's Chantry in
Christ Church, Canterbury, vac. by res. of Mr. Robert Dokett, in the
abp.'s collation. I. prior of Christ Church. Lambeth, 18 May 1493.

571 Inst. of Mr. John Gry, S.T.B., as second cantarist of the Black Prince's
Chantry (subtus le undrecroft) in Christ Church, Canterbury, vac. by
res. of Mr. James Curson, in the abp.'s collation. I. the other
cantarist. Lambeth, 18 May 1493.

572 Inst. of Mr. Benedict Dodyn to church of Bishop's Waltham (Southwaltham
Episcopi), Ha., Winchester dioc., vac. by res. of Mr. John Mytton by
reason of exchange for the church of Coquelles (Calkewell) in the
marches of Calais. P. Thomas bp. of Salisbury, elect of Winchester,
by reason of the grant to him by the king of custody of the
temporalities. I. archd. of Winchester. Lambeth, 20 May 1493.

573 Inst. of Mr. John Mytton to church of Coquelles (Calkewell), Thérouanne
dioc., vac. by res. of Mr. Benedict Dodyn by exchange. P. the king.
I. Commissary of the Calais jurisdiction. Lambeth, 20 May 1493.

574 Inst. of Richard Sympson, chaplain, in the person of his proctor
Thomas Aston, to church of Campe (Gempe), Thérouanne dioc., vac. by
res. of Mr. Robert Wyseman. P. the king. I. Commissary of the
Calais jurisdiction. Knole, 31 May 1493.

575 [fo.155v] Inst. of Mr. Roger Downevyle, B.C.L., to vic. of SS Cosmus
and Damian in the Blean, vac. by d. of John Egent. P. archd. of
Canterbury. Lambeth, 20 June 1493.

576 Inst. of John Parker, chaplain, to vic. of Seasalter (Sesalter), vac.
by d. of Richard Amott. P. prior and conv. of Christ Church,
Canterbury. Lambeth, 31 July 1493.

577 Inst. of Mr. William Cusshon, M.A., to church of Slindon (Slyndon),
Sx., in the abp.'s immediate jurisdiction and collation, vac. by d.
of last incumbent. I. dean of Pagham. Knole, 4 Sept. 1493.

578   Inst. of Richard Idon, in the person of his proctor John Copland, notary public, to church of Wootton (Wotton), vac. by d. of Robert Neuton. P. Henry Halle, generosus. Knole, 5 Sept. 1493.

579   Inst. of Mr. Robert Stalys, M.A., to church of Brasted (Brastede), in the abp.'s immediate jurisdiction and collation, vac. by d. of last incumbent. I. dean of Shoreham. Knole, 5 Sept. 1493.

580   Inst. of Robert Taylor alias Gybson to vic. of Westwell, vac. by res. of Mr. Robert Stalys, in the abp.'s collation. I. Commissary General of Canterbury. Knole, 7 Sept. 1493.

581   Inst. of Mr. William Axbrigge, M.A., to vic. of East Peckham (Estpecham), in the abp.'s immediate jurisdiction, vac. by d. of William Elyott. P. Hugh Spalding, r. of East Peckham. I. dean of Shoreham. Knole, 7 Sept. 1493.

582   Inst. of Mr. John Hawkyns, M.A., to church of Woodchurch (Woodchirch), vac. by d. of last incumbent, in the abp.'s collation. I. Commissary General of Canterbury. Lambeth, 17 Sept. 1493.

583   Inst. of Richard Hudson, chaplain, to church of Ruckinge (Rokynge), vac. by res. of Mr. John Hawkyns, in the abp.'s collation. I. Commissary General of Canterbury. Lambeth, 20 Oct. 1493.

584   [fo.156] Inst. of Mr. Humphrey Hawardyne, D.C.L., to church of St. Mary Aldermary in the City of London, in the abp.'s immediate jurisdiction and collation, vac. by d. of Mr. Thomas Cook. I. Mr. Hugh Peyntwyn and Mr. Thomas Rowthall. Lambeth, 20 Oct. 1493.

585   Inst. of Mr. William Sutton, S.T.P., to vic. of Ashford (Asshford), vac. by d. of last incumbent, in the abp.'s collation by devolution, according to the decree of the Lateran Council. Lambeth, 20 Oct. 1493.

586   Inst. of Hugh Hegh, chaplain, to vic. of Minster in Thanet (Mynstre), vac. by d. of last incumbent P. abbot and conv. of St. Augustine, Canterbury. Lambeth, 22 Oct. 1493.

587   Inst. of Roger Coltherst, chaplain, to church of Hinxhill (Hengshill), vac. by res. of Robert Taylor. P. William Kempe. Lambeth, 3 Dec. 1493.

152

588 Inst. of Christopher Lytton, chaplain, to church of St. John the
Evangelist, Watling Street (<u>Wattelyng Streete</u>), London, in the abp.'s
immediate jurisdiction, vac. by d. of last incumbent. P. Robert
Lytton, <u>generosus</u>, by virtue of the concession made to him by the
prior and conv. of Christ Church, Canterbury. I. dean of Arches.
Lambeth, 15 Dec. 1493.

589 Inst. of John Medwell, chaplain, to vic. of Elmstead (<u>Elmysted</u>), vac.
by res. of John Lawnde. P. prior and conv. of St. Gregory,
Canterbury. Lambeth, 16 Dec. 1493.

590 Inst. of Mr. John Millett, Decr.D., to church of Charlwood (<u>Charlwod</u>),
Sy., in the abp.'s immediate jurisdiction and collation, vac. by d.
of last incumbent. I. dean of Croydon. Lambeth, 20 Feb. 1494.

591 [<u>fo.156v</u>] Inst. of William Dalton, chaplain, to vic. of Farningham
(<u>Farnyngham</u>), in the abp.'s immediate jurisdiction and collation, vac.
by d. of Nicholas Spencer. I. dean of Shoreham. Lambeth, 3 March
1494.

592 Inst. of Mr. Hugh Peynthwyn, D.C.L., to church of Eynsford (<u>Eynisford</u>),
in the abp.'s immediate jurisdiction and collation, vac. by d. of last
incumbent. I. dean of Shoreham. Lambeth, 10 March 1494.

593 Inst. of Mr. Peter Marshall, S.T.B., to vic. of Tenterden (<u>Tentwarden</u>),
vac. by d. of last incumbent. P. abbot and conv. of St. Augustine,
Canterbury. Lambeth, 11 March 1494.

594 Inst. of Henry Harvy, chaplain, to St. Margaret's hospital for poor
priests in the city of Canterbury, with the parish church thereto
annexed, in the abp.'s collation. Lambeth, 5 May 1494.

595 Inst. of Thomas Halywell, chaplain, to the wardenship of the hospital
of St. Thomas the Martyr at Eastbridge (<u>Eastbrygg</u>), Canterbury, vac.
by res. of Mr. John Burther, in the abp.'s collation. Croydon, 24 May
1494.

596 Inst. of Mr. Robert Heton, M.A., as one of the cantarists of the
Buckingham Chantry in Christ Church, Canterbury, vac. by res. of
Thomas Halywell, in the abp.'s collation. I. his fellow cantarist.
Lambeth, 10 June 1494.

597 [<u>fo.157</u>] Inst. of Mr. John Hawkyns, M.A., to vic. of Lynsted (<u>Lynsted</u>),

vac. by res. of Nicholas Treble. P. archd. of Canterbury. Lambeth, 15 July 1494.

598 Inst. of Mr. John Staunford, M.A., to church of Barfreston (Berverston), vac. by res. of George Chadworth. P. Roger Lichfeld, generosus. Lambeth, 18 Aug. 1494.

599 Inst. of George Chadworth to church of Campe, Thérouanne dioc., vac. by res. of Mr. Richard Newport. P. the king. I. Commissary of Calais jurisdiction. Maidstone, 17 Sept. 1494.

600 Inst. of Thomas Prest, chaplain, to vic. of Rodmersham (Redmarsham), vac. by res. of James Chyrch. P. Br. John Kendall, Prior of the Hospital of St. John of Jerusalem in England. Lambeth, 9 Oct. 1494.

601 Inst. of William Couper to church of Ripple (Ryphill), vac. by res. of Philip Thomas alias Canton [sic, cf. no.474]. P. John, Lord Clinton and Saye. Lambeth, 20 Oct. 1494.

602 Inst. of Roger Norton, chaplain, to church of Oye, Thérouanne dioc., vac. by d. of last incumbent. P. the king. I. Commissary of the Calais jurisdiction. Lambeth, 30 Oct. 1494.

603 Memorandum of receipt of the certificate of Thomas bp. of Rochester concerning an exchange between Robert Segeford, chaplain, v. of Frindsbury (Frinysbury), Rochester dioc., and Richard Smyth, chaplain, v. of Meopham (Mepham), in the abp.'s immediate jurisdiction and collation. The bp. has examined and approved the exchange, and on behalf of and by the authority of the abp. has received from Robert [sic, recte Richard] his resignation of the vic. of Meopham (Mepeham) and has collated the vic. to Richard [sic, recte Robert]. I. dean of Shoreham. Lambeth. 18 Jan. 1495.

604 [fo.157v] Inst. of Thomas Balfre, chaplain, to vic. of Brabourne (Braborne), vac. by d. of Thomas Howlett. P. prior and conv. of Monks Horton (Hortun). Canterbury, 20 Jan. 1495.

605 Inst. of Thomas Hicson, chaplain, in the person of his proctor John Richardson, notary public, to church of St. Mary de Castro, Canterbury, vac. by d. of John Yeman. P. abbot and conv. of St. Augustine, Canterbury. Lambeth, 11 Feb. 1495.

606 Inst. of Thomas Grete, chaplain, in the person of his proctor

Mr. Christopher Middylton, notary public, to church of Seaton (Seyton), Ru., Lincoln dioc., vac. by res. of Edmund Brownyng. P. Humphrey Cunnyngesby, generosus, on this occasion by virtue of the grant of the advowson by Richard Burton and William Sheffield, feoffees of William Beaufo, deceased, and by the concession of Philippa Beaufo his widow, to whom William had bequeathed the advowson for the term of her life, and also by the concession of Elizabeth and Joan his heirs, as was proved by letters patent. I. archd. of Rutland [sic, recte of Northampton]. Lambeth, 14 Feb. 1495.

607 Inst. of William Hicson, chaplain, to the priestly scholarship in the College of the Holy Trinity, Bredgar (Bradgare), vac. by res. of Thomas Balfar, the collation having devolved upon the abp. according to the statutes of the college. I. Thomas Colley, chaplain of the college. Lambeth, 21 Feb. 1495.

608 [fo.158] Inst. of Mr. John Cosshen, M.A., to the Brenchley Chantry in Christ Church, Canterbury, vac. by d. of last cantarist, in the abp.'s collation. I. Commissary General of Canterbury. Canterbury, 29 Apr. 1495.

609 Inst. of John Michell, chaplain, to the perpetual chantry in the church of Reculver (Recolver), vac. by d. of last incumbent, in the abp.'s collation. I. Commissary General of Canterbury. Canterbury, 29 Apr. 1495.

610 Inst. of Leonard Eglesfeld, chaplain, to vic. of Reculver (Recolver), vac. by res. of Mr. John Nutkyn, in the abp.'s collation. I. Commissary General of Canterbury. Canterbury, 29 Apr. 1495.

611 Inst. of Thomas Percy, Augustinian canon, in the person of his proctor Peter Ottley, literate, to vic. of Bexley (Byxle), in the abp.'s immediate jurisdiction, vac. by d. of last incumbent. P. Lewis Hampton, generosus, on this occasion by virtue of the grant of the prior and conv. of Holy Trinity Aldgate, as shown by letters patent. I. dean of Shoreham. Lambeth, 9 May 1495.

612 Inst. of Mr. Clement Hardyng, B.C.L., to vic. of St. Dunstan-without-the-walls, Canterbury, vac. by d. of Richard Long. P. prior and conv. of St. Gregory, Canterbury. Lambeth, 12 May 1495.

613 Inst. of Edmund Lankastre, chaplain, to vic. of Petham, vac. by d. of Thomas Foster. P. abbot and conv. of St. Osyth. Lambeth, 12 May 1495.

614   Inst. of Mr. William Squyrer, M.A., to church of Treborough, So.,
       Bath and Wells dioc., vac. by d. of John Boteller. P. abbot and
       conv. of Cleeve. I. archdeacon of Taunton. Lambeth, 23 May 1495.

615   Inst. of Mr. John Camberton, S.T.P., to the mastership of the
       collegiate church of All Saints, Maidstone (Maydeston), vac. by d. of
       Mr. John Lee, Decr.D., to which he was legitimately elected and
       nominated by Mr. John Freston, M.A., the submaster, and the fellows
       of the college. I. the submaster. Lambeth, 4 June 1495.

616   [fo.158v] Inst. of Mr. Hugh Peynthwyn, D.C.L., to church of Bocking
       (Bockyng), in the abp.'s immediate jurisdiction and collation, vac. by
       res. of Mr. John Camberton. I. dean of Bocking. Mortlake, 9 June
       1495.

617   Inst. of George Thomson, priest, in the person of his proctor, John
       Darell, literate, to church of St. Peter, Canterbury, vac. by d. of
       John Colyns. P. prior and conv. of Christ Church, Canterbury.
       Lambeth, 13 June 1495.

618   Inst. of Owen ap Davit, chaplain, to church of Holy Trinity, Ardley
       (Yerdeley), Ox., Lincoln dioc., vac. by res. of Mr. Richard Blodwell,
       D.C.L. P. Nicholas Cromer, esq. I. archd. of Oxford. Lambeth,
       17 June 1495.

619   Inst. of Thomas Sydrak, chaplain, to church of Pevington (Pevyngton),
       vac. by d. of Thomas Ware. P. William Brent, generosus. Lambeth,
       17 July 1495.

620   Inst. of Mr. Macelinus Ramesey, M.A., to vic. of Patrixbourne
       (Patrikesborn). P. prior and conv. of Merton. I. Commissary General
       of Canterbury. Lambeth, 7 Aug. 1495.

621   Inst. of William Holyngborn, canon regular, in the person of his
       proctor, Mr. John Reed, to church of St. George, Ham by Sandwich
       (Hammys), vac. by res. of Thomas Brand. P. prior and conv. of Leeds.
       Lambeth, 16 Aug. 1495.

622   [fo.159] Inst. of John Kendill to vic. of Hollingbourne (Holyngborn),
       vac. by d. of last incumbent, in the abp.'s collation. I. Commissary
       General of Canterbury. Lambeth, 27 Aug. 1495.

623   Inst. of Mr. Nicholas Treble, B.C.L., deacon, to vic. of St. Mary,

Sandwich (<u>Sandewico</u>), vac. by d. of Mr. John Lee. P. John Bourgchier, archd. of Canterbury. Lambeth, 7 Sept. 1495.

624   Inst. of William Elys, clerk, to church of St. Nicholas, Barton-in-the-Clay (<u>Barton</u>), Bd., Lincoln dioc., vac. by res. of Thomas Yngilby, bp. of Rathlur. P. abbot and conv. of Ramsey. I. archd. of Bedford. Lambeth, 26 Sept. 1495.

625   Inst. of Mr. John Pevyngton, M.A., to church of St. Alphege, Canterbury, vac. by res. of Mr. John Cosshen, M.A., in the abp.'s collation. I. Commissary General of Canterbury. Lambeth, 2 Oct. 1495.

626   Inst. of Thomas Mawdisley to church of Newenden, vac. by res. of William Tredys, in the abp.'s collation. Lambeth, 6 Nov. 1495.

627   Inst. of Mr. Thomas Morton, archd. of Ely, in the person of his proctor, Mr. Henry Cooper, J.U.B., to the mastership of the collegiate church of Wingham, vac. by d. of Mr. Robert Coppyng, in the abp.'s collation. I. Commissary General of Canterbury. Lambeth, 21 Nov. 1495.

628   [fo.159v] Inst. of Mr. Hugh Peynthwyn, D.C.L., to the archdeaconry of Canterbury, vac. by d. of John Bourgchier, in the abp.'s collation. I. Commissary General of Canterbury. Lambeth, 26 Nov. 1495.

629   Inst. of Mr. Thomas Routhall, Decr.D., in the person of his proctor Mr. Thomas Maddis, S.T.P., to church of Bocking (<u>Bockyng</u>), Ess., in the abp.'s immediate jurisdiction and collation, vac. by res. of Mr. Hugh Peynthwyn, D.C.L. I. dean of Bocking. Lambeth, 29 Nov. 1495.

630   Inst. of William Wittilsey, canon regular of the priory of St. Mary, Ravenstone (<u>Ravenston</u>), Bk., as prior of that house, vac. by res. of Br. Ralph Bleese, in the abp.'s gift by devolution and by reason of the vacancy of the see of Lincoln. I. archd. of Buckingham. Lambeth, 1 Dec. 1495.

631   Inst. of Mr. Ralph Hanneys, Decr.B., to church of Marck (<u>Marque</u>), Therouanne dioc., vac. by d. of Thomas Holand. P. the king. I. Commissary of the Calais jurisdiction. Lambeth, 1 Dec. 1495.

632   Inst. of Mr. Edward Underwod, S.T.P., to church of North Crawley, Bk., vac. by d. of Robert Burgon. P. William, bp. of Coventry and Lichfield, and Sir Reginald Bray, by virtue of the grant of John Bohun,

esq., deceased, as demonstrated by letters patent. I. John Bedall, chaplain. Lambeth, 7 Dec. 1495.

633 [fo.160] Inst. of Mr. William Robynson, Decr.D., in the person of his proctor, Mr. John Nans, J.U.D., to church of Latchingdon (Lachyngdon), Ess., in the abp.'s immediate jurisdiction and collation, vac. by res. of Mr. Ralph Haneys, Decr.B. I. dean of Bocking. Lambeth, 7 Jan. 1496.

634 Inst. of Mr. Robert Lynley, M.A., to church of Easington (Esyngton), Ox., vac. by res. of James Willy, in the abp.'s collation by the vacancy of the see of Lincoln. I. archd. of Oxford. Lambeth, 10 Jan. 1496.

635 Inst. of Christopher Lowyn, chaplain, to church of Bonnington (Bonyngton), vac. by d. of Henry Spenser. P. Br. John Kendal, Prior of the Hospital of St. John of Jerusalem in England. Lambeth, 22 Jan. 1496.

636 Inst. of Richard Symson, chaplain, to church of Guisnes (Guysnes), Thérouanne dioc., vac. by res. of Mr. William Shaldo. P. the king. I. Commissary of the Calais jurisdiction. Lambeth, 5 Feb. 1496.

637 Inst. of Mr. John Frankelyn, M.A., to church of Great Mongeham (Mongeham), vac. by d. of John Baly, in the abp.'s collation. I. Commissary General of Canterbury. Canterbury, 9 Apr. 1496.

638 Inst. of Thomas Kyry, chaplain, to a prebend in the collegiate church of Wingham (Wyngham), in the abp.'s collation. I. provost of the college. Canterbury, 10 Apr. 1496.

639 [fo.160v] Inst. of Mr. John Williamson, Decr.B., to the prebend in the collegiate church of Wingham (Wyngham), vac. by d. of Mr. William Pyd, in the abp.'s collation. I. provost of the college. Canterbury, 10 Apr. 1496.

640 Inst. of Thomas Knyght, chaplain, to the perpetual chantry of St. Mary in the parish church of Bocking, in the abp.'s immediate jurisdiction, vac. by res. of Thomas Gothe. P. Thomas Fynys, esq. I. dean of Bocking. Lambeth, 10 Apr. 1496.

641 Inst. of Mr. Stephen Douce, S.T.B., master of the College of St. Michael Royal (in Riola), to church of St. Michael, Paternoster Royal, in the abp.'s immediate jurisdiction and collation by devolution

according to the decree of the Lateran Council, vac. by res. of Mr. Edward Underwood. I. dean of Arches. Knole, 19 Apr. 1496.

642 Inst. of Richard Wyatt, chaplain, in the person of his proctor, Mr. John Barett, notary public, to church of Old Romney (Vetere Rumney), vac. by res. of Mr. John Franklyn. P. the king. I. Commissary General of Canterbury. Lambeth, 11 May 1496.

643 Inst. of Mr. Simon Smyth, Decr.B., to church of Otterden (Otrynden), vac. by res. of Thomas Emmison. P. Thomas Ancher, generosus. Lambeth, 9 June 1496.

644 [fo.161] Inst. of William Ryngsawle, chaplain, to vic. of West Tarring (Terryng), Sx., in the abp.'s immediate jurisdiction, vac. by d. of Richard Smyth. P. Mr. John Thwytes, S.T.B., r. of West Tarring. I. dean of Pagham, or in his absence Christopher Lightbon, literate. Lambeth, 10 June 1496.

645 Inst. of Ralph Blynston, chaplain, to vic. of Ewell, vac. by d. of Henry Ramesay. P. Br. John Kendall, Prior of the Hospital of St. John of Jerusalem in England. Lambeth, 27 June 1496.

646 Inst. of William Water, chaplain, to church of Orlestone (Orlaston), vac. by d. of Adam Rideley. P. Sir William Scott, kt. Lambeth, 27 June 1496.

647 Inst. of Mr. Robert Lathes, S.T.B., in the person of his proctor, Mr. John Richardson, notary public, to church of Bersted (Berghsted), Sx., with chapel of Bognor, in the abp.'s immediate jurisdiction and collation, vac. by res. of William Ryngsaul. I. dean of Pagham. Lambeth, 9 July 1496.

648 Inst. of Richard Symon, B.A., to church of Upper Hardres (Hardis Magna), vac. by d. of last incumbent, in the abp.'s collation by devolution, according to the decree of the Lateran Council. Lambeth, 30 July 1496.

649 Inst. of Mr. Richard Trapp, S.T.P., to church of Eynsford, in the abp.'s immediate jurisdiction and collation, vac. by res. of Mr. Hugh Peynthwyn. I. dean of Shoreham Lambeth, 29 Sept. 1496.

650 [fo.161v] Inst. of John Parker, chaplain, to vic. of Woodnesborough (Wodnesbergh), vac. by d. of Nicholas Bremengham. P. prior and conv. of Leeds. Lambeth, 7 Oct. 1496.

651 Inst. of Thomas Hicson, chaplain, in the person of his proctor, Thomas Hicson junior, to church of St. Peter, Canterbury, vac. by d. of George Thomson. P. prior and conv. of Christ Church, Canterbury. Lambeth, 22 Oct. 1496.

652 Inst. of Thomas Richardson, chaplain, to church of Fordwich (Fordewich), vac. by d. of John Bayle. P. abbot and conv. of St. Augustine, Canterbury. Lambeth, 26 Oct. 1496.

653 Inst. of Thomas Denny, chaplain, in the person of his proctor, Thomas Woodruff, literate, to vic. of Rolvenden (Rollynden), vac. by res. of Ralph Reyner. P. the master and fellows of Cobham College. Imposition of oath to pay the retiring incumbent an annual pension of ten marks for the duration of his life. Lambeth, 18 Jan. 1497.

654 Inst. of Mr. John Smarte, B.C.L., to vic. of Seasalter (Sesalter), vac. by res. of John Parker. P. prior and conv. of Christ Church, Canterbury. Lambeth, 19 Jan. 1497.

655 [fo.162] Inst. of John Whyte, chaplain, to the perpetual chantry of St. Stephen, Selling (Sellyng iuxta Seldwich), vac. by res. of Christopher Lowyn. P. John Langley, generosus. Lambeth, 19 Jan. 1497.

656 Inst. of William Grave, chaplain, to vic. of Boughton Monchelsea (Bocton Monchesey), vac. by res. of John Walker. P. prior and conv. of Leeds. Lambeth, 25 Jan. 1497.

657 Inst. of David Flemyng, chaplain, to church of Ostenhanger (Ostynghanger), vac. by res. of John Whyte. P. Sir Edward Ponynges, kt. Lambeth, 26 Jan. 1497.

658 Inst. of Henry Ediall as master of the collegiate church of Wingham (Wyngham), vac. by d. of Mr. Thomas Morton, in the abp.'s collation. I. Commissary General of Canterbury. Lambeth, 26 Jan. 1497.

659 Inst. of Thomas Haymys, chaplain, to the perpetual chantry commonly called Kent's Chantry (Kentyschauntry), in the church of Headcorn (Hedcron), vac. by res. of John Emson. P. Mr. William Coyne, v. of Headcorn, and John Thomherst and Roger Lityll, wardens. Lambeth, 28 Jan. 1497.

660 Inst. of Mr. John Cook, Decr.B., to church of Norton, vac. by res. of

Richard Harper. P. the king, by virtue of the temporalities of the see of Rochester in his hands during the vacancy of the see[1]. Lambeth, 7 Feb. 1497.

[1. CPR 1494-1509, p.84. This represents an exchange with the church of Runton, Nf.]

661 Inst. of John Bradgar, canon regular of Leeds, to vic. of Marden, vac. by res. of John Flecher. P. abbot and conv. of Lessnes. Lambeth, 24 Feb. 1497.

662 [fo.162v] Inst. of Mr. John Cole, M.A., to church of St. Blaise in Melak (Blasy), Thérouanne dioc., vac. by d. of last incumbent. P. the king. I. Commissary of the Calais jurisdiction. Lambeth, 10 March 1497.

663 Inst. of William Bukley, chaplain, to church of Milstead (Myllsted), vac. by d. of last incumbent, in the abp.'s collation by devolution, according to the decree of the Lateran Council. Canterbury, 11 March 1497.

664 Inst. of Robert Rimer, chaplain, to vic. of East Peckham (Estpecham), in the abp.'s immediate jurisdiction, vac. by res. of Mr. William Axbrygge. P. Mr. Thomas Rothall, Decr.D., proctor of Mr. Hugh Spaldyng, r. of East Peckham. I. dean of Shoreham. Lambeth, 13 March 1497.

665 Inst. of Mr. Roger Church, D.C.L., to church of Sangatte alias Slymes (Sandgate alias Slymys), Thérouanne dioc., vac. by d. of last incumbent. P. the king. I. Commissary of the Calais jurisdiction. Lambeth, 25 March 1497.

666 Inst. of Mr. Thomas Water, S.T.B., to the hospital for poor priests with the church of St. Margaret thereto annexed, Canterbury, vac. by res. of Henry Harvi, last warden, by reason of an exchange for Arundel's Chantry in Christ Church, Canterbury. P. archd. of Canterbury. Lambeth, 22 Apr. 1497.

667 [fo.163] Inst. of Henry Harvi, chaplain, to Arundel's Chantry in Christ Church, Canterbury, vac. by res. of Thomas Water by exchange, as above, and in the abp.'s collation. I. prior of Christ Church. Lambeth, 22 Apr. 1497.

668 Inst. of Mr. John Cole, M.A., to church of Merstham, Sy., in the abp.'s immediate jurisdiction and collation, vac. by res. of Mr. John Ruddyng.

I. dean of Croydon. Lambeth, 11 May 1497.

669   Inst. of John Golson, B.A., to church of Cheam (Cheyham), Sy., in the abp.'s immediate jurisdiction and collation, vac. by res. of Mr. Robert Yong. I. dean of Croydon. Lambeth, 11 May 1497.

670   Inst. of Mr. Thomas Maddeys, S.T.P., to church of Wrotham, in the abp.'s immediate jurisdiction and collation, vac. by d. of Mr. William Pykinham. I. dean of Shoreham. Lambeth, 22 May 1497.

671   Inst. of Richard Weston, chaplain, to church of St. Blaise in Melak (Sancti Blasii), Thérouanne dioc., vac. by res. of Mr. John Cole. P. the king. I. Commissary of the Calais jurisdiction or his deputy. Lambeth, 25 May 1497.

672   Inst. of John Pereson to vic. of Brabourne (Brayborn), vac. by res. of Thomas Balfer. P. prior and conv. of Monks Horton. Lambeth, 4 June 1497.

673   Inst. of Mr. Roland Philipps to vic. of Croydon, vac. by d. of Mr. William Shaldoo, in the abp.'s collation on this occasion by virtue of a grant of Abbot John and the conv. of St. Saviour, Bermondsey (Barmondsey), waiving the normal composition [cf. no.388], and granting the abp. at the next vacancy, for that occasion, complete freedom in presentation. I. dean of Croydon. Lambeth, 18 Nov. 1497.

674   [fo.163v] Inst. of William Kyrkby, canon regular, to vic. of Postling (Postlyng), vac. by d. of last incumbent. P. abbot and conv. of St. Radegund. Lambeth, 19 June 1497.

675   Inst. of Thomas Fyssh, B.A., to church of Hayes (Hese), in the abp.'s immediate jurisdiction, vac. by d. of last incumbent. P. Thomas Wilkynson, r. of Orpington (Orpyngton). I. dean of Shoreham. Lambeth, 22 June 1497.

676   Inst. of William Ratclyff, chaplain, to vic. of Glynde, Sx., in the abp.'s immediate jurisdiction, vac. by d. of last incumbent. P. dean and chapter of the royal free chapel of St. George, Windsor. I. dean of South Malling. Lambeth, 26 July 1497.

677   Inst. of Mr. John Rice, B.C.L., to church of Hadleigh (Hadley), Ess., in the abp.'s immediate jurisdiction and collation, vac. by d. of Mr. William Pykenam. I. dean of Bocking. Lambeth, 26 July 1497.

678 [fo.164] Inst. of Robert Moton, chaplain, to church of Burmarsh (Burwarmarsh), vac. by d. of last incumbent. P. abbot and conv. of St. Augustine, Canterbury. Lambeth, 25 Sept. 1497.

679 Inst. of Robert Peele, chaplain, to vic. of Chilham (Chylham), vac. by d. of last incumbent. P. abbess and conv. of Syon. Lambeth, 27 Sept. 1497.

680 Inst. of Thomas Rose, chaplain, to church of Lower Hardres (Parva Hardys), vac. by res. of Robert Moton. P. prior and conv. of Merton. Lambeth, 14 Oct. 1497.

681 Inst. of John Yong, chaplain, to the perpetual chantry of St. Mary in the parish church of Bocking (Bockyng), in the abp.'s immediate jurisdiction, vac. by res. of Richard Knyght. P. Thomas Fenys. esq. I. dean of Bocking. Lambeth, 7 Nov. 1497.

682 Inst. of Mr. Henry Rawlyns, B.C.L., to church of Lyminge, (Lymnynge), vac. by res. of Mr. Thomas Maddys, in the abp.'s collation. I. Commissary General of Canterbury. Lambeth, 18 Nov. 1497.

683 Inst. of Mr. David Byford, M.A., to church or vic. of Monkton, vac. by d. of Mr. Edward Payne, in the abp.'s collation. I. Commissary General of Canterbury. Lambeth, 18 Nov. 1497.

684 Inst. of Thomas Wryght, chaplain, to the perpetual chantry of Dependen (Depden) in Petham, vac. by res. of William Abraham. P. abbot and conv. of St. Osyth. Lambeth, 22 Nov. 1497.

685 Inst. of William Rosse, chaplain, to church of Auderne (Audern), Thérouanne dioc., vac. by death of John Curson. P. Sir John Turburvyle, kt., by virtue of the grant made to him by the king, as demonstrated by letters patent. I. Commissary of the Calais jurisdiction or his deputy. Lambeth, 25 Nov. 1497.

686 [fo.164v] Inst. of Oliver Crane, chaplain, to vic. of Tong (Tonge), vac. by d. of John Chamber. P. abbot and conv. of Langdon. Lambeth, 7 Dec. 1497.

687 Inst. of William Fayrewey, chaplain, to church of Milstead (Mylsted), vac. by d. of last incumbent. P. the king. Lambeth, 15 Dec. 1497.

688 Inst. of John Newell, chaplain, in the person of his proctor Clement Clerk, to vic. of Moulton (Molton), Sf., in the abp.'s immediate jurisdiction and collation, vac. by d. of last incumbent. Lambeth, 18 Dec. 1497.

689 Inst. of William Ketillysden, chaplain, to vic. of Preston next Wingham (Preston iuxta Wyngham), vac. by d. of Thomas Wattes. P. abbot and conv. of St. Augustine, Canterbury. 26 Jan. 1498 [cf. no. 694].

690 Inst. of John Turbarvyle, chaplain, to church of St. Mary Magdalen, Escalles (Scales), Thérouanne dioc., vac. by res. of Henry Caton. P. the king. I. Commissary of the Calais jurisdiction or his deputy. Lambeth, 13 Feb. 1498.

691 Inst. of Mr. Edward Repe, M.A., to church of Stonar (Stoner), vac. by res. of Mr. Hugh Unge. P. abbot and conv. of St. Augustine, Canterbury. Lambeth, 16 Feb. 1498.

692 [fo.165] Inst. of Thomas Kyrittes, chaplain, to church of Sevenoaks (Sevynoke), in the abp.'s immediate jurisdiction and collation, vac. by d. of last incumbent. I. dean of Shoreham. Lambeth, 21 Feb. 1497.

693 Inst. of Thomas Fogges, clerk, to church of Cheriton (Ceryton), vac. by d. of Thomas Bolney. P. John Fogges, esq. Lambeth, 22 Feb. 1498.

694 Inst. of William Ketyllisden to vic. of Preston next Wingham, vac. by d. of last incumbent. P. abbot and conv. of St. Augustine, Canterbury. Lambeth, 27 Feb. 1498 [cf. no.689].

695 Inst. of Richard Trappe, S.T.P., to church of Newchurch (Newchyrch). vac. by res. of Mr. Henry Rawlyns, in the abp.'s collation. I. Commissary General of Canterbury. 3 March 1498.

696 Inst. of Mr. John Camberton, S.T.P., to church of Eynsford (Aynisford), in the abp.'s immediate jurisdiction and collation, vac. by res. of Mr. Richard Trappe. I. dean of Shoreham. Canterbury, 20 Apr. 1498.

697 Inst. of William Marshall, chaplain, to church of Warehorne (Warehorn), vac. by d. of last incumbent. P. James Pecham, esq. Lambeth, 9 June 1498.

698 Exchange, on the certificate of the bp. of Lincoln, between Mr. Andrew Bensted, M.A., warden of the collegiate church of Northill (Northeyeville), Bd., and Mr. Thomas Randulph, Decr.Lic., r. of Moulton (Multon), Sf., in the abp.'s immediate jurisdiction and collation. I. dean of Bocking. Lambeth, 15 June 1498.

699 Inst. of Christopher Daniell, chaplain, to church of Little Mongeham (Parva Mungeham), vac. by res. of Edmund Brydgill. P. abbot and conv. of St. Augustine, Canterbury. I. Commissary General of Canterbury. Lambeth, 21 June 1498.

700 [fo.165v] Inst. of John Maryet, chaplain, to church of Kingsnorth (Kyngesnorth), vac. by res. of Richard Idon. P. abbot and conv. of Battle. Lambeth, 22 June 1498.

701 Inst. of Mr. William Mody, B.C.L., in the person of his proctor, Mr. John Richardson, to church of St. Mary de Castro, Canterbury, vac. by res. of Thomas Hicson, chaplain. P. abbot and conv. of St. Augustine, Canterbury. Lambeth, 4 July 1498.

702 Inst. of Robert Spersall, chaplain, to church of St. Paul-without-the-walls, Canterbury, vac. by d. of last incumbent. P. abbot and conv. of St. Augustine, Canterbury. Lambeth, 1 Aug. 1498.

703 Inst. of William Chevenyng, chaplain, to church of Kingston (Kyngston), vac. by d. of last incumbent. P. Sir Henry Wentworth, kt. Lambeth, 21 Aug. 1498.

704 Inst. of Br. John Fantyng, O.E.S.A., to church of Blackmanstone (Blakmanston), vac. by d. of last incumbent. P. Thomas Hawte, esq. Lambeth, 11 Sept. 1498.

705 Inst. of Mr. Thomas Andrue, prior of Bilsington (Bilsingdon), to church of Hernhill, vac. by d. of last incumbent, in the abp.'s collation. I. Commissary General of Canterbury. Lambeth, 12 Sept. 1498.

706 Inst. of Mr. Richard Gardiner, M.A., to church of Chiddingstone (Chidingston), in the abp.'s immediate jurisdiction and collation, vac. by d. of last incumbent. I. dean of Shoreham. Knole, 24 Sept. 1498.

707 Inst. of Robert ap John, chaplain, to vic. of Tong, vac. by d. of last incumbent. P. abbot and conv. of Langdon. Knole, 11 Oct. 1498.

708 Inst. of Mr. William Assh, S.T.B., to church of Biddenden (Bydinden), vac. by d. of last incumbent, in the abp.'s collation. Lambeth, 12 Oct. 1498.

709 [fo.166] Inst. of Mr. Hugh Hope, M.A., to church of High Halden (Halden), vac. by d. of Mr. Thomas Copeland, in the abp.'s collation. Lambeth, 28 Oct. 1498.

710 Inst. of Robert Pynnell, chaplain, to the perpetual chantry in the church of St. Bartholomew, Waltham, vac. by d. of last incumbent. P. Thomas Hawte, esq. Lambeth, 15 Nov. 1498.

711 Inst. of Mr. John Holte, M.A., to church of Smarden, vac. by d. of last incumbent, in the abp.'s collation. Lambeth, 15 Nov. 1498.

712 Inst. of Thomas Rilyng, chaplain, to church of Newington (Newyngton), Sy., in the abp.'s immediate jurisdiction and collation, vac. by d. of last incumbent. I. dean of Croydon. Lambeth, 25 Nov. 1498.

713 Inst. of Mr. William Portland, S.T.B., to vic. of Lydd (Lyd), vac. by d. of last incumbent, in the abp.'s collation. I. Commissary General of Canterbury or his vicegerent. Lambeth, 28 Nov. 1498.

714 Inst. of Mr. Nicholas Leyns, B.C.L., to church of St. Blaise in Melak (Sancti Blasii), Thérouanne dioc., vac. by d. of Richard Weston. P. the king. I. Commissary of the Calais jurisdiction or his deputy. Lambeth, 29 Nov. 1498.

715 Inst. of Mr. Peter Marsshal, S.T.B., to church of Faversham (Feversham), vac. by d. of last incumbent. P. abbot and conv. of St. Augustine, Canterbury. Lambeth, 30 Nov. 1498.

716 Inst. of Thomas Graunt, chaplain, to vic. of Rodmersham, vac. by d. of last incumbent. P. Br. John Kendall, Prior of the Hospital of St. John of Jerusalem in England. Lambeth, 4 Jan. 1499.

717 [fo.166v] Inst. of Maurice Tyndale, chaplain, to the office of penitentiary in the collegiate church of South Malling (Southmallyng), Sx., with the church of Stanmer thereto annexed, in the abp.'s immediate jurisdiction and collation, vac. by res. of William Par. I. dean of the college. Lambeth, 29 Jan. 1499.

718   Inst. of Mr. John Wodhowse, J.U.B., to Roper's Chantry, vac. by d. of last incumbent. P. John Roper, <u>generosus</u>. Lambeth, 6 Feb. 1499.

719   Inst. of Mr. Thomas Haukyns, M.A., to church of Luddenham (<u>Ludenham</u>), vac. by d. of last incumbent. P. abbot and conv. of Faversham. Lambeth, 6 Feb. 1499.

720   Inst. of Mr. Thomas Marke, M.A., to church of Wilcote (<u>Wyvilcote</u>), Ox., vac. by d. of last incumbent, in the abp.'s collation by devolution, according to the decree of the Lateran Council. I. archd. of Oxford. Lambeth, 13 Feb. 1499.

721   Inst. of William Geffrey, chaplain, to church of Boughton Aluph (<u>Bocton Alluph</u>), vac. by d. of William Weyte. P. master and fellows of the College of SS Gregory and Martin, Wye. Lambeth, 13 Feb. 1499.

722   Inst. of Mr. Gilbert Carleton, Decr.B., to church of Farningham (<u>Fernyngham</u>), in the abp.'s immediate jurisdiction and collation, vac by d. of last incumbent. I. dean of Shoreham. Lambeth, 14 Feb. 1499.

723   Exchange, on the certificate of Edward bp. of Chichester, between William Ringsall, v. of West Tarring (<u>Tarryng</u>), Sx., in the abp.'s immediate jurisdiction and collation, and John New, chaplain, v. of West Firle (<u>Fyrle</u>), Sx., Chichester dioc. Inst. of New in the person of his proctor, Mr. John Holt. I. dean of Pagham. Lambeth, 14 Feb. 1499.

724   [<u>fo.167</u>] Inst. of Mr. John Fraunklyn, M.A., in the person of his proctor, Mr. Thomas Maddeys, S.T.P., to church of Ickham (<u>Ikham</u>), vac. by d. of last incumbent, in the abp.'s collation. I. Commissary General of Canterbury. Lambeth, 15 Feb. 1499.

725   Inst. of Mr. Thomas Syms, Decr.B., to church of Great Mongeham (<u>Magna Mongeham</u>), vac. by res. of Mr. John Fraunklyn, in the abp.'s collation. Lambeth, 20 Feb. 1499.

726   Inst. of William Hicson, chaplain, to vic. of St. Nicholas, Sturry (<u>Sturrey</u>), vac. by d. of last incumbent. P. abbot and conv. of St. Augustine, Canterbury. Canterbury, 28 March 1498.

727.   Inst. of Thomas Squier, chaplain, to church of St. Peter, Dover (<u>Dovor'</u>), vac. by d. of last incumbent. P. prior and conv. of St.

Martin, Dover. I. Commissary General of Canterbury. Canterbury, 4 Apr. 1499.

728   Inst. of Robert Reyfelde, abbot of St. Mary, Boxley, to vic. of Headcorn (Headcron), vac. by d. of last incumbent, in the abp.'s collation. Lambeth, 24 Apr. 1499.

729   Inst. of William Kettilsden, B.A., to church of Frittenden (Frityndon), vac. by d. of last incumbent. P. abbot and conv. of St. Augustine, Canterbury. Lambeth, 25 Apr. 1499.

730   Inst. of Mr. Thomas Mugworthi, J.U.B., to vic. of Sevenoaks (Sevinoke), in the abp.'s immediate jurisdiction and collation, vac. by d. of last incumbent. I. dean of Shoreham. Lambeth, 25 Apr. 1499.

731   [fo.167v] Inst. of Ambrose Payne, chaplain, to the prebend in the collegiate church of Wingham (Wyngham), vac. by d. of Mr. Thomas Coopland, in the abp.'s collation. I. provost of the college. Lambeth, 27 Apr. 1499.

732   Inst. of Thomas Hungerford, chaplain, to vic. of Preston next Faversham (Preston iuxta Faversham), vac. by d. of last incumbent, in the abp.'s collation. Lambeth, 28 Apr. 1499.

733   Inst. of Lawrence Skoye, chaplain, to church of Stockbury (Stokbury), vac. by d. of last incumbent. P. prior and conv. of Leeds. Lambeth, 29 Apr. 1499.

734   Inst. of William Kempe, chaplain, to vic. of St. Mary Northgate, Canterbury. P. prior and conv. of St. Gregory, Canterbury. Lambeth, 8 May 1499.

735   Inst. of Henry Bowrege, chaplain, to the priestly scholarship in the College of the Holy Trinity, Bredgar (Bradgar), vac. by the acceptance by William Hicson of another benefice, in the abp.'s collation according to the statutes of the college. Lambeth, 16 May 1499.

736   Inst. of William Erkelys, chaplain, to church of Kingsdown (Kyngisdown), vac. by d. of last incumbent. P. abbot and conv. of St. Augustine, Canterbury. Lambeth, 21 May 1499.

737   Inst. of Hugh Huntlow, chaplain, to vic. of Preston next Wingham

(Preston iuxta Wyngham), vac. by res. of William Ketillisden. P. abbot and conv. of St. Augustine, Canterbury. Lambeth, 8 June 1499.

738   Inst. of John Rikthorn, chaplain, to church of Isfield (Isefeld), Sx., in the abp.'s immediate jurisdiction and collation, vac. by d. of last incumbent. I. dean of South Malling or his deputy. Lambeth, 16 June 1499.

739   [fo.168] Inst. of John Maynell, chaplain, to the perpetual chantry of St. Nicholas at Croydon, in the abp.'s immediate jurisdiction, vac. by res. of Thomas Grene. P. Robert Weldon. I. dean of Croydon. Lambeth, 17 June 1499.

740   Inst. of Thomas Baschyrch, B.A., to church of Halton, Bk., in the abp.'s immediate jurisdiction and collation, vac. by d. of last incumbent. I. dean of Risborough. Lambeth, 18 June 1499.

741   Inst. of William Brownsop to church of St. Omer alias Oldekyrk (St. Audoman alias Oldekyrk), Thérouanne dioc., vac. by d. of last incumbent. P. the king. I. Commissary of the Calais jurisdiction. Lambeth, 1 July 1499.

742   Inst. of Robert Reyfeld, abbot of St. Mary, Boxley, to church of Hunton (Huntyngdon), in the abp.'s immediate jurisdiction and collation, vac. by d. of last incumbent. I. dean of Shoreham or his deputy. Lambeth, 15 Oct. 1499.

743   Inst. of Henry Wilson, chaplain, to church of Hayes (Heyse), in the abp.'s immediate jurisdiction, vac. by res. of Mr. Thomas Fyssh. P. Mr. Thomas Wilkynson, r. of Orpington. I. dean of Shoreham. Lambeth, 15 Oct. 1499.

744   Inst. of John Knowdysin, chaplain, to the perpetual chantry of St. Mary in the church of Croydon, vac. by res. of Thomas Thomilynson, in the abp.'s immediate jurisdiction and collation in this instance by devolution, according to the statutes of the chantry. I. dean of Croydon. Lambeth, 16 Oct. 1499.

745   Inst. of Mr. Reginald Philippis, M.A., to vic. of Wadhurst (Wadeherst), Sx., in the abp.'s immediate jurisdiction and collation, vac. by d. of last incumbent. I. dean of South Malling. Lambeth, 2 Nov. 1499.

746   [fo.168v] Inst. of William Weynwright, chaplain, to vic. of Graveney,

vac. by d. of last incumbent. P. prior and conv. of St. Mary Overy, Southwark. Lambeth, 8 Nov. 1499.

747   Grant to Richard Symons, priest, in commendam, of the church of Tunstall (Dunstall), vac. by d. of last incumbent and in the abp.'s collation, for a period of six months, according to the constitution of Pope Gregory X promulgated at the Council of Lyons[1]. Lambeth, 5 Dec. 1499.

      [1. c. 15, VI i 16.]

748   Inst. of Richard Kesell, chaplain, to vic. of Coldred (Colred), vac. by d. of last incumbent. P. prior and conv. of St. Martin, Dover. Lambeth, 5 Dec. 1499.

749   Inst. of James Freyle, chaplain, to vic. of Lydden (Lyden), vac. by d. of last incumbent. P. abbot and conv. of Langdon. Lambeth, 6 Dec. 1499.

750   Inst. of Mr. Adam Facet, Decr.D., to church of Patching (Pachyng), Sx., in the abp.'s immediate jurisdiction and collation, vac. by res. of Mr. William Holmysley. I. dean of Pagham. Lambeth, 16 Dec. 1499.

751   Inst. of John Wilkynson, chaplain, to vic. of Headcorn (Headcron), vac. by res. of the abbot of Boxley, in the abp.'s collation. Lambeth, 20 Dec. 1499.

752   Inst. of Mr. Richard Gardyner to church of Shoreham (Shorham), with the dependent chapel of Otford, in the abp.'s immediate jurisdiction and collation, vac. by res. of Mr. Humphrey Hawardyn, D.C.L. I. dean of Shoreham and Mr. Peter Bradshawe. Lambeth, 9 Sept. 1500.

753   Inst. of Mr. Robert Wodwarde, Decr.D., to church of Adisham (Adesham), vac. by d. of Mr. Henry Cooper, in the abp.'s collation. I. Commissary General of Canterbury or his deputy. Lambeth, 9 July 1500.

APPENDIX I

THE ARCHBISHOP'S SECULAR COMMISSIONS

Although only one such commission is included in the Lambeth register, a large number were transcribed in Priory Register S, now in the custody of the Dean and Chapter of Canterbury, as by custom they were confirmed by the prior and convent of Christ Church. The following list is arranged in alphabetical order, and the folio of Register S is given.

Ashborne, Henry	Joint custodian, parks and woods at Pinner, Mx., 3 March 1489	355v
Bagster, George	Custodian of park of Burstow, 30 Jan. 1500	434
Bolney, Edward	Joint bailiff of Wingham, 3 Jan. 1488	435
Bourne, John	Custodian of park of Lyminge, 6 Jan. 1495	404v
Bradkyrke, William	Custodian of palace of Canterbury, 2 Jan. 1498	417v
Brownsopp, John	Custodian of manor of Lambeth, Sy., 24 Feb. 1491	364
	Seneschal of the priory hall, 24 May 1495	396
Brownsopp, William	Custodian of the great north door, 24 May 1495	396
Butler, John	Custodian of woods of Buckholt and North Bishopsdene, 2 Jan. 1498	417
Byrde, Richard	Custodian of woods of Buckholt and North Bishopsdene, 2 Apr. 1494	388v
David, William	Custodian of woods of Drovedens, 16 Jan. 1495	405v
Ensyng, William	Custodian of capital manse of Maidstone, 30 Sept. 1487	351v
Ferrers, Edward	Custodian of park of Knole, 6 Jan. 1496	404v
	Bailiff of Otford, 9 Sept. 1500	438v
Frye, Matthew	Joint custodian of Bersted, Sx., 6 Jan. 1500	432v
Havard, John	Custodian of woods of Drovedens 2 Jan. 1488	354
	Custodian of manor of Knole, 1 Dec. 1495	403v

171

Heede, William	Bailiff of Maidstone, 2 Jan. 1488	350v
Langton, John	Custodian of manor and park of Mayfield, Sx., 6 March 1493	388
Malmayn, John	Custodian of town and lordship of Hythe, 27 Apr. 1499	355
Maryner, William	Joint custodian of Pinner, Mx., 3 March 1489	355v
	Bedel of the Court of Arches, 9 Sept. 1493	387
Michell, John	Custodian of the ferry at Lambeth, 9 Sept. 1500	438v
Morleye, William	Custodian of the liberty of Southwark, Sy., 15 Aug. 1500	438
Morton, John	Bailiff of Aldington, 20 Apr. 1500	435
Morton, Thomas, generosus	Bailiff of Croydon, Sy., 4 Feb. 1499	420v
Nethynfoll, John	Joint bailiff of Wingham, 3 Jan. 1488	435
Parker, Peter	Custodian of manor of Otford, 19 Nov. 1495	403v
Parys, William	Custodian of manor of Lambeth, Sy., 12 Aug. 1495	401v
Pekham, Reginald	Custodian of park at Wrotham, 9 Sept. 1500	438v
Perham, Lawrence	Custodian of park of Burstow, Sy., 2 Jan. 1488	351
Perham, Robert	Joint bailiff of Wingham, 3 Jan. 1488	435
Portar, Richard	Custodian of manor of Ford, Canterbury, 6 March 1493	388
Rye, John	Custodian of park of Broyle and the fords and waters near Lewes, Sx., 22 Feb. 1493	371v
Suston, George	Custodian of Otford, 9 Sept. 1500	438v
Talbot, William	Seneschal of the priory hall, 20 May 1493	384v
Ware, John	Joint custodian of the park of Broyle, Sx., 6 Jan. 1500	432v
Whatson, John	Custodian of the park of Frankham in Sussex, and of all forinsec woods in that county, 2 Jan. 1488	354v

INDEX OF PERSONS AND PLACES

Abbats, John, chap. of Northmoor, 330

Abraham, William, chap. of Depeden chantry, 684

Acastre, Richard, r. of St James, Dover, 427

Accoltis de Arctio, Peter de, papal chap., auditor of the Rota, 192, 195-6, 200, 203

Acrise (Acrese), Kent, ch., 140, 165, 494

Adam, Thomas, 379

Adamson, William, v. of Newington near Sittingbourne, 481

Adisham (Addesham, Adesham), Kent, ch., 167, 514, 753

Ady, Thomas, r. of Acrise, 494

Aisshe, see Ash

Aisshford, see Ashford

Aisshton, see Ashton

Alba, cardinal bp. of, see Costa

Alcock (Alkok, Alkoke):
John, bp. of Ely, 89-90, 114, 188, 201
Richard, r. of Goodnestone, 483
Thomas, v. of Chertsey, 360

Aldington, Kent:
ch., 166, 531
estate of abp., app. A

Aldington next Maidstone, Kent, chapel, 143

Alessandria (Alexandrinus), bp. of, see Sancto Georgio

Alexander IV, pope, 24

Alexander VI, pope, 39, 41, 52, 185, 187-8, 199, 201-2, 204-9, 211-21

Alexander, John, r. of Hinxhill, 459

Alexiis, Paul de, 198

Alkham (Alkeham), Kent:
ch., 138
vic., 164, 349

Alkok, see Alcock

Alphege, St, abp. of Canterbury, 23

Alton (Altoun), Ha., 265

Alyn, Thomas, can. of Wingham, 566

Amott, Richard, can. regular, v. of Seasalter, 452, 576

Amynewe, see Bartelott

Ancher, see Anger

Ancona, marches of, 47

Andover (Andevere), rural dean of, 234

Andreae, Johannes, canonist, 181

Androsone, John, r. of St Peter's Canterbury, 386

Andrue, Thomas, prior of Bilsington, v. of Hernhill, 705

Anger (Ancher):
John, 454
Thomas, 643

Annselme (Ansell), Thomas, m. of Christ Church Canterbury, 443a, 444b, 445c, 447d

Anselm, St, abp. of Canterbury, 211

Anthony, John, 198

Antony, John, m. of Christ Church Canterbury, 438d

ap Davit, see Davit

ap John, see John

Appledore (Appuldore, Appuldur'):
ch., 133
tithes, 69
vic., 166, 382
See also Ebony

Appuldur (Appuldre), John, m. of Christ Church Canterbury, 443a, 444b, 445c

Appulton, Roger, 70

Appylby, Thomas, 549

Archdeacon, the (Guido de Baysio), canonist, 181

Arches, court of, see Canterbury

Ardley (Yerdeley), Ox., ch. of Holy Trinity, 818

Argentyne, John, r. of St Vedast's London, 408

Arundel (Arundell), earl of:
Thomas, 286
William, 184, 286

Arundel (Arundell):
Henry, m. of Christ Church Canterbury, 438d
John, bp. of Chichester, 184
Thomas, abp. of Canterbury, 54, 346

Ash (Esh), ch., 141

Ash (Aisshe, Assh, Aysshe):
  Thomas, m. of Christ Church
    Canterbury, 438d, 439c, 444d
  William, r. of Biddenden, 708
Ashbocking (Assh), Sf., ch., 176
Ashborne, Henry, custodian of
  Pinner, app. A
Ashby (Asshby), Thomas, master of
  Ospringe hospital, 425
Ashford (Asshford, Esshetesford,
  Estchestesford):
  ch., 140
  vic., 179, 585
Ashford (Aisshford, Asshford),
  John, m. of Christ Church
    Canterbury, 441a, 443b, 444c,
    447d
Ashmynton, William, 433b, 434c,
  435d
Ashton (Aisshton, Asshton), alias
  Catt, John:
  r. of Teynham, 405
  v. of Gillingham, 401
Asshby, see Ashby
Asshford, see Ashford
Asshton, see Ashton
Assisi, bp. of, see Vulterris
Astle, Richard, m. of Christ Church
  Canterbury, 441d
Aston, Thomas, 574
Atherton, Robert, 337
Att Hasill, see Hasill
At Wood, atte Woode, see Wood
Aubre, see Brounebrede
Auderne (Audern), Thérouanne dioc.,
  ch., 685
Audley, Edmund:
  bp. of Hereford, 40-2, 201
  bp. of Rochester, 85, 88-90, 99,
    102, 114
Austen, James, m. of Christ Church
  Canterbury, 446b, 447c
Autun (Eduen') dioc., 192, 200
Avignon, 37, 234, 252
Awbrey:
  Richard, 322
  William, 322
Awood, see Wood
Axbrigge, William, v. of East
  Peckham, 581, 664
Ayloffe:
  Edmund, 267
  Eleanor, 267
  Thomas, 267

Aylsham (Aylesham), Nf., 339
Aynesford, see Eynsford
Aysshe, see Ash

Bacchild, see Bapchild
Badeslee, John de, 232
Badlesmere (Baldesmere), Kent,
  ch., 171
Bagster, George, app. A
Bakchild, see Bapchild
Baker, John:
  chap. of St Mary's chantry,
    Harrow, 482
  r. of Eythorne, 475
  r. of North Petherton, 63
Baldesmere, see Badlesmere
Balfrer (Balfar, Balfre), Thomas:
  scholar of Bredgar coll.,
    492, 607
  v. of Brabourne, 604, 672
Balgeswy, James, v. of Linsted,
  472
Balinghem (Balyngham), Pas de
  Calais, ch., 542
Baly (Bayle, Bayly):
  John, r. of Fordwich, 652
  Thomas, r. of Great Mongeham,
    523, 637
Balyngham, see Balinghem
Bamberg (Bambergen'), Germany:
  ch. of St Bangolf, 228
  ch. of St Stephen, 223
  dioc., 223, 228
Bampton, Lewis, 611
Banaster, see Banester
Banes (Banys):
  Giles, r. of Halstead, 369
  Thomas, prior of Folkestone,
    76-82
Banester (Banaster):
  John, can. of South Malling
    coll., 550
  William, chap. of St Mary's
    chantry, Harrow, 482
Bangor (Bangoren'), Carn.:
  bp., 432c
  dioc., 119, 128
  see, 127
Banham, Richard, abbot of
  Tavistock, 72
Banys, see Banes

Bapchild (Bacchild, Bakchild), Kent:
  ch., 170
  vic., 170, 461
Baptista, John, 198
Bardunen' dioc., (probably
  Barchinonen', Barcelona), 198
Barett (Baret), John, notary public,
  registrar of the abp. and the
    Prerogative, 54, 61, 71, 81, 99,
      187-8, 195-6, 217, 227-9,
        236-8, 240-1, 243-5, 642
Barfreston (Berverston), Kent, ch.,
  162, 598
  See also Hartanger
Barham, Richard, O.E.S.A., 440a
Barkeley, John, 191
Barker, William, Official of archd.
  of Surrey, 390
Barking (Berkyng), Ess., 191
Barlings (Barlyng), Li., 232
Barmondsey, see Bermondsey
Barnererio, Christopher, 255
Barnes (Bernes), Sy.:
  ch., 175
  temp. of bp. of London, 152
Barnwell (Barnewell), Ca., priory,
  433d, 444d
Barradon, Henry, r. of Harbledown,
  568
Barrington (Beryngton'), Ca., 268
Barry, John, 521
Bartelott, alias Amynewe, Simon, 287
Barton-in-the-Clay (Barton), Bd.,
  ch. of St Nicholas, 624
Baschyrch, Thomas, r. of Halton, 740
Basingstoke, William de, m. of
  Winchester, 230
Baskett, John, 298
Bastard, Elizabeth, 345
Batrychisden, see Bethersden
Bath and Wells (Bathon' et Wellen'),
  So.:
  bp., 37-8
    See also Fox, Richard
  dioc., 119, 128
  see, 127
Battle (Bellum), Sx., abbey, 134,
  488
Battle, John, 471
Baxter (Baxster):
  Simon, r. of St Michael Crooked
    Lane, London, 364
  Thomas, 436a

Bayham (Begham), Sx., abbey, 151
  can. (named), 440d
Bayle, see Baly
Baysio, Guido de, see Archdeacon
Beaconsfield (Bekennefeld), Bk.,
  314
Beall, see Beele
Beatrichden, see Bethersden
Beauchamp, Thomas, 298
Beaufo:
  Elizabeth, 606
  Joan, 606
  Philippa, 606
  William, 606
Beauford (Beaufort):
  Henry, bp. of Winchester,
    235, 258-60, 264
  John, earl of Somerset, 235
Beaugfeld, see Beauxfield
Beautre, John, 234
Beauxfield (Beaugfeld, Beuxfeld,
  Bewsfelde), in Whitfield, Kent:
  ch., 143
  vic., 164
Becket, Thomas, abp. of Canterbury,
  23, 44
Bedall, John, chap., 632
Bedford, archd. of, 624
Bedyngden, see Biddenden
Bee, Simon, 262, 264
Beele (Beall, Beel):
  John, chap. of Holy Cross
    chantry, St Nicholas Calais,
      548
  John, notary public, abp.'s
    registrar, 26, 43, 237-8, 417
  William, v. of Newnham, 462,
    495
Begham, see Bayham
Beke, Robert, v. of Eynesford,
  418
Bekennefeld, see Beaconsfield
Bakesbourne (Lethyngesbourne,
  Lyvingesburn), ch., 141, 167
Bekett, Peter, chap., 316
Bekley, Br Stephen, r. of
  Knowlton, 370
Bell (Belle), John, notary
  public, 236-7
Bellum, see Battle
Benedict XII, pope, 24
Benett (Benet):
  John, chap., 288

175

Roger, m. of Christ Church
Canterbury, 439d
Benfold, Michael, O.F.M., 444d
Bensted (Benstede), Andrew:
r. of Moulton, 698
r. of Stonar, 516
warden of Northill coll., 698
Berghstede, see Bersted
Berkyng, see Barking
Bermondsey (Barmondesey,
Barmondsey, Bermondeseye), Sy.,
abbey, 180, 388-9, 431c, 432c,
673
abbot, 199, 202, 221
account of litigation despatched
to, 247-66
Berne (Burne), John, m. of Christ
Church Canterbury, 443a, 444b,
445c
Bernes, see Barnes
Berse, Thomas, 440b
Bersted (Berghstede, Bergstede),
Kent:
ch., 140
vic., 169
Bersted, South (Southberghstede),
Sx.:
estate of abp., app. A
vic., 172, 647
Berverston, see Barfreston
Beryngton, see Barrington
Besancon (Bisunten') dioc., 194
Bethersden (Batrychisden,
Beatrichden, Betrysden), Kent:
ch., 141
vic., 179, 506
Betteshanger (Betteshangre), Kent,
ch., 162, 569
Beuxfeld, see Beauxfield
Beverley (Beverlacum), Yk ER,
Hospitaller preceptory, 370
Beverley (Beverle, Bevyrle,
Beyveley):
John, 327
Robert, v. of West Hythe, 413
Robert, 327
Roger, O.E.S.A., 433b
Bewsfelde, see Beauxfield
Bicknor (Biknor), Kent, ch., 170
Biddenden (Bedyngden, Bydinden),
Kent, ch., 179, 708
Bilford, David, r. of Monkton, 683

Biggleswade (Bikkylyswade),
Bd., 284
Biknor, see Bicknor
Billyngton, John, O.F.M., 446a
Bilsington (Bilsingdon), Kent:
ch., 144
priory, 144
can. (named), 438b, 440d
prior, 705
Bilton (Bylton), Robert, r. of
Shadoxhurst, 363, 457
Bingham, Simon, 250
Bircholde:
John, 309
Matilda, 309
Bircholt (Byrcholt), Kent, ch.,
165
Bishop (Bysshop), Richard, chap.
of Coldred chantry, 549
Bishopsbourne (Bisshopisborn),
Kent, ch., 141, 167
Bishopsden, North, see Dunkirk
Bisunten', see Besançon
Blackmanstone (Blakmanston),
Kent, ch., 168, 704
Bladwell, see Blodwell
Blagge, John, chap., 270
Blake, John, r. of Shadoxhurst,
363
Blakmanston, see Blackmanstone
Blean, St Cosmus and St Damian
in the, Kent, vic., 575
Bleese, Ralph, prior of Ravenstone,
630
Blodwell (Bladwell, Bladywell),
Richard:
advocate of Court of Canterbury,
Commissary General of bp. of
London, 191, 196, 202
r. of Ardley, 618
Blois, Henry of, bp. of Winchester,
252
Blynston, Ralph, r. of Ewell, 645
Boardfield (Bordefeld), in
Otterden, Kent, vic. 508
Bocking (Bockyng, Bokking,
Bokkyng), Ess:
ch., 176, 497, 616, 629
chantry of BVM, 421, 640, 681
curate, 497
dean, 421, 469, 552, 616, 629,
633, 640, 677, 681, 688, 698
dy., 176

Bockingfold (Bokkingfold), in Goudhurst, Kent, free chapel, 559
Bocton, see Boughton
Bognor, Sx., chapel, 647
Bohun, John, 632
Bokking, see Bocking
Bokkingfold, see Bockingfold
Bokyngham, Richard, m. of Christ Church Canterbury, 445a, 446b
Bolley (Boly):
　Gertrude, 313
　John, 313
　William, 273
Bolney:
　Edward, app. A
　Thomas, r. of Cheriton, 693
Boly, see Bolley
Bonde, John, r. of Old Romney, 450
Boneauntor, Richard, v. of Herne, 463
Boniface VIII, pope, 199
Boniface IX, pope, 24
Bonnington (Bonyngton, Bonynton), Kent, ch., 166, 635
Bononia, Alexander de, 222
Bonyngton, see Bonnington
Boold, John, notary public, 346
Boparc, John, O.F.M., 433b
Bordefelde, see Boardfield
Borden, Kent, ch.:
　ch., 140
　vic., 170
Borstowe, see Burstow
Borwermerssh, see Burmarsh
Boston (Bostone), John:
　can. of West Langdon, 438d
　r. of Denton, 393
　v. of Lenham, 391
Bote, Thomas, v. of East Peckham, 399
Boteler, see Butler
Bottern, William, notary public, 195
Boughton Aluph (Bocton Alulphi, Alluph), Kent, ch., 167, 721
Boughton under Blean (Bocton), Kent:
　ch., 135
　vic., 171
Boughton Malherbe (Bocton Maleherbe, Boghton Maleherbe), Kent, ch., 179, 358
Boughton Monchelsea (Bocton Chenesey, Chensy, Monchesey), Kent: ch.,
　ch., 140
　vic., 169, 656

Bourgchier (Burgchyer, Burther):
　John:
　　archd. of Canterbury, 628
　　warden of Eastbridge hospital, 595
　.Thomas, abp. of Canterbury, cardinal priest of St Ciriac in Thermis, 1, 24
Bourne, John, app. A
Bowre, Roger, r. of Aldington, 531
Bowrege, Henry, scholar of Bredgar coll., 735
Bowsy, Edmund, 335
Bowthe, Thomas, 297
Box, Thomas, 448a
Boxford (Boxforde), Sf., ch., 176
Boxley (Boxle), Kent:
　abbey, 121, 123, 136
　　abbot, 728, 731, 742
　　monks (named), 431b, c, 435a, b, 442a, c, 443c, 445a
　ch., 139
　vic., 169, 460
Boxwell, John, m. of Christ Church Canterbury, 439a, 442b
Brabourne (Braborne, Brayborn), Kent:
　ch., 142
　vic. 165, 604, 672
Bradestede, see Brasted
Bradford, Br James, v. of River, 373
Bradgar (Bradgare):
　John, can. of Leeds, v. of Marden, 661
　Robert, founder of Bredgar coll., 346
Bradkyrke, William, app. A
Bradshawe, Peter, 752
Bardsole, Kent, abbey of St Radegund, 138, 349, 372-3, 431c, 432c, 674
　can. (named), 435c, 437b, d, 438a, 439a, 440b, d, 441d, 447c
Brancheley, John, m. of Boxley, 442c
Brand, Thomas, r. of Ham, 433d, 621

Brasted (Bradestede, Brastede),
Kent, ch., 173, 415-6, 579
Bray, Henry, 632
Brayborn, see Brabourne
Bredgar (Bradgar, Bradgare),
Kent:
ch., 170
coll. of Holy Trinity, 346
chaplains (named), 455, 491-2,
607, 735
scholars (named), 346, 455, 492,
607, 735
Breknok, William, prior of
St Andrew's Northampton, 14-5, 71
Bremengham, Nicholas, v. of
Woodnesborough, 650
Brensete, see Brenzett
Brent, William, 619
Brenzett (Brensete, Brensett,
Brensette), Kent:
ch., 156
vic., 166, 503
Bridge (Bregge), Kent, dy., 130,
132, 134, 141, 145, 147, 153,
167
Bristol (Bristoll'), Gl., 274-5,
304
hospital of St Mark, Billeswick,
alias Gaunt's, 275
Briston, Walter, v. of Patrixbourne,
62
Broadhurst (Brodehirst), Sx., 326
Bromefeld, Richard, can. of
Hereford, 519
Bromeshell, see Broom Hill
Bromham (Brumham), Wlt., 319
Brook (Broke, Brooke), Kent, ch.,
167, 385
Brookland (Brokeland, Brokelond),
Kent:
ch., 132
vic., 166
Broom Hill (Bromeshell), Kent, ch.,
156
Broune, Thomas, can. of St Paul's,
196
Brounebrede alias Aubre, Christopher,
290
Brouns, Thomas, chancellor of Abp.
Chichele, 346
Brown (Browne), John, O.F.M., 444a,
445b

Brownebaker, Robert, v. of
Eynesford, 484
Brownsopp:
John, app. A
William:
custodian of great north
door, app. A
r. of St Omer, 741
Brownyng, Edmund, r. of Seaton,
606
Broyle, see Ringmer
Brug, Andrew de, 232
Brumham, see Bromham
Bryan, William, master of Higham
Ferrers coll., 378
Bruyn, Walter, 344
Brydgill, Edmund, r. of Little
Mongeham, 699
Bubwith, Nicholas, keeper of
Privy Seal, 235
Buckholt, see Petham
Buckingham, archd. of, 630
Buckland (Buklonde), Kent, ch.,
133, 171
Bukley, William, r. of Milstead,
663
Bukstede, see Buxted
Bulbeke, William, 250, 258, 263
Bulfynch, Nicholas:
r. of Ikham, 406
r. of St Michael's Crooked Lane,
London, 406, 561
Bull, John, 262
Burbach, John, notary public,
346
Burgele, John, v. of Newnham,
495
Burges:
Arnold, O. Trin., 440a
Peter, papal scribe, 197
Burgchyer, see Bourgchier
Burgon, Robert, r. of North
Crawley, 632
Burmarsh (Borwermerssh,
Burwarmarsh), Kent, ch., 166,
678
Burne, see Berne
Burnell, Henry, 298
Burstow (Borstowe), Sy.:
ch., 175, 493
estate of abp., app. A
Burther, see Bourgchier

178

Burton:
  John, r. of Withington, 26
  Richard, 606
Burton-upon-Trent (Burton super
  Trent), St., abbot of, 58
Burtwesyll, Thomas, r. of Ockley,
  362
Burwarmarsh, see Burmarsh
Bury, Thomas, 274
Buryell, John, v. of Boardfield,508
Butler (Boteler, Boteller, Botiler):
  Alice, 338
  John:
    custodian of abp.'s estates,
      app. A
    r. of Treborough, 614
  Morgan, 338
  William, 346
Butte, Thomas, 441a
Buxted (Bukstede), Sx., ch., 174
Bydinden, see Biddenden
Bydinden, William, m. of Faversham,
  448a
Bygood, Roger, chap., 346
Byllyngton, John, O.F.M., 446a
Bylton, see Bilton
Bynnor, John, 312
Byrcholt, see Bircholt
Byrde:
  Richard, app. A
  Thomas, r. of Stowting, 498
Bysshop, see Bishop
Byxle, see Bexley

Cabell, John, v. of Wadhurst, 387
Cager, Richard, 264-5
Calais (Calesia), dep. Pas de Calais:
  ch. of St Mary, 426, 509
  ch. of St Nicholas:
    chantry of Holy Cross, 548
  commissary of abp., 357, 384, 394,
    398, 414, 426, 509, 533, 535, 542,
    548, 573-4, 599, 602, 631, 636,
    662, 665, 690, 714, 741
  rs. and chaps., 348, 409
  See also Hames; Marck
Calixtus III, pope, 24
Calkewell, see Coquelles
Camberton, John, 61, 190
  master of Maidstone coll., 615
  r. of Bocking, 497, 616
  r. of Eynesford, 696
  r. of Latchingdon, 469
Cambrai (Cameracen') dioc., 192,
  194, 200, 203

Cambridge (Cantebr') university:
  colleges and appropriated
    benefices, 120
  King's College, warden and
    fellows, 543
  poor students, 95, 124
Cameracen', see Cambrai
Campe (Gempe), Therouanne dioc.,
  ch., 357, 574, 599
Cant, John, 320
Canterbury (Cantuariensis), Kent:
  abp., see Alphege; Anselm;
    Arundel; Becket; Bourgchier;
    Chichele; Courtenay; Kemp;
    Morton; Rich; Savoy; Stafford;
    Walter
  apparitor general, 20, 70
  apparitor, in City of London,
    21
  auditor of causes, 16, 18, 26,
    43, 61, 65, 78, 81
  benefices in collation of,
    347, 351, 364-5, 369, 371,
    376-8, 380, 387, 390, 397,
    404, 406, 408, 410, 415,
    422-3, 430, 449, 451, 453,
    459, 463, 465, 467, 469,
    473, 477-8, 482, 486, 489-93,
    496-7, 499-502, 511-5, 518,
    520, 522-3, 525-32, 537-8,
    550-2, 554, 561-4, 566-8,
    570-1, 577, 579-80, 582-5,
    590-2, 594-6, 603, 608-10,
    616, 622, 625-30, 633-4,
    637-9, 641, 647-9, 658, 663,
    667-70, 673, 677, 682-3,
    688, 692, 695-6, 698, 705-6,
    708-9, 711-3, 717, 720,
    722-5, 728, 730-2, 735, 738,
    740, 742, 744-5, 747, 750-3
  chancellor, 7, 87, 101
  Commissary General, 62, 69,
    75, 77, 98
    as inductor, 347-430 passim,
      449-753 passim
  commissions:
    ecclesiastical, 16-8, 20-2,
      33, 42, 66, 69-70, 74, 84,
      86, 98, 100
    to proctors, 61, 189-90,
      224, 226, 249
    secular, 35, app. A
    to tax collectors, 123,
      125-6

conservator of privileges of
Carthusian Order, 37–8
court of (Court of Arches):
advocates (named), 76, 191,
196, 202
bedel, app. A
Official Principal, 196, 232
practitioners in, misconduct
of, 196, 201–2
proctors (named), 47, 225
registrar, 61, 196, 202
court of Audience, 23
cross, 7
palace, 66, 488–9, 523, 562,
604, 608–10, 637–9, 663, 696,
726–7
custodian, app. A
Prerogative (testamentary), 58,
267–345
commissary general, 17, 84,
227–8, 236, 239, 245–6
litigation concerning, 191–203
papal confirmation, 204, 213,
219
registrar, 187–8, 195–6, 217,
227–9, 236–8, 240–1, 243–5
registry, 227
prison, 89
proctors (named), 61, 189–90,
197–8, 222, 224–9, 236, 246,
249
receiver, 35
registers, 230–5
registrars (named), 81, 99,
187–8, 195–6, 217, 227–9, 232,
236–8, 240–1, 243–5
registry, 229–46
clerks (named), 236–41
sede vacante jurisdiction:
acts by reason of, 73, 83, 352,
355–6, 360–2, 502, 511–2,
519, 540, 543, 560, 572, 606,
614, 618, 624, 630, 632, 634,
720
litigation concerning, 221–66
officials exercising, 263–6
aquittance, for recepts,
232, 234
appointment, 42, 230,
232–3, 235, 243
nomination, 34
revocation of appointment,
230, 234–5, 243
papal confirmation, 205–6,
215, 217

servitia to pope, due from,
210
suffragan, 431, 433–7,
529–30
tenants, 53–4
vassals, 4
visits ad limina apostolorum
208, 210
archd.:
appointed, 628
collector of charitable
subsidy, 125
or Official, inductor,
348–430 passim, 450–753
passim
patron, 405, 413, 417, 472
485, 575, 597, 623, 666
possessions, value of, 131
See also Bourgchier; Mooteron;
Peyntwyn
cathedral church of Christ
Church:
almoner, 163
chantries:
Arundel's, 403, 537, 570,
667
Black Prince's, 478, 527,
571
Brenchley, 608
Buckingham's, 596
chapter house, 44
great north door, custodian
of, app. A
monks (named), 433d, 438b, d,
439a, c–d, 441a–d, 442b–d,
443a–d, 444b–d, 445a–d,
446b–d, 447a, c–d
prior, 403, 537, 570, 667
(named), 7, 65, 346
prior and conv.:
litigation of, 69
orders to title of, 439b
patrons, 385–6, 403, 424,
452, 544, 576, 617, 651,
654
possessions, value of, 130
visitation, 65–6
priory hall, seneschal of,
app. A
subprior and conv., 44
churches in or near:
All Saints, 31, 161, 468
Holy Cross, Westgate, 141, 161

St Alphege, 161, 371, 625
St Andrew, 161
St Dunstan-without-the-Walls,
   141, 161, 612
   chantries:
      St Nicholas, 350
      Roper's, 718
St Edmund, 161
St George, 161
St John, 161
St Margaret, 161
St Martin-without-the-Walls, 161
St Mary Bredin (Bredden, de
   Bredon), 161, 381
St Mary Bredman (de Brednam),
   161
St Mary de Castro, 161, 605, 701
St Mary Magdalene, 161, 539
St Mary Northgate, 141, 161, 734
St Michael Burgate, 161
St Mildred, 161
St Paul-without-the-Walls, 132,
   161, 702
St Peter, 161, 386, 617, 651
St Stephen Hackington (Hakenton,
   Hakyndon), 131, 161, 487
diocese, 271
   clergy, 5, 98
   people, 6
   processions, 75
   value of ecclesiastical
      possessions, 119, 128, 130-79
dy., 131-2, 141, 161
friars, Orders or houses of:
   Augustinian (named), 433b, d,
      436a
   Dominican (named), 431d, 433a,
      435b, 440a, 441b, 446b, d,
      447b-c, 448a
   Franciscan (named), 433b-d,
      435c, 436a-b, d, 443d, 444a,
      445b, 446a, c
hospitals in or near:
   St Margaret, for poor priests,
      161, 594, 666
   St Thomas the Martyr,
      Eastbridge, 595
province:
   Convocation, 85-126
      constitutions, 24, 31
      prolocutors (named), 88, 102
   licence to celebrate in chapels
      throughout, 28

licence to preach throughout,
   27, 29
processions to be organised
   throughout, 33, 74
suffragans, 3
   professions of obedience,
      45, 196, 234-5
religious houses in or near:
   St Augustine's abbey:
      abbot, 199, 202, 214, 216,
         218, 247-9, 253-6
      proctors (named), 247,
         253-6
      abbot and conv., patrons,
         353, 374-5, 391, 399,
         456, 468, 476, 516-7,
         524, 539, 586, 588, 593,
         605, 652, 678, 689, 691,
         693, 699, 701-2, 715,
         726, 729, 736-7
      chamberlain of Deal, 132
      chapel of St Andrew, 254
      chapter house, 255
      monks (named), 432a, c,
         433d, 436a, c, 437d,
         439b-d, 442d, 443b-c,
         444d, 445b, 446b-c, 447c
      possessions, value of, 141
   St Gregory's priory:
      can. (named), 435a, 437d,
         438b, 440c, 446a, 447b
      orders to title of, 431c,
         433d, 434d, 436b
      possessions, value of, 141
      prior and conv., patrons,
         396, 458, 506, 589, 612
         734
   St Sepulchre's priory:
      orders to title of, 433b-c,
         434c, 435d, 437c, 438b,
         439d, 440b, 442d
      prioress and conv., patrons,
         381
Canton, see Phillip
Caprinis, Adrian de, notary
   public, 222
Capua, abp. of, see Lopez
Careys, Nicholas, chap. of
   St Nicholas chantry in ch. of
   St Dunstan-without-the-Walls,
   Canterbury, 350
Carleton:
   Gilbert, v. of Farningham, 722

Robert, 340
Carpenter, Henry, v. of Croydon, 388
Carteryd, Thomas, v. of Hever, 464
Carthusian Order:
conservators of privileges of, 37
exempt from taxation, 120
See also Sheen; Witham
Casimir, king of Poland, 47
Castellesi (Castellensis):
Adrian:
abp.'s proctor at curia, 189–90, 224
papal protonotary, nuncio and collector, r. of St Dunstan in the East, London, 525
Robert, papal protonotary, 187
Castellimare, bp. of, see Flores
Castilione, Leonard de, 203
Caton:
Henry, r. of Escalles, 690
John:
chap. of St Mary's chantry, Herne, 453
v. of Herne, 463
Catt, see Ashton
Caune, Richard de, m. of Winchester, 252
Caunterbury:
Thomas, can. of Bradsole, 435c, 437d
Walter, can. of St Gregory's Canterbury, 435a, 438b, 440c
Cednor, see Cutnor
Chadworth:
George:
r. of Barfreston, 598
r. of Campe, 599
Joan, 57
Chamber (Chambre), John:
chap., 333
v. of Tong, 686
Chamberleyn (Chambirleyn), Thomas, notary public, 225, 227–9, 236, 244
Chapman:
Miles, r. of Knowlton, 370
Oliver, v. of St Margaret's Cliffe, 359, 395
William, 327

Charing (Charryng, Charyng), Kent:
ch., 179, 564
rural dy., 129–30, 132, 134, 140–1, 143, 148, 179
Charlton by Dover (Charleton), Kent, ch., 164
Charlwood (Charlwod, Cherlwoode), Sy., ch., 175, 590
Charryng, see Charing
Chart, Great (Magna Chart alias Est Chart), Kent, ch., 179
Chart, Little (Parva Chart), Kent, ch., 179
Chart Sutton (Charte), Kent, ch., 140
Chartham, Kent, ch., 167
Chartham (Charteham), William, m. of Christ Church Canterbury, 438b, 439c, 442d
Chaunceler, William, r. of Ruckinge, 347
Cheam (Cheyham), Sy., ch., 175, 669
Chedingston, see Chiddingstone
Chepstede, see Chipstead
Cheramo, Lelius de, lector of Audience of Contradicted Letters, 194
Cheriton, Kent, ch., 164, 693
Chertsey (Chertesey), Sy.:
abbey, 186
abbot and conv., patrons, 360
ch., 360
Cheshunt (Chesthunte), Hrt., 232
Chester, archd. of, 512, 543
Chesterlett, see Chislett
Chetham, Richard, can. regular, chap. of Bockingfold and Newstead, 559
Chevening (Chevenying), Kent:
ch., 173, 567
estate of abp., 53–4
Chevening:
Adam de, kt., 53
John de, 53
Simon de, 53
William, 431c, 432c, 435a
r. of Kingston, 703
Chichele, Henry, abp. of Canterbury, 24, 346

Chichester (Cicestren'). Sx.:
  bp., 461, 723
    See also Arundel; Story
  cathedral ch.:
    dean, 61
    dioc., 119, 128–30
  see, 127
Chichonis, Aymo, notary public, 198
Chiddingstone (Chedyngston,
  Chidingston), Kent, ch., 173,
  376, 423, 706
Children, John, 68
Chilham (Chillham, Chylham), Kent:
  ch., 153
  vic., 167, 679
Chilham, William, m. of Faversham,
  439a, 440b, 443c, 444d
Chilinden, Thomas, prior of Christ
  Church Canterbury, 346
Chillenden (Chillynden), Kent,
  ch., 167
Chillham, see Chilham
Chipman, Mr, v. of East Meon, 253,
  258
Chipstead (Chepstede), Kent, estate
  of abp. at, 53–4
Chipstede (Chepstede):
  John, 54
  John de, 53
Chirch, see Church
Chislet (Chestelett, Chistelett),
  Kent:
  ch., 132
  vic., 163
Choo, John, r. of Dowdeswell, 26
Church (Chirch, Churche, Chyrch):
  James, v. of Rodmersham, 600
  Roger, 440b
    advocate of Court of
      Canterbury, 196
    r. of Kenardington, 479
    r. of Sangatte, 665
Chylham, see Chilham
Cicestren', see Chichester
Cleeve, So., abbey, 614
Clefe, see Clive
Clement:
  John, m. of Christ Church
    Canterbury, 433d
  Nicholas, m. of Christ Church
    Canterbury, 439a, 441b, 442c,
    444d

Clerk (Clerke):
  Clement, 688
  John, 431a, 432b
    v. of Newington (near
      Folkestone), 420
  Richard, bp. of Ross, 251–2
  William, v. of Bethersden, 506
Clerkenwell, see London, religious
  houses
Cleve, see Cliffe, Clive
Cliffe (Cleve), (Shoreham dy.),
  Kent, ch., 139, 173
Cliffe (Cliff iuxta Dovorr',
  Clyffe), Kent, St Margaret's
  ch., 133, 164, 359, 395
Cliffe, West (Westcleve), Kent,
  ch., 130
Clifford (Clyfford):
  Richard, 437a
    bp. of Worcester, 235
  Thomas, 255
Clifton, He. (unid., possibly
  Clifton upon Teme, Wo.), 330
Clinton, John, lord Clinton and
  Saye, 601
Clive (Clefe, Cleve, Clyve),
  Michael:
    chancellor of bp. of
      Winchester, 107
    Official sede vacante
      Winchester dioc., 243
    warden of Winchester coll., 250
Cloose, John, dean of Chichester,
  61
Clyfe, see Clive
Clyfford, see Clifford
Cobham, Kent, coll. ch., 653
Coblenz (Confluencia), John of,
  friar, 440b, 441c
Cockys, William, 334
Cok, Nicholas, 446a
Cokett:
  James, 268
  John, 268
Coldred (Colred, Colrede), Kent,
  ch., 133, 137
  chantry, 549, 748
Cole:
  John:
    r. of Merstham, 668
    r. of St Blaise in Melak,
      662, 671
  William, 345

183

Colfox, Richard, r. of St Peter's
Dover, 402
Colley, Thomas, 433c, 434d
chap. of Bredgar coll., 491-2,
607, 735
Colman, Thomas, notary public, 366
Cologne (Colonien') dioc., 200,203
Colred, see Coldred
Colrede, John, 279
Colstenestoke, Hugh, 341
Coltherst:
Brian, v. of Newington (near
Hythe), 420
Peter, r. of Brook, 385
Roger, r. of Hinxhill, 587
Colyns (Colynys), John, r. of
St Peter's Canterbury, 386, 617
Comb (Combe), John, precentor of
Exeter cath., 72
Combwell (Combewell), in Goudhurst,
Kent, priory:
can. (named), 436a, 438b, 439a-c,
443a, 444c, 445a-b, d, 446c,
447b, d
possessions, 143
prior and conv., patrons, 383, 464
Confluencia, see Coblenz
Consell, Nicholas, notary public,
251-2
Cooke:
Alexander, curate of Latchingdon,
496
John, 352
r. of Norton, 660
Richard:
O. Carm., 445a-b, 446c
r. of Chiddingstone, 423
Thomas:
Auditor of Causes, 16, 18, 26,
43, 61, 66, 78, 81
chancellor of abp., 7, 87, 101
commissary of the Prerogative,
17
prolocutor of Convocation, 88
r. of Lyminge, 377
r. of St Mary Aldermary,
London, 584
Walter, chap., 307
William, 307
Copland (Copeland, Coppeland,
Coupland):

Copland (Cont'd):
alias Jhonson, John, notary
public, 195, 225, 228, 236,
246, 578
Thomas:
can. of Wingham, 731
r. of High Halden, 532, 709
Coppyng, Robert, master of
Wingham coll., 627
Coquelles (Calkewell), in the
marches of Calais, ch., 627
Corbrand, William, chap. of
Bockingfold and Newstead, 559
Cordemaker, Robert, r. of
St Mary Bothaw, London, 544
Coricio, John, 223, 228
Cornewelle (Cornell):
John, m. of Dover, 435d
William, r. of Wormshill,
368, 412
Cornyssh, John, r. of St Mary
Magdalene, Canterbury, 539
Corpusty, Richard, 339
Corunte (Corrunti), Anthony,
192, 200
Cosshen (Cosshon), John:
chap. of Brenchley chantry,
Canterbury cath., 608
r. of St Alphege, Canterbury,
371, 625
Costa, George, cardinal bp. of
Alba, abp. of Lisbon, 197
Cotes, Humphrey, 301
Cottebery, Thomas:
cantarist in St Nicholas's
hospital, Harbledown, 417
v. of St Stephen Hackington,
487
Couper, see Cowper
Coupland, see Copland
Courawgh, John, r. of Betteshanger
569
Courtenay:
Peter:
bp. of Exeter, 46, 85, 88-90
bp. of Winchester, 46, 114,
221, 243, 258-66, 354-5
William, abp. of Canterbury,
54, 346
Coventry (Coven'), Wa., 235
hospital of St John the Baptist,
507

184

Coventry and Lichfield (Coven' et
   Lich'), Wa.:
   bp., 445b, 632
      See also Halse; Smith
   dioc., 119, 128
   see, 127
Cowper (Couper):
   Henry, 476, 627
      can. of Wingham, 501, 562-3
      Commissary General of Canterbury,
         69, 75, 77
      r. of Adisham, 514, 753
      r. of Great Mongeham, 490, 523
   William, 433d
      r. of Ripple, 601
Coyne, William, v. of Headcorn, 659
Crage, Andrew, v. of Grain, 419
Cranbrook (Cranebrook), Kent,
   ch., 129
Crane, Oliver, v. of Tong, 686
Cranebrook, see Cranbrook
Crawley, North, Bk., ch., 632
Crayford alias Earde, Kent, 342
   ch., 173
Creme, Thomas, 346
Cremona, John de, 222
Cresham, George, O.P., 448a
Cretyng, William:
   dean of Westbury-on-Trym coll., 509
   r. of St Mary Calais, 426
Crofte, Richard, 200
   See also Crosse
Cromer, Nicholas, 618
Crosby:
   alias Roger, lady Anne, 57
   John, 57
Crosse:
   alias Crofte, Nicholas, 433b, 435c
   John:
      m. of Christ Church Canterbury,
         447a
      O.E.S.A., 440a
Crowmer (Crowmere), Alexander:
   chap. of Radfield, 367, 541
   r. of Tunstall, 486, 538
   scholar of Bredgar coll., 455
Croydon (Croydoun), Sy.:
   almshouse, 180
   ch., 175, 180, 388-90, 434, 673
      chantry of St Nicholas, 392,
         547, 739
   dean of peculiar jurisdiction, 22,
      392, 404, 482, 493, 545, 551

553, 590, 668-9, 673, 712,
   739, 744
dy., 152, 175
manor of abp., 56, 129,
   360-1, 527, 530-5, 595
Crundale (Crumdale), Kent, ch.,
   167
Culford, Richard, kt., king's
   comptroller, 188
Culpeper:
   Elizabeth, 362
   Margaret, 362
   Nicholas, 362
   Richard, 362
Curson:
   James:
      cantarist of Arundel's
         chantry, Canterbury cath.,
         537
      chap. of Black Prince's
         chantry, Canterbury cath.,
         527, 571
   John, r. of Auderne, 685
   Robert, r. of Harbledown, 568
Curteys, William, 195
Cusshon, William, r. of Slindon,
   577
Cutler, William, O.F.M., 444a,
   445b
Cutnor (Cednor), Thomas, O.F.M.,
   444a, 445b

Dady, Robert, chap. of
   St Nicholas's chantry, Croydon,
   392
Dale, see Deal
Dalton:
   Ralph, r. of Snargate, 410
   Robert, 498
   William, v. of Farningham,
      591
Daniell (Danyell):
   Christopher, r. of Little
      Mongeham, 699
   Ralph, 55
Darell:
   Ivo, r. of East Lavant, 520
   John, 617
Darenth (Darent, Darunth), Kent:
   ch., 139
   vic., 173

Dartford (Dertford), Kent, 70
  priory, 536
Darunth, see Darenth
Datell, Jerome, 223
Daubeny, see Dawbeny
David, William, app. A
Davington, Kent, priory, 462, 495,
  508
Davit, Owen ap, r. of Ardley, 618
Davy:
  Ellis, mercer of London, 180
  John, 264
  Thomas, v. of Sittingbourne, 556
Dawbeny (Daubeny), Giles lord,
  chamberlain to the king, 188
Dawncy:
  Hugh, 310
  Margaret, 310
Dawson (Dauson), Robert, O.E.S.A.,
  434b
Deal (Dale), Kent:
  chamberlain of, 132
  ch., 162
Dean (Dene), Bd. or Ox., 288
Dean, West (Westdene), Sx., 265
Deane, Henry, prior of Llanthony,
  278
Debekyn (Dobekyn), Robert, O.F.M.,
  440a, 441b
Demechurch, see Dymchurch
Dene, see Dean
Denny, Thomas, v. of Rolvenden, 653
Denton (Denynton), Kent, ch., 165,
  393
Denwey (Denneway), Thomas, chap.,
  of Bredgar coll., 455, 491
Denynton, see Denton
Dependen (Depden), see Petham
Derby:
  Henry de, Commissary General of
    Canterbury, 252
  Thomas earl of, 103, 108
Dertusen', see Tortosa
Desiderii, John, 222
Dingley (Dyngley), Peter:
  chap. of Radfield, 367
  r. of Snave, 374
  v. of Milton (near Sittingbourne),
  375
Dinham (Dynham), John:
  lord, Treasurer of England, 30, 90,
    103, 108
  r. of Hareway, 348, 411, 429

Ditton, Long (Longditton), Sy.,
  ch., 560
Dobekyn, see Debekyn
Dobson, Robert, 191
Doddiscombsleigh (Doddescome Lye),
  De., 302
Dodyn, Benedict:
  r. of Bishop's Waltham, 572
  r. of Coquelles, 573
Doebull, William, 443d
Dokett, John:
  cantarist of Arundel's chantry,
    Canterbury cath., 537
  r. of Chevening, 567
Dolfyn, Nicholas, O.P., 433a
Don:
  Edward, 35
  John, kt., 35
Donyngton, William, 288
Doo, Margaret, 321
Dorset, marquis of, see Grey
Dorturer, William le, notary
  public, 252
Douce, Stephen, master of
  St Michael Royal coll., London,
  641
Dover (Dovoria, Dovorr'), Kent:
  churches in:
    St James, 164, 427
    St John, 164
    St Mary, 164
    St Nicholas, 164
    St Peter, 164, 402, 727
  dy., 130, 133, 137-8, 143,
    154, 156, 164
  hospital of St Mary (domus Dei):
    can. (named), 433d
    master and brethren, 433c,
      434d
  priory of St Martin:
    monks (named), 431a, 435d,
      438b, d, 439b, 440c
    possessions, 133
    prior, 81, 212
    prior and conv., 359, 382,
      395, 402, 427, 549, 727,
      748
  revenues of prior of Lewes, 158
  temporalities of abbess of
    Guisnes, 156
Dover (Dovor, Dovorr):
  John, m. of Christ Church
    Canterbury, 443a, 445b, 446c

186

Dover (Cont'd):
  Richard, m. of St Martin's Dover,
    439b, 440c
  William, m. of St Martin's Dover,
    435d
Dowdeswell (Dowdyswell), Gl., ch.,
  26
Downe:
  John, m. of St Augustine's
    Canterbury, 446b, 447c
  Thomas, r. of East Peckham, 399,
    428
Downes, James, r. of Wickham, 565
Downevyle, Roger, v. of St Cosmus
  and St Damian in the Blean, 575
Drake, John, r. of Ripple, 474
Drakelow (Drakelowe), Db., 276
Draper:
  John, see Grousmouth
  Richard, advocate of court of
    Canterbury, Official of bp. of
    London, 191, 195-6, 202
Drovedens woods, app. A
Dubreuquet, John, 200
Duceti, Jaspard, notary public, 197
Dudan, Natrelus, 194
Dunelm', see Durham
Dunes, in Flanders, abbey of, 136
Dunkirk, Kent, North Bishopsden
  wood in, app. A
Dunstall, see Tunstall
Dunster, John:
  can. of West Langdon, 442a, 445b
  m. of St Augustine's Canterbury,
    432a, 439c, 442d
Dunston, John, m. of Christ Church
  Canterbury, 438b, 441c, 442d
Durant, see Wayneflete
Durham, bp. of, see Fox, Richard
Dutton, James, 47
Dymchurch (Demechurch), Kent, ch.,
  166, 476
Dynes, Alexander, 433d
Dyngley, see Dingley
Dynham, see Dinham

Easington (Esyngton), Ox., ch., 634
Eastbridge (Eastbrige, Eastbrigg),
  Kent, ch., 168
Eastchurch (Estchurch), Kent:
  ch., 136
  vic., 170
Eastling, Kent, ch., 171

Eastry, Kent:
  ch., 130
  vic., 162
Eastry, Christopher, m. of Christ
  Church Canterbury, 445a
Eastwell (Estwell), Kent, ch.,
  179
Ebony (Ebney), Kent, chapel,
  382
Edburton, Sx., ch., 174
Ede, John, v. of Elmstead, 396
Edendon, see Edington
Ediall (Edyall), Henry, 371
  master of Wingham coll., 658
  r. of Pluckley, 380
  r. of Saltwood, 365
Edington (Edendon), William, bp.
  of Winchester, 234, 258
Edmondson (Emmison), Thomas, r.
  of Otterden, 454, 643
Eduen', see Autun
Edward I, king, 231, 252
Edward III, king, 252
Edward IV, king, 186
Edwardes, John, 200
Edy, Edmund, 300
Edyall, see Ediall
Egent, John, v. of St cosmus and
  St Damian in the Blean, 575
Egerton, Thomas:
  can. of Leeds, 442a, 443b,
    445c
  m. of St Augustine's Canterbury,
    445b, 447c
Egham, Sy., 298
Eglesfeld (Egilsfeld):
  Leonard, v. of Reculver, 610
  Robert, preceptor of Beverley,
    deputy of Prior Provincial
    of Hospitallers, 370
Elcok, Thomas, 253-4, 256
Eleigh, Monks (Ilegh, Illegh
  Monachorum), Sf., ch., 176,
  554
Elham, Kent:
  ch., 165
  dy., 138, 140, 142, 165
Elham (Eleham), John, m. of
  Christ Church Canterbury, 438b,
  441c, 444d
Elien', see Ely
Elizabeth of York, queen, 8, 11,
  43

Elliott (Elyott), John or William,
  v. of East Peckham, 428, 581
Elmley, Kent, ch., 170
Elmstead (Elmestede, Elmstide,
  Elmysted), Kent:
  ch., 141
  vic., 396, 589
Elmstone (Elmerstone, Elmestone),
  in Preston hundred, Kent, ch.,
  167, 536
Elmysted, see Elmsted
Ely (Elien'), Ca.:
  bp., see Alcock; Morton
  dioc., 119, 128
  prior, 199, 202
  see, 1, 6, 127
Elyott, see Elliott
Elys:
  Thomas, v. of Grain, 407
  William, r. of St Nicholas,
    Barton-in-the-Clay, 624
Emlyn, John, notary public, 236,
  238
Emmison, see Edmondson
Emson, John, chap. of Kent's
  chantry, Headcorn, 659
Enderby, Richard, kt., 284
Engerst, Richard, 437a
Englissh:
  John, can. of St Chad's
    Shrewsbury, 511
  Thomas, can. of St Chad's
    Shrewsbury, 511
Ensyng, William, app. A
Entingeham, Roger de, m. of
  Winchester, 252
Erkelys, William, r. of
  Kingsdown, 736
Erle, Nicholas, r. of Wormshill,
  412
Eryk:
  John, 191
  Robert, 191
Escalles (Scales), Thérouanne dioc.,
  ch. of St Mary Magdalen, 690
Esh, see Ash
Essart (Essarde), Peter, 247, 254
Essex, archd. of, see Jane
Esshetesford, see Ashford
Estchurch, see Eastchurch
Estfarlegh, see Farleigh, East
Estlangdon, see Langdon, East
Estlavent, see Lavant, East

Estmallyng, see Malling, East
Estmeane, see Meon, East
Estmonde, Richard, 321
Estpecham, see Peckham, East
Estwell, see Eastwell
Esyngton, see Easington
Eton, Brk., coll. of St Mary, 120
Eugenius IV, Pope, 24
Evere, see Iver
Ewell, Kent, vic., 164, 645
Ewen, John, 283
Exere, see Westbury
Exeter (Exon'), De.:
  bp., see Courtenay; Fox; King
  cath.:
    canons (named), 540
    dean and chapter, 540
  dioc., 28-9, 72, 119, 128
  see, 127
Eye (Eey), Sf., priory, 441a
Eynsford (Aynesford, Aynisford,
  Eynesford, Eynisford), Kent:
  ch., 173, 418, 484, 592, 649,
    696
  vic., 418, 482
Eythorne (Eythorn), Kent, ch.,
  162, 475

Facet, Adam, r. of Patching, 750
Fairehede, John, scholar of
  All Souls, 64
Fairfield (Feyrfeld), Kent, 69
Falk (Falke), William, notary
  public, 196, 225, 228, 236
Fantyng, John, O.E.S.A., r. of
  Blackmanstone, 704
Faram, John, m. of Boxley, 445a
Farlegh, Thomas, m. of Christ
  Church Canterbury, 433d
Farleigh, East (Estfarlegh,
  Farlegh), Kent:
  ch., 173
  vic., 558
Farley, Henry, v. of Newnham, 462
Farnham (Farneham), Sy., 264,
  290, 328
Farningham (Farnyngham,
  Ferningham, Fernyngham), Kent:
  ch., 173
  vic., 173, 513, 591, 722
Farragene, Anthony, proctor of
  Audience of Contradicted
  Letters, 194

188

Faversham (Feversham), Kent:
  abbey:
    abbot, 212
    abbot and conv., 441c, 719
    monks (named), 433c-d, 434d,
      439a, 440b, 441c, 443c, 444a,
      d, 445b, 446c, 447d, 448a
    possessions, 135
  ch., 132
  vic., 132, 171, 715
Fayreway, William, r. of Milstead,
  687
Fayting, Richard, 431a, 432b
Feld, Walter, can. of Exeter, 540
Fenne, Robert, 299
Fenys, Thomas, 421, 557, 640, 681
Ferningham, see Farningham
Ferrers, Edward, app. A
Ferynges, Richard de, 230
Feversham:
  Edmund, can. of St Gregory's
    Canterbury, 431b, 437d
  Richard, m. of Christ Church
    Canterbury, 443a, 445b, 446c
  Robert, m. of Faversham, 448a
  See also Faversham
Feyrfeld, see Fairfield
Feytzherbert, see Fitzherbert
Fidelibus, James de, 222
Findon (Fyndon), Sx., 265
Firle, West (Fyrle), Sx., vic., 723
Fitzherbert (Feytzherbert):
  Nicholas, 293
  Roger, 293
Fitzjames, John, 298
Fitzjohn, William, r. of Leaveland,
  480
Fleccher, see Fletcher
Flemyng, David, r. of Ostenhanger,
  657
Fleshmonger (Flesshmonger), William,
  250, 258, 266
Fletcher (Fleccher), John:
  v. of Boxley, 460
  v. of Marden, 546, 661
Flete, Robert, v. of St Mary Bredin,
  Canterbury, 381
Flores, Anthony, protonotary of
  apostolic see, auditor of causes
  of the Rota, subsequently bp. of
  Castellamare, 221
  proceedings conducted on authority
    of, 223-66

Foche, Thomas, 431c, 432c, 435a
Fogges:
  John, 693
  Thomas, r. of Cheriton, 693
Folkestone (Folkeston'), Kent:
  ch., 154, 164, 212
  priory, 76-82, 154, 212
Folon, William, v. of Waltham,
  458
Ford, see Herne
Ford, Thomas, notary public,
  236, 241
Fordwich (Fordewich, Fordewicum),
  Kent, ch., 161, 652
Forebas, Robert:
  r. of Stowting, 498
  v. of Brenzett, 503
Forest, Thomas, 252
Forster, Robert, 285
Foster:
  Richard, 196
  Thomas, v. of Petham, 366, 613
Fownten, John, 81
Fox:
  Humphrey, 274
  Richard:
    bp. of Bath and Wells, 51
    bp. of Durham, 185, 188, 211,
      221
    bp. of Exeter, 44-5, 51, 99,
      102
  Robert, 191
Framsfield, Sx., ch., 174
France, 108, 186
  king, 74-5, 103, 108, 186
Frankelyn, see Franklyn
Frankham, see Wadhurst
Franklyn (Frankelyn, Franklion,
  Fraunklyn), John, 443d
  r. of Great Mongeham, 637, 725
  r. of Ickham, 724
  r. of Old Romney, 555, 642
Fraunces:
  Ingram, lately abbot of
    Bradsole, v. of Postling,
    372
  Nicholas, O.F.M., 443d
Fraunch, Thomas, O.Carm., 446a
Fraunklyn, see Franklin
Frende, Thomas, master of Higham
  Ferrers coll., 378
Frenstede, see Frinstead
Frere, William, O.E.S.A., 434c

189

Freston, John, submaster of
   Maidstone coll., 615
Freyle, James, v. of Lydden, 749
Frindsbury (Frinysbury), Kent, ch.,
   603
Frinstead (Frenstede), Kent, ch.,
   179
Frinysbury, see Frindsbury
Frittenden (Frithenden, Fritynden),
   Kent, ch., 179, 729
Froell, see Froyle
Frotyngham, Alexander, chap. of
   Holy Cross chantry, St Nicholas
   Calais, 548
Froyle (Froell'), Ha., 263
Frye, Matthew, app. A
Fulham, Mx., 86, 100
Fuller, Robert, v. of Brenzett,
   503
Furnes:
   Beatrice, 320
   Robert, 320
Fyndon, see Findon
Fyrle, see Firle, West
Fyssh, Thomas, r. of Hayes, 675,
   743

Garard:
   John, m. of Christ Church
      Canterbury, 443a, 445b, 446c
   Stephen, O.E.S.A., 440a
   William, 445d
Gardiner (Gardyner, Gardynere):
   John, 314
   Richard:
      r. of Chiddingstone, 706
      r. of Shoreham, 752
Garston, Thomas, 314
Garthe, Thomas, 315
Gaynesford, Walter, 434a
Geffrey, William, r. of Boughton
   Aluph, 721
Gelytard, William, r. of
   Dymchurch, 476
Gempe, see Campe
George, Thomas, v. of West Hythe,
   413
Gerhard, Gerard, 192, 200, 203
German, John, chap. of St Nicholas
   chantry, St Dunstan-without-the-
   Walls, Canterbury, 350

Germyn, Elena, prioress of
   St Mary de Prae, 50
Gerona, John de, clerk of
   apostolic camera, 61, 189-90,
   224
Gerveys, Thomas, 324
Giglis (Gyglis, Lilliis):
   John de, papal collector in
      England, 47
   Silvester de, bp. of Worcester,
      222
Giles (Gylis), Robert, can. of
   Bradsole, 447a
Gillingham (Gillyngham), Kent,
   vic., 173, 401
Glassynbury, Robert, m. of
   Boxley, 445a
Glynde, Sx.:
   ch., 155
   vic., 676
Godmersham, Kent:
   chapel, 130
   ch., 130
   vic., 167, 465
Godstone (Godston), Sy., 269
Godyn, John, scholar of Bredgar
   coll., 346
Goldwell:
   James, bp. of Norwich, 85, 88-90,
      99, 102, 109-10, 114-5
   Thomas, m. of Christ Church
      Canterbury, 443a, 444b, 445c
Golson, John, r. of Cheam, 669
Goode, William, 328
Goodhewe (Gudhew), John, fellow
   of Merton coll., 432a 444b
Goodnestone (Goodneston,
   Gudneston), Kent, ch., 171, 483
Goodwyn, William, 443b
Goold, Henry, r. of Elmstone, 536
Gooldston (Gooldstone), John:
   can. of Leeds, 433d
   r. of High Halden, 451
   r. of Ivychurch, 526
   r. of Old Romney, 450
Goss, John, 262
Gossage, John, 265-6
Gothe (Gouge), Thomas, chap. of
   St Mary's chantry, Bocking, 640
Gotinden, Richard, v. of Hernhill,
   473

Goudhurst (Goutherst, Gouthirst),
  Kent:
  ch., 140
  vic., 169
  See also Bockingfold
Gouge, see Gothe
Goutherst, see Goudhurst
Grafton, Adam, r. of St Dionis
  Backchurch, London, 499
Grain, Isle of (Greane, Grene),
  Kent:
  ch., 139
  vic., 173, 407, 419
Grasonn, William, 85
Graunt, Thomas, v. of Rodmersham,
  716
Grave, William, v. of Boughton
  Monchelsea, 656
Graveney (Greane), Kent:
  ch., 171
  vic., 746
Greane, see Grain, Isle of; Graveney
Greenwich (Grenwicum), Kent,
  Observant Franciscan conv., 188
Grene, Thomas:
  chap. of St Nicholas chantry,
    Croydon, 547, 739
  v. of Hartlip, 466
Grenehode, Robert, chap. of
  Sheering, 429
Grenewich, Thomas, can. of Bayham,
  440d
Grenwicum, see Greenwich
Greseley:
  John, kt., 276
  Richard, 276
Grete, Thomas, r. of Seaton, 606
Gretham, Robert, r. of St Dionis
  Backchurch, London, 430, 499
Grey, Thomas, marquis of Dorset,
  300, 331
Grousmouth alias Draper, John, 312
Growte, Robert, abp.'s registrar,
  237
Growght, William, 283
Groxolos, see Wroxfield
Gry, John, cantarist of Black
  Prince's chantry, Canterbury cath.,
  571
Gudhew, see Goodhewe
Gudneston, see Goodnestone
Guisnes (Guynce, Guysnes),
  dep. Pas de Calais:
  abbess, 156
  ch., 409, 636

Gulson, John, 446d
Guston, Kent:
  ch., 133
  vic., 164
Guynce, see Guisnes
Gyan, Thomas, m. of Winchester,
  248
Gybbys, John:
  r. of Hastingleigh, 470, 504
  r. of Sevington, 471
Gybson (Gybsonne):
  John, O.Carm., 447d
  Robert, 437a
    r. of Hinxhill, 518
Gyglis, see Giglis
Gylis, see Giles
Gyllingham (Gylingham,
  Gylyngham), m. of Christ Church
  Canterbury, 445a, 446b, 447c

Hackington, see Canterbury
Hacomblen, Robert, v. of
  Prescott, 543
Hadleigh (Hadlee, Hadley),
  Ess., ch., 176, 677
Hadley:
  Elizabeth, 272
  Thomas, 272
Hagnaby (Hagneby), Li., abbey,
  443d
Haines, see Haynes
Halden, High (Halden), Kent,
  ch., 179, 451, 532, 709
Haliday, Thomas, r. of Monks
  Eleigh, 554
Haliwell (Halywell, Holiwell),
  Mx., 342
  See also London, religious
    houses
Hall (Halle):
  Henry, 578
  Ricard, abbot of Hyde,
    proceedings before, 247-66
Halse, John, bp. of Coventry
  and Lichfield, 39
Halstead (Halstede), Kent,
  ch., 173, 369
Halstow, Lower (Halstowe),
  Kent, ch., 170
Halton, Bk., ch., 177, 740

Halywell, Thomas:
  chap. of Buckingham's chantry,
    Canterbury cath., 596
  warden of St Thomas's hospital,
    Eastbridge, 595
Ham by Sandwich (Hamme, Hammys),
  Kent, ch., 140, 162, 621
Hambledon (Hameldon, Hamyden), Ha.,
  ch., 221-66 passim
Hames (Hammeswell), Pas de Calais,
  ch., 414, 535
Hamme, see Ham
Hampden, John, 333
Hamptonia, see Southampton
Hamyden, see Hambledon
Hanys, see Haynes
Hanfeld (Henfeld), John, m. of
  Christ Church Canterbury, 438b,
    441c, 445d
Hannes, see Haynes
Hanselape (Hanslope), Thomas, m.
  of St Martin's Dover, 431a, 438d
Harall, John, v. of Boardfield, 508
Harbledown (Harbaldon, Harbaldown,
  Herbaldowne), Kent:
  chantry in St Nicholas's
    hospital, 417
  ch., 161, 568
Harding (Hardyng), Clement:
  fellow of New College, Oxford,
    442c, 443d
  v. of St Dunstan-without-the-
    Walls, Canterbury, 612
Hardres, Lower (Nether Hardys,
  Parva Hardes, Parva Hardys),
  Kent, ch., 161, 351, 680
Hardres, Upper (Magna Herdys),
  Kent, ch., 167, 648
Hardyng, see Harding
Hareway (Harway, Herwey), in
  marches of Calais, ch., 348,
  411, 429
Harford (Hertford):
  John, m. of Faversham, 444a,
    445b, 446c, 447d
  William, m. of Christ Church
    Canterbury, 445d
Hariettsham, see Harrietsham
Harington, Ralph, r. of Wichling,
  379
Harnehill, William, 434d
Harowe, see Harrow

Harper, Richard, r. of Norton,
  660
Harrietsham (Heriettysham,
  Heriottisham), Kent, ch., 169
Harrietsham (Hariettsham,
  Herriettesham), Thomas, can. of
  Leeds, 433c, 437d
Harrow-on-the-Hill (Harowe,
  Harrowe super le Hille), Mx.:
  chantry of St Mary, 482
  ch., 175
Harrys, Robert, v. of Thornham,
  383
Harryson, Thomas, v. of Chertsey,
  360
Harsett, Robert, r. of Newington,
  404
Hartanger (Hertangre), in
  Barfreston, Kent, ch., 140
Hartley Wespall (Hartley Waspall),
  Ha., 308
Hartlip (Hartlepe, Hertlepp),
  Kent:
  ch., 139
  vic., 170, 466
Harvey (Harvi, Hervey, Hervi,
  Hervy):
  Henry:
    chap. of Arundel's chantry,
      Canterbury cath., 667
    warden of St Margaret's
      hospital, Canterbury, 594,
      666
  John:
    can. of Hereford, 7
    can. of Wingham, 563
    r. of Ickham, 406, 529
    r. of Monks Risborough, 522
    r. of St Michael Crooked Lane,
      London, 364
Harway, see Hareway
Hasill, Thomas att, 250, 258-9,
  261
Haslach, Magnus, de, 228
Hastingleigh (Hastinglegh,
  Hastingligh), Kent, ch., 165,
  470, 504
Hastyng, John, O.F.M., 446a
Hatton, Richard, r. of Guisnes,
  409
Havard, John, app. A

192

Hawarden (Hawardyn, Hawardyne),
  Humphrey, 87, 101
  auditor of abp.'s Court of
    Audience, 18
  commissary of Prerogative, 17
  Official Principal of Court of
    Canterbury, 196
  prolocutor of Convocation, 102
  r. of St Mary Aldermary, London,
    584
  r. of Shoreham, 397, 752
Hawes:
  Margery, 301
  Thomas, 301
Hawkhurst (Hawkeherst, Hawkehurst),
  Kent, ch., 134, 179
Hawkhurst (Hawkherst):
  Thomas, m. of Christ Church
    Canterbury, 447a
  William, m. of St Augustine's
    Canterbury, 432a, 439c, 442d
Hawkinge (Hawkyng), Kent, ch., 164
Hawkyns:
  John:
    r. of Ruckinge, 449
    r. of Woodchurch, 582
    v. of Linsted, 597
  Thomas, r. of Luddenham, 719
Hawte, Thomas, 704, 710
Hayes (Heese, Hese, Heyse), Kent,
  ch., 173, 675, 743
Hayes (Heese), Mx., ch., 175
Hayles, Walter, clerk, 298
Haylsham (Haylisham), John, m. of
  St Augustine's Canterbury, 446b,
  447c
Haymer, John, r. of Long Ditton, 560
Haymys, Thomas, chap. of Kent's
  chantry, Headcorn, 659
Haynes (Haines, Haneys, Hannes,
  Hannyes, Haynyes):
  John, r. of Eynsford, 418, 484,
    592
  Ralph:
    can. of Reigate, 83
    Official sede vacante, Rochester
      dioc., 42
    r. of Latchingdon, 522, 633
    r. of Marck, 631
Haywarde, John, can. of Lanthony,
  278

Headcorn (Headcron, Hedcron,
  Hedcrone), Kent:
  ch., 179, 659, 728, 751
  Kent's chantry, 659
Headcrone, Thomas, O.Trin., 435d
Hebbing, John, can. of domus
  Dei, Dover, 433d
Hedcron, see Headcorn
Heede, William, app. A
Heese, see Hayes
Hegh, Hugh, v. of Minster, 586
Hemiot, Thomas, r. of
  Hervelinghen, 384
Henfeld, see Hanfeld
Hengshill, see Hinxhill
Henley, Brian, O.F.M., 444a,
  445b, 446c
Henrici, Cornelius, O.F.M.,
  438b
Henry V, king, 186
Henry VI, king:
  alleged sanctity, 185
  letters patent, 180
  relics, 186
Henry VII, king:
  grants, 354, 540, 572, 685
  papal concessions to, 8, 11-12,
    43, 187
  patron, 348, 357, 384, 394,
    398, 409, 414, 426, 450,
    507, 509, 519, 533-5, 542,
    548, 555, 573-4, 599, 602,
    631, 636, 642, 660, 662,
    665, 687, 690, 714, 741
  petitions to pope, 185-6, 188,
    211
  prayers for, 33, 56, 74-5
Henxhill, see Hinxhill
Hereford (Hereforden'), 312
  bp., 441b; see also Audley;
    Myllyng.
  cath.:
    can. (named), 7, 519
    dean and chapter, 519
  dioc., 119, 128
  priory of St Guthlac, 439b
  see, 127
Herfeld, John, m. of Christ
  Church Canterbury, 441c
Heriettysham, see Harrietsham

Herne, Kent:
    chantry of St Mary, 453
    vic., 463
    manor of Ford, app. A
Hernhill (Harnehill, Harnhill),
    Kent, vic., 171, 473, 477, 705
Hertford, see Harford
Hertlepp, see Hartlip
Hervelinghen (Herveningham), in
    parts of Picardy, ch., 384
Hervey, see Harvey
Herway, see Hareway
Hese, see Hayes
Hether, Richard, 250, 258-9
Heton, Robert, chap. of
    Buckingham chantry, Canterbury
    cath., 596
Hever, Kent, ch., 173, 464
Heyse, see Hayes
Hewett, William, r. of Hames, 414
Hicson (Hikson, Hycson):
    Thomas, 443b
        junior, 651
        r. of St Mary de Castro,
            Canterbury, 605, 701
        r. of St Peter's Canterbury,
            651
    William, 436b, 437d, 438c
        scholar of Bredgar coll., 607,
            735
        v. of St Nicholas, Sturry, 726
Hida, see Hyde
Higham Ferrers, Np., coll. ch., 378
Hikson, see Hicson
Hildyche, William, v. of East
    Farleigh, 558
Hill (Hille, Hyll, Hylle):
    John, 290
        can. of St Paul's London, 196
    Richard, bp. of London, 191-2,
        196-7, 199-203
Hilp (Hilpp), Thomas:
    r. of Snave, 374
    v. of Lenham, 353, 391
Hinxhill (Hengshill, Henxhill),
    Kent, ch., 168, 459, 518, 587
Hodingfellys, Henry, 338
Hofkyrk, see Offekerque
Hoggan, Simon, 279
Hoggis, Simon, v. of St Stephen,
    Hackington, 487
Hokty, Thomas, 311

Holand, Thomas, r. of Marck, 631
Holbeme:
    Christopher, 302
    John, 302
Holcombe, Mr William, 28-9
Holden:
    Mr Bernard, 257
    Thomas, 250, 258, 264
Holer (Hollere), Robert, chap.
    of St Nicholas's chantry,
    Croydon, 392, 547
Hollingborn (Holingborn,
    Hollyngborn, Holyngborn):
    Robert, m. of Christ Church
        Canterbury, 439a, 441b, 445d
    Thomas, m. of St Augustine's
        Canterbury, 432c
    William:
        can. of Leeds, 433b, 438c,
            443d
        r. of Ham, 621
Hollingbourne (Holyngborn),
    Kent, 346
    ch., 169
    vic., 622
Holme, James, 302
Holmysley, William, r. of
    Patching, 750
Holt, John, 723
    r. of Smarden, 711
Holyngborn, see Hollingbourne
Holywell, see Haliwell
Hony, John, r. of Sevington, 521
Honynden, Mr Edward, 255
Honywod, Mr Robert, 444c
Hooke, Thomas, 432c
Hookes, Thomas, r. of
    Hastingleigh, 504
Hoope, Thomas, r. of Shoreham,
    397
Hoorne, see Horne
Hope All Saints (in marsh of
    Romney), Kent:
    ch., 168
    tithes, 142
Hope, Hugh, r. of High Halden,
    709
Hopton:
    David, can. of Hereford, 519
    William, r. of Burstow, later
        Carthusian, 493

Horne (Hoorne):
  Gervase, 271
  Henry, 479
Horsey, Herman, O.F.M., 436b
Horsham (Horseham), Sx., 332
Horsham, John, O.Carm., 436c, 438d
Horsley (East Horstleigh), Sy.,
  ch., 175
Horsley, John, 291
Horton, Monks (Hortun), Kent:
  ch., 165
  priory, 142
    prior and conv., 604, 672
Hospital of St John of Jerusalem:
  privileges, 89-90, 107
  prior provincial, 61, 90, 107,
    370, 600, 635, 645, 716
  See also Kendall
Hostiensis (Henry de Segusio,
  cardinal bp. of Ostia), canonist,
  181
Hostinghanger, see Ostenhanger
Hothfield (Hotfelde), Kent, ch., 179
Hoton, Robert, 447d
Hougham by Dover (Hucham, Hugham),
  Kent, ch., 133, 164
Houghton (Hogton), Mr J., 232
Hovar, John, 264
Howlet, Thomas, v. of Brabourne,
  604
Hucham, see Hougham
Hucking (Huckinge), Kent, 346
Huddeston, Oliver, can. of West
  Langdon, 439d
Hudson, Richard, r. of Ruckinge, 583
Huett, William, r. of Pluckley, 380
Hugham, see Hougham
Hull, Nicholas, m. of Christ Church
  Canterbury, 447a
Hunbolde, Simon, 308
Hunden, John, bp. in the Universal
  Church, v. of Lenham, 353
Hungerford:
  Eleanor, see Manyngham
  Thomas, v. of Preston next Faversham,
    732
Huntingdon, archdeaconry, 129
Huntlow, Hugh, v. of Preston near
  Wingham, 737
Hunton (Huntyngdon), Kent, ch.,
  173, 742

Hurst:
  Richard, 332
  Robert, 332
Hustwayte, Thomas, r. of Oye,
  398
Hutton:
  Mr James, 26
  Thomas, archd. of Lincoln,
    226-9, 236
Hyde (Hida, Hyda), near
  Winchester, Ha., abbey, 258
  abbot, papal mandatory, 247-
    66
Hyll, see Hill
Hyndemarsh (Hyndemerssh), Alan,
  r. of All Saints, Canterbury,
  31, 468
Hyne, Richard, v. of St Clement,
  Sandwich, 485
Hythe, Kent, town and lordship,
  app. A
Hythe, West (Westhith), Kent,
  vic. 413

Ickham (Icham, Ikham), Kent,
  ch., 167, 173, 406, 529, 724
Idon, Richard:
  penitentiary of South
  Malling and r. of Stanmer,
  422, 488-9
  r. of Kingsnorth, 488, 700
  r. of Wootton, 578
Ifield (Ifeld), Kent, ch., 173
Ikham, Thomas, m. of Christ
  Church Canterbury, 439d
Ile-Dieu (Insula Dei), Normandy,
  abbey, 157
Ilegh, see Eleigh, Monks
Imbroke, William, notary public,
  225, 227-9, 236, 244, 247,
  257
Imola, bp. of, see Pasarella
Inena, Alphonsus Fernandus de,
  notary public, 200
Inglisthorp, Joan, 565
Innocent VIII, pope, 1-6, 8-12,
  40, 43, 46-51, 185, 187
Insula Dei, see Ile-Dieu
Ireland, 43, 89

Isaak:
  Mary, 343
  Richard, 343
Isfield (Isefeld), Sx., ch.,
  174, 738
Ispalen', see Seville
Ivechurch, see Ivychurch
Iver (Evere), Bk., 322
Ivychurch (Ivechurch), Kent,
  ch., 166, 526

James (Jamys):
  John:
    clerk of royal chancery, r.
      of Old Romney, 534
    r. of Peuplingues, 533
  Sybil, 281
  Walter, 280-1
Jane (Jayn), Thomas, archd. of
  Essex, 34, 101, 126
Jareterii, Venetus, 194
Jayn, see Jane
Jeakyn, Thomas, clerk, 346
John, king, 53
John XXIII, pope, 39, 252
John, Robert ap, v. of Tong, 707
Johnson:
  Richard, v. of St Nicholas at
    Wade, 500
  Br Robert, v. of River, 373
Jowre, Thomas, 441a
Jupsi, Paul, 197

Kadmore, Everard:
  can. of St Stephen's Bamberg,
    223
  prior of St Bangolf, Bamberg,
    228
Keamys:
  John, 304
  Thomas, 274
Kempe:
  John, abp. of Canterbury, 24
  Thomas:
    bp. of London, 34, 85-6, 97,
      99-100, 124
    esq., 483, 498
  William, 587
    v. of St Mary Northgate,
      Canterbury, 734

Kemsyng, Peter de, clerk, 53
Kenardington (Kenardynton,
  Kenarton), Kent, ch., 166, 479
Kendall, John, prior provincial of
  Hospitallers, 61, 370, 600, 635,
  645, 716
Kendill, John, v. of Hollingbourne,
  622
Kennington (Keniton, Kenynton),
  Kent, ch., 132, 179
Kentwell, John, can. regular, r.
  of East Langdon, 456
Kenynton, see Kennington
Ker, John, 255
Kerver, John, v. of East Peckham,
  428
Kesell, Richard, v. of Coldred,
  748
Keston (Kestane), Kent, ch., 173
Kettilsden (Ketillysden), William,
  444a
  r. of Frittenden, 729
  v. of Preston near Wingham, 689,
    694
King (Kyng, Kynge):
  John, O.P., 446b, 447c
  Oliver:
    bp. of Bath and Wells, 221
    bp. of Exeter, 52
    can. of Exeter, 540
Kingsdown (Kyngesdon, Kyngisdown),
  Kent, ch., 170, 736
Kingsnorth (Kingesnorth,
  Kyngesnorth, Kyngisnorth), ch.,
  134, 166, 488-9, 700
Kingston (Kyngeston, Kyngston),
  Kent, ch., 167, 703
Kirkeby, Nicholas, 336
Knaptofte (unid.), Coventry and
  Lichfield dioc., 282
Knight (Knyght):
  Richard or Thomas, chap. of
    St Mary's chantry, Bocking,
    640, 681
  Thomas, m. of Winchester, 248-9,
    255
  William, r. of Brook, 385
Knole, Kent, abp.'s manor, 421,
  454, 475, 477, 574, 577-81, 641,
  706-7, app. A
Knolton, see Knowlton

Knowdysin, John, chap. of St
  Mary's chantry, Croydon, 744
Knowlton (Knolton), Kent, ch.,
  162, 370
Knyght, see Knight
Knyveton, Matthew, v. of
  Ospringe, 425
Kyng, see King
Kyngesdowne, William, 54
  See also Kingsdown
Kyngesnorth, see Kingsnorth
Kyngiston, Richard, m. of Christ
  Church Canterbury, 441a, 442b,
  443c
Kyngston, see Kingston
Kyrbither, Thomas, v. of
  Postling, 372
Kyrittes, Thomas, 439b
  r. of Sevenoaks, 692
Kyrkby:
  Thomas, O.P., 439a
  William:
    can. of Bradsole, 432c, 435c
    v. of Postling, 674
Kyry, Thomas, can. of Wingham,
  638

Lachedon, see Latchingdon
Lackingdon, see Latchingdon
Lacy:
  Richard, m. of Winchester, 248
  Mr Robert, 230
Lamberhurst, see Lambherst
Lambeth (Lamhithe), Sy, abp.'s
  manor, 13-14, 16, 18-23, 25-9,
  31-3, 35, 38, 43, 47, 50, 54-5,
  57, 60-1, 63-4, 67-71, 73-4,
  76-7, 79, 81-4, 86, 90, 97-100,
  121-2, 124-6, 187, 189-90, 224,
  226, 232, 234-5, 243, 267-91,
  293-346, 347-430 passim,
  449-753 passim
  chamber of Mr Peyntwyn, 229
  court session in chapel, 13-5,
    71, 79
  custodian, app. A
  ferry, app. A
  janitor's dwelling, 237-40
  Morton's Tower, 241
  prison, 89
  registry, 227, 229, 236-46

Lambherst (Lamberhurst, Lamherst,
  Langeherst), Edmund, 436a,
  437c, 438b, 439d
Langdon, East (Estlangdon),
  Kent, ch., 132, 162, 456
  See also Pising
Langdon, West (Langdon,
  Westlangdon), Kent:
  abbey, 137
  abbot and conv., 686, 707,
    749
  can. (named), 438d, 439b,
    442a, 445b, 446c, 447d
  ch., 137
Langdon, John, m. of Christ
  Church Canterbury, 447a
Lange, John, r. of Burstow, 493
Langeherst, see Lambherst
Langley, Kent, ch., 169
Langley:
  John, 655
  Thomas:
    Chancellor of England, 235
    can. of Leeds, 437b, 438a,
      442c
    v. of Northbourne, 517
Langriche, John, master of St
  Mark's hospital, Bristol, 275
Langthorn, Mr John, 252
Langton, Li., 300
Langton:
  John, app. A
  Thomas:
    bp. of Salisbury, 85, 88-90,
      99, 102, 104
    bp. of Winchester, 243,
      260-6
    elect of Winchester, 572
Lankastre, Edmund, v. of Petham,
  613
Lanthony (Lanthon' iuxta
  Gloucestr'), Gl., priory:
  prior, 278
  can. (named), 278
Lany, see Lawny
Large, Thomas, 59
Lasnon, see Losenham
Lasynby, Robert:
  chap. of St Nicholas's chantry,
    Harbledown, 417
  v. of St Peter's, Isle of
    Thanet, 400

Latchingdon (Lachedon, Lachindon, Lachyndon, Lackingdon, Lackyndon), Ess., ch., 176, 469, 496, 552, 633
Lathes, Robert, v. of South Bersted, 647
Laudevell, Robert, v. of Godmersham, 465
Launde (Lawnde):
  John, v. of Elmstead, 396, 589
  Thomas, 448a
  William, 446b
Launey, see Lawny
Laurencii, Mr John, 190, 203, 224, 228
Lavant, East (Estlavent, Lavent), Sx., ch., 172, 520
Lawe, John:
  r. of Teynham, 405
  v. of Gillingham, 401
Lawnde, see Launde
Lawny (Lany, Launey), John, can. of Combwell, 439a-b, 444c, 445d
Leanham, see Lenham
Leaveland (Leveland, Loveland), Kent, ch., 171, 480
Ledane, see Lydden
Lee (Legh):
  Henry, m. of Faversham, 433c, 434d
  John:
    master of Maidstone coll., 615
    v. of St Mary's Sandwich, 623
  Thomas, m. of Christ Church Canterbury, 447a
Leeds (Ledes, Ledys), Kent:
  ch., 140
  priory, 140
    can. (named), 433b-d, 437a-b, d, 438a, c, 439b-c, 442a, c-d, 443a-b, d, 445b-c, 446b, 661
    prior and conv., 440d, 448a, 494, 559, 621, 650, 656, 733
Legh, see Lee
Leicester (Leicestr'), Le., coll. ch. of Newark, 378
Leicester (Leycestre), Mr Roger de, 53
Leisden, see Leysdown

Le Man:
  Joan, 346
  John, 346
Lenham (Leanham), Kent:
  ch., 132
  vic., 169, 353, 391
Lenn, see Lynn
Lenster, Robert, 273
Lessness (Lesenes), Kent, abbey, 146
  abbot and conv., 481, 546, 661
Lethyngesbourne, see Bekesbourne
Lewes, Sx., abbey, 158
Lewis, chap. of St Stephen's chantry, Selling, 505
Ley, John, v. of Tooting, 361
Leycestre, see Leicester
Leynham, Thomas, m. of Faversham, 448a
Leyns, Nicholas, r. of St Blaise in Melak, 714
Leysdown (Leisdon, Leysden), Kent, ch., 138, 170
Lichfield (Lychefeld):
  Richard:
    archd. of Mx., 87, 101, 126, 228
    Official sede vacante, London dioc., 33-4, 56
  Roger, 569, 598
  See also Coventry
Lightbon, Christopher, 644
Lightfoote, John, r. of St Nicholas, Weybridge, 352
Liliis, see Giglis
Lincoln, co. Li.:
  archd., see Hutton
  bp., 37-8, 431a, 432b, 433b, d, 435c, 436b, 440a, 443b, 445d, 698
    See also Russell; Smith
  dioc., 119, 128-30, 318, 321
  see, 127
Lincoln, Richard, r. of Prescott, 543
Lisbon, abp. of, see Costa
Litleborn (Litilborn), Edmund, m. of St Augustine's Canterbury, 436a, 439b, 443c, 444d
Littlebourne (Litelborn), Kent, ch., 132

Littleover (Parva Ovre), Db., 58
Littleton (Littelton), Ha., 252
Lityll, Roger, 659
Llandaff (Landaven'), Glam.:
  dioc., 119, 128
  see, 127
Lodenham, see Luddenham
London, 34, 191, 196, 354
  aldermen and sheriffs, 89
  archdeaconry, 129
  bp., 86, 100, 429, 439b
    See also Hill; Kempe; Savage.
    Commissary General, 191, 196,
      202
    manor, at Fulham, 86, 100
    Official, 191, 195-6, 202
    proctors (named), 191-2,
      194-6, 200, 202-3
    testamentary jurisdiction,
      191-2, 194
  cathedral church of St Paul,
    31, 34, 85, 97, 99, 126,
    192-3, 196-7, 228
    can. (named), 196
    chapel of St Mary, 85
    chapter house, 101
    dean, 88, 102
    dean and chapter, 34, 152
    Long Chapel, 195, 225, 227-8,
      242-6
  churches in or near:
    All Hallows, Lombard St (in
      Graschurch), 178
    All Hallows the Less, 191
    All Hallows London Wall (in
      muro), 296
    St Botolph Aldersgate, 337
    St Clement Danes (extra barras
      novi Templi), 291
    St Dionis Backchurch, 430, 499
    St Dunstan in the East, 178,
      525
    St Edmund King and Martyr,
      279
    St John the Evangelist,
      Watling St, 588
    St Leonard Eastcheap, 178
    St Magnus the Martyr, 192-3
    St Martin in the Fields (in
      campo), 291
    St Martin, Ludgate, 313
    St Mary Aldermary (de Aldermary
      Chirch), 178, 252, 584

London (Cont'd):
    St Mary Bothaw (de Bothawe),
      544
    St Mary le Bow (de Arcubus),
      178
      dean (of Arches), 364, 406,
        408, 424, 430, 499, 525
        561, 588, 641
      dy., 21, 70, 178, app. A
    St Michael Crooked Lane (in
      Crokid Lane), 178, 364,
      406, 561, 588, 641
    St Michael Paternoster Royal
      (in Riola), 424, 641
    St Michael Queenhithe (apud le
      Quenehithe), 60
      Whittington coll., annexed
        to, 67, 641
    St Nicholas Shambles (ad
      Macellas), 191
    St Pancras, 178
    St Swithin, 287
    St Vedast, 178, 408
  clergy, 89, 92
  dioc., 33, 56, 119, 128-30, 305,
    338
    Official sede vacante, 33-4,
      56
  friars, 89
    O.E.S.A. (named), 434b-d
  hospitals in or near:
    St Mary without Bishopsgate,
      59, 445d
    St Thomas the Martyr of Acon
      or Acre, Cheapside, 23-5,
      447d
    St Thomas the Martyr, Southwark,
      73
  mayor, 90
  Mercers Company, 180, 424
  places in or near:
    Ely Inn, 7
    Gray's Inn, 302
    Ivy Lane, 196
    palace of bp. of Exeter, 354
    palace of bp. of Winchester,
      235
    Paul's Cross, 70, 89-91
    Paul's Wharf, 99
    Tower, 89
  religious houses in or near:
    Holy Trinity or Christ Church,
      Aldgate, 611

London (Cont'd):
    can. (named), 611
   St John the Baptist, Haliwell,
    433b, 445b
   St Mary de Fonte, Clerkenwell,
    556
   St Mary Overy, Southwark, 232
    361, 746
  see, 127
London:
  George, O.E.S.A., 433b
  John de, 232
  Mr Reginald de, 53
  Robert, m. of Faversham, 433d
Long, Richard, v. of St Dunstan-
  without-the-Walls, Canterbury,
  612
Long Ditton, see Ditton
Lopez, John, abp. of Capua,
  cardinal priest of St Mary
  Transtiber, 221-2
Losenham (Lasnon), Kent,
  Carmelite friary:
  friars (named), 438b-c
Lovelasse, Richard, 367, 541
Lovell, Lord, 89
Lovyer (Lovier), Mr John, 248,
  250-1, 253
Lowen (Lowyn), Christopher:
  chap. of St Stephen's chantry,
   Selling, 505, 655
  r. of Bonnington, 635
Luca, Mr Peter de, 192, 194, 196,
  200, 203
Lucas, Henry, 436b, 438c
Luddenham (Lodenham, Lodyngham,
  Ludenham), Kent, 149
  ch., 135, 171, 719
Ludwhich, Richard, chap. of
  Arundel's chantry, Canterbury
  cath., 403
Lugdunen', see Lyons
Luknor (Lukenor):
  Richard, 326
  Roger, kt., 326
  Thomas, kt., 326
Lullingstone (Lyllyngton), Kent,
  ch., 169
Lute, Richard, can. of St Thomas,
  Southwark, 73
Luvel, Henry, 53
Lyall, James, v. of Bapchild, 461

Lychefeld, see Lichfield
Lydd (Lyd, Lydde), Kent:
  ch., 168
  vic., 168, 713
Lydden (Ledane, Lyden), Kent:
  ch., 137
  vic., 749
Lylle, John, r. of Leaveland, 480
Lyllisden, Thomas, clerk, 346
Lyminge (Lymmynge, Lymnynge),
  Kent:
  ch., 165, 377, 682
  park, app. A
Lympne (Lymmene), Kent:
  ch., 131, 166
  dy., 131-4, 142, 144, 156, 160,
   166, 168
Lyndesey, see Lynsey
Lynley (Lyndeley):
  John, r. of Wittersham, 530
  Robert, r. of Easington, 634
  Thomas:
   r. of Chiddingstone, 376, 423
   r. of St Michael Paternoster
    Royal, London, 424
Lynn, King's (Lenn Episcopi), Nf.,
  310, 335
Lynn, South (South Lyn'), Nf., 329
Lynne, Mr Gregory, 225, 228, 236,
  246
Lynsey (Lyndesey), John, can. of
  Combwell, 443a, 445b, 446c, 447d
Lynsted (Lynstede), Kent, vic.,
  171, 472, 597
Lynsted, Bartholomew, can. of
  Leeds, 445a, 447b
Lynton, Robert, anchorite, 297
Lyons (Lugdunen') dioc., 197
Lytton:
  Christopher, r. of St John the
   Evangelist, Watling St, 588
  Robert, 588
Lyvingesburn, see Bekesbourne

Maddes (Maddeys, Mades), Thomas,
  50, 99, 190
  r. of Lyminge, 682
  r. of Wrotham, 670
Magfeld, see Mayfield
Magna Chart, see Chart, Great
Magna Herdys, see Hardres, Great

Magna Muncham, see Mongeham, Great
Maidstone (Maidiston, Maydenestane,
  Maydeston), Kent, 478-80, 599
  coll. ch. of All Saints, 169,
    615
    master and fellows, 568
    submaster and fellows, 615
  hospital of SS Peter, Paul and
    Thomas, 68
  manor of abp., app. A
Maldon, William de, notary public,
  252
Malintiis, Perseus de, dean of
  St Michael de Profeto, Bologna,
  47
Malling, East (Estmalling), Kent:
  ch., 148
  vic., 173
Malling, South (Southmallyng), Sx.:
  coll. ch. of St Michael, 174
    can. (named), 550
    dean, 387, 489, 550, 676, 717,
      738, 745
    dy., of abp.'s immediate
      jurisdiction, 129, 155, 174
    penitentiary in, 422, 488-9,
      717
Malmayn, John, app. A
Malmesbury (Malmysbury), Roger,
  abp.'s registrar, 237-8, 240-1
Malta, 47
Mannyng, Robert, chap., 334
Manwood, William, m. of Winchester,
  229, 236, 242, 244, 247-50, 255,
  257
Manyngham alias Hungerford, Lady
  Eleanor, 333
Mapulsden, James, 292
Marchall, see Marshall
Marck (Marque), in parts of
  Picardy, ch., 631
Marden (Merden, Merdon), Kent:
  ch., 146
  vic., 169, 546, 661
Mareshall, see Marshall
Margate, Kent, ch., 163
Marke, Thomas, r. of Wilcote, 720
Marshall (Marchall, Mareshall,
  Marshal):
  John, O.E.S.A., 438b
  Peter:
    r. of Faversham, 715
    v. of Tenterden, 593

Marshall (Cont'd):
  William:
    r. of Warehorne, 697
    v. of Appledore, 382
Marshe (Mershe):
  Agnes, 289
  Thomas, 289
Martyn (Marten):
  Richard:
    bp. in the Universal Church,
      431, 433-7, 529
    r. of Ickham, 529
    r. of Wittersham, 530
    v. of St Peter's, Isle of
      Thanet, 400
  Thomas, r. of Peuplingues, 394
Marwell (Merewell), Ha., 252
Maryet, John, r. of Kingsnorth,
  700
Maryner, William, 70, 236, 240,
  279, 298, 345, app. A
Mascall, John, O.E.S.A., 436a
Mason, John, r. of Acrise, 494
Massey, John, 340
Materes, Christopher, 448a
Matheu, Gerard, O.E.S.A., 434d
Mauleverer:
  Joan, 393
  William, 393
Mawdisley, Thomas, r. of
  Newenden, 626
Maxey, Peter, chap. of Black
  Prince's chantry, Canterbury
  cath., 527
Maydenhith, Mr John, 235
Maydeston (Maydston), Thomas:
  m. of Boxley, 442a, 443c
  m. of St Augustine's Canterbury,
    432a, 439c, 442d
  See also Maidstone
Maye, William, 504
Mayfield (Magfeld, Maghfeld),
  Sx.:
  ch., 129, 174
  manor, app. A
Maynell, John, chap. of
  St Nicholas chantry, Croydon,
  739
Mayo, Erasmus, 440a
Meath (Miden') dioc., Ireland,
  437a, 442d
Mediolanen', see Milan

Medwall (Medewall):
  Henry, 438a
    notary public, 50
    r. of Balinghen, 542
  John, abp.'s apparitor in
    London, 21
Medwell, John, v. of Elmstead,
  589
Menstre, see Minster
Menys, John, m. of Christ Church
  Canterbury, 438d
Meon, East (Estmeane, Estmene),
  Ha., ch., 221-66 passim
Meopham (Mepeham, Mepham), Kent:
  ch., 130
  vic., 173, 603
Mercelli, Mr John, 194
Merewell, see Marwell
Mersham, Kent, ch., 168
Merstham (Merstan, Sy., ch.
  175, 668
Mershe, see Marshe
Merston, Kent, ch., 170
Merton (Merten), Sy., priory,
  145, 232
  prior and conv., 560, 620, 680
Michell, John:
  chap. of Reculver chantry, 609
  custodian of Lambeth ferry, app.A
Middilbourgh, Cornelius, O.F.M.,
  436a
Middilton, see Middelton, Milton
Middlesex:
  archd. of, 87, 101, 126, 228
    Official, 72
  archdeaconry, 129
Middleton (Middelton, Middilton,
  Myddleton, Myddylton):
  Christopher, notary public, 606
  Gilbert de, Official of Court
    of Canterbury, 232
  Robert, 26
    r. of St Dionis Backchurch,
      London, 430, 499
  Thomas, v. of St Margaret's,
    Cliffe, 395
  See also Milton
Midley (Mydley), Kent, ch., 168
Milan (Mediolanen') dioc., 203
Millett, John:
  Official of archd. of Middlesex,
    72
  r. of Charlwood, 590

Milstead (Milstede, Myllsted,
  Mylsted), Kent, ch., 170, 663,
  687
Milton next Canterbury (Middelton),
  Kent, ch., 161
Milton near Sittingbourne
  (Middilton), Kent:
  ch., 132
  vic., 170, 375
Milton, Thomas, m. of St
  Augustine's Canterbury, 446b,
  447c
Minden dioc., 194
Minster in Thanet (Menstre,
  Mynstre in Thaneto), Kent:
  ch., 132
  vic., 163, 524, 586
Miryk, James, 258
Miscua, Pampulus de, notary
  public, 194
Mody, William, r. of St Mary de
  Castro, Canterbury, 701
Mokarum, Bernard, 222
Molence, Anne, 333
Moleton, see Moulton
Monachus, Johannes, canonist, 181
Mongeham, Great (Magna Muncham,
  Magna Mungeham, Mongeham,
  Moungeham), Kent, ch., 162, 490,
  523, 637, 725
Mongeham, Little (Parva Mungeham),
  Kent, ch., 162, 699
Monkton in Thanet (Monketon),
  Kent:
  ch., 130, 163
  vic., 683
Mooteron, Adam, archd. of
  Canterbury, 346
More, see Northmoor
Moreton Magna (unid.), He., 282
Morleye, William, app. A
Mortlake (Mortelake), Sy., 17-8,
  232, 371, 464, 529, 616
Morton:
  Cecily, 342
  John:
    bp. of Ely, translated to
      Canterbury, 1-6
    cardinal priest of St
      Anastasia, 207-9
    See also Canterbury, abp.
    bailiff of Aldington, app. A

202

Morton (Cont'd):
  Nicholas, r. of Newington, 404
  Robert:
    archd. of Winchester, 354-5
    bp. of Worcester, 85, 88, 90,
      99, 102, 114, 354-5
    can. of Wherwell, 356
    Master of the Rolls, 7
  Roger, 342
  Thomas:
    archd. of Ely, 562
    can. of Wingham, 562
    master of Wingham coll., 627,
      658
    generosus, app. A
Mortymer, John, O.F.M., 433c
Moryce, Mr Walter, 275
Mosden, William, 292
Moton, see Motton
Mottenden (Motynden), Kent,
  Trinitarian priory:
  can. (named), 433c, 435d, 440a
  prior and conv., 363, 457
Motton (Moton), Robert:
  r. of Burmarsh, 678
  r. of Lower Hardres, 351, 680
Moulton (Moleton, Multon), Sf.:
  ch., 176, 698
  vic., 688
Moungeham, see Mongeham, Great
Mountford, Edmund, kt., 7
Mowbrey, Mr John, 191
Mugworthy, Thomas, v. of
  Sevenoaks, 730
Multon, Richard, v. of Appledore,
  382
  See also Moulton
Munden, John, v. of Boxley, 460
Myddleton, see Middleton
Mydley, see Midley
Mylle, Thomas, master of hospital
  of St John the Baptist,
  Coventry, 507
Myllyng, Thomas, bp. of Hereford,
  40, 85, 88, 99, 102, 109-10,
  114-5
Mylsted, see Milstead
Mynster, Christopher, m. of
  St Augustine's Canterbury, 432a,
  436c, 437d
Mynstre, see Minster

Mytton, John:
  r. of Bishop's Waltham, 572
  r. of Coquelles, 573

Nackington (Nacynden), Kent:
  ch., 141
  vic., 161
Nancothon, John, 287
Nans, Mr John, 631
Naugh (Naughley), Walter, 437a,
  442d
Navenby, Li., 232
Nawte, Thomas, O.P., 431d, 433a,
  435b
Nepolis, John de, 61
Nether Hardys, see Hardres, Lower
Nethynfoll, John, app. A
Nettleham (Netleham), Li., 232
Neuenton, see Newington
New, John:
  v. of West Firle, 723
  v. of West Tarring, 723
Newbrigge, William, v. of Farnham,
  328
Newchirch, Henry, m. of Boxley,
  431b, 435a
Newchurch (Newchyrch), Kent, ch.,
  166, 695
Newell, John, v. of Moulton, 688
Newenden (Newendon), Kent, ch.,
  179, 626
Newenham, see Newnham
Newenton (Newyngton), John, m. of
  Faversham, 444a, 445b, 446c
Newington (Newenton iuxta Heth),
  Kent:
  ch., 156
  vic., 164, 420
Newington (Neuenton, Newenton),
  near Sittingbourne, Kent:
  ch., 146
  vic., 170, 481
Newington (Newenton), Ox., ch.,
  177
Newington (Newyngton), Sy., ch.,
  175, 404, 712
Newnham (Newenham), Kent:
  ch., 135
  vic., 462, 495
Newport, Richard:
  r. of Campe, 357, 599
  r. of Offekerque, 357

Newstead (Newstede), Kent, free
chapel, 559
Newton:
John, v. of Tooting, 361
Robert, r. of Wootton, 578
Nicholson, William, notary public,
257
Nix (Nikkys), Mr Richard, 26
Nobill, Theodoric, O.F.M., 446c
Nocera (Nucerin'), bp. of,
see Ubaldis
Norbury, St., 293
Norbury, John, m. of Christ
Church Canterbury, 443a
Norchand, John, 499
Norman:
John, r. of St Nicholas,
Weybridge, 352
Robert, 319
Thomas, 319
Northampton, Np., priory of St
Andrew, 14-5, 71
Northbourne (Northborn, Northborne),
Kent, vic., 162, 517
Northeyeville, see Northill
Northfleet (Northflete), Kent,
ch., 141
Northill (Northeyeville), Bd.,
coll. ch. of St Mary, 698
Northmoor (More), Ox., 330
Northpederton, see Petherton, North
Norton, Kent, ch., 139, 171, 660
Norton:
John, 505
Roger, r. of Oye, 602
Norwich (Norwicum), Nf., 307, 339
bp., 443d
See also Goldwell
dioc., 119, 128, 130, 311, 345
see, 127
Norwich (Norwiche), Edmund, can.
of Bradsole, 439a, 440b, 441d
Notingham (Notyngham), John, 437a,
443b
Nucerin', see Nocera
Nudery, Thomas, v. of St Margaret's
Cliffe, 359
Nutkyn, John, v. of Reculver, 610

Oare (Ores), Kent, ch., 139-41
Ockley (Okeley), Sy., ch., 362
Offargall, Theobald, r. of Alkham,
349

Offekerque (Hofkyrk), in parts
of Picardy, ch. of St Mary
Magdalen, 357
Ogbourne St George (Okerborn,
Okerborne), Wlt., priory, 155,
175
Oke, Thomas, abbot of Titchfield,
papal mandatory, proceedings
before, 247-66
Oldekyrke, see St Omer
Okeley, see Ockley
Okerborn, see Ogbourne St George
Olcombe, see Ulcombe
Ores, see Oare
Orchfounte, see Urchfont
Orgarswick (Orgarswik), Kent,
ch., 168
Orlestone (Orlaston), Kent, ch.,
168, 645
Orpington (Orpenton, Orpyngton),
Kent, 437a
ch., 173, 545, 553, 675, 743
vic., 545, 553
Osney, Ox., abbey, 431a, 432b
Ospringe (Ospring), Kent:
dy., 131-2, 135, 139-41, 153,
171
hospital of SS Mary and John
the Baptist, 424, 436b, 438c
vic., 171, 425
Ostenhanger (Hostinghanger,
Ostynghanger), Kent, ch., 166,
657
Ostia, see Hostiensis
Oterynden, see Otterden
Otford (Otteford), Kent, 232
abp.'s manor, 54, app. A
Otham, Kent, ch., 169
Otterden (Otryndon), Kent,
ch., 171, 454, 643
Ottery (Oterey) St Mary, De.,
collegiate ch., 28
Ottley, Peter, 611
Oudeby, Mr Walter, 34
Ousteby, Thomas, r. of Weston-
super-Mare, 502
Overton, Br Robert, v. of
Appledore, 382
Oxford (Oxon'):
archd., 618, 684, 720
John earl of, 103, 108
University, 294
colleges of, exempt from
royal taxation, 120
colleges and halls:

Oxford (cont'd):
    All Souls, 64, 444c, 510
    Merton (Marton), fellow
      (named), 432a, 444b
    New College (Beate Marie
      Winton' in Oxonia), 442c,
      443d
    poor students, exempt from
      charitable subsidy, 95, 124
Oxney (Oxene), Kent, ch., 137
Oye, in Thérouanne dioc., ch., 398,
   453, 602

Pachyng, see Patching
Pagden, see Pugden
Page:
  Henry, 295
  William, 448a
Pagham (Paggeham), Sx.:
  ch., 130
  dean of immediate jurisdiction,
    520, 577, 579, 644, 647, 723,
    750
  dy., 129-30, 172
  vic., 172
Panormitanus 9Nicholaus de
  Tudeschis), canonist, 181
Par, see Parre
Parham, Thomas, can. of St Chad's,
  Shrewsbury, 511
Parker:
  John:
    v. of Seasalter, 576
    v. of Woodnesborough, 650
  Peter, app. A
Parma, Nicholas de, papal procurator
  fiscal, 61, 197-8, 222
Parre (Par):
  penitentiary of South Malling and
    r. of Stanmer, 489, 717
  r. of Kingsnorth, 288-9
Parsalt, Robert, 441a
Parterych, John, chap. of bredgar
  coll., 455
Parva Chart, see Chart, Little
Parva Mungeham, see Mongeham,
  Little
Parva Ovre, see Littleover
Parys, William, app. A
Pasarella, James, bp. of Imola, 12

Pastor, John, r. of East Langdon,
  456
Patching (Pachyng), Sx., ch., 172
  750
Patrixbourne (Patriksborne,
  Patrykisborn, Patryksborn),
  Kent:
  ch., 145
  vic., 62, 167, 620
Patynson, Robert, v. of
  Orpington, 553
Paul II, pope, 24, 188
Pavy, Hugh, bp. of St Davids,
  99, 102
Pawlett, Thomas, r. of Wotton,
  306
Payne:
  Ambrose, can. of Wingham, 731
  Edward:
    Commissary General of
      Canterbury, 62, 98
    v. of Hernhill, 477
    v. of Monkton in Thanet, 683
    v. of St Clement's Sandwich,
      485
Paynell, William, chap., 306
Paynethwyn, see Peyntwyn
Pecham, James, 697
Peckham, East (Estpecham,
  Estpekham, Pecham), Kent:
  ch., 173, 399, 428, 581, 664
  vic., 399, 428, 581, 664
Peeke, John, 284
Peele, Robert, v. of Chilham, 679
Peese, John:
  r. of Lyminge, 377
  r. of Saltwood, 365
Pekham, Reginald, app. A
Pemberton, Robert, r. of
  Brasted, 416
Penhalse, John, clerk of Oxford
  University, 294
Penshurst (Penseherst), Kent,
  ch., 173
Penwortham, John, clerk, 346
Percy, Thomas, can. regular, v.
  of Bexley, 611
Pereson:
  John, v. of Brabourne, 672
  Richard, chap. of Black
    Prince's chantry, Canterbury
    cath., 478, 527

Perham:
  Lawrence, app. A
  Robert, app. A
Perry Barr (Pery), St., 293
Perusio, Mr Bartholomew de, 61,
  228
Pery, John, 443a
Peryn, John, chap., 334
Pesemede (Pesemed, Pesemeth),
  John, 439a, 444b, 445d
Petham, Kent:
  ch., 147
  vic., 167, 366, 613
  places in:
    Buckholt woods, app. A
    Depeden, chantry at, 684
Petham, John, m. of Christ Church
  Canterbury, 441a, 443b, 444c
Petherton, North (Northpederton),
  So.:
  ch., 63
  chapel of St Gabriel, 63
Pett, in Charing, Kent, ch., 179
Pett (Pette), William 433d
  r. of Brasted, 415-6
Petyte, William, v. of Milton
  near Sittingbourne, 375
Peuplingues (Pitham, Pytteham),
  in parts of Picardy or marches
  of Calais, ch., 394, 533
Pevensey, Richard, m. of Faversham,
  433d
Pevington (Pevyngton, Pevynton),
  Kent, ch., 179, 619
Pevington (Pevyngton),
  John:
    can. of Combwell, 436a, 438b,
    439c
    r. of St Alphege, Canterbury,
    625
  Thomas, v. of Orpington, 545, 553
Peyntwyn (Paynetwyn, Peynthwyn
  Peytwyn), Hugh, 443d, 584
  arch. of Canterbury, 628
  Commissary General of the
    Prerogative, 227-8, 236,
    245-6
  r. of Bocking, 616, 629
  r. of Eynsford, 592, 649
Peyto, William, can. of South
  Malling coll., 550
Peyton, Thomas, 393

Philipps, see Phillips
Phillip, Thomas, alias Canton,
  alias Thomas, Philip, r. of
  Ripple, 474, 601
Phillips (Philippis, Philipps,
  Philips):
  Reginald, v. of Wadhurst, 387
  Roland, v. of Croydon, 673
Pinner, Mx., abp.'s estate,
  app. A
Pising (Pissing), in East
  Langdon, Kent, ch., 132
Pistio, James de, abp.'s
  proctor, 61
Pius II, pope, 24, 188
Playston:
  Alice, 269
  Richard, 269
Pluchett, John, chap., 331
Pluckley (Plukle, Pluklee,
  Plukley), Kent, ch., 141, 179,
  331
Plumstead (Plumstede), Kent, 132
Pluntesdon, Henry de, archd. of
  Dorset, 252
Pogden (Pagden, Pugden), Matthew,
  O.F.M., 440a, 441b, 444d
Pole:
  John, 317
  Richard, 317
Poley:
  John, 296
  Richard, 296
Poleyn, Polayne, Mr Peter, 232
Pons Roberti, see Robertsbridge
Pontefract (Punfrait'), Richard
  de, kt., 53
Pontigny (Pontenace), abbey, 160
Pontissara, John de, bp. of
  Winchester, 252
Pontow (Punto), John, can. of
  West Langdon, 446c, 447d
Ponynges (Ponynggis), Edward,
  kt., 470, 480, 504, 657
Pope, William, chap. of Arundel's
  chantry, Canterbury cath., 403
Popeshale, Kent, ch., 133
Porsmouth, John, r. of Hareway,
  411
Portar, Richard, app. A
Porter, Christopher, r. of
  Boughton Malherbe, 358

Portland, William, v. of Lydd,
713
Postling (Postlying) Kent
ch., 138
vic., 165, 372, 674
Potkyn, William, notary public,
227-9, 236, 246
Prae (Pre), St Mary de, Hrt.,
priory, 50
Pratt, John, v. of Thornham, 383
Pre, see Prae
Prentise, Christopher, v. of
Hever, 464
Prescot (Prescote), La., vic.,
543
Prest, Thomas, v. of Rodmersham,
600
Preston next Faversham (iuxta
Faversham), Kent:
ch., 135
vic., 171, 515, 732
Preston, near Wingham (iuxta
Wyngham), Kent:
ch., 132,
vic., 167, 689, 694, 737
Preston, Peter, O. Carm., 438b
Preston Candover (Candever),
Ha., 265
Price:
Alice, 305
Richard, 305
Privett (Pryvett), Ha., 259
Puchelle, Mr John, 346
Punfrait', see Pontefract
Punt:
Cecily, 58
Henry, 58
Thomas, 58
Punto, see Pontow
Purdy:
John, chap., 339
Nicholas, chap., 339
Pycia:
Ducius de, notary of court of
apostolic camera, 222
Francis de, notary of court of
apostolic camera, 222
Pydd (Pyd), William:
can. of Wingham, 639
r. of Wickham, 565
Pyke, John, 297
Pykinham (Pyknam), William:
r. of Hadleigh, 677
r. of Wrotham, 670
Pynk, Richard, 265

Pynnell, Robert, chap. of St
Bartholomew's chantry, Waltham, 710
Pysok, Henry, v. of Bapchild, 461
Pytteham, see Peuplingues

Quelnelo, Peter, clerk, 194

Raby (Rabye), John:
v. of Eynsford, 418, 484
v. of Grain, 407, 419
Radfield (Rodefeld, Rodevild), in
Bapchild, Kent, 367, 541
Rainham (Renham, Reynham), Kent:
ch., 140
vic., 170
Ramesay, see Ramsey
Ramsey, Hu., abbey, 624
Ramsey (Ramesay):
Henry, v. of Ewell, 645
John, 432a, 444d
Macelinus, v. of Patrixbourne,
620
William, 340
Randulph, Thomas:
r. of Moulton, 698
warden of Northill coll. ch., 698
Ratclyff, William, v. of Glynde,
676
Rathur (Rathhirensis) bp. of, see
Yngilby
Raustowe, John, 250, 258, 260
Ravenstone (Ravenston), Bk.,
priory, 630
Rawlyns, Henry:
r. of Lyminge, 682
r. of Newchurch, 695
Raynold, John, 436a
Reach (Rich, Riche), Ca., 283
Reculver (Recolver, Reculvere),
Kent:
ch., 129
chantry, 609
vic., 163, 610
Redeshefe (Redsheff), Adam:
commissary for Calais, 19
dean of Westbury-on-Trum coll.,509
r. of St Mary Calais, 509
r. of Campe, 357
r. of Offekerque, 357
Redman, Richard, bp, of St Asaph,
99, 102, 104, 114
Redmersham, see Rodmersham
Redsheff, see Redeshefe

Reed, Mr John, proctor of Court
of Canterbury, abp.'s proctor,
225–9, 236, 246, 249, 621
Regis, Thomas, 222
Reigate, Sy., priory, 83
can. (named), 83
Renham, see Rainham
Repe, Edward, r. of Stonar, 691
Revesby (Revisby), Li., abbey, 443b
Reyfeld (Reyfelde), Robert, abbot
of Boxley:
r. of Hunton, 742
v. of Headcorn, 728, 751
Reyner, Ralph, v. of Rolvenden,
653
Reynham, Robert, can. of Leeds,
443a, 445b
See also Rainham
Reynolds, Walter, abp. of
Canterbury, 232
Riall, William, r. of St James
Dover, 427
Riario, Raphael, cardinal deacon
of St George in Velabro, papal
chamberlain, 210
Rice, see Ryse
Rich, Edmund, abp. of Canterbury,
44, 53
See also Reach
Richard II, king, 346
Richard III, king, 186
Richardson:
John:
notary public, 247, 605, 647,
701
proctor of abbot of St Augustine's
Canterbury, 254–5
Thomas, r. of Fordwich, 652
Richemond, William, r. of
Hervelinghen, 384
Rideley, Adam, r. of Orleston, 646
Ridingweld, see Ringwould
Rikthorn, John, r. of Isfield, 738
Rilyng, Thomas, r. of Newington,
712
Rimer, Robert, v. of East
Peckham, 664
Ringmer, Sx., Broyle park in, app. A
Ringsall (Ryngsaul, Ryngsawle),
William:
v. of South Bersted, 647
v. of West Firley, 723
v. of West Tarring, 644, 723

Ringwould (Ridingweld), Kent,
ch., 162
Riparia, see River
Ripple (Riple, Ripley, Ryphill,
Rypill), Kent, ch., 132, 16?,
474, 601
Ripple, William, chap. of
St Mary's chantry, Bocking,
557
Risborough Monks (Risebergh,
Ryesbourgh), Bk:
ch., 177, 522
dean of immediate jurisdiction,
522, 554, 740
dy., 177
Rise, see Ryse
Risheborne, see Rushbourne
River (Riparia, Riperia), Kent:
ch., 138
vic., 164, 373
Roberd, John, 267
Roberdes, Richard, v. of Preston
next Faversham, 515
Robertsbridge (Pons Roberti),
Sx., abbey, 150
Robyns, Thomas, 191
Robynson, William:
abp.'s proctor, 190, 224
r. of Latchingdon, 633
Roche, John, 47
Rocheford:
Agnes, 316
Patrick, 316
Rochester (Roffen', Rowchester),
Kent, 324
bp., 603
See also Audley; Savage
bridge, 66
cath. ch., prior and conv.,
of, 175, 460, 466
dioc., 42, 119, 128–30
see, 127
Rochestre, Thomas, can. of
Leeds, 437a, 439b, 442c
Rodefeld, see Radfield
Rodmersham (Redmarsham), Kent,
vic., 600, 716
Roffen', see Rochester
Roger, John, 57
Rolvenden (Rollynden,
Rolveden), Kent:
ch., 179
vic., 653
Romagna, 47

Rome (Roma):
  apostolic see or church:
    Audience of Contradicted
      Letters, 192, 194, 197
      lector, 194
      proctors, 194
      scribe, 194
    camera, 222
      chamberlain, 47, 210
      clerk, 61, 189-90, 224
      collector, in England, 47,525
      court of causes, proctor
        of, 222
      servitia due to, 210
    canonisation by, 181-3
      185, 211
    cardinals, 181-3, 197
      See also ᴆourgchier; Morton,
        John; Riario; Sancto
        Georgio
    confirmation, to be sought, 67
    indulgences, 47, 187
    nuncio, to England and
      Scotland, 12
    patrimony, 47, 187
    procurator fiscal, 61,
      197-8, 222
    protonotary, 187, 189-90, 211,
      223-4
    Rota or Court of the Sacred
      Palace, 346
      proceedings in, 192, 195-6,
        200, 203, 221, 223-66
      scribe, 197
    scriptor of apostolic letters,
      194
    visits to (ad limina apostolorum),
      208, 210
  bulls or letters dated at, 1-6,
    8-12, 24, 38-41, 43, 46-52,
    185, 187-8, 192, 194, 197-223,
    228
  churches:
    St Anastasia, 189, 209
    St Celsus, 194
  court of:
    appeals to or processes in:
      191-200, 221-66
    proctors of abp. at, 61,
      189-90, 224
  hospital of St Thomas the
    Martyr and the Holy Trinity, 23

Rome (Cont'd):
    warden, 61, 189-90, 210,
      224
    popes, see Alexander VI;
      Boniface VIII and IX;
      Eugenius IV; Innocent IV
      and VIII; John XXII;
      Paul II; Pius II; Sixtus
      IV; Urban V
Romney, New (Romene), Kent:
    ch., 160
    vic., 510
Romney, Old (Rumney, Rumpney,
    Veter Romenale, Veter Rompney),
    Kent, ch., 166, 450, 534,
    555, 642
Romney, St Mary-in-the-Marsh
    (in Marisco), Kent, ch.,
    168
Romney, Adam, m. of Christ
    Church Canterbury, 443a
    444b, 445c, 446d
Rompayne (Rumpayne), Mr John,
    43, 50, 540
Rooper, see Roper
Roose, Thomas, 439a
    r. of St Mary Bothaw,
    London, 544
Roper (Rooper), John, 350,
    718
Rose, Thomas, r. of Lower
    Hardres, 680
Ross (Rossen'), hp. of, see
    Clerk
Rosse, William, r. of
    Auderne, 685
Rostherne (Rosthorne), Ch.,
    ch., 512
Rothal, see Rowthale
Routhale, see Rowthale
Rowchester, see Rochester
Rowthale (Rothall, Routhale,
    Routhall), Thomas, 584, 664
    Commissary General of the
      Prerogative, 84
    proctor of abp. 189, 224
    r. of Bocking, 629
Ruckinge, Kent, ch., 166,
    347, 449, 583
Ruddyng, John, r. of
    Merstham, 668

Rumney, see Romney
Rumpayne, see Rompayne
Rumpney, see Romney
Runton, Nf., ch., 660
Rushbourne (Risheborne), Kent,
  ch., 141
Russell, John, bp. of Lincoln,
  85, 88-9, 99, 114
Ruthyn, Mr Ellis, 250-1, 253
Ryche, John:
  can. of Wingham, 528
  clerk, 43, 270
  r. of Elmstone, 536
  r. of High Halden, 451, 532
Rye, John, app. A
Ryngeston, Richard, m. of Christ
  Church Canterbury, 446d
Ryngsaul, see Ringsall
Rypill, see Ripple
Ryse (Rice, Rise), John:
  abp.'s clerk, r. of Hadleigh,
    677
  r. of Sampford Courtenay, 32
Rysebourgh, see Risborough, Monks

Saddokysherst, see Shadoxhurst
St Albans, Hrt., abbey, 50
  abbot, 50, 214, 216, 218
  jurisdiction, 119, 128
  monk (named), 50
  tithes, 130
St Andrew's dioc., 436a
St Asaph (Assaven'), Denbigh and
  Flint:
  bp., see Redman
  dioc., 119, 128
  see, 127
St Audoman, see St Omer
St Blaise in Melak (Sancti Blasii),
  Thérouanne dioc., ch., 662, 671,
  714
SS Cosmus and Damian, see Blean
St David's (Meneven'), Pembroke:
  bp., see Pavy
  dioc., 119, 128
  see, 127
St George in Velabro (ad Velum
  Aureum), cardinal deacon of,
  see Riario
St Laurence in the Isle of Thanet,
  Kent, ch., 163
St Mary-in-the-Marsh, see Romney
St Mary Trantiber, cardinal priest
  of, see Lopez

St Neots (Sanctum Neotum),Hu.,
  232
St Nicholas at Wade (Woode),
  Isle of Thanet, Kent:
  ch., 163
  vic., 500
St Nicholas (Seint Nicholas,
  Seintnycoles):
  Juliana, 368
  Roger, 412
St Omer (St Audoman) alias
  Oldekyrk, in parts of Picardy,
  ch., 741
St Osyth, Ess., abbey, 147
  abbot and conv., 366, 613, 684
St Peter Extra, in the Isle of
  Thanet, Kent:
  ch., 163
  vic., 400
St Radegund, see Bradsole
Salforde, Richard, 58
Salisbury (Sarum), Wlt., 287, 299
  bp., 442c, 443d
  dioc., 119, 128
  see, 127
Salmyston, Henry, m. of St
  Augustine's Canterbury, 436a,
  439b, 443c, 444d
Salop, see Shrewsbury
Saltwood (Saltwode), Kent, ch.,
  165, 365
Sampford Courtney (Courteney), De.:
  ch., 32
  chapel, 32
San Geminiano, Dominic de,
  canonist, 181
Sancto Georgio, John Anthony de,
  cardinal priest of SS Nereus and
  Achilleus, bp. of Alessandria,
  auditor of the Rota, 192, 197,
  223
Sandgate, see Sangatte
Sandhurst (Sandhirst), Kent, ch.,
  179
Sandwich (Sandewico, Sandwico),
  Kent:
  Carmelite friars (named), 436c
    438d, 445a-b, 446a, c, 447c-d
  ch. of St clement, 131
    vic., 162, 485
  ch. of St Mary, 131-2
    vic., 162, 623
  ch. of St Peter, 162
  dy., 130, 132-3, 137-40, 162

Sandwiche, William, m. of Boxley, 431b, 435a
Sangatte (Sandgate) alias Slymes, Guisnes, ch., 665
Sangwen, Richard, 344
Sapwell, see Sopwell
Sarre (Serre, Serrey), Kent:
  ch., 140
  vic., 163
Sarum, see Salisbury
Saunder:
  John, r. of Dymchurch, 476
  Thomas, can. of Mottenden, 433c
Saunders, John, can. of Wingham, 556
Savage, Thomas:
  bp. of Rochester, 41-2, 201
  r. of monks Risborough, 522
  r. of Rostherne, 512
Sawle, John, chap. of St Mary's chantry, Bocking, 421
Saxlyngham, Richard, r. of Hames, 535
Saynte, Mr Thomas, 191
Scales, see Escalles
Scott, William, kt., 646
Scotus, Richard, notary public, 252
Seasalter (Seesalter, Sesalter, Sesaltre), Kent, vic., 163, 452, 576, 654
Seaton (Seyton), Ru., ch., 606
Secheford, Gilbert de, 232
Sednor, Richard, 440d
  See also Cednor
Sedyngborne, see Sittingbourne
Seesalter, see Seasalter
Seggeford (Segeford), Robert:
  v. of Frindsbury, 603
  v. of Meopham, 603
  v. of New Romney, 510
Segovia (Segobien') dioc., 222
Selling (Selling iuxta Sheldewich, Sellyng), Kent:
  ch., 132
  chantry of St Stephen, 505, 655
  vic., 171
Sellinge, Kent, ch., 168
Sellyng, William:
  m. of Christ Church Canterbury, 445a, 446b, 447c
  prior of Christ Church Canterbury, 7, 65

Semer, Stephen, 250
Senden, Walter, 438a
Serre, see Sarre
Serro, Didacus del, clerk, 222
Sesalter, see Seasalter
Sethingborn, see Sittingbourne
Sevenoaks (Sevenoke, Sevinoke), Kent, ch., 173, 692, 730
Seville (Ispalen') dioc., 200, 222
Sevington (Steventon), Kent, ch., 168, 471, 521
Sevinoke, see Sevenoaks
Sewall, Henry, 337
Sewte, Robert, O.E.S.A., 442a
Seyton, see Seaton
Shadoxhurst (Saddokysherst, Shaddokesherst, Shaddokysherst), Kent, ch., 168, 363, 457
Shaftesbury (Shaffesbury), Do., 319
Shaldoo, William:
  commissary of Calais, 19, 509
  dean of Croydon, 22
  r. of Guisnes, 409
  r. of Hareway, 348
  v. of Croydon, 388-90, 673
Sheel, Michael, notary public, 223, 228
Sheen (Shene), Sy., Charterhouse, 493
Sheering (Sheryng), Ess., chapel, 429
Sheffield (Sheffeld):
  John, notary public, 236, 239
  Robert, can. of Wingham, 528
  William, 606
Sheldwich (Sheldwhich), Kent, ch., 171
Shelley, Roger, 70
Shene, see Sheen
Sheppey (Shepey), Kent, priory of St Sexburga at, 401, 407, 419
Sheppey, John, m. of Faversham, 439a, 440b, 441c
Sherborne, Do., 319
Sherborne (Shirborne, Shirburne):
  Robert:
    collector of charitable subsidy, 126

Sherborne (Cont'd):
    Official sede vacante, Bath
        and Wells dioc., 265
    Official sede vacante,
        Winchester dioc., 243,
        263-6
    nominated as v. of Croydon,
        388
    Mr Roger, 326
Sherfield (Shirefeld), Ha., 308
Sheryng, see Sheering
Shirborne, see Sherborne
Shirehampton (Shirenhampton),
    Gl., 274
Shirwood (Shirewood, Shirwoode),
    Robert, m. of Christ Church
    Canterbury, 439a, 441b, 443c,
    445d
Shoreham (Shorham), Kent:
    ch., 173, 397, 752
    dean of immediate jurisdiction,
        369, 376, 397, 399, 407, 415,
        418-9, 422, 428, 464, 513,
        558, 567, 581, 591-2, 603,
        611, 649, 664, 670, 675, 692
        696, 706, 722, 730, 742-3, 752
    dy., 130, 139, 141, 148, 173
Shotforde, Henry, 340
Shrewsbury (Salop), Sa., coll.
    ch. of St Chad, 511
    can. (named), 511
Sibburn, Thomas de, 53
Sibertswold (Sibertiswode), Kent,
    ch., 138
Sibill, John, 280
Sicily, 47
Sigar (Sygar):
    John, chap., 318
    Stephen, 318
Sion, see Syon
Sittingbourne (Sedyngborne,
    Sethingborn, Syddingborn,
    Sydingbourne), Kent, dy., 132,
    136, 139, 146, 157, 170
    vic., 170, 556
Sittyngborn (Siddingborn,
    Sydingborn), John, can. of Leeds,
    437b, 438a, 442d
Sixtus IV, pope, 24, 188
Skoye, Laurence, v. of Stockbury,
    733
Skyby, Mr, r. of St Vedast,
    London, 408

Sleaford (Sleford), Li., 232
Slindon (Slyndon), Sx., 230
    ch., 172, 577
Slymes, see Sangatte
Smarden (Smerden), Kent, ch.,
    179, 711
Smardon, Richard, m. of Boxley,
    443c
Smarte, John, v. of Seasalter,
    654
Smerden, Alexander, m. of
    Boxley, 431c, 435b
    See also Smarden
Smith (Smyth):
    Catherine, 335
    John, 433a
        chap. of St Mary's chantry,
            Bocking, 421
    Richard:
        v. of Frindsbury, 603
        v. of Meopham, 603
        v. of West Tarring, 644
    Robert:
        r. of St Michael Paternoster
            Royal, London, 424
        r. of Wath, 424
    Simon:
        r. of Otterden, 643
        v. of Charing, 564
    Thomas, r. of St Mary, Calais,
        426
    William:
        archd. of Winchester, 354-4
        bp. of Coventry and Lichfield,
            39
        can. of Wherwell, 356
        r. of Ruckinge, 347
Snargate (Snaregate, Snergate),
    Kent, ch., 166, 410
Snave (Snaves), Kent, ch., 166,
    374
Snaw, William, 445d
Snell, Laurence:
    can. of Bilsington, 438b, 440d
    can. of Leeds, 439c
Snergate, see Snargate
Somerfeld, Richard, m. of
    St Augustine's Canterbury,
    432a, 436c, 439d
Somerham alias Story, Br Thomas,
    v. of East Peckham, 399
Sondes, Reginald, 358

Sondland, Roger, m. of Boxley,
445a
Sopwell (Sapwell), Hrt., priory,
50
Southampton (Hamptonia), Ha., 258,
281, 323, 325
churches:
Holy Cross, judicial proceedings
conducted at, 247–57
St Michael, 250
Southberghstede, see Bersted, South
Southchurch, Ess., ch., 176
Southmallyng, see Malling, South
Southougri:
John, 304
Margery, 304
Southwaltham Episcopi, see Waltham,
Bishop's
Southwark (Sowthwerk, Suthwerck,
Suthwerk), Sy., 252
abp.'s liberty, app. A
See also London, religious houses
Southwick (Suthwyk), Ha., 266
Sowthwerk, see Southwark
Spain, 200
Spalding (Spaldyng), Hugh:
r. of East Peckham, 581, 664
warden of English hospice at
Rome and abp.'s proctor, 61,
189–90, 210, 224
Spekington, Richard, v. of
Linsted, 472
Spencer:
George, 282
Laurence, 282
Nicholas, v. of Farningham, 513,
591
Richard, notary public, registrar
of Court of Canterbury, 61,
196, 202
Spenser, Henry, r. of Bonnington,
635
Spersall, Robert, r. of St Paul-
without-the-Walls, Canterbury,
702
Springet, William, 442a
Spycer, John, 271
Squier (Squyrer):
Roger, r. of All Saints,
Canterbury 468
Thomas, r. of St Peter's, Dover,
727
William, r. of Treborough, 614

Stale, see Stalys
Stalisfield (Stalfeld,
Stallesfeld), Kent:
ch., 141
vic., 171
Stalys (Stale), Robert:
r. of Brasted, 579
v. of Westwell, 467
Stanefeld, Ralph de, r. of
Wootton St Lawrence, 252
Stanes, William, r. of Ockley,
362
Stanmer, Sx., ch., 174, 422, 488–
9, 717
Stanmore, Mx., 303
Staple (Stapill), Alexander, m.
of Christ Church Canterbury,
439a, 441b, 442c, 444d
Staplehurst (Staplehirst,
Stapulhurst), Kent, ch., 169
See also Newstead
Staunford, John, r. of Barfreston,
598
Steep (Stepe, Stupe), in East
Meon parish, Ha., 258–66 passim
Stempe, see Stympe
Stephinson, Robert, O. Carm.,
438c
Stepney (Stevenhithe), Mx., 252,
338
Stevenage, Hrt., 327
Stevenhithe, see Stepney
Steventon, see Sevington
Stevyns, William, 442a
Stisted (Stystede), Ess., ch.,
176
Stockbury (Stokbury), Kent:
ch., 140
vic., 733
Stokes (Stokys), John, warden of
All Souls College, Oxford, 64
Stokton (unid.), Kent, ch., 162
Stonar (Stonor), in Isle of
Thanet, Kent, ch., 162, 516,
691
Stone, in Oxney, Kent, ch., 132,
166
Stonor, see Stonar
Stony Stratford, Bk., 301
Storke, John, 319
Storton, see Stourton
Story, Edward, bp. of Chichester,
99, 102, 109, 114
See also Somerham

213

Stourmouth, Kent, ch., 167
Stourton (Storton), William lord, 184
Stowting (Stutyng), Kent, ch., 165, 498
Strangways, Thomas, r. of Denton, 393
Stratford, John, bp. of Winchester, 252, 258
Stratton, John, auditor of causes in Rota, 346
Strenger, William, r. of Betteshanger, 569
Stupe, see Steep
Sturdy, Robert:
  r. of Aldington, 531
  r. of Ivychurch, 526
Sturry (Turrey), Kent:
  ch., 132
  vic., 726
Stutyng, see Stowting
Stympte (Stempe), Richard, 250, 258, 265
Stystede, see Stisted
Sudborough (Sudburg), Np., 334
Sudbury, Sf., 267
Sudbury:
  John, m. of Christ Church Canterbury, 438b, 439c, 443d
  Simon, abp. of Canterbury, 346
  Thomas:
    m. of St Alban's, 50
    pretended prior of St Andrew's Northampton, 14-5, 71
Sunderhesse, Alan de, 53
Sundridge (Sundrisshe), Kent, ch., 173
Surrey, archd. of, 360-2, 390, 560
Suston, George, app. A
Suthwerk, see Southwark
Suthwyk, see Southwick
Sutton, Kent, dy., 132, 139-40, 143, 146, 169
Sutton:
  Mr Henry, 298
  John, 329
    m. of Christ Church Canterbury, 439a, 441b, 442c, 443d
  Thomas:
    Mr, 329
    r. of Otterden, 454
  William, v. of Ashford, 585

Sutton Valence (Sutton), Kent, ch., 169
Swalecliffe (Swaleclyve), Kent, ch., 163
Swanton, Gilbert de, 346
Swarder, John, 191
Swayne, Robert, r. of Shadoxhurst, 457
Sweden(?) (Sudeden'), 437a
Swingfield (Swynesfeld, Swyntyngfeld), Kent:
  ch., 164
  Hospitaller preceptory, 159
Syday, Alexander, v. of Bethersden, 506
Syddingborn, see Sittingbourne
Sydrak, Thomas, r. of Pevington, 619
Sygar, see Sigar
Symon, Richard, r. of Upper Hardres, 648
Symons, Richard, r. of Tunstall in commendam, 747
Symonds, William, priest, 89
Sympligham, Henry de, can. of Wherwell, 252
Sympson (Symson), Richard, 191
  r. of Campe, 574
  r. of Guisnes, 636
Syms, Thomas, r. of Great Mongeham, 725
Symson, see Sympson
Syntyngefeld, see Swingfield
Syon (Sion), near Isleworth, Mx., abbey, 120, 153
  abbess and conv., 438b, 679

Tachbrook (Tachebrok'), Wa., 230
Tailard, William, 284
Tailor, see Taylor
Talbot (Talbott):
  John, chap., 541
  William, app. A
Taliour, see Taylor
Tangmere, Sx., ch., 172
Tanner, Richard, v. of Petham, 366
Tanyngton, see Thanington
Tarring, West (Tarryng, Terring, Terryng), Sx.:
  ch., 172, 644
  vic., 644, 723

Tarry:
  Arnulf, 441c
  John, r. of East Lavant, 520
  Thomas, O.P., 447b
Taunton, So., 265
  archd. of, 614
Tavernere, William, 305
Tavistock (Tavistok'), De.,
  abbey, 72
Taylor (Tailor, Tailour, Taliour,
  Tayllor, Taylour):
  John, 311, 335
  Ralph, v. of New Romney, 510
  Robert:
    r. of Hinxhill, 587
    v. of Orpington, 545
    v. of Westwell, 580
  William:
    can. of St Gregory's
      Canterbury, 446a, 447b
    m. of Christ Church
      Canterbury, 447a
Teneham (Thendham, Thenham),
  Richard, m. of St Augustine's
  Canterbury, 436a, 443b, 446c
Thenham, see Teynham
Tenterden (Tentwarden), Kent:
  ch., 132
  vic., 179, 593
Tentwarden, Stephen, m. of
  St Augustine's Canterbury,
  446b, 447c
Terring, see Tarring, West
Terry, John, r. of Peuplingues,
  394, 533
Teynham (Tenham), Kent;
  ch., 131, 405
  vic., 171
Teynham, Thomas, m. of Faversham,
  448a
Thanet, Isle of, Kent, churches in,
  see Margate; Minster; St Laurence;
  St Nicholas at Wade
Thanington Within (Tanynton), Kent:
  ch., 141
  vic., 161
Thendham, see Teneham
Thomas, see Phillip
Thomherst, John, 659
Thomilynson, Thomas, chap. of
  St Mary's chantry, Croydon, 744
Thomson, George, r. of St Peter's
  Canterbury, 617, 651

Thorley (Thorele iuxta Ware),
  Hrt., 232
Thorndon, Robert, m. of Christ
  Church Canterbury, 441a, 443b,
  444c
Thornham (Thorneham), Kent:
  ch., 143
  vic., 383
  See also Aldington next
    Maidstone
Throwle, Nicholas, m. of Christ
  Church Canterbury, 447a
Throwley (Trughle, Trulegh),
  Kent:
  ch., 153
  vic., 171
Thwytes, John, r. of West
  Tarring, 644
Tichefelde, see Titchfield
Tiknes, James, r. of Wormshill,
  368
Tilmanstone (Tilmanston,
  Tylmanston), Kent, ch., 162
Titchfield (Tichefelde), Ha.,
  abbot of, proceedings before,
  247-66
Toby, William, O. Carm., 436c,
  438d
Tonbridge (Tunbrigge), Kent,
  priory, 431a, 432b, 443b
Tong (Tonge), Kent:
  ch., 137
  vic., 170, 686, 707
Tooting (Totyng), Sy., v. of 361
Tortosa (Dertusen') dioc., 190,
  203, 224, 228
Totyng, see Tooting
Trappe (Trapp):
  Nicholas, notary public, 270
  Richard:
    r. of Eynsford, 649, 696
    r. of Newchurch, 695
Treble, Nicholas:
  v. of Linsted, 597
  v. of St Mary Sandwich, 623
Treborough, So., 614
Tredys, William, r. of Newenden,
  626
Trenniell:
  Henry, 299
  Margery, 299
Trier (Treveren') dioc., 223,
  228

Tring, Hrt.:
  abp.'s manor, 35
  ch., 129
Tripland, Richard, 191
Trughle, see Throwley
Trulegh, see Throwley
Tunbrigge, see Tonbridge
Tunstall (Dunstall, Dunstalle),
  Kent, ch., 170, 486, 538, 747
Turbarvyle (Turburvyle), John:
  kt., 685
  r. of Escalles, 690
Turner, Nicholas, proctor of
  Court of Canterbury, 47
Turrey, see Sturry
Twitham, Nicholas de, 53
Tylmanston, see Tilmanstone
Tyndale, Maurice, penitentiary
  of South Malling and r. of
  Stanmer, 717

Ubaldis:
  Baldus de, legist, 181
  Matthew de, bp. of Nocera,
    papal chap., auditor of the
    Rota, 221
    proceedings conducted by
      authority of, 247–66
Ulcombe (Olcombe), Kent, ch., 169
Underwood (Underwod, Underwoode),
  Edward:
  r. of North Crawley, 632
  r. of St Michael Royal, warden
    of Whittington coll., 67, 641
Unton:
  Catherine, 336
  Thomas, 336
Upchurch, Kent:
  ch., 157
  vic., 170
Urban V, pope, 234
Urchfont (Orchfounte), Wlt., 299
Urilband, Peter, clerk, 194

Vaghan, see Vaughan
Valence, Thomas, m. of
  St Augustine's Canterbury, 433d
Vasor, Peter, r. of Newington
  near Sittingbourne, 481

Vaughan (Vaghan, Waghan, Waughan):
  Edward, advocate of the Court
    of Canterbury, 196, 202
  James, notary public, 247–8, 257
  John, 441b
    can., 306
  William, 411
Venice (Venetiarum) dioc., 197
Verona, John de, abp.'s proctor, 61
Veter Romenale, see Romney, Old
Veysy, Mr John, 27
Vielstone, Hamo de, kt., 53
Vincent (Vyncent):
  Robert, 300, 331
  Thomas, can. of Leeds, 446b
Veneria, John de, O.F.M., 436d
Viterbo (Viterbien') dioc., 222
Voes, Nicholas, notary public, 200,
  203
Volterra (Vulteran') dioc., 187
Vulterris, Jeremias Contugi de,
  bp. of Assisi, 222
Vyncent, see Vincent

Wade, Richard, v. of Sittingbourne,
  556
Wadhurst (Wadeherst, Wadehirst,
  Wadehurst), Sx., 174, 387
  Frankham park in, app. A
Waghan, see Vaughan
Waillant, Igrobus, 198
Waldershare (Waldershar), Kent:
  ch., 137
  vic., 162
Waley, Lumnus, O. Carm., 447c
Walingford, see Wallingford
Walker, John, 323, 325
  v. of Boughton Monchelsea, 656
Walkerne, John de, notary public,
  252
Walle, Richard, r. of St Mary
  Magdalen, Canterbury, 539
Wallingford (Walingford), Brk.,
  priory, 177
Walmer (Walmere), Kent, ch., 137
Walsh (Walshe, Walsshe):
  John, proctor of abbot of
    St Augustine's Canterbury, 254
  Philip, r. of Boughton Malherbe,
    358
Walteham, see Waltham

Walter:
  Hubert, abp. of Canterbury, 53
  William, O.E.S.A., 442a
Waltham (Walteham), Kent:
  ch., 141
  chantry of St Bartholomew, 710
  vic., 167, 458
Waltham, Bishop's (Southwaltham
  Episcopi), Ha., ch., 572
Waltham Holy Cross (Sancte Crucis),
  Ess., abbey, 13
  abbot, 13, 221
Waltham, John, m. of Christ Church
  Canterbury, 442d
Wamberg, Robert de, Official sede
  vacante in Winchester dioc., 232
Ward (Warde):
  John, 323, 325
    v. of St Mary Bredon, Canterbury,
    381
    v. of Waltham, 458
  Robert, v. of East Farleigh,
    558
Warden (Wardon), in the Isle of
  Sheppey, Kent, ch., 170
Ware:
  John:
    custodian of Broyle park, app.A
    O.F.M., 435c
  Thomas, r. of Pevington, 619
Wareham, see Warham
Warehorne (Warehorn), Kent, ch.,
  166, 697
Warham (Wareham):
  Laurence, 341
  Mr William, 61, 76
Warner:
  John, 303
  Thomas, 303
    clerk, 294
Warwick, earl of, 89-90
Water:
  Thomas:
    second cantarist of Arundel's
      chantry, Canterbury cath.,
      570, 667
    warden of St Margaret's
      hospital, Canterbury, 666
  William, r. of Orleston, 646
Waterladde, Thomas, v. of
  Hartlip, 466
Wath, N. Yk., ch., 424

Wathyngton, Mr Richard de, 53
Watnoo (Watno), John, 295
Wattes, Thomas, v. of Preston
  near Wingham, 689
Waughan, see Vaughan
Waynflete (Wayneflete):
  alias Durant, Robert, v. of
    Minster, 524
  William, bp. of Winchester,
    46, 184, 258-66
Webster, Robert, 283
Week, see Woodland
Weldon (Welden):
  Elizabeth, 392, 547
  Robert, 739
Weller, Robert, O.F.M., 440c
Welles (Wellys):
  Geoffrey, 433c, 435d
  Robert de, Official sede
    vacante in Winchester dioc.,
    252
  Thomas, can. of St Gregory's
    Canterbury, 437d, 438b
Wells (Wellen'), So., archd. of,
  502
  See also Bath
Wellys, see Welles
Welythwode, Richard, notary
  public, 252
Wengeham, see Wingham
Wentworth, Henry, kt., 703
Westbere, Kent:
  ch., 163
  dy., 129-30, 132, 140-1, 163
Westbrok, Peter, 443b
Westbury (Exere), Ha., chapel,
  258-66
Westbury-on-Trym (Westbury),
  Gl., coll. ch., 509
Westcleve, see Cliffe, West
Westden, see Dean, West
Westhith, see Hythe, West
Westlangdon, see Langdon, West
Westminster (Westm', Westmon'),
  Mx., 79, 86, 97, 121, 180,
  188, 252, 297
  abbey, 149, 186
    abbot, 214, 216, 218, 221
Weston-super-Mare, So., ch., 502
Weston:
  John, 262, 264
  Richard:

Weston (Cont'd):
    r. of St Blaise in Melak, 671,
      714
    r. of Snargate, 410
    William, 250, 258, 262
Westwell, Kent:
    ch., 130, 148
    vic., 179, 467, 580
Weybridge (Weybrigge), Sy., ch.
    of St Nicholas, 352
Weynwright, Nicholas, v. of
    Graveney, 746
Weyte, William, r. of Boughton
    Aluph, 721
Whatson, John, app. A
Wherwell (Wherewell), Ha., abbey,
    356
    prebendaries (named), 356
Whetely, Robert, r. of
    Tunstall, 538
White (Whyte), John:
    chap. of St Stephen's chantry,
      Selling, 655
    r. of Ostenhanger, 657
Whitmore, John, chap., 507
Whitstable (Whitestaple), Kent,
    ch., 163
Whittington, Richard, 67
Whyte, see White
Wich, Richard, chancellor of
    Abp. Edmund Rich, 53
Wichling (Wycheling), Kent, ch.,
    170, 379
Wickham (Wykham), Kent, ch., 167,
    565
Wigley, John, 308
Wigorn', see Worcester
Wikham (Wykham):
    John, m. of Christ Church
      Canterbury, 445a, 446b, 447c
    Stephen, 431c
Wilcote (Wyvilcote, Wyvilcott),
    Ox., ch., 720
Wilkes (Wylkes), Roger:
    r. of St Peter's Dover, 402
    r. of Hames, 414, 535
    r. of Monks Eleigh, 554
    r. of Old Romney, 534, 555
Wilkinson (Wilkynson, Wylkynson):
    John, v. of Headcorn, 751
    Thomas, r. of Orpington, 545,
      553, 675, 743
Willesborough (Willysborgh,
    Wyvelesberh), Kent:

Willesborough (Cont'd):
    ch., 132
    vic., 168
William, Herman, O.F.M., 444a
Williams (Willyams):
    David, 7
    r. of Adisham, 514
    r. of St Dunstan-in-the-East,
      London, 525
    Thomas, 541
Williamson (Wyllyamson), John, 255
    can. of Wingham, 639
    v. of Minster, 524
Willoughby (Wylleby):
    Elizabeth, Lady, 30
    Robert, baron Willoughby de
      Broke, 30
Willy, James, r. of Easington, 634
Willysborough, see Willesborough
Wilson (Wylson):
    Clement, 440a
    Henry, r. of Hayes, 743
    John, r. of Wichling, 379
Wilton, Wlt., 317, 331
Wilton (Wylton), Richard, 442a,
    443b, 444d
Wimbledon (Wymbaldon), Sy., ch., 175
Winchester (Winton'), Ha., 234-5
    archd., 354-6, 572
    bp., 434a, 438a, 443b
      suffragan of, 184
    See also Beaufort; Blois;
      Courtenay; Edington; Langton;
      Pontissara; Sandale; Stratford;
      Wayneflete; Woodlock
    cath. priory of St Swithun, 184,
      258
      chamberlain, 263
      monks (named), 229, 236, 242,
        244, 247-50, 252, 255, 257
      prior, 184, 230, 235, 261, 355
      prior and conv., engaged in
        litigation against abp.,
        221-66 passim
      subprior, 263, 265-6
    coll. of St Mary, exempt from
      royal taxation, 120
    Fromond's chapel in, 250
    dioc., 119, 128-30, 222, 228
      sede vacante administration of,
        73, 83, 221-66 passim
    see, 127
Windsor (Windesore), Brk., coll.
    ch. of St George, 185-6
    dean and chapter, 676

Wingham (Wengeham, Wyngham),
  Kent, 230, 346
  abp.'s estate, app. A
  coll. ch. of St Mary, 167
    can. (named), 501, 528,
      562-3, 566, 638-9, 731
    master, 501, 528, 562-3,
      566, 627, 638-9, 658, 731
Wingham (Wingeham, Wyngham),
  William, can. of Bradsole,
  437b, 438a, 440c
Winteneye, see Wintney
Winterborn, Thomas, Commissary
  of the Prerogative, 239
Wintersel, see Wintresell
Winto, John, chap., 307
Winton', see Winchester
Wintresell' (Wintersel'), Henry de,
  kt., 53
Wintney (Winteneye), Ha., priory,
  232
Wisbech (Wisebech), Ca., 320
Wiseman (Wyseman):
  Gerard, O.F.M., 438d
  Robert, r. of Campe, 574
Witham (Wytham), So.,
  Charterhouse, 38
Withington (Wythyndon), Gl.,
  ch., 26
Withipoll (Wythypoll), John, 274
  senior, 275
Wittersham (Witersam,
  Wytrechysham, Wyttesham), Kent,
  292
  ch., 166, 530
Wittey, Br Nicholas de, 444d
Wittilsey, William, prior of
  Ravenstone, 630
Wodechurch, see Woodchurch
Wodenesbergh, see Woodnesborough
Wodeton, see Wootton
Wodwarde, see Woodward
Wolhop, Walter de, prior of
  Mottisfont, 232
Wolshawe, Thomas, 272
Wood (Woode):
  John:
    kt., 315
    r. of Chiddingstone, 376
  John atte, 346
  Thomas at (alias Awood):
    r. of Eythorne, 475
    r. of Kennardington, 479

Wood (Cont'd):
  William atte:
    r. of Hastingleigh, 470
    r. of Sevington, 471, 521
Woodchurch (Wodechurch,
  Woodchirch), Kent, ch., 166, 582
Woodeford, William, 438b
Woodell, John, 439a
Woodhouse (Wodhowse), John, chap.
  of Roper's chantry in
  St Dunstan-without-the-Walls,
  Canterbury, 718
Woodland, in East Meon parish,
  Ha., 259
Woodland (Wodlond), alias Week,
  Kent, ch., 173
Woodlock, Henry, bp. of Winchester,
  231
Woodnesborough (Wodenesbergh,
  Wodnesbergh, Wodnesberth,
  Woodnesbergh), Kent, 140
  ch., 139-40
  vic., 162, 650
Woodruff, Thomas, 653
Woodward (Wodwarde), Robert, r.
  of Adisham, 753
Wootton (Wodeton, Wotton), Kent,
  ch., 165, 578
Wootton St Lawrence (Woton',
  Wotton), Ha., ch., 252
Worcester (Wigorn'):
  bp., 432b, 433a, 443d, 509
    See also Clifford, Richard;
      Giglis, Silvester de; Morton,
      Robert
  dioc., 119, 128
  see, 127
Worcettor, Richard, master of
  St John the Baptist's hospital,
  Coventry, 507
Worme, William, 291
Wormenhale, John de, commissary
  of bp. of Winchester, 234
Wormeshill, see Wormshill
Wormingford (Wormyngforde), Ess.,
  296
Wormshill (Wormeshill), Kent,
  ch., 169, 368, 412
Worsley (Worsle) alias Worse,
  Thomas, O.P., 440a, 441b, 446d
Wotton (unid.), Lincoln dioc., 306
  See also Wootton St Lawrence

Wredilsforth, Richard, v. of
Ospringe, 425
Wright (Wryght):
John, penitentiary of South
Malling and r. of Stanmer,
422
Nicholas:
master of Wye coll., 420
v. of St Nicholas at Wade,
500
Thomas, chap. of Depeden
chantry, 684
Wroteham, see Wrotham
Wrotely, John, can. of St Thomas's
hospital, Southwark, 73
Wrotham (Wroteham), Kent:
ch., 173, 670
park, app. A
Wroxfield (Groxolos, Wroxfeld),
in East Meon parish, Ha.,
258-66 passim
Wryght, see Wright
Wurzburg (Herbipolen') dioc.,
223, 228
Wyatt (Wyett, Wyott):
John, 265
Richard, r. of Old Romney, 642
Wycheling, see Wichling
Wycombe, Bk., 232
Wye (Wy), Kent:
ch., 134
coll. ch. of SS Gregory and
Martin, 420, 440b, 503, 721
vic., 167
Wyett, see Wyatt
Wykham, see Wickham, Wikham
Wykeham, William, bp. of
Winchester, 234-5, 258
Wylkynson, see Wilkinson
Wylleby, see Willoughby
Wylles (Wyllys), Stephen, r. of
Alkham, 349
Wyllyamson, see Williamson
Wylson, see Wilson
Wylton, see Wilton
Wymbaldon, see Wimbledon
Wynchepe (Wynchypp, Wynshepe),
William, m. of Christ Church
Canterbury, 443a, 445b, 446c

Wyndar, John, 250, 258
Wyndisborogh, John, m. of Christ
Church Canterbury, 447a
Wynfeld, Thomas, 441a, 442b
Wyngham, see Wingham
Wynnesbury (Wynnysbury),
Nicholas, 272
abp.'s apparitor, 20
Wynshepe, see Synchepe
Wyreham, Richard, chap. of
St Mary's chantry, Herne, 453
Wyrell, Thomas, r. of Oye, 453
Wyseman, see Wiseman
Wytham, see Witham
Wythyndon, see Withington
Wythypoll, see Withipoll
Sytrechesham, see Wittersham
Wyttesham, see Wittersham
Wytton, William, advocate of
Court of Canterbury, 196
Wyvelesberh, see Willesborough
Wyvilcote, see Wilcote

Yate, William, v. of Clifton, 330
Yeman, John, r. of St Mary de
Castro, Canterbury, 605
Yerdeley, see Ardley
Yerford:
James, 277
Pax, 277
Yngilby, Thomas, bp. of Rathlur
and r. of Barton-in-the-Clay,
624
Yonge (Yong):
Hugh, r. of Stonar, 516, 691
John, chap. of St Mary's chantry,
Bocking, 681
Nicholas, r. of Weston-super-
Mare, 502
Robert:
r. of Cheam, 551, 669
r. of Long Ditton, 560
r. of Latchingdon, 496
r. of St Michael Crooked Lane,
London, 561
York (Ebor', Eboracen'), abp. of,
447d
Yorke, William, m. of St Martin's
Dover, 431a, 438b, 440c

INDEX OF SUBJECTS

Abbeys, see Barking; Battle; Bayham;
  Bermondsey; Boxley; Bradsole;
  Burton-upon-Trent; Canterbury,
  St Augustine's; Chertsey; Cleeve;
  Faversham; Guisnes; Hagnaby;
  Hyde; Ile-Dieu; Langdon, West;
  Lessness; Malling; Osney;
  Pontigny; Revesby; Robertsbridge;
  St Albans; St Osyth; Syon;
  Tavistock; Titchfield; Waltham
  Holy Cross; Westminster; Wherwell
Absolution:
  of contributors to papal appeal,
    47, 187
  of molestors of Witham, 38
  of monks of Winchester, 230
  of rebels against king, 11
  reserved, 193, 203, 223
  right claimed by Hospitallers,
    107
Alien priories, dissolved,
  taxation of possessions of, 96,
    120, 153, 155-7
Alms:
  distribution neglected, 50
  exhorted by abp., 23-5, 55, 59
  requested by pope, 47, 187
Almshouse, foundation statute of,
  180
Anchorite, 297
Apple trees, to be planted, 346
Archdeaconry, institution to,
  354-5, 628
Armies, prayers for success of,
  33, 74

Bailiffs, abp.'s, 35, app. A
Benefices:
  admission to, 252, 347-430,
    450-753
  appropriation, 252
  collation by abp., 347, 364-5, 371,
    376-7, 380, 387, 390, 397, 404,
    406, 408, 410, 415, 422-3, 430
    449, 451, 453, 463, 465, 467,
    469, 473, 477-8, 486, 489-90,
    493, 496-7, 500-1, 513-5,
    518, 520, 522-3, 525-6, 528-32,

Benefices (Cont'd):
    537-8, 550-2, 554, 561-4,
    566-8, 570-1, 577, 579-80,
    582-4, 590-2, 594-6, 603,
    608-10, 616, 622, 625-9,
    633, 637-9, 647, 649, 658,
    667-70, 677, 682-3,688, 692
    695-6, 698, 705-6, 708-9,
    711-3, 717, 722-5, 728,
    730-2, 738, 740, 742, 745,
    747, 750-3
  according to decrees of
    Lateran Council, 351, 459
    482, 499, 512, 585, 630,
    641, 648, 663, 720
  according to statutes of
    foundation, 378, 491-2, 527,
    607, 735, 744
  during vacancy of see, 502,
    511-2, 630, 634
  through composition, 673
  exchange, 357, 401, 405-6, 429,
    470-1, 488-9, 509, 572-3,
    603, 660, 666-7, 698, 723
  commission to examine, 429
  held in commendam, 747
  held by religious, 372-3, 452,
    456, 529, 611, 621, 661,
    674, 704-5, 726, 742
  pension payable to outgoing
    incumbent, 26, 382, 416,
    430, 463, 499, 502, 507,
    511, 524, 550, 566-7, 653
  presentation to, 252, 347-430
    passim, 450-753 passim
  composition concerning,
    388-90, 424, 675
  concession of, 540, 588,
    606, 611, 632, 685
  residence ordered, 31, 62
  resignation, 252, 347-430
    passim, 450-753 passim
  because incumbent has
    become Carthusian, 493
Bishop:
  consecration, elsewhere than
    Canterbury, 44
  election, 231-2
  obsequies, 92-3

Bishop (Cont'd):
   profession of obedience, 45,
      196, 234–5
   provision, 39, 41, 52
   translation, 1–2, 40, 46, 51
   in the Universal Church, see
      Hunden; Martyn
   suffragan, 184, 624
Bond, 265–6
Books, not to be used outside
   college, 346
Bridge, repair of, 55
Butcher, see Weston, William

Canonisation, 181–3, 185, 211
Canon law, citation of, 62, 181,
   351, 459, 482, 499, 512, 585,
   630, 641, 648, 663, 720, 747
   See also Judicial procedure
Cardinals:
   in consistory, 197
   to be consulted concerning
      canonisation, 181–2
   dignity of, 197
   See also Costa; Lopez; Morton;
      Sancto Georgio
Carthusian Order:
   monk, 493
   privileges, 37–8
Chantries, institution to, 350,
   392, 403, 417, 421, 453, 478,
   482, 505, 527, 537, 547–9,
   557, 570–1, 596, 608–9, 640,
   655, 659, 667, 681, 684, 710,
   718, 739, 744
Chapel:
   annexed to churches of episcopal
      mensa, 258–66
   licence for celebration of mass
      in, 32, 63
   licence for marriage in, 30
Chaplains, liable to payment of
   charitable subsidy, 95, 112,
   124
Chest:
   common, for corporation, 180,
      346
   for storing charitable subsidy,
      126
Coadjutor, appointed to aid sick
   superior, 83

Collectors:
   of alms, 24, 47, 55, 59
   of subsidy, 95, 119–21, 123–6
Colleges, see Bredgar; Cobham;
   Higham Ferrers; London,
   Whittington;   Maidstone;
   Malling, South; Ottery St Mary;
   Shrewsbury; Westbury-on-Trym;
   Windsor; Wingham; Wye
   academic, exempt from royal
      taxation, 120
      See also Cambridge; Eton;
         Oxford; Winchester
Commissions, abp.'s:
   to apparitor general, 20
   to apparitor in City of London,
      21
   to Auditor of Causes, 16, 18
   to bailiffs, 35, app. A
   to bp. of London, or Official
      sede vacante, as dean of
      province, 33, 74, 86, 100
   to commissary in Calais, 19
   to commissary of Prerogative,
      17, 84
   to dean of Croydon, 22
   to proctors, 61, 189–90, 224,
      226
   to administer Reigate priory, 83
   to administer vacant sees, 42
      230–5
   to announce death of intestate,
      70
   to collect charitable subsidy,
      125–6
   to collect royal subsidy, 123
   to determine tithe dispute, 69
   to examine election, 72, 232
   to examine state of Folkestone
      priory, 76
   to summon clergy to Convocation,
      98
   to visit religious house, 66,
      232
Confessors, to be chosen by
   contributors to papal appeal,
   47, 187
Consanguinity, dispensation for,
   8, 12
Conservators:
   of Prerogative of church of
      Canterbury, 214, 220

Conservators (Cont'd):
  of privileges of Carthusian
    Order, 37–8
  of sede vacante jurisdiction
    of Canterbury, 216, 218
Constitutions, provincial:
  concerning obsequies of bps., 93
  concerning privileges of
    St Thomas Acon, 23
  regulating residence of
    incumbents, 31
Convocation of Canterbury, 31,
  97–126
Corrody:
  appointment to, 68
  chaplains in receipt of, liable
    to payment of charitable
    subsidy, 95, 124
Court:
  Audience of abp., 23
  of Canterbury (i.e. of Arches),
    196, 201–2
  of commissary of bp. of London,
    191
  of Rome, 61, 189–202, 221–66
    passim
  manorial, 262, 264–5
  See also Judicial procedure
Crusade, indulgence for, 47

Dilapidation of ecclesiastical
  property, 13, 50, 80–2
Dining, communal, enjoined for
  priests, 92
Dispensation:
  for marriage within prohibited
    degrees, 8, 12
  for religious to hold benefice,
    373, 452
Dress, regulations concerning:
  of clergy, 92, 94
  of those beneficed in Bredgar
    college, 346

Excommunication, 11, 38, 191–2,
  197, 203, 221–3, 230
Executors of last testaments, 57–8,
  191, 204, 267–345
  laws of England relating to, 204

Exemplification by notaries
  public:
  of papal bulls, 43, 47, 187–8
  of other documents, 50, 71,
    189–91, 194–8, 200, 203,
    222–3, 228, 252, 255, 346
Exempt religious houses:
  chaplains of, liable to payment
    of charitable subsidy, 95,
    124
  proceedings against, 13–15
  visitation, 9, 48, 50
Expenses:
  of canonisation, 183
  of litigation at Court of Rome,
    222

Faculties, papal:
  to cardinal abp., 207–9
  to collectors, 47, 187
Feast:
  of Name of Jesus, 118
  of the Transfiguration, 94
  of a newly canonised saint, 181
Fine payable:
  if legal expenses not paid, 222
  if pension not paid, 416
Fire, in church, 60
Franciscan Order, reformation of,
  188
Friaries, see Canterbury; Greenwich; London; Losenham; Sandwich

Gavelkind, 53–4
Guild, 67

Hair, short, enjoined for priests,
  92
Harvest, 56
Homage, 4, 54
Hospitals:
  institution to, 507, 594–5, 666
  liable to payment of charitable
    subsidy, 95, 124
  See also Bristol; Cambridge;
    Canterbury; Coventry; Dover;
    London, St Mary Bishopsgate;
    Maidstone; Ospringe; Rome;
    Southwark; Winchester

223

Hospitallers:
  churches appropriated to, 90
  privileges allegedly abused,
    89–90, 107
Husbandmen, 259–60, 263–6

Indulgences:
  archiepiscopal, 23–5, 27, 33,
    55, 60, 67, 74–5
  papal, 8, 24, 47, 187
  hostility towards, 23
  suspension of, 47, 187
Interdict, 24
Intestates, 70, 268–9, 271, 274,
  276, 278–9, 282–4, 286–9,
  291–8, 300–1, 303, 305–12,
  314–5, 317, 319–27, 329–30,
  333, 339–40, 343, 345
Invasion:
  French, 108
  Turkish, 47
Inventory of goods:
  of college, 346
  of deceased, 58, 267–345

Judicial procedure:
  appeal:
    to Court of Rome, 191–2,
      196–7, 199, 201–2, 221
    to metropolitan, 192
    letters of, 81
  citation:
    by abp., 13–15, 31, 57–8, 62,
      70, 77, 79, 83, 191
    by commissary of bp. of
      London, 191
    by papal judges, 192–7, 200,
      202, 223, 227–9, 242
  expenses:
    of commissary of papal judge
      delegate, 255
    of litigation at Rome, 221–2
  inhibition, by papal judges,
    192, 195–7
  instrument excusatory, 254–5
  letters compulsory, for
    production of documents,
    203, 227–8
  rotulus remissorius, proceedings
    in accordance with, 247–66

Judicial procedure (Cont'd):
  witnesses produced, 200, 250,
    253, 258–66

Knight's fee, 53–4

Lepers, excluded from almshouse,
  180
Letters dimissory, 73, 431–3,
  435–6, 442–3, 445–7
Liberties of the English church,
  89, 102–3
Licence:
  alibi, 44
  archiepiscopal:
    for celebration in chapel,
      32, 63
    to celebrate throughout
      province, 28
    for marriage in chapel, 30
    to preach throughout
      province, 27, 29
  papal, for religious to hold
    benefice, 373, 452
  See also Faculties
Litany, see Procession
Literates, 47, 59, 81, 191, 195–6,
  236, 247, 250, 254, 262, 264–5,
  274, 411, 504, 611, 617, 644,
  653

Mad persons, excluded from
  almshouse, 180
Marriage:
  banns, 107
  in chapel, licence for, 30
  contrary to law of church,
    celebrated by Hospitallers,
    107
  within prohibited degrees, 8,
    12, 47
Marshland, 69
Martyrs, 181
Mendicants:
  chaplains of, liable to payment
    of charitable subsidy, 95, 124
  of London, 89
  See also Franciscan Order;
    Friaries

Mensa, episcopal:
  churches appropriated to, 206,
    215
  dispute concerning revenues of,
    sede vacante, 221-66
Mercenaries, papal, 187
Miracles, 181, 185-6, 211

Notaries public:
  at court of Rome, see Caprinis;
    Castilione; Chichonis; Coricio;
    Corrunti; Dubreuquet; Duceti;
    Gerhard; Haslach; Inena; Kadmer;
    Sheel; Voes
  in England, temp. Morton, see
    Barett; Barkely; Beele; Bell;
    Blomvile; Bottern; Carmelianus;
    Chamberleyn; Colman; Colt;
    Copland; Emlyn; Falke; Ford;
    Imbroke; Medwall; Middleton;
    Nicholson; Potkyn; Reed;
    Richardson; Sheffield;
    Spencer; Trappe; Turner;
    Vaughan
  in England, attesting earlier
    documents, see Boold; Burbach;
    Consell; Dorturer; Maldon;
    Scotus; Walkerne; Welythwode

Obsequies of bishops, 92-3
Ordination, 431-48
  below canonical age, absolution
    from penalties for, 47
Ornaments:
  necessary for service of
    canonisation, 182-3
  not to be used outside college,
    346

Papal bulls, 1-6,8-12,37,39-41,43
  46-52, 185, 187-8, 199, 201-2,
  204-9, 211-21
  publication of, 43, 47, 50, 187-8
Papal judges delegate, 199, 201-2,
  212, 221, 247
Papal legate, 8, 12
Parish churches:
  annexed to priory, 80, 212
  appropriated, 252

Parish churches (Cont'd):
  boundary dispute between, 69
  distinguishing marks of, 259-60
  indulgence for, 60
  residence in, ordered, 31, 62
  revenues of, farmed, 265-6
  rights of, safeguarded, 28, 32,
    63
  taxable value of, 129-79
  See also Benefices; Pension
Patrimony of St Peter, 187
Penance, suitable, to be imposed,
  11, 47
Penitentiary, institution to
  office of, 422, 489, 717
Pension:
  chaplains in receipt of, liable
    to payment of charitable
    subsidy, 95, 124
  due from one parish ch. to
    another, 26
  due from parish ch. to religious
    house, 132, 134-5, 137, 139-40,
    155, 160, 163, 165, 167,
    175-7
  due to retiring incumbent, see
    Benefices
Pilgrimage:
  to St Thomas Acon, 24-5
  to threshold of the apostles, 47
Prayers:
  for good weather, 56
  for king and army, 33, 74
  stipulated in foundation
    statutes, 180, 346
Preachers:
  at Paul's Cross, 89-91
  of crusade indulgence, 47
  throughout province, 27, 29
Preaching, guild established to
  foster, 67
Prebendal churches, institution
  to, 356, 378, 501, 511, 519,
  528, 540-1, 550, 562-3, 566,
  615, 627, 638-9, 658, 731
Prerogative, testamentary, of
  church of Canterbury:
  commissary general, see
    Peyntwyn; Winterborn
  commissions issued by virtue of,
    57, 70, 267-345

Prerogative (Cont'd):
 dispute with bp. of London
  concerning, 191-203
 infringed by abbot of Burton-
  upon-Trent, 58
 papal confirmation, 204, 213,
  216, 218-9
 registrar, see Barett
 registry, 227
Prison, abp.'s, 89
Priories, see Barnwell; Bilsington;
 Canterbury, Christ Church,
 St Gregory's , St Sepulchre;
 Combwell; Dartford; Davington;
 Dover; Ely; Folkestone;
 Hereford; Horton, Monks; Lanthony;
 Leeds; Lewes; London, Holy
 Trinity Aldgate, St John the
 Baptist Haliwell, St Mary de
 Fonte Clerkenwell, St Mary Overy
 Southwark; Merton; Mottenden;
 Northampton; Ogbourne St George;
 Prae; Ravenstone; Reigate;
 Rochester; Sheen; Sheppey;
 Sopwell; Tonbridge; Winchester;
 Wintney; Witham
Procession:
 ordered by abp., 33, 56, 74-5
 for canonisation, 182
 for translation of relics, 184
Proctors:
 of abbot of St Augustine's
  Canterbury, 254
 See also Elcok; Essarde;
  Richardson, John; Walsh,
  John
 of abp., 61, 189-90, 196, 224,
  226, 249
 See also Castellesi, Adrian;
  Cloose; Gerona; Kendall;
  Laurencii; Nepolis; Parma;
  Perusia; Pisio; Reed;
  Robynson; Rowthale;
  Spaldyng; Venetiis; Verona
 of bp. of London, see Luca
 of clergy in Convocation, 87,
  98, 101
 of papal procurator fiscal, 198
 See also Anthony; Baptista
 of prior of Folkestone, see
  Fownten
 of prior of Winchester, 222

Proctors (Cont'd):
 See also Bononia; Desiderii;
  Fidelibus; Mokarum; Parma;
  Pycia; Regis
 of prior and conv. of
  Winchester, 229, 248, 250
 See also Gyan; Knight, Thomas;
  Lacy, Richard; Lovyer;
  Manwood; Perusio; Ruthyn;
  Semer; Vaughan, James
 of warden of English hospice
  at Rome, 664
 institution to benefices in
  person of, 366, 371, 411,
  417, 476, 498-9, 504, 540,
  549, 574, 578, 605-6, 611,
  617, 621, 627, 629, 633,
  642, 647, 651, 653, 688,
  701, 723-4
Prolocutor of clergy in
 Convocation, 88, 94, 102, 118
 See also Cooke, Thomas;
  Hawarden

Questors, see Collectors

Rebels:
 against abp.'s decrees, 23
 against king, 11, 43, 89-90,
  187, 195
Receiver, abp.'s, 35
Reform, discussion of, 89-92, 94
Registers, of previous abps.,
 230-5
Registrar, abp.'s, see Barett;
 Beele; Growte; Malmysbury;
 Secheford
Registry, abp.'s, 227, 229,
 236-46
Relics, translation of, 184, 186
Religious holding benefices, see
 Benefices
Religious houses:
 dilapidated, 13, 50, 80-2
 immorality, 50
 indebted, 13, 76-82
 investigation of, by papal
  authority, 13-15, 50, 71,
  188
 internal dispute, 14

Religious houses (Cont'd):
  maladministration, 13, 50, 76–82
  poor, exempt from royal taxation,
    96, 120
  sequestration of revenues, 81
  spoliation of goods, 38
  visitation, 65–6
  by papal authority, 9, 48
  Heads:
    absent from house, 76–82
    appointment, 630
    coadjutor appointed, 83
    deprivation, 82
    election, 72, 232
    proceedings against, by papal
      authority, 13–15, 50, 71
    resignation, 71
    summoned to Convocation, 98
  See also Abbeys; Alien Priories;
    Exempt religious houses;
    Friaries; Hospitals; Priories
Residence, monition for, 31, 62
Royal Officials:
  Chamberlain, see Dawbeny
  Chancellor, see Morton, John
  Chancery clerk, see James, John
  Comptroller, see Culford
  Master of the Rolls, see Morton,
    Robert
  orators at court of Rome, 211
  Treasurer, see Dinham
Rule:
  of St Augustine, 13, 83
  of St Benedict, 50, 76

Saints, catalogue of, 181, 185, 211
  See also Canonisation
Sanctuary, 10, 49
Scholars, appointment of:
  at All Souls College, Oxford, 64
  at Bredgar college, 346, 492,
    607, 735
Secular arm, invocation of, 10, 49
Sede Vacante administration:
  archiepiscopal jurisdiction:
    disputed, 221–66
    papal confirmation of, 205–6,
      215, 217
    documents relating to, 73, 83,
      352, 355–6, 360–2, 502, 511–2,
      519, 540, 543, 560, 572, 606,

Sede Vacante (Cont'd):
    614, 618, 624, 630, 632,
    634, 720
  lay keepers of temporalities,
    252
  Officials sede vacante, 263–6
    acquittance for receipts,
      232, 234
    appointment, 42, 230, 232–3,
      235, 243
    nomination, 34
    revocation of appointment,
      230, 234–5, 243
  revenues of churches
    appropriated to episcopal
    mensa during vacancies, 206,
    215, 221–6
  visitation, 231–2, 234–5, 243
    expenses of, 206
    resistance to, 232
  See also Vacancies
Sequestration:
  of revenues of Folkestone
    priory, 81
  of tithes, 223
  to enforce payment of subsidy,
    95, 120
Sermons, 85, 99, 184
Servitia, due to apostolic
  camera, 210
Shrine:
  of St Alban, 50
  of St Swithun, 184
Simony:
  absolution from penalties for,
    47
  of abbot of St Albans, 50
Statutes:
  of Bredgar coll., 346
  of Croydon almshouse, 180
Subsidy, see Taxation
Suffragans, see Bishops

Taverns, prohibited for priests,
  92
Taxation, clerical:
  charitable subsidy, due to
    abp., 94–5, 112, 117–8,
    124–6, 128
  subsidy due to king, 90, 94,
    96, 103, 108, 117–23, 128

Taxation, clerical (Cont'd):
　assessment of benefices for,
　　129-79
　assessment of dioceses for,
　　119, 128
　assessment of episcopal
　　possessions for, 127
Temporalities of bishopric:
　concession by king, 354-5, 572
　in hands of king, 660
　restored, 231, 234
Tenure, on abp.'s lands, 53-4
Testamentary jurisdiction, see
　Prerogative
Theologians, of London, 89
Tithes, 69, 221-66 passim
　assessed for taxation, 140-2
Tithe barn, 262-6
Translation, see Bishops
Treasurer, royal, 90, 103, 108
　and Barons of Exchequer, 96,
　　119-21
Treasury, royal, 95, 252

Universities, poor chaplains in,
　exempt from charitable subsidy,
　95
　See also Cambridge; Oxford
Usury, 50

Vacancy of see of Winchester:
　1280-82, 230
　1304-5, 231
　1316, 232
　1319-20, 232
　1323, 232
　1333, 252, 258
　1345-6, 258
　1404, 235, 258
　1447, 252, 258-61, 264
　1486-7, 258-66
　1492-3, 73, 221-66 passim
　See also Sede Vacante
　　administration
Vestments:
　for canonisation service, 182-3
　not to be used outside college,
　　346

Vicarage:
　established in Folkestone ch.,
　　212
　established in Northfleet ch.,
　　129
　See also Benefices
Visit ad limina apostolorum, 208
　210
Visitation:
　of dioceses sede vacante, 206,
　　231-2, 234-5, 243
　of province, 66
　of religious houses, 9, 48, 65-6
　by wardens of Mercers Company,
　　180
Vows, commutation of, 47

War:
　prayers for success in, 33, 74
　royal taxation for, 119
Woods:
　to be felled for upkeep of
　　college, 346
　wasted, 50
Writs, royal, 86, 97, 121-2